Musical Life in a Changing Society

"Politica." Plate from the instruction manual Empress Maria Theresia had prepared for her son Ferdinand in 1769. Painted by Charles Joseph Roëttiers. The political order assigns the very lowest rank to beggars, actors, and musicians. Österreichische Nationalbibliothek, Vienna.

Musical Life
in a Changing Society

Aspects of Music Sociology

by
Kurt Blaukopf

translated by
David Marinelli

AMADEUS PRESS
Reinhard G. Pauly, General Editor
Portland, Oregon

ISBN 0-931340-52-7 (cased)
ISBN 0-931340-55-1 (paper)
Printed in Singapore

AMADEUS PRESS
(an imprint of Timber Press, Inc.)
9999 S.W. Wilshire, Suite 124
Portland, Oregon 97225

Library of Congress Cataloging-in-Publication Data

Blaukopf, Kurt.
　　[Musik im Wandel der Gesellschaft. English]
　　Musical life in a changing society : aspects of music sociology /
by Kurt Blaukopf ; translated by David Marinelli.
　　　　p. cm.
　　Includes bibliographical references and index.
　　ISBN 0-931340-52-7. — ISBN 0-931340-55-1 (paper)
　　1. Music and society.　2. Music—History and criticism.
I. Title.
ML3795.B6313　1992
306.4'84—dc20
　　　　　　　　　　　　　　　　　　　　　　　　　92-17805
　　　　　　　　　　　　　　　　　　　　　　　　　CIP
　　　　　　　　　　　　　　　　　　　　　　　　　MN

Contents

Preface

This century has witnessed a major revolution in scholarly and professional thinking with respect to the nature and determinants of human
conduct as reflected in institutions connected with music. The rise of
music-sociology as a recognized discipline has been a gradual process
that gained momentum toward the end of the last century. Continued
progress in the field is attested through recent advances in our knowledge of diverse musical cultures. The ramifications of music-sociology
are observable throughout the intellectual world but are most notable
in such disciplines as aesthetics, the history of music, music education,
and musicology.

Kurt Blaukopf has achieved renown in Europe both as a critical
observer of these developments and as an influential force in shaping
them. It is gratifying to realize that this English-language edition of his
acclaimed *Musik im Wandel der Gesellschaft* will spread knowledge about
him and his accomplishments among English-speaking readers as well.

Growing up and studying in Vienna, Blaukopf was exposed to the
extraordinary breadth of musical life in the city where Viennese classics
from Haydn, Mahler, Berg, and Schoenberg can be heard in restaurants
and on the radio along with Johann Strauss, Franz Lehár, currently popular hits, and regional folk music. He also heard the music of political
assemblies and observed efforts by socialist education associations that
were aimed at elevating musical culture for the working people. These
were the late 1920s and early 1930s, before the Anschluss, when Guido

Adler reoriented musicology from within, and sociology—in the footsteps of Georg Simmel and Max Weber—cried for reorientation from without. Moreover, the Frankfurt musicologist T. W. Adorno, who later switched to social theory, was in Vienna during part of this period. At a time when composers and musicians who had been officially denounced in Berlin were moving Vienna's audiences to enthusiastic applause, the city was strategically positioned to make intellectuals aware of the significance of the emerging sociological perspective.

The distillation of Blaukopf's formative experiences and formal studies into the first German-language book ever to use *Musiksoziologie* in its title had to wait until Austria was freed and he could return from his refugee years in France and Palestine. A series of articles and entries on the sociology of music in influential encyclopedias quickly established Blaukopf in post–World War II Vienna. His growing reputation led to another first: in 1965 an institute for the sociology of music was created at the Wiener Hochschule fur Musik where subsequently, in 1972, a formal chair dedicated to this field was established. His teaching spawned empirical research that not only helped refine concepts and theory in sociological study but also influenced musical *praxis* through the founding of the Commission on Music in Culture, Educational and Mass Media Policies, for *ISME* (the International Society for Music Education). Blaukopf also pursued further application of sociological research outside academia through his involvement in UNESCO and his creation of MEDIACULT—the International Institute for Audio-Visual Communication and Cultural Development. Results of these activities are condensed in Blaukopf's remarkable bibliography. In the pages of this book he shares with us his sociological discoveries and insights on music.

Challenged by changing empirical questions, Blaukopf found that the intellectual resources of his associates in his various Institutes provided a fertile environment for winnowing from sociological tradition whatever is applicable and testing it for contemporary relevance. He shows that accomplishments in sociology depend upon both theory and research techniques and that facts about music derive their import from the ongoing interchange between questions and answers. The accomplishments and facts do not speak for themselves; one may liken them to the planets whose light is merely a reflection of external and more powerful sources.

Changes in the music of this century have been an outgrowth of changes in technology and social structure. For example, at the turn of the twentieth century, opera in Europe was performed in houses scaled in size to the customs of their principal sponsors, the royal lords, families of nobility, and the rising bourgeoisie. Now, at the end of the century, opera is broadcast from Europe or New York City, recorded for global audiences that number in the millions, and sponsored for economic gain by multi-national corporations. *Mediamorphosis*, Blaukopf's term for technologically instigated transformations in the arts, draws attention to the analytic power of sociological concepts by relating the more obvious dimensions of change to underlying institutional adaptations. The effects of mediamorphosis are evident in the need for a reexamination of intellectual property rights, in the economic threat to the survival of small opera ensembles, in the growth of new musical specializations, and in the changing requirements for musical education in the age of electronic media music. Further examples of mediamorphosis at work include the cross-marketing of live musical productions with mass media and the substitution of quantitative indicators for qualitative aesthetic criteria in evaluating musical performances, as when the sales figures of a recording carry more weight than the critical acclaim of the recorded piece.

Blaukopf's analyses are not restricted to the world of the present. His discussions elsewhere on the changing fates of the Vienna Philharmonic, or of individual composers such as Gustav Mahler, engage us for their substantive content and analytic insight. Under his guidance, the sociology of music opens avenues of creative inquiry among the interconnected institutional networks of our changing world. He offers us tools for understanding how the arts function in modern society in their diverse and multiethnic manifestations, including non-Western music, music in shopping malls and airport lounges, advertising art, music videos, and popular music, as well as music regarded as "serious." He documents the struggles to preserve high culture and to provide opportunities for composers who, in their old-fashioned manner, still write down musical notes to be performed by live musicians for live audiences.

It is a credit to Blaukopf's scholarly sophistication that neither is his book dated nor is its applicability limited to the European context from which it emerged. The mark of Kurt Blaukopf, gifted scholar and concerned individual, is that his analyses transcend temporal and geographic limits, offering insights into the empirical world of music as well as outlining the policy implications of mediamorphosis.

I am privileged to introduce the English-language edition of Kurt Blaukopf's seminal book, and I do so with the expectation that his new circle of admirers will grow to include intellectuals, practicing musicians, arts administrators, and others from many walks of life who are concerned with the fate of musical culture, in addition to scholars from the social sciences, ethnomusicology, musicology, and aesthetics.

—K. Peter Etzkorn, Professor and Chair
Department of Sociology, University of Missouri • St. Louis

Introduction

The first edition of this book appeared in German in 1982. The English-language edition is largely unchanged, with the exception of chapters 28 and 29, which have been completely rewritten in light of recent developments.

In this book I attempt to demonstrate that there have been and are a number of different forms of musical activity, that is, many "musics," which differ not only in their tonal material—how it is used, how the music is structured—but also in the role musical activity plays in social life.

The sociology of music attempts to track down various factors of musical activity and behavior: material and spiritual, economic, political, and many others. This intention of the sociology of music has more often been stated than fulfilled. Howard S. Becker was quite correct when he somewhat sarcastically pointed out:

> To say that art or music is a social product, or that they are affected by social forces, or that they reflect the structure of a society—to use any of these common platitudinous formulae—is simply to claim the domain of the arts for sociology in return for a promissory note for an analysis to be delivered, if all goes well, on some later occasion. Sociologists have left so many of these obligations unredeemed that artists and humanistic scholars have become justifiably wary of their pretensions. (Becker 1977, xiii)

Recently the criticism has also been leveled that socio-musicology lacks a "core of literature and a unifying body of theory" (White 1987, 1). Some have attributed this deficit to the musicologists' reluctance to deal with sociological questions (e.g., Shepherd 1987, 75), while others have attributed it to the sociologists' failure to consider the special aspects of music in their projects.

Anyone who deals with the questions posed by the sociology of music soon recognizes that answers must be derived not only from sociology and musicology, but also from anthropology, communications, psychoacoustics, room acoustics, and a number of other disciplines. The time has come to accept this necessary convergence and to discover what interdisciplinary research can yield.

This type of strategy is also advocated by some musicologists who reject limiting their discipline to historical and philological questions. Gilbert Chase maintains that

> the view that history is the essential core of musicology, to which all other disciplines are marginal, represents a regression from the wider, more inclusive concept of musicology formulated by Guido Adler in 1885, which included not only historical, systematic, and comparative branches, but also musical theory, pedagogy, didactics, aesthetics, and psychology of music. (Chase 1975, 233)

This reference to the comprehensive concept of Guido Adler (1856–1941), the founder of Austrian musicology, shows the path that must also be taken by socio-musicology. Adler's method, which took its orientation from both the natural sciences of his time and the findings of the Vienna school of art history requires us not to subscribe to a preconceived system of thought but rather to start from empirical data.

Such an approach differs from much of the contemporary literature in socio-musicology, which is characterized by a superabundant use of grandiose terminology and a frequently compulsive urge to systematize at all costs, as demonstrated by the pains taken to discover laws that apply to "music" as such. Yet once we have recognized that there are many possible forms of musical behavior, it is easy to understand that there are few valid general propositions about this behavior and that these are usually "medium-range theories," valid only for given musical cultures and given time periods. Advocates of system in all things are wont to regret that "the devil is in the nuts and bolts." As I understand it, the sociology of music professes the idea that a detailed analysis is a scientific blessing and not a potentially mortal peril.

Despite the trail blazed by Max Weber at the beginning of this century, the sociology of music is still a young, to some extent rudimentary, discipline. Nothing could be simpler than to combine its many doctrines into a new, subjective "system." I have tried to resist this temptation, deeming it more important to examine the utility for research of the ideas that have been developed in sociology since Auguste Comte. Standing on the shoulders of predecessors, one is able to see farther. It was important to me to show that over the course of approximately 150 years, thought in the sociology of art and music has clearly evolved in a single direction—from philosophical speculation to empirically supported science. Of course, I must also mention the contribution of those musicologists who, although they did not fly the banner of sociology, were indispensable as guides on the socio-musicological expedition.

This account not only concentrates on theory but also seeks to deal with the musics themselves. For that reason I have combined a discussion of the history of socio-musicology with an examination of the social changes of musical life.

I began to study the sociology of music during the thirties, inspired by the work of an American, Joseph Yasser. In my *Musiksoziologie,* first published in 1950 and reissued in 1972, I tried to reconcile the ideas in Yasser's *Theory of Evolving Tonality* with the sociological thought of Max Weber. The present book goes far beyond the problems of tonal systems, tracing the history of socio-musicological thought and attempting to describe some characteristic behavior patterns of various musical cultures.

I was concerned from the start with including the experiences of as many countries as possible in the socio-musicological discourse. This would have been impossible without the many years of patient work performed since 1965 by my colleagues at the Vienna Institute of Socio-Musicology. The incorporation of these efforts into a comprehensive research project was significantly advanced by the founding of the Mediacult Institute in 1969. This Vienna-based institute began under the presidency of the Belgian socio-musicologist Robert Wangermée, who was later succeeded by the Canadian music and media expert John P. L. Roberts. Because of their initiative, we were able to begin research into the transformation of Western musical life under the influence of the audio-visual media. The results of that work are also, in part, reflected in the present book. These interdisciplinary and international endeavors have been essential to my own efforts to identify problems, analyze earlier attempted solutions, and draw on an extensive literature in a number of languages.

The aforementioned cooperation made it easy to avoid the temptation of stewing in the juices of my own research. By providing a means of access to the scholarship of other countries, it brought considerable intellectual profit. I found the North American tradition particularly enriching; the reader will quickly see the important role in the development of my own thought played by the sociological concepts of William J. Ogburn, Thorstein Veblen, Talcott Parsons, and others. Much the same applies to the ethnomusicological writings of, for example, Alan P. Merriam or Bruno Nettl.

Despite this variety of sources of socio-musicological thought, my tie to the sociology of Max Weber persists. Weber taught us not to direct our attention exclusively toward the musical work of art in its notated form (in order to decipher its relationship to "society"), but to train our sights on musical activity—activity which may or may not lead to a notated work of art. Admittedly, Max Weber was not the only one to espouse this view. Ethnomusicologists have always been dedicated to it. And if a sociologist who is also a musician describes art as activity, he is simply steering the same course that others may have learned from Max Weber. Here I allude to Howard S. Becker, who pointed out that works of music and the performing arts must also be understood as directions for social activity: "Many art works exist in the form of directions to others telling them what to do to actualize the work on a particular occasion" (Becker 1982, 210).

This example is intended to demonstrate that the sociology of music is capable of producing similar or even identical results in different countries or from different points of departure. The same is true for the concept, developed in this volume, of "mutations" of musical activity and their dependence on the changing technological conditions. When I first expounded the notion of the "technologizing of music," I was unaware of the ideas that Walter J. Ong had developed in *The Technologizing of the Word* (Ong 1982). Since then, musicologists have also discovered the significance of Ong's theory (e.g., Tokumaru 1985), providing an incentive for me to pursue the thought of the technical-social change further—to that change brought about by the electronic media, which is described in Chapter 29 as a worldwide "mediamorphosis of music."

—K. B.
Vienna
October 1990

Abbreviations used in this book

GARS = Weber, Max. 1972. *Gesammelte Aufsätze zur Religionssoziologie*, 6th ed. vol. 1. Tübingen: J. C. B. Mohr. [vol. 2: 1976, vol. 3: 1978.]

GAWL= Weber, Max. 1973. *Gesammelte Aufsätze zur Wissenschaftslehre.* 4th ed. Tübingen: J. C. B. Mohr.

IRASM = *International Review of the Aesthetics and Sociology of Music.* 1970– . Zagreb: Institute of Musicology.

MEB = Marx, Karl, and Friedrich Engels. 1953. *Ausgewählte Briefe 1843–1895* (MEB). Berlin (East): Dietz.

MGG = Blume, Friedrich, ed. 1949–1979. *Die Musik in Geschichte und Gegenwart. Allgemeine Enzyklopädie der Musik.* 16 vols. Kassel: Bärenreiter.

MGÖ = Flotzinger, Rudolf, and Gernot Gruber, eds. 1977 and 1979. *Musikgeschichte Österreichs.* 2 vols. Graz, Vienna, Cologne: Verlag Styria.

Chapter 1 *Goals of the Sociology of Music*

*From time to time, one must return to investigate words;
for the world can move away while words stand still.*
—Georg Christoph Lichtenberg

*Thus words too serve to express new ideas
without changing their orthography.*
—Émile Durkheim

As a rule, one attempts to circumscribe the field of the sociology of music by starting with the idea, which must be defined more exactly, of how sociology should treat certain aspects of music. Assuming that existing disciplines already deal adequately with several aspects of music (for example, music theory, musical aesthetics, psychology of music, and so on) the only way to legitimize the sociology of music would be to describe its methods and area of application in such a way that its particular task is identified. For many years I regarded this as superfluous, because in my opinion every method of dealing with music involves sociological aspects, and a separate sociology of music could be justified as a "transient science" only as long as scholarship did not integrate it into musicology. I soon revised this interpretation (Blaukopf 1972a, 5–6), because theory and methodology (primarily that of the empirical sociology of music) had evolved and become more refined, as reflected in an extensive literature on the subject (cf. Kneif 1966, Elste 1975).

To be sure, that dubious tendency which, over the last thirty years, has been called "the fight for a place in the academic sun" (Acham 1979, 135) has also been responsible for socio-musicology's claim to recognition as a separate discipline. This trend should not be supported. On the contrary, we would do well to assign no more than a modest place to the sociology of music, because establishing it as a special area of study carries with it two potential dangers.

The *first* danger is that sociology may operate with its own ready-made categories, failing to regard music, the object of its research, as the criterion for their usefulness. According to some scholars, sociology concerns itself solely with studying the social involvement of art, and this study cannot be used to "explain the nature and essence of the arts themselves" (Silbermann 1973A, 20). Adorno correctly pointed out that this process neglects the actual object and that, in so doing, academic sociology tries to get around methodological difficulties by "classifying in agenda style." In Silbermann's opinion, sociology "has to do with the social effects of music, not with music itself" (Adorno 1976, 196). This type of socio-musicology, carried out in anything but splendid isolation, operates according to a method that not only is regarded as largely fruitless by musicology but has long since lost validity in sociology as well. Talcott Parsons has indicated that

> *every* important empirical field of social science is a field of application for the conceptual schemes of all the relevant theoretical disciplines. No academic organization of the disciplines can overcome this inherent logical cross- and inter-penetration. In which disciplinary category a given empirical field is predominantly placed is usually mainly a matter of historical accident and pragmatic convenience, not of scientific principle. (Parsons 1949, 329)

Gunnar Myrdal addressed himself in a similar fashion to the strict divisions between the various social sciences, emphasizing that "in reality there are not economic, sociological, or psychological problems, but simply problems, and as a rule, they are complex" (Myrdal 1969, 10). Every sociology of art and music seems therefore to demand an inter-disciplinary approach, for "a division of labor between disciplines such as philosophy, sociology, psychology, and history is not contained in the subject but is imposed on it from the outside" (Adorno 1967 A, 101).

The *second* danger in detaching the sociology of music from the music itself is that the dialogue between disciplines may be suppressed, and the long-established disciplines may imagine that sociological reflection on music is no longer within their purview. If a separate discipline already exists to deal with the sociological aspects of music, it might be argued that musicology need not concern itself with the task. In this case, establishing the sociology of music as a separate discipline would stifle the interdisciplinary investigations demanded by the subject itself. Of course, this risk has gradually become less acute. Musicologists such as Guido Adler and Jules Combarieu long ago acknowledged the sociological dimension of their discipline, and the rapid development of comparative musicology and ethnomusicology since the end of the nineteenth century has sensitized musicologists not only to anthropology but to sociology as well.

Musics as Types of Social Activity

These developments have also paved the way for a new definition of the term *music*. For a long time, the definition took as its primary point of departure the concept of music as a work of art. A typical example is the definition given as late as 1961 by the most prestigious German encyclopedia of music: "Music is the artistic discipline whose material consists of sounds" (Hüschen in MGG9, 970). This definition is derived from a preconceived idea of "art" rather than from the verifiable phenomena of musical activity, which extend far beyond art music. A definition of this kind says little about the phenomenon of music, while saying a great deal about a musicology that is preoccupied with art music. Recent musicological literature goes beyond the restrictions inherent in this definition. There is a growing awareness that we cannot speak simply of "music" but must speak instead about various types of "musics" and about differing historical structures of musical behavior. Studies of the development of European folk music and of pre-Renaissance European music, analyses of the technologically disseminated popular music of modern industrial civilization, and explorations of the musical life of non-European peoples seem to indicate that the subject of musicological research—and therefore the sociology of music—must be defined in a different, more comprehensive way.

All the above considerations direct attention to types of musical behavior that can be regarded as social behavior. (By behavior we mean the observable acts and omissions of people.) Sociology seeks to identify patterns of cultural behavior because these patterns reveal the behavior expectations characteristic of each social structure. The sociology of music is properly concerned with cultural types of behavior, too, for these rules are considered binding for musical behavior as well.

The task of the sociology of music—in keeping with a basic idea of Max Weber's—is to understand musical activity as a social activity, thereby explaining how it originated. Defined in the broadest sense, a *musical activity* is any activity directed toward the production of sound-events intended for others. While this definition is broad enough to include everything—the acoustic utterances of cavemen as well as the writing of a modern score, the repetition of traditional musical formulas as well as the performance of a *res facta*—it is too broad because it also includes all verbal communication, which would contradict our current knowledge as well as the conventional terminology resulting from that knowledge. We are accustomed to distinguishing between the aesthetic information conveyed by music and the semantic information reserved for speech. In our minds, music and speech are separate spheres. Furthermore, this definition of musical activity would lead to problems in defining what we—and all cultures—generally call musical behavior.

Semantic and Aesthetic Information

The problems in defining musical behavior can be overcome by taking into consideration that the logical separation of aesthetic and semantic information (Moles 1968, 124–125) came about relatively recently, whereas both elements were originally linked. In most African cultures, for example, it is impossible to separate the "purely musical" from the spiritual, terpsichorean, and linguistic elements. In these societies, "understanding music" means reacting to music in a culturally defined fashion, which usually includes a dance reaction as well (Nketia 1975, 11–12). Since music is not detached from speech communication and gestural expression, these societies usually lack words that correspond to our idea of "music":

> Most African languages do not have a word wholly equivalent to the Western term "music." The terms used often mean a combination of music and dance. We frequently find expressions for "song" and "singing" on the one hand and for "dance," "type of dance" and "type of music" on the other. (Kubik 1973, 172–173)

This close connection between linguistic-semantic and musical-aesthetic communication has also been stressed in studies on the culture of ancient Greece. Although the word *music* is derived from the Greek *musiké*, the two terms actually have little to do with one another. "It is incorrect to translate musiké with music; these two terms designate different things" (Georgiades 1954, 7). *Musiké* is the name for something which we would today regard as a joining of poetry and music:

> Ancient Greek verse was a curious form, for which there is no analogy in the Occident. It was, so to say, music and poetry in one; and it is precisely for this reason that it cannot be broken down into the two tangible components of music and poetry." (Georgiades 1954, 6)

The history of the words *musiké* and *music* clearly demonstrates how the function of an expression changes and to what extent it can be filled with new content. In Arab cultures, for example, until the nineteenth century the term *musiqa* was reserved for theoretical treatises on music theory, tonal systems, musical instruments, the aesthetics of music, and so on (Touma 1975, 28). In this instance, then, the word designates, not musical practice but theoretical reflection about music.

All scholarly consideration of non-European and ancient European cultures must therefore pay attention to the indivisible connection between linguistic, gestural, and musical elements. When we speak of music in these areas, we must be aware that we are making a mental distinction that does not, in general, exist in either social practice or the thought associated with it. Is it then meaningful, in such instances to speak of music? Yes, but only if we mentally view the isolated musical forms of behavior in conjunction with the predominant types of cultural behavior associated with them.

Musical Practice

This, albeit rather major, limitation will enable us to use the terms *types* of musical behavior, *patterns* of musical behavior (i.e. rules of behavior), and musical behavior *expectations*. Classifying these three concepts under the term musical *practice*, allows us to define the sociology of music as "the compilation of all social data relevant to musical practice, the classification of this data according to its importance for musical practice, and the recording of data of crucial significance in altering practices" (Blaukopf in Bernsdorf/Bülow 1955, 342). This description of socio-musicology stresses *practice* and the *change* of practice. Rather than starting from music as a work of art, a phenomenon that appeared later in history, it takes as its point of departure music as a social activity, something older than notated music that eventually brought forth the "musical work of art" at a given stage of socio-technological development. (Of course, the composition of such a work of art at this stage is, in its turn, also part of musical practice.) I would like to note again that the word *practice* should not be taken in the narrow sense of referring only to "what is actually heard." It should be extended to include all musical acts and omissions, as well as observable behavior patterns. Theoretical reflection on this musical practice—that is, thought about music based on each practice and capable of influencing it—will also be considered part of this socio-musical practice.

Another important aspect of the foregoing definition is the special attention devoted to the changes in musical practice. As a rule—to which there are, of course, possible exceptions—the sociology of music is unable to explain all parts of a given musical practice from a sociological point of view. It can, however, localize social data which make a given musical practice possible or directly cause it to change. In short, *the sociology of music explains, not why musical practice is the way it is, but how it changes.*

The curious onlooker who expects the sociology of music to "explain" why a certain composer is a great genius will be disappointed, and rightly so, because although the sociology of music is able to list several of the conditions necessary for this greatness, it is by no means able to account for all of them. Even brilliant philosophical attempts (such as Adorno's) to "decipher" musical works of art "sociologically" are unable to alter this fact. Contrary to our definition of the sociology of music, these efforts—which have been emulated by others, with lesser results—start with the work of art and trace their way back

---

to the social background. The exceptional instances in which this has been successful may reinforce the false impression that sociology is able to derive the concrete form of musical artworks from the structure of the society in which these works were created. This misunderstanding has recently been fostered by a number of authors trying to reach that goal by following in Adorno's footsteps. The pseudo-sociology used for such efforts largely employs analogy and metaphor as a speculative means of tying social facts to aesthetic phenomena. They tend to ignore Adorno's warning against this method: "Sociological concepts applied to music are not binding when not founded in the music" (Adorno 1959, 11).

Hans Engel also noted in 1965 that a mere linking of artworks and society is unproductive: "Aesthetic speculation and a mere synchronic listing of musical and social data serve no purpose" (MGG 12, 966). However, Engel also took Max Weber, the founder of the sociology of music in Germany, to task, maintaining that Weber's fragmentary yet fundamental essay on the rational and sociological bases of music, first published in 1921, had produced "no results." Engel overlooked the fact that Weber was not trying, in this or other studies, to establish at any price a correspondence between music and social system but was concerned instead with discovering the conditions under which musical activity changed. Weber focused his attention on the development of tonal systems, on the conflicts inherent in any rationalization of tonal systems, and on the significance of musical instruments for musical practice—all of which make him a pioneer of socio-musicological thought. As I will show, Weber's socio-musicological thought is closely linked to the musicological and aesthetic thought of his age.

Chapter 2 *The Search for the Origins of Music*

"It is customary to commence a study at the beginning, except in history." This admonition by Jacob Burckhardt in his *Weltgeschichtliche Betrachtungen* [Reflections on World History] (1978, 4) also applies to the history of music. We are all too inclined to succumb to the temptation of using our musical experiences as our guiding principle in understanding the music of the past. This temptation can only be resisted by seeking opportunities to become acquainted with musical cultures outside the Occidental which exist to the present day. Curt Sachs wrote to this effect, referring to the musical culture of European antiquity: "Is it really admissible to interpret the numberless dark passages in Greek authors with the conceptions of modern European music? Or is it not more logical and promising to ask for information where tradition is still alive?" (Sachs 1943, 202). Despite the fact that ethnomusicology is unable to provide us with a picture of our Occidental musical past, we can nonetheless open our minds to the possibility of different musical practices.

Nor can the attempt to determine the social rank of musical activity in the early phases of human history dispense with the help of ethnology. This becomes evident when one investigates the question of the so-called origins of music.

There are many theories concerning the origins of music. Charles Darwin (1809–1882) and Herbert Spencer (1820–1903) dealt with this question; subsequently historians and psychologists also devoted themselves to the problem. Walter Graf (1967) has written an informative survey demonstrating the essentially hypothetical character of the theses advanced on this subject. The most plausible of these are the reflections of Robert Lach (1874–1958), based on empirical evidence. According to Lach, the development of music proceeds by stages "from purely sensual pleasure derived from sound (first stage) to simple groups of notes (first aesthetic stage), and finally to architectonic structure (architectonic stage)" (Graf 1967, 4). One advantage of this interpretation would seem to be that it can be demonstrated both ontogenetically and phylogenetically. This does not, however, mean that interpretations by other authors should be entirely dismissed, for they emphasize aspects that could be quite relevant: Darwin concentrates on the role of sexual courtship, Spencer traces musical expression to "surplus energy," and others speak of the "instinct of play" (Karl Groos) or the "primitive cry" (Fausto Torrefranca).

Aesthetic Consciousness

With the exception of Robert Lach, these authors all start from the experiential frame of modern Western civilization and, in some sense, seek the origins of what we understand as music. The only possible scientific method for dealing with this problem is to reconstruct the role of musical utterances within the context of overall cultural behavior at a certain early stage of human history. Such an attempt could find its bearings by determining the position of music in this kind of society:

> Music is not autonomous "art" in the early phases of human history, but . . . woven into general social activity: into work, into worship. It strives to control and acquire strange, scarcely known, and therefore apparently frightening, nature; this is why what is perhaps its most important function is to organize, harmonize, and intensify physical and mental powers in the interest of satisfying vital interests of the community. It is impossible at this primitive level of culture to speak of aesthetic consciousness, autonomous artistic creation, and aesthetic enjoyment. (Suppan 1977A, 12)

By following these basic principles we avoid the error of viewing music at this early phase as having been something independent. Although we apply our concept "music" to it, the autonomy contained in that term is simply a matter of our interpretation. In sociology, understanding must start from the subjective interpretation of those who act, without, however, ignoring the possibility of a different objective meaning. To be sure, it is hard to follow Wolfgang Suppan's reasoning in assigning primary importance to "vital needs" in the early phases of culture while denying the existence of an aesthetic consciousness. This widespread idea postulates that because living conditions during those stages of culture were so harsh, one can assume that musical activity was undeveloped. But although Stone Age people are rightly regarded as having only the simplest of tools at their disposal, it would be premature at best to conclude, therefore, that living conditions were harsh, either by their subjective or our objective standards. The banal question also arises as to whether the harshness of living conditions really made it so difficult to satisfy vital needs that Stone Age men and women had little time left for play. The discovery of a bone pipe approximately forty thousand years old suggests a "time budget" that permitted not only the production of notes but the creation of musical instruments as well. Although we have a fragmentary knowledge of some of these instruments, we know nothing about how they were used—nothing, that is, about the "music" of this cultural period. Given, however, the examples of cave painting which have come down to us, we are compelled to ask about the relationship between the state of toolmaking and artistic activity. Lewis Mumford pointed out the long-distorted interpretation of this relationship:

> In our museums the facts were long staring us in the face, without our having the will or the gift to interpret them. In the very hall of our museums of natural history, for example, where there is a great array of tools and weapons, some so early and primitive that they are hardly to be identified as such, one sometimes finds reproductions of the early cave paintings from Altamira and the Dordogne. The contrast between these two sets of artifacts should long ago have impressed us. One has only to compare the cave paintings of the Aurignacian hunters with the tools that they used to see that their technical instruments, even if eked out with wood and bone instruments that have disappeared, were extremely primitive, while their symbolic arts were so advanced that many of them stand on a par, in economy of line and esthetic vitality, with the work of the Chinese painters of the Sung dynasty. (Mumford 1952, 39)

Much as we admire the high aesthetic standard of the most impressive cave paintings from the Magdalenian culture (before 10,000 B.C.), we must not regard these works as autonomous art. Everything we know seems to indicate that these manifestations stemmed from a view of life determining all activity, one which was seen as "rational" by those belonging to it. In this sense, a painted animal had a magical significance; it did not have an aesthetic function separate from reality. According to Max Weber, "Magic activity cannot be separated from practical everyday activity, especially as its aims are also largely economic" (Weber 1956a, 317). Nonetheless, we are permitted, in retrospect, to consider separately the artistic abilities that went into creating such manifestations as the cave paintings. We are more inclined to do so following the discovery of stones containing scratches that can be interpreted as sketches or preliminary studies to cave paintings. Whatever social function and intended meaning these "sketches" may have had, they do show that exercise and repetition were part of the practice that produced the cave paintings.

Artistic Intent and Division of Labor

The thesis maintaining that we cannot postulate the autonomy of art and the independence of musical activity in the early stages of society does not appear to exclude aesthetic elements in the musical behavior of Stone Age people. Ethologists also suggest this thought:

> In Homo sapiens the divers subsystems of skill and knowledge, of the individual acquired and accomplished types of motion and the cumulative abilities of acquiring knowledge contained in tradition, attain a degree of independence greater than that of any other being. These subsystems are independently available and can therefore be freely combined by purposeful men and women. They all become conceptualized, and people begin to *play* with them. As early as making the simplest objects of use, human beings at the lowest cultural stage cannot help creating *beauty*. (Lorenz 1978, 34)

The essentially correct view that the early phases of human culture did not possess a separate aesthetic sphere will therefore have to be modified. The search for the "origins of music," modified in light of behaviorism and archaeological findings, is the search for the development of activity that does not directly serve practical purposes—that is, artistic activity—although within the structure of a primitive society's dominant outlook on life, such activity may appear to be subjectively utilitarian.

Gordon Childe (1946, 37) relates the activity of the cave painters to the social structure of Magdalenian culture. He considers these artistic manifestations as proof that this culture had already developed the first "specialists"—that there were those who were exempted by the others from earning their own livelihoods so that they could pursue their "profession." In other words, they practiced a division of labor having economic premises and aesthetic consequences.

These findings are also important for understanding musical activity in early cultures. Although we have examples of prehistoric painting, our reconstruction of early musical behavior is dependent on the remains of musical instruments that have survived because they were made from material that has resisted the ravages of time. Apart from the remains of musical instruments, the only possibility of supplementing our sparse knowledge on the subject is by analogy with the development of painting or through the findings of ethnomusicology. Here the question often arises as to whether we must understand musical activity at an early cultural stage as wholly collective or whether we can imagine individual initiative or even specialization in this area as well as in cave painting.

Community and Individual

The concept of "collective production" is of interest beyond its use in the early history of the human race or in connection with the musical practice of certain non-European peoples. The concept also lurks in writings on the sociology of art and assumes propagandistic dimensions in some programmatic theories of art. After all, a theory of art that promotes collective production ("stimulating the audience," "releasing general creative forces," "overcoming the individuality of the creative process influenced by the closed form") could be made more plausible if it could be proved that so-called collective production was a "natural," primeval practice that had been perverted by the subsequent division of labor, economic exploitation, and the transformation of art into a commodity. Yet a writer who traced the relationship between the work of art and its form as commodity writes explicitly that "the example of a hypothetical primitive state in which the generation and utilization of works of art coincide in collective, simultaneous processes is atypical even in a historical context" (Leithäuser 1978, 25).

Nonetheless, vestiges of the notion that early musical activity was nonspecialized appear in the ethnomusicological literature. Bruno Nettl (1956, 10) believes that initially there was little specialization and that the music of the group was equally known by all of its members. At the same time, other interpretations based on ethnological findings reveal an early division of labor, thereby contradicting the idea of collective production. It must be assumed that the concept of folk song, first coined by Herder and also significant in the theories of the Brothers Grimm, has led others to explain the origins of linguistic and musical forms as the result of collective efforts by "the people." This interpretation has also become popular in sociological speculation. The findings of ethnomusicology, however, seem to bear out the fact that despite the existence of collective contributions and creative cooperation between individuals, we are in fact dealing with "individuals working creatively" (Merriam 1964, 166). Moreover, it has been shown that nonliterate peoples often understand "composition" as a distinct act, about which they are even able at times to speak (ibid.). These ethnomusicological and archaeological findings lead us to conclude that it is likely that "the beginnings of the development of the artist's profession may go back to the Neolithic period." (Meyer 1977, 39).

Life and Art in the New Stone Age

If we posit a specialization of artistic and musical activity as early as this phase of human history, we must ask ourselves whether an economy based on hunting and gathering also had room for specialists of this kind, with those engaged in labor creating a surplus product that went toward the specialists' livelihood.

We will only come closer to answering this question if we analyze an extant culture that is economically similar to the Stone Age cultures of hunters and gatherers. Analyses of the Australian aborigines and the African bushmen show that these two cultures do not experience a scarcity of resources and a hard struggle for existence (Sahlins 1974). Australian aborigines require between four and five hours a day to acquire and prepare what they need to live; the bushmen in Botswana need little more than two hours per day. This stage of economic development is characterized by an "underutilization" of economic opportunities; that is to say, no effort is made to maximize economic yield as would be the natural tendency in a society whose production is directed toward goods rather than artifacts. More revealing than the way in which time is allotted for work is the rhythm of life peculiar to these cultures. They lack our familiar rhythm regulating work, recreation, and sleep. Instead, rest and sleep are used to separate activities. Marshal Sahlins goes so far as to call this type of culture an "affluent society," for its most salient feature is that people do not have to work hard (Sahlins 1974, 17).

These considerations lead us to conclude that during certain periods of the Stone Age people were in a position to create the economic conditions that appear to be necessary for artistic and musical specialization; that is, they were able to produce the surplus product needed to guarantee the existence of specialists. If, as ethology indicates, human beings at simple stages of culture cannot avoid "creating beauty" (Lorenz), the economic analysis confirms that cultures at similar stages (with exceptions caused by such phenomena as the Ice Age, natural catastrophes, receding flora and fauna) could create the foundation for such specialized activity.

Situation as Sociographical Category

This example demonstrates that, despite all the means at its disposal, sociology is not in a position to characterize the types of early musical behavior. Its task is interdisciplinary: even in our example it was necessary to supplement the findings of ethnology and archaeology with those of economics and ethology. Only then, albeit in a rudimentary form, could we characterize the situation of people at a given stage of culture. Characterizations of this type include not only economic and psychological data (which have not yet been dealt with), but data concerning the rhythms of everyday life and how people allocate their time.

This method requires "situation physiognomies," including these and other kinds of data. Otto Neurath first proposed "situation" [the German *Lebenslage*] as a category for the social sciences (Neurath 1937). He took "situation" to mean "standard of living," but not in the narrow, income-dependent sense: "In the definition of 'standard of living' suggested here, food, housing, clothing, theater, health, occupational fatigue, and leisure time are all to be included" (Neurath 1937, 141). Going back to the concept of the inventory approach originated by the French sociologist Frédéric Le Play (1806–1882) has proved especially useful in sociography. Le Play elevated situation inventory to a method that he then applied to his comprehensive study on work, home life, and the cultural situation of European workers. In recent empirical social research, situation is characterized by a profusion of quantitative data taken from special surveys. Only by combining this data with the "natural" data found in statistics, documents, or other types of source material is it possible to arrive at generalized formulas needed to describe a particular situation.

The classical example of a study that follows this method is *Die Arbeitslosen von Marienthal* [The Unemployed of Marienthal], first published in 1933. The work's methodological significance was elucidated by Paul F. Lazarsfeld in a "Prologue to the New Edition" (Jahoda et al., 1978). Attempts have recently been made to apply this method of empirical survey, developed in Austria, to the sociology of music; definitions have been advanced for the theoretical framework in which such an inventory of musical practice could be carried out in a given situation (Ostleitner 1980). One aspect that seems to have received insufficient attention is the emotion associated with a given musical practice, that is the psychic "ear" for music, which can be crucial for the role and rank of musical practice in a given society, social stratum, or group. In most cases, the interest of empirical research is directed primarily at musical activity, and much less at the ideas and emotions associated with this activity (cf. Klausmeier 1963, Blaukopf 1974). The significance of the psychic factor has more frequently been touched upon in studies that, going far beyond music, deal with more general cultural phenomena (Bontinck 1974, 1977; Willis 1978). Studies of this kind are striking proof that "what people feel is as important as what they do" (Lazarsfeld in Jahoda 1978, 16). Empirical sociology has developed subtle methods with which to analyze and quantify the feelings connected with social activity. The success of these methods suggests the value for historical analysis of developing ways to characterize the subjective feelings connected with musical activity as well. We could then avoid a speculative answer to the question about the origins of music by drawing a picture of early musical practice that includes the subjective feelings associated with this practice.

Ancient Reinterpretations of the Origins

As we have already shown, one of the main obstacles to this approach is the thesis of the inexorable "harshness" of economic conditions during the early phases of human history. If this thesis is accepted, music would only seem to be possible at a more developed stage of culture in which surplus economic product creates the freedom necessary for musical activity. This interpretation was set forth during Greek antiquity in the opinions of Democritus (fifth century B.C.) as related by Philodemus. According to them, music is a young art which owes its existence not to "want" but to "abundance." Aristotle (fourth century B.C.) gave a similar interpretation in Book 8 of *Politics*, asserting that music and the performing arts came into being when people "received more leisure due to affluence."

The structure of society during this epoch suggests that this interpretation linking the origins of music to the existence of leisure was an attempt to revise the view of history to make it conform to ancient society. Work, and productive activity in general, tended to be regarded as undignified in a society built upon slavery. Theorizing about music was considered suitable only for free citizens. This is illustrated most clearly in a passage from Aristotle's *Politics*:

> There is a meaning also in the myth of the ancients that tells how Athena invented the flute and then threw it away. It was not a bad idea of theirs that the Goddess disliked the instrument because it made the face ugly; but with still more reason may we say that she rejected it because the acquirement of flute-playing contributes nothing to the mind, since to Athena we ascribe both knowledge and art. (Aristotle 1988, 194)

Physical activity, deemed suitable only for slaves, was typically held in contempt by the free of that epoch. Although this mentality permitted music to be included in the educational system, a careful distinction was made between music fit for free citizens and the kind of music "even animals and the mass of slaves and children enjoy." Here is another example of the changes in meaning that the word "music" can undergo. In this case, attention is directed at the ideal education of the free as well as at understanding music. This attitude leads to certain instruments being excluded from the acceptable type of music. The reasons given by Aristotle for one case clearly demonstrate this educational character: wind instruments are to be avoided in teaching because they are constructed in such a way as to make it impossible to "speak with them" (i.e. explain while playing).

Thus the theory that the late acquisition of leisure time was the precondition for the origins of music appears to be a particular interpretation based on the outlook, or mental situation, of a slave society. Furthermore, the concept is colored by notions of education and an understanding of music which for us only partly define music.

Paradigms of Musical Activity

This digression into Greek antiquity is meant to illustrate how mental attitudes—which in this case rest on the characteristics of a slave society—can color the interpretation of musical activity. Historical and intercultural comparisons are therefore ideally suited to showing the given social context in which musical practice takes place. Here, too, it will be useful to outline the "ideal types" that could serve as instruments for measuring given examples of musical activity. Carl Dahlhaus (1978), for example, has shown the concept of absolute music to be an aesthetic paradigm belonging to a particular period in the history of European music; and Walter Benjamin (1963, 17) starts on the assumption that the way in which human sensory perceptions are organized "is not only determined by nature but also by history."

The concept of "paradigm," which was introduced to the history of science by Thomas Kuhn (1970), is especially fruitful for the sociology of music. Paradigms, which are "fundamental ideas . . . capable of directing musical perception and musical thought, form one of the central themes of musical aesthetics that do not lose themselves in speculation but represent some clarification of conditions that (unobtrusively and receiving scant attention) support everyday musical habits" (Dahlhaus 1978, 7–8). In my opinion, Dahlhaus's emphasis on the nonspeculative character of working out paradigms is especially positive. This is precisely why the challenge of revealing paradigms for musical behavior is not only applicable to the aesthetics of music, but to the sociology of music as well. In the sociological sense, the concept of paradigm seems in part identical with that of "ideal type"; it is therefore encouraging to note that reflection on the history of art and music approaches this task of extracting ideal types, or paradigms, of musical behavior from more than one side.

Paradigms of this kind can also be found for the "origins of music," that is, for the musical practice of human beings at early stages of culture. Most of these come from two sources: the general mental situation of the people in that culture and the particular investigation of the tools used for music-making.

Nor should the concept of mental situation be understood as speculation. Through the findings of ethnology, which for this purpose must assume those tasks performed in contemporary studies by empirical sociological surveys, the outlook in stages of culture as far back as the Old Stone Age can be ascertained. These findings reveal the dominance of magic and animistic ideas; certain powers are assigned to given objects, certain effects are assigned to given actions, and so forth. Thought is determined by analogy: "Mythical thought is human thought which thinks reality by analogy" (Godelier 1973, 297). It is difficult for us to retrace these kinds of thought processes because they very often contradict our own. Such thought processes are able to prevail by virtue of their inner consistency: all thoughts, acts, and omissions are intertwined in a closed network or "structure." According to Jean Piaget's definition, "a structure is a totality; that is, it is a system subject to laws which apply to the whole system and not merely to some element or other within the system" (Piaget 1973, 30).

Prescriptions assigning given musical practices to given individuals and groups are very frequent in animistic cultures. If we apply our terminology to such conditions, we can say that given musical processes ("compositions") are linked to specific people. Jaap Kunst (1953, 2) has shown that there are three main types of such assignments in primitive societies: music that "belongs" to a given person, music that may be performed only by one given person, and music that may be performed only by a given group (caste, tribe). This kind of assignment is consistent with the animistic system of thought that forms a coherent unity. Sigmund Freud, who investigated such systems of thought on the basis of the ethnological writings of his period and his own psychological experiences, insists on the structural unity of this system of thought: "Animism . . . not only gives an explanation of individual phenomena but makes it possible to explain the whole of the world as a single continuum, from one point of view" (Freud 1956, 88).

The Coherence of Magic Musical Thought

Musical practice conforms to this system not only outwardly—for example, through the assignment of given musical processes—but, as remains to be demonstrated, inwardly as well. This can be surmised from the way people use the musical instruments they create. Hornbostel and Sachs divide the instruments into four groups: idiophones, aerophones, membranophones and chordophones. In this context, Sachs asks the probably unanswerable question as to which musical instruments are the earliest, arriving at the conjecture that certain idiophones (e.g. rattles, scrapers, stamping tubes) and aerophones (e.g. bull-roarers, flutes without holes) are the oldest (Sachs 1940, 63–64). Far more important than this effort at chronological order is his attempt to analyze the effects of individual instruments in an animistic context. According to Sachs, the drum derives its ritual function from its powerful rhythmic effect. Yet a number of instruments that do not satisfy motoric impulses still play important roles in tribal ritual. How do these instruments acquire their magic significance? Sachs answers this question by reconstructing animistic thought:

> When a primitive man blows into a cane or whirls a bull-roarer about, he does not obey a rhythmic impulse, nor is his vitality stimulated by any rhythmic response. The bare fact is identical; a man's act is answered by sound. But there is a difference. It is obvious to everyone that stamping, pounding, and striking have an audible effect. They are as inextricably connected with sound as men with their shadows. It is not self-evident, on the contrary, that whirling a small slab of wood should produce a stormlike rumbling, or breathing into a bone, a shrill whistle. In both cases there is an audible response; but with stamping and striking the sound seems to be produced by the instrument, in the second case by some strange force living inside it. In the former group a motor impulse finds an expected audible result; in the latter an action which is scarcely expected to cause an audible result is unexpectedly followed by a sound, which consequently has an unexplained and frightening character, appearing to be aggressive and hostile. Something living, a spirit or a demon, must have answered. (Sachs 1940, 37)

This attempted reconstruction of animistic argumentation (which fits into a system of thought starting from analogy) is of crucial importance in understanding early cultures. Among other things, Sachs's achievement consists in his having discovered the particular effect of a number of musical instruments within a paradigmatic, ideal type of culture. He thereby demonstrates that the particular character of a musical practice is not only the result of the general mental situation, but of that culture's approach to musical instruments as well. In other words, a people's predominant philosophy of life is further confirmed by the particular effect of various instruments on their consciousness. Thus the approach to these musical instruments once again seems to reinforce the inner coherence of the system of thought for the consciousness of animistic culture. Or, to quote Sachs again, "Other ritual objects must be spiritualized; the musical instrument is spirit" (Sachs 1928, 2).

The dominance of the animistic explanation over the rational one is a sociological phenomenon whose significance can also be understood from the history of the bow as a hunting tool and as a musical instrument. To the best of my knowledge, science has yet to provide a satisfactory answer as to whether the bow was invented first for hunting or for musical purposes. The history of technology pays tribute to the inventor(s?) of the bow as a historical achievement of the Neolithic period, for "the bow was the first machine for storing energy; when the archer draws the bow, his strength gradually flows into it and is released the instant he shoots" (Lilley 1952, 12). Surprisingly enough, the numerous myths concerning the creation of the musical bow (Belvianes 1951, 47) make no reference to the hunt or to war but only to the voice of the spirits that sing from the musical bow. This may be further evidence of the all-pervasive importance of the animistic system of thought, which reveals more about early forms of musical practice than all speculation about the "origins of music."

Chapter 3 *The Beginnings of Sociology*

Even an examination of music that devotes its attention entirely to the *res facta*, the autonomous musical artwork fixed for all time in notation, cannot avoid dealing with different versions of these works and seeking an explanation for the changes—be it the immediate surroundings in which the work was created, the zeitgeist, or the particular type of society, however this "particularity" may be characterized.

A survey of interpretations that attempt to relate music in the strict sense of the term to extra-musical factors, or have it depend on such factors, shows that over the course of many decades musicology has come closer to the way in which sociology poses its questions. Nevertheless, the instances in which such interpretations have succeeded have been due, not to ready-made sociological concepts, but rather to the painstaking analysis of notated works of music, their preconditions, and their effects. The modes of behavior underlying the notes were uncovered. And what is more, knowledge about the notated musical artwork was supplemented by the investigation of its realization in sound by reconstructing historical performance practice from textual and visual sources. In this way musicology, which originally concentrated primarily on musical philology, gradually also incorporated the study of musical practice as it related to changing social conditions. Later, I will come back to this historical convergence of musicology with sociology, because this seems to be more important than the contribution sociology, as such, has so far been able to make in elucidating socio-musicological problems. Nonetheless, it is a good idea to take a look at the doctrines of sociology to see whether they have something useful to offer to the sociology of music.

Auguste Comte

The first author I must consider is Auguste Comte (1798–1857), who placed "social physics" at the head of his hierarchical system of the sciences. He soon called this "sociology." Although he gave the science its name, he did not, as has often been pointed out, discover the discipline of sociology (Gould in Raison 1969, 36). One of Comte's fundamental ideas is the three stages of humankind: the theological, the metaphysical, and finally, the positive (i.e. the modern, scientific). This model of the history of philosophy—it is unclear whether it is meant to refer to the history of the West or to the entire history of the human race—contains the force of a philosophical dictum similar to Hegel's "world spirit." This paradigm reveals more about the ideology of its creator, who wishes to present a formula for saving the world, than it does about the nature of human society. The fact that Comte labeled his theory of three stages a "law" does not alter the fact that we are dealing, at best, with an unconfirmed hypothesis.

History without Great Names

Nonetheless, this philosophy of history is based on an idea useful in dealing not only with society or politics but with culture as well. Comte challenges a view of history devoted largely or wholly to the influence of great figures with an interpretation that concentrates on society as a whole:

> In the development of science or art, the human mind follows a definite line that is stronger than the greatest intellectual forces, which for their part, as it were, only appear as chosen instruments in order to make the necessary discovery at the given time. (Comte, quoted in Massing's version, in Käsler 1976, 1, 35)

Even if one ignores the fact that Hegel's expression of this orientation toward totality is more convincing, brilliant, and profound, and that Hegel's idea of the "guile of reason" is a more imaginative description of the relationship between society and individual, one is still forced to concede that incorporating the idea of social totality into the first sociology bearing the name is of lasting importance. In place of a history composed of great names, Comte—at least in his intentions—advocates a history of society as a whole.

It is impossible to separate Comte's sociology from the bizarre personality of its creator. He was a man who referred to observable reality in his thought, and yet regressed into the role of someone founding a religion; a man who for a long time earned his living as a mathematician, and yet was opposed to mathematics becoming too powerful in science; a thinker who advocated the notion of progress, and yet believed that the history of the human race would be concluded "once and for all" when the last of his three stages (the positive, scientific stage) had been attained. A sociologist who dealt with Comte more than once in his writings aptly characterized the three stages this way:

> [Comte's] . . . famous law of the three stages has nothing to do with a causal relationship as such. Even if it were correct, it is merely empirical and can be nothing more. It is a summary survey of past history. Comte's designation of the third stage of history as the final stage of humankind is wholly arbitrary. (Durkheim 1976, 199)

Comte also forces the arts into his paradigm. Objectively speaking, he has very little indeed to say about music (Comte 1969, 37–40). The relationship between language, gesture, music, and poetry is depicted in such a way as to fit into the paradigm. Although Comte speaks of the original unity of music and poetry, alluding to the process of differentiation Herbert Spencer will later attempt to show, the Frenchman is referring solely to ancient music and poetry, as can be seen from an analysis of his texts. His attempt to establish a hierarchy (law of three stages, hierarchy of sciences) is also reflected in his considerations on the arts: poetry holds first place, music second, and all other arts follow. Certainly these theses provide little in the way of knowledge. I would refrain from mentioning them here had they not been uttered by the man who founded sociology and gave the discipline its name.

Intercultural Comparison

Nevertheless, one aspect of Comte's method looks far beyond his own time and is still of interest today: he recommended that historic and intercultural comparisons in the science of culture be regarded as methods comparable to experimentation in the natural sciences. Just as the possibility exists in experimentation to study specific phenomena under particular conditions,

> in the same way and for a similar reason, the many epochs in which political permutations more or less tended to interrupt cultural development can be regarded as a means of providing social physics with genuine experiments which are, in part, more apt than simple observation. (Comte, quoted by Massing, in Käsler 1976, 43–44)

Using this statement, Massing goes so far as to maintain that Comte's sociology is equally oriented toward history and ethnology. Of course, this is not noticeable in individual instances, such as when Comte deals with music; yet we must admit that Comte developed the idea of linking historic and ethnological research to at least a rudimentary degree. This is perhaps the most important lesson (also for the sociology of music) to be learned from the founder of sociology, whose system of thought was otherwise arbitrary and subjective.

Herbert Spencer

The idea of historical and intercultural comparisons also lies at the heart of the thought of Herbert Spencer (1820–1903). His "comparative method" has, of course, also been subject to criticism: his detractors contend that Spencer did not critically analyze the material he gathered from ethnological research and travel accounts but chose, instead, that which fit into his theory. Spencer's thought was grounded in a notion of development rather like Comte's, though he was, to be sure, able to support its results in the natural sciences and the humanities far more systematically than his French predecessor. Herbert Spencer's encyclopedic efforts, which embraced philosophy, psychology, biology, sociology, and ethics, were responsible for his becoming one of the most popular writers of his own generation and the next. By the end of the nineteenth century it seemed as though "there could hardly be another social science than Spencer's" (Wiese 1964, 54). The subsequent neglect accorded, with few exceptions, to Herbert Spencer's works is therefore all the more surprising.

Spencer's *On the Origin and Function of Music*, first published in an English journal in 1857 (reprinted in Spencer 1966) is still quoted occasionally. This essay reveals a certain familiarity with musical terminology. In it Spencer refers, if only superficially, to Mozart, Mendelssohn, and Chopin; he even goes so far as to speak of the characteristic tremolo of the Italian tenor Enrico Tamberlik, who performed in London at the time. On the whole, however, Spencer's familiarity with musical problems does not yet appear to have been very great.

For Spencer all music is originally vocal music. Every type of vocal utterance can be explained by the relationship between mental and muscular stimulation. He attempts to prove this for various aspects of vocal utterances: volume, tone color, pitch, interval, and change of pitch (in that order!). Thus, according to Spencer, vocal phenomena have a common physiological basis. This basis points to the origin of music and to its function, which consists not only of providing direct pleasure but of developing the "language of the emotions" (Spencer 1966, 327).

Spencer's Law of Progress

The essay also contains an allusion to Spencer's general "law of progress," formulated elsewhere, that is easily lost on the uninitiated reader. Illustrating this law through music, he holds that progression from the homogeneous to the heterogeneous is confirmed by the separation of dance, poetry, and music into their component elements (Spencer 1966, 320). According to Spencer, initial homogeneity diverges into separate activities. In the course of history (i.e., the development from the homogeneous to the heterogeneous), dance, poetry, and music, originally one, developed into distinct areas of activity. Although these branches with a single root develop according to their own laws—this is where sociology comes in—they are not truly independent of one another, but affect each other in various ways (Spencer 1966, 326).

The idea of progressing from the homogeneous to the heterogeneous, touched upon briefly in the aforementioned essay, is the heart of the genuinely sociological study entitled *Progress: Its Law and Cause*, which Spencer published in 1857. The importance he attached to this essay can be seen from the fact that he later incorporated it into his *First Principles* (1862), a book in which he presents his methods and which went through a number of printings. In the preface to the fourth edition (Spencer 1893, v–vi), Spencer makes a point of noting that his ideas on evolution could not have been influenced by Charles Darwin, as the first edition of Darwin's *Origin of Species* was published in 1859, two years after the appearance of Spencer's essay on progress.

According to Spencer, the fundamental principle of progress (he later spoke of the law of evolution) is the constant transition from the homogeneous to the heterogeneous. He said that, while the law can be demonstrated equally as well in the differentiation of the earth's climatic zones as in the development of the human embryo, it is especially applicable to the history of human society.

The claim to totality of this law, which Spencer extends to all areas of nonorganic, organic, and superorganic social activity, has been called into question, and rightly so. The most incisive critique is probably that of the English philosopher and mathematician Bertrand Russell. In a letter to the English social researcher Beatrice Webb, written in 1923, Russell asked whether Spencer had not been made less sure by the second law of thermodynamics, which says that everything aspires to homogeneity, not heterogeneity (see Webb 1938, 1, 112). This surely calls the comprehensive character of Spencer's theory into doubt. If, however, we apply this idea of Spencer's only to sociology, the utility of viewing evolution from the homogeneous to the heterogeneous, not as an eternal law but as a useful analytical point of departure, becomes apparent.

Critique of Comte

This approach enables us to follow Spencer's philosophy, which was not uniform and rigid but changed over the many decades he was active. Spencer regarded models unsupported by empirical data as dubious. No later than 1873, he came out against Auguste Comte's paradigm of three-stages. Comte sought to interpret all observable forms of society as rungs of a ladder, with the "positive," scientific stage of present-day society as the highest phase of social development. Spencer challenged this speculative construction with an idea reaching far beyond his own century: he asserted that types of society "are classifiable only in divergent and re-divergent groups" rather than in consecutive stages (Spencer 1873, 329).

The notions of "structure" and "function," which Spencer contributed to sociology, prove helpful. Spencer's use of these terms can be accounted for by his idea of treating society as an "organism," his analogy between society and a living being. Many critics have therefore accused Spencer of sociological "biologism," failing to see that he intended this analogy to be, not a substantial comparison between the organism and society, but merely an illustration. Guy Rocher has correctly pointed out that, as Spencer stated in the third volume of his *Principles of Sociology* (1896), analogy is merely intended as a didactic framework in order to erect a coherent sociological system; the scaffolding can be removed once the system has been created, and sociology would be able to stand of its own accord (Rocher 1968, 2, 179).

Spencer's Ideas on Music

That many twentieth-century authors in general sociology have used the concepts of "structure" and "function" — albeit with different nuances of meaning — confirms the fruitfulness of Spencer's approach. I will concern myself, however, not with this influence, but rather with the perspectives Spencer may have created for socio-musicology. To test the matter I will use the previously mentioned 1857 essay on progress and the 1893 fifth edition of his philosophical "debut," *First Principles*.

1. The predominant interpretation of progress was teleological. Spencer strives for an analysis of development "apart from our interests" (1966, 154). This method sets him apart from those advocating speculation on the history of philosophy and also distinguishes him from Comte. Spencer's requirement was also important for the methodology of the art history and musicology of his time, if one considers the extent to which thought about the world history of music (up to Hugo Riemann) was dominated by the idea that the musics of all other periods and regions were to be viewed merely as preliminary stages to our own music.

2. The common origin of poetry, music, and dance, and their step-by-step differentiation, illustrates the law of the transition from the homogeneous to the heterogeneous (1893, 354).

3. The development of instrument-making is further proof of heterogenization. This development contributes to the creation of music independent of gestures and words, that is, to further differentiation (1893, 355).

4. The advance from the homogeneous to the heterogeneous is manifest not only in the separation of the arts but also in the differentiation to which each individual art is subject (1893, 356).

5. This differentiation is manifest not only in the greater number of subjects but also in the structure of each individual work of art (1966, 169). Here Spencer applies the concept of structure to each individual picture; there is no reference to music, although there is at another point.

6. Spencer considers the advance to the conscious use of polyphony as additional confirmation of his "law." In his opinion, polyphonic music was not created all at once but was reached in a continuous, "inconspicuous" process of differentiation (1893, 357).

7. Although Spencer starts from the idea that purely "melodic music" came before "harmonic music" (1893, 357), he is also able to use his philosophical paradigm to distinguish consciously used polyphony on the one hand and unconsciously polyphonic practice on the other. His description of this practice is rather awkward, yet he clearly means a kind of homophony. (Continuing Spencer's argumentation, one could say that musical heterophony represents a more homogeneous state than musical homophony, which could be called more heterogeneous in the sociological sense. One sees how easy it is for musicological and sociological terminology to encroach on each other's territory!)

I believe that Spencer's significance lies, not in his comprehensive system, but in the possible fruitfulness of single ideas for the sociology of art and music. The idea of the differentiation process is confirmed *grosso modo* by historical and ethnological data, although we cannot ignore the countertendencies in popular music, for example the fusion of dance, music, and language in the urbanized folklore of the twentieth century. Thus Spencer's paradigm cannot be regarded as a prefabricated model into which to force data, but rather as an instrument with which to measure processes of assimilation and differentiation.

Moreover, Spencer usually, though not always, interprets the differentiation process as continuous. The causes of sudden changes in musical practice (e.g., church laws and prohibitions, the rise of music printing, the founding of organizations for musical theater and concerts) would have to be ignored by this kind of examination. Spencer's sociology, otherwise extremely eager to extend to every aspect of life, sometimes reveals a tendency to view the course of artistic evolution in a certain isolation. However, it should be mentioned in all fairness that Spencer demonstrated the interrelationship of causes and effects with such clarity in other instances that his considerations of this kind can also be applied to music. I am referring to his insistence on the thesis that "every active force produces more than one change—every cause produces more than one effect" (1966, 176). Using the example of the locomotive, he applies his experience as a former railroad engineer to discuss the multitude of effects on England's industrial system (1966, 192–193). As is his habit, and to increase his examples, Spencer also turns to art: the influence of Pre-Raphaelite painting on other schools of painting, the revolutionary role of John Rushkin's art theory, and the effect of photography on painting. Technical innovation, artistic effect, and art theories are labeled as factors that cause a "multiplication of effects." In Spencer's opinion, the reader's patience would be overtaxed by a description of all ramifications of the various changes, almost impossible to follow in their intricate and subtle interconnections (1966, 195). Indeed, one task of the sociology of art is to overcome these difficulties. Nor can socio-musicology be content with tracking down "general tendencies of development" but must go on to analyze the details. Only then is it possible to check the validity of general paradigms that may be justified as hypotheses. Spencer's ideas can be of some help here, particularly in applying the notion of structure not only to society as a whole but also to musical behavior and therefore to musical structure and to notated works of music. Applied in this way, Spencer's sociology, which has suffered a great deal of misinterpretation and been pronounced dead a number of times, is still very much alive for the sociology of music.

Dance, Music, and Liturgy

In the third volume of *The Principles of Sociology*, first published in 1896, Spencer expanded upon his ideas about the sociology of music originally set forth in his works of 1857 ("Progress: Its Law and Cause" and *On the Origin and Function of Music*). By this time not only was new ethnological literature available, of which Spencer made use, but the first edition of Sir George Grove's four-volume *Dictionary of Music and Musicians* (1879–1889) had also been published. Spencer quoted Grove a number of times in *The Principles of Sociology* (Spencer 1896, 210ff.). Besides giving lengthy explanations of earlier ideas, he introduces a new chain of thought on the relationship between dance and music, which Spencer had originally characterized as "twinlike." He also deals with a phenomenon which will play a part in his later considerations on socio-musicology: the separation of dance from the medieval Christian liturgy. Spencer asks why the twinlike relationship between dance and music was interrupted by Christianity; why music, unlike dance, found a place in religious services. He interprets dance as a manifestation of excess energy used primarily to express joy. This expression was incompatible with "the awe, the submission, the penitence, that form large parts of religious worship in advanced times" (Spencer 1896, 209).

Spencer's comment anticipates an important idea of subsequent music sociology—that the disciplinary demands of the Christian liturgy are one of the prerequisites for the separation of music from bodily movement. This paves the way for the disassociation of music from the sensual and corporal that will become crucial in the development of Occidental music (see chapter 18). Spencer does not consider this process further, because he is primarily interested in dance and music as proof for his thesis of heterogenization and differentiation as illustrated, inter alia, by the separation of vocal music from instrumental and of composing from performing. Nonetheless, his search for the social motives of the separation of music and dance is pioneering because, as I will show later, his train of thought was followed by a great many musicologists and socio-musicologists. That this usually took place without reference to Spencer is further proof of the extent to which Spencer's ideas, so popular during his own time, have passed into oblivion.

Chapter 4 A Conception of the Sociology of Art: Taine

The ideas of Comte and Spencer, insofar as they deal with the arts, still retain a bias toward historical-philosophical speculation. They primarily use the vicissitudes of the arts as examples for illustrating their paradigms, and they were not interested in studying the origin and evolution of artistic phenomena. The first impetus in this area came not from sociologists but, so far as I can tell, from a thinker dedicated to the arts—principally literature and the visual arts. Hippolyte Taine (1828–1893), who since 1864 held the chair for aesthetics and art history at the École des Beaux Arts in Paris, took the initiative in the direction of a sociology of the arts in his chief work on the philosophy of art (the first chapter of which appeared in 1865, the complete work in 1882). Although he titled the book *La Philosophie de l'art*, the sections of the work dealing with methodology contain a wealth of ideas that should be considered a contribution to the sociology of art.

Natural and Social Environment

The novelty of Taine's conception consists in having utilized Darwin's notion of evolution. A work of art, an artist, or a group of artists can only be understood if one has a picture of the general intellectual and moral situation of the period. Taine calls this general situation the "moral temperature." As in biology the physical temperature (the environment) is responsible for natural selection, the moral temperature of society affects the selection of talented individuals. A certain moral temperature is required in order for certain talents to develop; should this be missing, talents fail to develop (Taine 1903, I, 55).

This formula is in keeping with Taine's basic attitude toward the philosophy of history, which makes the moral temperature, or as he says, the "milieu," responsible for the development or atrophy of individuals. If, for example, Oliver Cromwell had not lived in the milieu of the Great Rebellion, he would have remained what he had been—a stern Puritan concerned more with his farm and family than with public affairs. Had Louis XVI grown up in a middle-class family he would have led a quiet, circumspect life (Taine 1903, II, 319–320).

The milieu is also of crucial importance in determining the development of art and artists (Taine 1903, I, 7). Thus Taine establishes the primacy of milieu over all other explanations or factors. A number of Taine's critics who apparently have only a fleeting acquaintance with his writings prefer to overlook this fact. Leo Kofler, for example, writes (in Silbermann 1979 B, 20) that according to Taine "racial conditions fundamentally determine historical action."

This misunderstanding arises from the fact that once Taine has established the crucial importance of natural, social, and historical milieu, he also discusses other data in an order determined, not by the importance of the factors, but only by the course of the analysis. These factors are: heredity, environment, and historical moment (la race, le milieu, le moment). Taine does not use the French word *race* (heredity) in quite the same way we would use the English "race" today. The meaning that Taine assigns to this notion goes beyond a simple translation of the term. A large number of passages allow us to conclude that Taine is not consistent in his use of the term: in one instance he means nation; in another, national character; in yet another, biological or psychic traits resulting from environmental conditions. On the whole, it can be said that Taine most often uses the word *race* to denote natural aptitudes and skills. Although his most general statements remain unclear (and therefore contribute to the misunderstanding that Taine was a "racist"), when he does speak concretely about *race* his characteristic way of using the word becomes clear.

His meaning is unambiguous, for example, in the second volume of *La philosophie de l'art*, where he uses *race* in connection with ancient Greek sculpture. An entire chapter entitled *"La race"* clearly shows that Taine attributed the characteristics of *race* to natural environmental conditions. This led him to an important conclusion regarding the influence of the natural environment: technologically developed and socially differentiated civilizations are far less subject to the influence of the natural environment than are less developed societies. Human beings who are still largely unable to influence nature are "defenseless" against her, completely dependent upon her. At this stage nature has a determinant influence on people, whom it shapes without their being strong enough to counteract. This interpretation, which traces the characteristics of national character to conditions of natural and social environment, concretely sets Taine's sociology of art far apart from primitive racism. One must admit, however, that Taine's more general formulations are not sufficiently unequivocal to rule out a racist interpretation.

Taine's "Formulas"

Taine is at his best in the monographs. Methodological explanations make up only a small part of his *Philosophie de l'art*, which is largely devoted to Italian Renaissance painting, Dutch painting, and ancient Greek sculpture. Only when he applies his methods in these remarks, which are truly sociology of art, is it possible to discern the exact meaning of his ideas on methodology. This application reveals him to be an uncommonly knowledgeable, carefully reasoned thinker. It is a pity, then, that music comes off so badly in his writings. His statements on music (e.g., volume 1, 44–45 and 98ff.) do not go beyond generalities, indicating a rather limited knowledge of the history of music.

Taine's contribution to methodology for the sociology of art is, on the other hand, all the more revealing: he attempts to reduce methodology to a single formula. This formula characterizes in a general way the elements sociological analysis must undergo: the "general situation" (technological, economic, social, political); the needs, skills, and emotions developed in this situation; the image of man dominating this situation (the "ruling personality," as Taine calls it); and, finally, the artistic media ("sounds, shapes, colors, or words") that give expression to this image of man and harmonize with the aforementioned needs and abilities (Taine 1903, 1, 103–104).

Of course, this formula could be expanded upon; nonetheless, as Georgi V. Plekhanov remarked as early as 1896, it advances efforts of the sociology of art "a great deal in understanding the history of art" (Plekhanov 1946, 147). Taine refers to the factors that influence the concrete shape of a work of art and outlines a method of investigation that attempts to do justice to logic and historical facts. We can see in Taine's philosophy of art a first approximation of the theory of factors, as later developed by Antonio Labriola, and at the same time, a basis for Plekhanov's own formulas, which the Russian acknowledged as having resulted from his analysis of Taine.

Chapter 5　*History and Society as Reflected in Musicological Thinking*

Hippolyte Taine's ideas on the arts are much more definite than those of Comte's or Spencer's philosophical systems. That Taine makes little effort to concretely apply his ideas to music is to be explained not only by his education and interests, which were oriented toward the visual arts and literature, but also by the situation of musicological thought in France at the time. Even a superficial application of sociological concepts to music presupposes the availability of data and information, and most of all requires the development of clear ideas about history and evolution.

Cyclical and Linear Time

The concept of evolution itself is closely linked to that of historical time. Our familiar notion of linear time entered European thought during the fourteenth century. In his study on time as a problem of cultural history, A. J. Gurevich (1976) has shown how the transition from the *cyclical* idea of time to the *linear* came about in European thought: how the way was prepared at the end of the Middle Ages and how the transformation was accelerated by the Industrial Revolution. This change also has consequences for the idea of musical time, for the temporal organization of music since measured music began, for the consolidation of the beginning and end of musical time, and for the establishment of musical form as organized time. The awareness of cyclical time is closely linked to the cyclical rhythm of life in agrarian society; the emergence of the linear concept of time is favored, and ultimately demanded, by crafts, semi-industrial manufacturing, and industry. The difference between cyclical time and linear time, however, affects not only the way of thinking but also the life style, the characteristic structure of the "time budget" for day-to-day life. This effect is seen in the relationship between working time and leisure time. The separation of these two spheres is a late product of cultural development: it is a long way from the alternation of various activities—as still can be seen, for example, in the New Stone Age (see page 12)—to the rational allotment of time in the industrial age. This transformed concept of time is reflected in the separation of art from everyday life, and it forms one of the bases for the idea of the autonomy of art and for the ideology of liberation from the constraints of reality through art.

Changes in the Concept of Musical Development

Historical perspective springs from a way of thinking that is tied to the linear concept of time: the sequence of events is no longer viewed as cyclical activity but rather as linear history. The beginnings of this historical perspective can be seen in the first history of music in German. Written by Wolfgang Caspar Printz and published in Dresden in 1690, it bears the title:

> Historical Description of the Noble Art of Singing and Playing, in Which are Introduced and Described in Greatest Brevity its Origin and Invention, Progress and Improvement, Varied Use, Marvelous Effects, Multifarious Enemies, and Most Famous Practitioners from the Beginning of the World to our Times, Based on the Foremost Sources and Presented in Order.

"Progress and Improvement" alludes to the desired organizing principle, while the idea of evolution refers to those things created by God. To the best of my knowledge the word *evolution* does not appear until the following century, yet the idea is already outlined here. The first history of music in French (by Bourdelot and Bonnet, 1715) also speaks of "successive progress" (*progrès successifs*) in its title.

The most radical thinkers in the Age of Enlightenment linked the idea of progress and improvement with the idea of a law upon which this evolution could be based. Early proof of this belief is contained in the polemic of Melchior von Grimm, connoisseur of literature and music, against Jean-Jacques Rousseau. Grimm writes in his *Correspondance littéraire* of 15 February 1754:

You weak, unsure philosopher! Don't you see that the nations of this earth are guided by the almighty hand of fate and that you are subject to the same laws of the universal mechanism, despite your specious and arrogant arguments?

Grimm's thesis is directed against the subjective advice that Rousseau addresses to humanity. He wishes to replace such personal observations by tracking down the "laws of development." This intent is in line with the thought of the Encyclopedists, as most uncompromisingly manifest in the writings of Denis Diderot. The English Enlightenment, by no means as radical in philosophical matters as the French, also expounded the concept of development, although without a future-oriented thrust. Everything that has previously happened is considered to be the path to the present state. This is the concept presented in the histories of music by John Hawkins (1776) and Charles Burney (1777/ 1789). Both of these authors "consider the entire development of music from the point of view of the present, from the point of view that progress in their time had reached its height" (Einstein 1947, 352). Comte would have agreed with such a paradigm.

Kiesewetter's Idea of the History of Music

At the beginning of the nineteenth century, however, attempts were already being made to combine the refinement of the concept of history with the collection of data and facts, and to rely upon such collections. Of course, the field of musicology (which did not yet exist under this name) had to be delineated. Raphael Georg Kiesewetter (1773–1850) provides an example of combining both tasks. His very intense admiration for Beethoven is by no means combined with contempt for all previous art. On the contrary, he brings old music back to life in amateur concerts, he answers the prize question of the Dutch Scientific Society ("What are the merits of the Dutch in music, especially that of the fourteenth, fifteenth, and sixteenth centuries?"), he presents a study concerning *The Music of the Arabs* (1842), and one of his works indicates that he was not concerned with speaking about music as such but that he considers Occidental music as a special case in the history of music. Here, again, is the complete title:

History of Occidental or our Present-Day Music. Account of its Origin, its Growth, and its Step-by-Step Development. From the First Century of Christendom to Our Time.

Kiesewetter's historical essay is no longer of a purely philological nature but is combined with an interest in the musical occurrences of ages past. He seeks to bring those events back to life in his concerts (which were, in a sense, musical laboratories). His concept of "step-by-step development" appears to have nothing to do with the stages of development that Auguste Comte introduced into the historical discussion, at about the same time, as prefabricated philosophical elements. Instead, Kiesewetter attempts to trace development by examining the musical data themselves. His interpretation is based on the idea that there is no connection between political and artistic development: "I hold that art has created its own historical periods, which, as a rule, are not congruent with those of general world and political history, and actually have nothing in common with them" (Kiesewetter 1834, 10).

Chrysander, Spitta, and Adler

Kiesewetter's concept of musical history, which appears to form such a distinct contrast to the sociological concepts that came about elsewhere at the same time, was of decidedly positive significance for the later convergence of musicological and music-sociological thought. Kiesewetter freed musical research from philosophical and ideological bonds and circumscribed its field of study, thereby making—together with others—a decisive contribution to establishing what was soon to be known as musicology. The interpretation of music history, therefore, gradually began to get away from philosophical speculation, no matter how brilliant, such as that contained in Hegel's *Aesthetics*. From this point on, philosophy and musicology began to go down increasingly separate paths.

The path of musicology was forged thanks to musical enthusiasts and devotees of the history of music whose professional training was in totally different fields. Kiesewetter was a jurist; Friedrich Chrysander (1826–1901), a literary historian and teacher; and Philipp Spitta (1841–1904), an authority on Classical philology. Chrysander's and Spitta's decision to devote themselves to music was of crucial importance in establishing musicology as an academic discipline. The fruits of their labors were in large part the result of their not being satisfied with general statements concerning the nature and history of music, causing them to focus their attention (despite interest in universal aspects) on narrowly defined areas.

Chrysander placed Handel at the center of his activity. Characteristic of his approach was the combination of writing faithful biography, which he strove for in his unfinished Handel biography (1858/1867), with beginning to compile the complete edition of Handel's works. He was interested in concrete individual details—the shape of the work, performance practice, the embellishment of melodic lines—and at the same time, the musical panorama of the epoch: his scholarly interest was not confined to Handel but extended to the musical life of Handel's age. This strategy was suited to clearly exposing the concrete links between society and musical genius, which are usually ignored by accounts governed by a purely philosophical view of history. In 1863, Chrysander created a journal devoted to his discipline, the *Jahrbuch für die musikalische Wissenschaft*.

Spitta's importance for Bach research was similar to Chrysander's for Handel. His two-volume biography of Bach (1873/1880) is shaped by scientific, philological, and historical methods. Spitta's concept of development is significantly different from that of the Enlightenment in that he regards Johann Sebastian Bach as the culmination of musical history. Like Chrysander, Spitta also combined biographical-historical scholarship with an edition of the works—in this case, Bach's. Spitta and Chrysander prepared the ground for establishing musicology and detailed the requirements for testing the applicability of sociological theories to music. In 1885, Chrysander, Spitta, and the young Austrian musicologist Guido Adler founded the *Vierteljahrsschrift für Musikwissenschaft*. The first issue of this publication contained a programmatic essay by Adler entitled "Range, methods, and goals of musicology." Although the sociological systems of thought, by then long in vogue, are not discussed, Adler's argumentation does utilize a thoroughly sociological concept. For him the most important questions of musicology include

> the relationship of music to the culture, climate, and economic conditions of a nation, because in addition to the purely musical factors, other forces outside the specific constructive elements affect the progress of art, often having an incalculable influence on the development of art. (Adler 1885, 12)

The remarkable aspect of this convergence with sociological questions is that the still young discipline of musicology was not alerted to the importance of "extra-musical" factors by sociological theories; rather this point of view was the result of the work in musicology itself. The conscious link of German and Austrian musicology with sociology's world of ideas thus still seems to be missing. We would interpret this, not as a weakness of the musicology of this era, but as a strength: it concretely and independently formulated those sociological questions that the sociologists could only present as suggestions.

Bridges to French Sociology

The link to sociological thought, primarily French sociological thought, was soon established. At the end of the eighties a young Frenchman, who had a thorough grounding in music and had also read Comte and

Spencer, came to Spitta, who had been giving lectures on the history of music in Berlin since 1875. His name was Jules Combarieu. At the beginning of the twentieth century, he attempted to systematize what he had learned from Spitta and what he had achieved in his own research, taking into consideration the teachings of sociology without accepting them blindly.

Chapter 6 *Acoustics, Sociology, and Ethnology*

By incorporating sociological aspects into research, musicologists were able to provide more and more of the data and facts that had been missing in the speculative sociology of art. Nonetheless, musical journalism persisted in dealing with the basic ideas of these speculations. In the French-speaking countries, where the developmental paradigms of Comte and other authors had come to the public attention, the concepts of "progress" and "evolution" had received so much attention that it was impossible not to apply them to the history of art and music.

At about the same time that Kiesewetter advocated his idea of "step-by-step development" in Vienna, François-Joseph Fétis (1784–1871), a native of Brussels living in Paris, published a "Philosophical Resumé of the History of Music." This resumé is the introduction to Fétis's *Biographie universelle des musiciens*, the first volume of which was published in Paris in 1833. To use a concise definition, Fétis outlined "a history of tonal languages ordered according to logical associations" (Wangermée in MGG 4, 135). Fétis did not, however, order this logical series of musical languages according to the current idea of progress. Whereas Comte in his three-stage model assigned the highest development of art to the third (the "positive") stage, Fétis rejected the notion of music progressing to higher stages. In the preface to the second edition of the *Biographie universelle* (1868), he polemicized against applying the doctrine of progress to the history of music. In his opinion music simply changes ("la musique se transforme"), and one can only speak of progress in its material elements ("les éléments matériels").

This concept, in its own way, also contributed to broadening the horizons of music history. It is precisely the idea of the transformation of music, as Fétis understood it, that directed attention to the different structures of musical activity in European history and, even more, in non-European societies. The *Histoire générale de la musique* (5 volumes, 1869–1876), which Fétis did not live to complete, reveals that he interpreted the history of Occidental music as one of many special cases, not as a paradigm according to which the musics of other climes are to be measured.

All the same, an impediment remained to developing musicological thought. Most scholars were still inspired by the idea, stated or not, that general principles determined the relationship between musical notes. This thought was already vehemently expressed in Johann Friedrich Herbart's *Lehrbuch zur Einleitung in die Philosophie* (1813), in which he speaks of "harmonious and disharmonious relationships." Herbart sees these "with virtually total certainty" as the definite, recognized elements of music (Herbart 1891, 4, 128).

Helmholtz's Advice to Historians

This conviction, when combined with delight in one's own culture and music, formed an ideologically coherent unity and further strengthened the thoroughly ethnocentric view that the familiar musical culture must be the best of all musical cultures. Not until the physiological bases of music were investigated, in accordance with the principles of natural science, was a suitable instrument found to undermine this ideological bias; not until the physical and physiological aspects of sound perception were researched could the question be answered as to which "elements of music" were to be regarded as natural and which subject to social change. In retrospect it can be said that the analysis of auditory perceptions was one of the prerequisites for socio-musicology.

This prerequisite was fulfilled by Hermann von Helmholtz (1821–1894) in *Die Lehre von den Tonempfindungen als physiologische Grundlage für die Theorie der Musik* [On the Sensations of Tone as Physiological Basis for the Theory of Music], first published in 1862. In the introduction, the great naturalist writes that the purpose of his book is to unite the allied fields of physical and physiological acoustics with those of musicology and aesthetics. In the first two parts of the work, Helmholtz analyzes isolated sonic phenomena (overtones, tone colors, combination tones, beats, consonance, and dissonance); in the third part he turns to the musical use of these sonic phenomena—that is, the musical context into which they are placed. He concludes by separating the natural conditions of all music-making from the socially determined patterns of this music-making:

> The greater or lesser harshness of one chord with respect to another depends solely on the anatomical structure of the ear, not on psychological motives. The amount of harshness the listener is inclined to tolerate as a means of musical expression, however, depends on taste and habit; thus the boundary between consonance and dissonance has undergone great changes. Similarly, scales, tonalities, and their modulations have been subject to great changes, not only in uneducated and primitive peoples but also within those periods of world history and in those nations in which human education has reached pinnacles of achievement. This leads us to the maxim, which musical theorists and historians have yet to bear sufficiently in mind, that the system of scales, tonalities, and harmonies is not based entirely on unalterable natural laws but is also in part the consequence of aesthetic principles which, with the progressive development of humankind, are and will continue to be subject to change. (Helmholtz 1913, 380)

Far from trying to solve questions of music history by resorting to a purely scientific point of view, Helmholz made a strict distinction between natural laws and aesthetic principles. Consequently, science encountered a new task: to discover the genesis of aesthetic principles and, more important, the reasons these principles change. Helmholtz rightly assigned this task to musical theoreticians and historians, admittedly without being more specific about which methods could be used to accomplish this task. Subsequent decades have shown that musical ethnology and sociology were to play an important role in designing these methods.

Helmholtz's findings marked a break in the understanding of music history, a break from the preconceived idea of progress that flatters Occidental cultural vanity and, paradoxically, is also apt to interfere with an understanding of Occidental music. That idea of progress seeks to interpret all cultural events in the European past and in non-European areas as mere preludes, preliminary stages to the perfection achieved in Europe.

Hegel had already expressed this philosophical view of art history in its most general form, although he was sufficiently careful to attribute a degree of "perfection" to exotic art as well:

> At certain stages in the awareness of art and mimesis, the departure from and distortion of natural forms results, not from unintentional lack of technical skill and awkwardness, but rather from intentional change originating in the content, which is present in consciousness and demanded by the content. Thus there is imperfect art which can be quite perfect, both technically and otherwise, *in its own sphere* but

which appears to be imperfect with respect to the ideal. (Hegel 1970, 1, 105–106)

Hegel's insistence on the imperfection and inadequacy of artworks belonging to other "stages of artistic awareness" is characteristic of the mentality Helmholtz was seeking to overcome for music when he advocated an "historical interpretation of art." He regretted that this interpretation had not yet been accepted by most historians, claiming that

> they usually judge old music according to the rules of modern harmony, and are inclined to consider every deviation from the latter as a simple lack of skill on the part of the ancients, or even as a barbaric lack of taste. (Helmholtz 1913, 389)

In a note to this passage Helmholtz blames "R. G. Kiesewetter's writings on music history, otherwise so rich in diligently collected facts," for being animated by the zeal of rejecting everything "that does not fit into the pattern of m____ ¬d minor keys."

Alexander John Ellis

When Helmholtz's observations opened the door of acoustics to music sociology, the effects were but oddly circuitous. The social sciences' first step in the direction of musicology was taken, not by a sociologist or musicologist, but by an English jurist and philologist, Alexander John Ellis (1814–1890), a man with no particular interest in music who devoted himself to the questions raised by Helmholtz.

Ellis had long concentrated his attention primarily on changes in English pronunciation. His studies in phonetics soon led him to Helmholtz's writings. In 1875 he published an English translation of Helmholtz's *On the Sensations of Tone as Physiological Basis for the Theory of Music* with additions of his own. He then sought to supplement the writings of the German physicist with empirical evidence. The question of the existence of different tonal systems was already current in English writings on music. Yet the answers to this question lacked empirical foundations; they were influenced by the previously discussed Eurocentric ideology. John Pike Hullah, for example, wrote in his history of music, published in 1862, that "the European system, though the exigencies of practice prevent its being absolutely true, is nearer the truth than any other" (quoted in Allen 1962, 125).

Rather than proceeding from speculations of this kind, Ellis turned instead to testing and measuring various tonal systems. The result was *Tonometrical Observations on Some Existing Non-Harmonic Scales* (1884), republished the following year as *On the Musical Scales of Various Nations*. This work represented a step beyond Helmholtz's ideas while furnishing material for the realization of those "aesthetic principles" that Helmholtz regarded as subject to change. Ellis concludes from his measurements that "the Musical Scale is not one, not 'natural,' nor even founded necessarily on the laws of the constitution of musical sound so beautifully worked out by Helmholtz, but very diverse, very artificial, and very capricious" (Ellis 1985, quoted in Kunst 1954, 1286).

Ellis thereby pointed to the variety of existing tonal systems, at the same time drawing attention to the fact that this variety cannot be explained by the natural structure of musical sounds. Ellis's pioneering work—his scientific observation of existing systems, his measurement techniques, and his introduction of a logarithmic measurement system having 1,200 cent to the octave (i.e., 100 cent for our tempered semitone)—earned him the name "father of ethnomusicology." To be sure, Ellis did not identify factors that could account for the existence of different systems or for the historic change of a given system. But by departing from the usual reference to the "naturalness" of a system, Ellis dealt a blow against the speculations in history and aesthetics rooted in Eurocentrism. Ellis "opened the eyes of European musicologists to the fact that scale constructions based on principles entirely different from those in Europe could exist, scale constructions which will sound natural and logical to ears accustomed to them" (Kunst in MGG 3, 1286).

Logical Correctness and Social Validity

By this time at the latest, musicology also began to distinguish between that which can be called correct according to our level of knowledge and that which is valid in a particular cultural context where it is felt to be "natural and logical." Ethnomusicology would develop this idea still further during the decades to come. Ellis's important role in this process is illustrated by the fact that in 1922 Erich M. von Hornbostel, one of the founders of ethnomusicology, published a German translation of Ellis's aforementioned work in the first issue of *Sammelbände für vergleichende Musikwissenschaft*.

Ellis's approach led scientists to seek factors that could account for each type of musical communication in a given social context. Although the philosophical constructs of Comte, Spencer, Taine, and others often touched peripherally on music, and thus aroused interest in sociomusicological questions, the lack of empirical evidence meant that this interest could only be served through general statements. With the establishment and development of ethnomusicology came help in verifying the validity of paradigms in the sociology of art. Later, there was a convergence between ethnomusicology and the sociology of music.

Remarkably, not only ethnologists wanted this convergence; sociologists also wished to establish contacts with ethnology, as can be seen most clearly in the development of French sociology immediately before and after 1900.

Gabriel Tarde

During the last decade of the nineteenth century, French sociologists turned to the question of how individual behavior could be modified by clearly verifiable, socially valid norms. Gabriel Tarde (1834–1904) considered "imitation" to be responsible for social cohesion. His theory of imitation grew from the idea that uniform modes of behavior are caused by a kind of social hypnosis:

> The social condition, just like the hypnotic state, is simply a type of dream, an involuntary dream and a dream in action. To have nothing but suggested ideas and to consider these spontaneous—this is the illusion peculiar to both sleepwalkers and social beings. (Tarde 1895, 83)

In a note to the second edition of *The Laws of Imitation*, Tarde replaced the concept of sleepwalking with that of hypnosis. He also based his thesis on the results of psychological research, especially that of E. Bernheim, which showed that the effect of hypnosis depends on the social position of the subject hypnotized (cf. Cuvillier 1960, 32). Tarde seems to have quickly recognized the weak points in his argument, for in the preface to the second edition of his book he sought refuge in the concept of "counterimitation," claiming that it is as characteristic for society as imitation.

This strange new concept of counterimitation was already evident, in essence, in Tarde's statements on art: epochs of tradition produce a different art than epochs of fashion. This typology is limited to labeling traditional art as noninnovative and repetitive while crediting fashionable art with producing professional artists who are interested in innovation rather than imitation. These definitions are of limited use to the sociology of art, partly because Tarde wishes to reduce all social activity to the individual. His rejection of the concept that a system of behavioral norms exists independent of individual consciousness (cf. Tarde 1908, 93) is also the subject of his polemic against Émile Durkheim, the sociologist who was to assume the dominant role in this science.

Collective Norms in Durkheim's Sociology

For Émile Durkheim (1858–1917) the subject matter of sociology is the collective consciousness. "Collective ideas, emotions, and drives do not have their generating causes in states of individual consciousness but rather in the relationships in which the social organism as a whole exists" (Durkheim 1976, 189). In *Les règles de la méthode sociologique*, first published in 1895, Durkheim devotes his attention to the norms of social activity that exercise the compulsion Tarde labeled "hypnotic." Durkheim explains the collectivity of the principles of social activity:

> The system of symbols I use to express my thoughts, the system of coins I use to pay my debts, the documents I use in my business relations, the customs of my profession—these lead a life independent of the use I make of them. This is true for every aspect of social life. Thus we find a special type of action, thought, and feeling whose most important characteristic is that it exists outside individual consciousness. (Durkheim 1976, 105–106)

If we follow Durkheim, who emphasizes the validity of this idea for every area of social life, we will also be able to identify collective imprinting in the field of musical activity, thought, and feeling: the characteristic use of the singing voice, the available instruments and their utilization, the musical repertoire, the choice of tones from the continuum (the tonal system), and the different systems of notation developed in various cultures —all, as it were, are givens for those born into that society. In cultures with oral traditions, the ones ethnomusicology prefers to deal with, the individual acquisition of collective norms becomes manifest. For this reason, ethnomusicological research must not only investigate the sound of the music in question but also analyze the cultural learning processes that enable the individual member of society to acquire the prevailing norms (cf. Merriam 1964, 145–146). The idea of collective imprinting is also valid for the music of modern industrial societies; we can recognize a collective norm not only in the tonal system consisting of an octave divided into twelve equal sections but also in the institutionalized occasions and venues of music-making (concert, theater, church), in the predetermined organization of musical performance (e.g., orchestras with instrumentation that may actually be mandated), in predetermined musical events (e.g., the length of an orchestral concert), and even in the ritual of behavior that determines when the audience is allowed to express approval (or disapproval). Thus Durkheim's approach is also useful in the area of artistic and musical activity.

The Concept of "Fait Social"

Durkheim created a term for the "more or less prescribed way of acting that is able to coerce the individual" (Durkheim 1963, 14). He called it a *fait social*—translated literally, a social fact. It would be an easy matter to use this simple concept in the sociology of music, too. Unfortunately, however, as Parsons and later König have shown, Durkheim did not always use the term with the same meaning. Consequently, the concept *fait social* has recently been rendered in German as *soziologischer Tatbestand* (sociological statement of facts)—see König in Durkheim 1976, 38. Of course, this complicates matters further because the term *Tatbestand* (whose French equivalent is *éléments constitutifs*) has a standard meaning in law that really does not apply here. One can assume that Durkheim, who was well versed in law, would not have agreed with the new German term. I apologize to the reader for spending so much time with questions of terminology. I have done so to point out the trend in recent sociological literature to complicate relatively simple trains of thoughts, such as Durkheim's, with semantic hairsplitting. Those who use this literature should not allow themselves to be discouraged and should view with benevolence the linguistic efforts that usually serve only to conform to the jargon of academic sociology. This jargon, too, is a *fait social*, a social fact, meriting a study in the manner of Durkheim.

Understanding the social facts of which Durkheim speaks—the coercive nature of collective norms for behavior, thought, and feeling—is once again made more difficult by a change of terminology initiated by students of Durkheim. In the sociology entry of the French *Grande Encyclopédie*, published in 1901, Paul Fauconnet and Marcel Mauss proposed the concept "institution" for socially determined ways of acting. Institution is used here, not in the colloquial sense, but rather as an abstraction essentially identical with Durkheim's *fait social* (Mauss 1969, 16–17). Durkheim accepted this use of institution in the preface to the second edition of his *Rules of Sociological Method*. We therefore now have at least three terms for coercive collective norms: *social fact*, *sociological statement of facts*, and *institution*.

The Work of Art as Reflection of Social Activity

We would have no reason to investigate this verbal proliferation if Durkheim's concept were not ideally suited to serving the sociology of art and music. In chapter two of the aforementioned work, Durkheim names rules for observing social facts, that is, social behavioral norms. In doing so he points out that these *faits sociaux* find material expression: "Law exists in the law books; the activities of daily life are recorded in the figures of statistics and in memorable historical events, fashions in dress, taste in works of art." (Durkheim 1976, 127) Here the novel approach lies in interpreting works of art as products of social activity that crystallize the relationship of social subjects in such a way that the predominant principles of the social activity can be extrapolated from them. In these brief remarks, Durkheim also assigns a specific task to the sociology of art—something he did not otherwise deal with. Just as political economy is concerned with discovering the relations of human beings to one another, as expressed in the material form of "goods," so is sociology properly concerned with deciphering the social relations expressed in works of art. More recent sociology of art has—without, so far as I can tell, referring to Durkheim's basic ideas— incorporated this method to some extent.

Cultures without musical *res facta* (i.e., notated works of art) obviously create music that is the outcome of social activity. Yet neither the creation nor the reception of notated works of art can be separated from the social fabric. "All music, even the stylistically most individualistic, takes on a collective content: every single sound speaks in the plural" (Adorno 1959, 23).

Durkheim's concept of sociology as a science sui generis could easily lead to the misunderstanding that he has not sought to cooperate with other disciplines. But the opposite is true. He recommends comparative cultural research as early as in his *Rules*, insisting on the need to follow the development of the *fait social* through all social types. Only thus can one reach an explanation (Durkheim 1976, 216). Durkheim speaks even more clearly when he names two areas of research for investigating the "physics of morals and justice" (Durkheim 1950,5): (1) comparative historiography and ethnology, and (2) comparative statistics. The reference to ethnology is paralleled in the sociographic efforts of Frédéric Le Play (1806–1882), whose 1855 survey of the life of European workers is a pioneering achievement. In Le Play's opinion, traveling to other countries is for sociology what chemical analysis is for minerology and the observation of facts for all the natural sciences (cf. Raison 1969, 53).

If Durkheim raised intercultural comparison to a methodological imperative, his pupil Marcel Mauss (1873–1950) went one step further by attempting to combine Durkheim's basic sociological ideas with the efforts of ethnology. In his "Fragment d'un plan de sociologie générale descriptive" (Fragment of a Plan of General Descriptive Sociology) (Mauss 1969, 89ff.), Mauss first takes stock of the difficulties in evaluating the theses of armchair sociology through the results of ethnological field research and, conversely, in deriving benefits for ethnology from the findings of sociology. This line of thought from Durkheim's school once again confirms that the conceptions of science were converging.

The advantage of the tie to ethnology was demonstrated by the natural-science-oriented works of Helmholtz and Ellis, as well as by various sociological theories. Thus was the ground prepared for a sociology of music that was readily legitimized because it strove to synthesize field research and theoretical reflection by combining the history of music, ethnomusicology, and sociology. Although such a synthesis had already been advocated in a large number of philosophical systems—most notably Hegel's *Philosophy of History* and *Aesthetics*—it remained speculative. There was not yet sufficient data to provide a solid basis for the integration of the knowledge still to be collected in the various disciplines. So much the greater, then, was the need to look for a pattern in the history of philosophy that would be better suited for research in the sociology of art than Comte's law of three stages or Spencer's paradigm of evolution. This need was partly satisfied by borrowing from the theories of Karl Marx and partly by analyzing these theories.

Chapter 7 Art and the Materialistic View of History

A central notion in the teachings of Karl Marx (1813–1883) is the distinction between "infrastructure," or "base," on the one hand and "superstructure" on the other. According to Marx, everything related to production forms the basis of society. Upon this foundation rests a "legal and political superstructure" (Marx 1871, 15). Consequently, the entire social, political, and mental life process appears to be determined by the "method of producing material things necessary to life." Religion, art, and philosophy are considered part of the superstructure. "Once the economic base is modified, the entire superstructure is transformed more or less rapidly" (Marx 1871, 15). Artistic activity is thus ultimately subordinated to the economic foundation of society.

Many of those who believed themselves to be following in Marx's footsteps were content to assert this subordination of artistic activity without furnishing detailed evidence. The concepts "base" and "superstructure" encouraged them to discount the complex interactions among the various spheres of social activity and to believe that artistic phenomena could be adequately explained through economic circumstances. Numerous authors taking their orientation from Marx sought to solve the problems of historical interpretation by simply applying this concept as if it were a predetermined pattern into which one merely had to fit details and facts. It is clear from Marx's writings, however, that he did not envision an uncritical application of any kind of pattern in representing social phenomena.

On several occasions in the 1890s, long after Marx's death, Friedrich Engels undertook to protect from misrepresentation the notions he had shared with his friend. One such opportunity arose in 1890: the Austrian writer Hermann Bahr had begun a polemical battle with the German author Paul Ernst, accusing the latter of transforming Marxist literary history into a "dogmatic axiom to take the place of experience" (Demetz 1969, 140). When Ernst sought support from Engels, he was disappointed. In a letter dated 7 June 1890, intended solely for "private information," not publication, Engels reproached Ernst as follows:

> Above all, I have to say that the materialistic method turns into its opposite when it is used as a preconceived stereotype to which one tailors historical evidence rather than being employed as a guide to the study of history. And if Herr Bahr thinks he has caught you on this wrong track, it would seem to me that there is a grain of truth in what he says.

Soon afterward, on 5 August 1890, the same theme emerged in a letter Engels addressed to Conrad Schmidt. Part of this letter, sad to say, has fully retained its topicality up to the present day:

> In fact, the word "materialistic" is generally used by many young German writers as a cliche with which one labels anything and everything without further study; that is, one affixes this label and considers the matter closed. Our view of history is, however, first and foremost an introduction to further study, not a lever that works a mechanism. (MEB 1953, 501)

Peter Demetz (1969) sees these statements and other similar remarks as a departure from the basic attitudes adopted by Marx and Engels. In my opinion, Engels's choice of words rather indicates a refinement of the system of thought; while it still takes account of the primacy of economics, it also points to the interaction of the "superstructure" with the "base." It is notable that Engels assigns to himself and Marx part of the "blame" for the fact that the later neo-Marxist authors had accorded more significance to economic factors than was actually justified. Two letters support this view. The first, addressed to J. Bloch and dated September 21/22, includes this statement:

> Marx and I are in part to blame for the fact that the new generation lends more weight to the economic side than it merits. In our arguments with our opponents we had to emphasize this central principle, which they denied, and we did not always have the time, place, or opportunity to give the other interacting aspects their due. (MEB 1953, 504)

Engels wrote much the same thing to the German literary historian Franz Mehring, on 14 July 1893, regarding a point to which . . . Marx and I regularly failed to lend sufficient prominence, and for which we are equally to blame. That is to say, we all initially placed, and had to place, the main emphasis on the explanation of political, legal, and other ideological concepts, and the actions mediated by these concepts, in terms of basic economic realities. As a result, we neglected form in favor of substance—the manner in which these concepts come about, etc. (MEB 1953, 549)

Accepting both the thesis that the economic basis of society has primary importance and the thesis that interactions occurring in all areas of the superstructure have a retroactive effect on the base led Engels to conclude that the development of base and superstructure were not parallel in all phases. The dependence of the superstructure on the infrastructure applied only in the "last stage," and the two corresponded only in the long term:

> The further the area we happen to be investigating departs from economics and approaches purely abstract ideology, the more we shall find that it displays accidental aspects, the more its curve will describe a zigzag. If, however, you trace the average axis of the curve, you will find that the longer the period under observation and the wider the area dealt with, the more nearly this axis will run parallel to that of economic development. (MEB 1953, 561)

The Theory of Factors

Engels draws attention to the fact that the long-term congruency of base and superstructure does not exclude short-term divergences. It is just such divergences that remain relevant for the sociology of art, but characterizing them calls for detailed studies that go beyond applying a preconceived pattern. Antonio Labriola (1843–1904) dealt with the methodology of such individual studies, taking a Marxian conception of history as his starting point. Labriola's book on historical materialism was published in Italian in 1896 and in 1897 it became accessible to a wider readership with the French edition. The study breaks down complex social events into individual "historic-social factors."

Labriola's "theory of factors" is not a product of subjective opinion; rather it is an attempt to derive an understanding of the overall social process from academic disciplines that have evolved through a division of intellectual labor. The separate study of individual factors (be they economic, political, legal, ideological, technical, or other) is in no way regrettable, for an isolated examination by the individual disciplines has contributed to perfecting the instruments of observation and to recognizing each factor's link with the overall social context (Labriola 1902, 165).

A research strategy that proceeds according to the theory of factors is in a position to progress from merely theoretical assertions to concrete analyses of a given historical period. But the synthesis of individual factors is not a simple matter. Labriola insists that even acceptance of the materialistic view of history, which concedes a crucial influence to the role of society's economic framework, in no way guarantees that all the links between base and superstructure will be exposed. In his opinion, the economic base is not a simple mechanism that "automatically" generates institutions, laws, customs, thoughts, feelings, and ideologies. The lines that lead from the base to the rest of the social complex are often extremely subtle and circuitous. Labriola concludes his discussion by adding that these connections are not always "decipherable" (Labriola 1902, 168).

Such are the limitations encountered by all art-sociological analysis, including that which takes its cue from the materialistic view of history. Engels was alluding to these limits when he spoke of "the accidental" whose role becomes progressively greater with increasing distance from the economic infrastructure. According to Labriola, the theory of factors is "far less than science and much more than a gross error." It provides, he says, an important starting point for the decoding of interactions in the overall social process.

For the Russian Marxist Georgi Plekhanov (1856–1918), who took issue with Labriola's doctrine as early as 1897, the theory had been legitimate and useful in its day but could no longer hold up to critical examination (Plekhanov 1940). A "synthetic conception of social life" was needed to replace it. In reviewing Labriola's book, Plekhanov provides an account of Labriola's conception but also introduces accents of his own—among them his concept of "social psychology." If one wishes, he says, to understand the history of a country's art, it is not sufficient to know its economy; one must proceed from economy to social psychology, which must be carefully studied in order to arrive at a (materialistic) explanation for the history of ideologies (Plekhanov 1940, 17). Without an analysis of the state of consciousness, it is impossible to "progress one step further" in the history of art.

On the whole, Plekhanov seems to take a step backward from Labriola. Whereas Labriola leaves room for "accidents" and indecipherable interrelationships, Plekhanov goes so far as to state that "there is not a single historical fact that does not owe its origin to political economy" (Plekhanov 1940, 18). To be sure, the validity of this assertion depends upon what one regards as a historical fact. If he only means political upheavals, then Plekhanov's thesis will often, though not always, prove tenable. But it is highly unlikely that such evidence for "historical facts" can be provided in the arts. For example, the direct influence of the natural environment on human musical behavior in early cultures is certain to embarrass the intransigent proponent of such a theory, should he confine his efforts to the "economic factor."

Plekhanov and French Romanticism

Plekhanov's treatment of the basic ideas of Marx and Engels is less careful than that of Labriola. This is especially apparent when he ventures from the theoretical into a concrete investigation. An example can be found in an article by Plekhanov, the Russian version of which was first published in May 1908, the German translation in 1910. Here, he takes an example from French Romanticism, using Victor Hugo, Eugène Delacroix, and Hector Berlioz to illustrate what he regards as "social psychology":

> It is a simple matter to recognize that all ideologies have their common roots in the psychology of the era in question, as anyone with even a passing familiarity with the facts will be persuaded. Let us refer, for example, to French Romanticism. Victor Hugo, Eugène Delacroix, and Hector Berlioz were active in three utterly different fields of art, and none of the three was close to any of the others. In any event, Hugo did not like music, and Delacroix thought little of Romantic musicians. Yet these three remarkable men are rightly regarded as "the Romantic Trinity." One and the same psychology is revealed in their works. It may be said that Delacroix's painting *Dante and Virgil* expresses the same atmosphere that dictated *Hernani* to Hugo and the *Symphonie fantastique* to Berlioz. Their contemporaries felt this, too—those who had any interest in literature and art. (Plekhanov 1929, 82)

It is striking that a man like Plekhanov, who certainly imagined himself to be a consistent opponent of mysticism, should have chosen to advance a concept as vague as "psychology of the era" (merely another name for "zeitgeist") and to support it with the equally imprecise term "atmosphere." Such vagueness is strangely at odds with the logical stringency of Marx's economic theory. Even Plekhanov's attempt to treat the psychology of French Romanticism as the psychology of a specific class "living under specific social and historical conditions" does not make up for this lack of precision.

A further characteristic of Plekhanov's approach is his lack of attention to the technical, organizational, and social requirements of artistic communication. In making the leap from economics to psychology, it is exactly these prerequisites and "factors" he loses sight of. This leads him to claim for social psychology, regardless of how it is defined, an immediate and direct influence on the creation of paintings, novels, plays, and musical compositions—unaffected by the specific characteristic features of each art form, the organization of artistic life, the divergence between change and tradition, and the special technical characteristics of the profession. Whereas a painting is finished once and for all, a symphony must be "performed" in order to have a social impact. A play, on the other hand, can enter the communication process without being performed, simply by being printed. Precisely because Plekhanov withdraws into the mystical category of "social psychology" and does not undertake a concrete analysis of the factors which determine the creation of art and how it affects people, he runs into a problem which he describes thus:

> It is well known that Berlioz, like Hugo, had to fight outright battles. And it is also common knowledge that his ultimate victory demanded far more time and an incomparably greater effort than Hugo's. Why was this the case, since Berlioz's music expressed the same psychology as that found in Romantic poetry and drama? To answer this question, one would have to have a clear picture of many similar details in the comparative history of French music and literature, details which will perhaps remain hidden for a long time to come, *if not forever*. (Plekhanov 1929, 83)

To be sure, the question does not arise only because Plekhanov followed a preconceived pattern (namely, economic basis produces social psychology) rather than undertaking a detailed analysis. But Jacques Barzun, though not informed by declamatory notions of the "synthetic interpretation of social life," made a far greater contribution to this type of synthesis with his findings in *Berlioz the Romantic Century* (1950) than have any general statements about the relationship of base and superstructure. He remarks that Berlioz took part in the battle over Hugo's *Ernani* (first performed on 25 February 1830), but not because of the play's content:

> The point of the battle was not philosophic but strategic. The victory meant a public recognition of certain technical liberties which had already been wrested in print, and supporting the play meant the public affirmation of freedom for all the arts. (Barzun 1950, 127)

Berlioz regarded the demonstration for Hugo as preparation for the impending battle over his *Symphonie fantastique*, which was premiered on 5 December 1830.

It would be difficult indeed to derive the compositional structure of the *Symphonie fantastique* from "social psychology," no matter how we define it. Certainly, the work also contains socio-psychological assumptions, but it is virtually impossible to define these in a general way. Even if it were possible, the question would still remain as to how these same socio-psychological motives could be made responsible for the works of Berlioz on the one hand and the completely different creations of his friend Liszt on the other. Relying on an abstract construct such as "social psychology" (a more accurate expression would be "social psyche") will explain no more than will attributing everything to a vaguely defined "zeitgeist." Here, then, lies the affinity between the two concepts, and it is extremely surprising that Plekhanov's materialistic concept of base converges *in this respect* with an idealistic concept of history. His thesis that social psychology must be derived from the base does not make his concept any more sound.

Berlioz and His "Market"

Only when we trace the individual motives that may be crucial for a composer's work do the links connecting the social and intellectual life to the concrete form of musical creation become apparent. This applies, for example, to the compositional principle of the *idée fixe*, reflected in the visions of the *Symphonie fantastique*. This psychiatric term (which also appears in Georg Büchner's *Woyzeck*, written about the same time) was a fashionable word of the period, whose clinical meaning the medical school dropout Berlioz must have known. The role of opium, which is responsible for the hallucinations in the *Symphonie fantastique*, is also explained by the period's interest in drugs. Thomas De Quincey's (1785–1859) autobiographical *Confessions of an English Opium Eater* was widely read in France at the time. Justification of this tendency to the bizarre and the monstrous in literature was seen in the cult of Shakespeare. In Berlioz's case this is linked to his passion for the Irish actress Harriet Smithson. All these elements are contained in the symphony and in its rarely performed second part, *Lélio*.

These idea-related motives, however, say little or nothing about the actual form of the score. Significant as literary references may be to the content of a work of literature or the theater, such psychological or ideological aspects are not sufficient to interpret works of the visual arts or music. In these instances an understanding of the technical substratum of the art will be more crucial. This is especially true where the particular structure of the genre makes it difficult for the finished work to have an effect on society. Such impediments are greatest in works of music that require a large, expensive apparatus for their performance. The answer to Plekhanov's question (why the success of the "Romantic" Berlioz came so much later than that of the "Romantic" Victor Hugo) has a lot to do with the specifics of musical communication and the demands that Berlioz's artistic intentions placed upon the performance apparatus. Berlioz demonstrated in his oeuvre (and declared in his autobiography) that his expansion of the orchestra was aimed at producing something "grand" and "new." These aims made it even more difficult for him to have his work performed.

In the last part of his novel *Cousin Pons*, Honoré de Balzac sarcastically describes an artist's efforts to market his products. A tombstone mason is seeking a buyer for an unsalable sculpture depicting the heroes of the July Revolution of 1830. To help find a taker, the figures on the monument are adapted to the prospective buyer's interest: figures embodying the Revolution become symbols for army, wife, and family, suitable for adorning a politician's final resting place. Finally, for an artist's grave, the figures are turned into the genii of music, sculpture, and painting. Berlioz also had to await the suitable body for the already-completed gravestone. Commenting on the performance of a Requiem by Luigi Cherubini in 1825, Berlioz had said that composers of funeral music always found an opportunity to hear their works performed. In 1837 he was able to obtain a commission from the Parisian Ministry of Fine Arts to compose a Requiem to commemorate the heroes of the July Revolution, a "quarry I had long coveted." Although Berlioz was paid a considerable fee, the performance planned for July 1837 did not take place. Once again the search began for a "suitable corpse." General Damrémont, who had fallen in Algeria in October 1837, seemed to deserve the honor of a solemn Requiem. This time it was the Ministry of War that commissioned the work, divorced from its original purpose. Berlioz received another honorarium, and the *Grande Messe des Morts* was performed on 4 December 1837 in Les Invalides. The struggle to have the work performed—it requires 400 players— illustrates the difficulties confronting a composer of such monumental compositions when he sought to achieve public recognition.

Style: Instrument or Object of Research

The detailed description of these circumstances may also provide a partial answer to the question asked by Plekhanov: Why was Berlioz given a chance only *after* Victor Hugo? The question itself, however, already reveals the abstract nature of Plekhanov's train of thought. He obviously ignores the fact that the communication of a work of music, especially a monumental one, requires something different from what is required to succeed with a literary work. Any sociology of art that confines itself to investigating "social psychology" or "zeitgeist" cannot explain the different lengths of time it takes for works in different genres to find acceptance. There can be no doubt that acceptance of an artwork depends not only on psychological and social but also on technical, administrative, and even economic factors. For a long time Berlioz was forced to earn his living by writing reviews so that he would have time to compose. By so doing, he further affected the musical climate because his articles on music influenced musical taste. These observations clearly show that the "factors," as understood by Labriola, are interrelated in highly intricate ways. One task of the sociology of art is to follow these tangled paths. The method to be used is probably more complicated than merely applying a ready-made interpretation of history.

We must be especially careful in applying concepts of style to works of art. Plekhanov's use of the term "Romanticism" is an example of the dangers that can result from such use. The idea of "Romanticism" is abstracted from the works (more accurately, from several works) of a specific period in time. The question is then posed, after the fact, as to how Romanticism is expressed in individual works. This type of circular argumentation, based upon concepts of style thus created, can have only a declarative, not an explanatory, function.

One cannot, however, deny real, historical significance to all concepts of style—not when one can identify cases that subjectively affirm a specific manner of artistic creation. Two examples are the "New German" movement during the nineteenth century, in which the belief in program music was paramount, and the "New Viennese" school during the twentieth, in which the organizing principle of notes (the "twelve-tone technique") was primary. In the latter case I am more inclined to speak of "school" than "style," especially since the stylistic classification made by posterity may turn out to be different. There are already indications that Alban Berg's music has a different appeal for the general public than Arnold Schoenberg's or Anton von Webern's.

It will probably always be tempting to apply stylistic labels to musical characteristics shared by a number of composers, but the categories that serve to satisfy this need for order should not automatically be understood as sociological divisions. Rather than being analytical tools, these categories are themselves phenomena that form an object of sociological analysis. It is highly instructive, for example, to point out that Gustav Mahler was long classified as a "late Romantic," whereas more recently he has been seen in a number of ways as a "precursor" of many aspects of twentieth-century composition. Sociology is not called upon to choose one or the other interpretation. It has fulfilled one of its tasks, however, if it explains this very change in interpretations as determined by the social context of reception in which Mahler's music moves.

Chapter 8 *Technical Conditions of Musical Activity*

Representatives of the materialistic view of history were not the only ones to seek a regular, convincing connection between the creation and reception of art and the social system of the time. Consistent philosophical idealists have also tried to explain such links. They are more inclined than the advocates of a materialistic interpretation to make "spirit," "mood," or "psychology" responsible for individual manifestations of art. Alois Riegl's concept of "artistic intent" (*Kunstwollen*) still contains an element of these purely intellectual arguments. But when Riegl provides a detailed analysis of specific phenomena, he does not adhere to the mystical interpretation that attempts to raise artistic intent to the single force driving the development of art.

Virtually all historiography of art proceeds from the basic view that "not everything is possible in every period." This statement by Heinrich Wöfflin caused Ernst H. Gombrich to ask, "To explain this curious fact is not the art historian's duty, but whose business is it?" (Gombrich 1960, 4). Gombrich's question is a challenge for sociology, which has, after all, been entrusted with investigating social activity (including artistic activity) within the social sphere in which this activity takes place. The reconstruction of such events cannot be restricted to invoking the "spirit" of a society. Activity also takes place under very definite material and technical conditions, and sociology must also take these into account.

If the technical aspect is ignored, the assertion that not everything is possible at all times is reduced to a trite formula, such as the following statement: we cannot imagine Beethoven's "Eroica" having been composed at the beginning of the eighteenth century; it had to be written at the beginning of the nineteenth. A pronouncement of this kind, which relies wholly on "spiritual" aspects, consciously ignores material and technological conditions. But such a statement can be meaningful only when it is based on real data—that is, when it can be refuted—for only then, as long as it is not refuted, can it claim to be valid. It is easy to see that Beethoven's Third Symphony (1804) could not have been created prior to the development of the orchestra or without the long historical process leading to the sonata form and technical mastery of the compositional style which Beethoven called "obbligato accompaniment." The technical aspect refers to not only the performance apparatus but also the skills needed to handle this apparatus in a certain way. It also includes the composer's idiom, which, individual though it may be, rests on idioms developed by others over the course of history. That this idiom is influenced in turn by the technical characteristics of the available instruments (for example, the natural horn, which was not replaced by the valve horn until after Beethoven's death), once again defines the limits in time. In other words, it is not purely a spiritual desire to create that roots the "Eroica" in a specific period and place; it is also the grappling of artistic intent with the technical structure, the use of given material, and the application of historically developed skills governing this use. In short: "Scientific research must utilize everything that can shed light on the development of music. It must consider all aspects and causal factors connected with [musical] creation" (Adler 1919, 12).

The methodological importance of this realization, which science has strongly urged on the visual arts, can hardly be overrated. Discussing the views of Alois Riegl, Wilhelm Worringer, and Max Dvořák, Gombrich writes:

> I would assert that what is their greatest pride is in fact their fatal flaw: by throwing out the ideal of skill they have not only surrendered vital evidence, they have made it impossible to realize their ambition, a valid psychologyl of stylistic change. (Gombrich 1960, 21)

Gombrich insists on the importance of "technical ability" for an understanding of change in the visual arts. His thesis is also valid for music, applying not only for the technical ability in using musical instruments but also for changes in musical technology itself; the valve horn permits different skills than the natural horn. But progressing from one technology to another implies losses as well as gains. Richard Wagner, who stood at the threshold of this process of technical change, provides an example in *The Flying Dutchman*, which still employs both natural and valve horns. In his manual of instrumentation, published in 1844, Berlioz made a case for retaining the old natural horn alongside the new valve horn because he regarded the particular tone color of the earlier instrument to be indispensable.

Liszt and the Piano

Directing our attention to technology will not help us explain the individuality, or even the aesthetic quality, of a musical work; it will, however, allow us to point out factors influencing changes in composition. These factors occasionally include changes in instrument-making that clear the way for new procedures in composition. Franz Liszt's treatment of the piano reveals this relationship between the construction of the instrument and the concept of an ideal piano sound. Very rarely has the connection between an economic-technical (in this case, iron production) and a technological factor (piano action) been so forcefully revealed in a style of performance and composition. Liszt's *Études en forme de 12 exercices* of 1826, which the composer revised in 1837 (and once again in 1852), are a rare stroke of luck that clearly calls for sociological analysis. Robert Schumann compared the 1826 and 1837 versions in a review, aptly writing that in the second version of the Études "the composer had to wring them from the piano with his hands."

The best pianos available to Liszt during the 1830s were distinctly different from their predecessors. The evolution of the instrument is characterized by two technical innovations:

1. A cast-iron frame permitting greater string tension and volume
2. The so-called double escapement action with repetition, which catches the returning hammers so as to enable a new attack immediately without having to release the key completely

Liszt's particular achievement consisted of "fully exploiting" the new tonal possibilities, for example, chords using all fingers, passages in octaves and double-stops, and rapid repetition of a single note (Kurt von Fischer in MGG 7, 1160).

Schumann's Analysis of the Liszt Études

A comparison of the first version of the Études (1826) with that of 1837 illustrates the greater sonority resulting from the piano's reinforced frame and more responsive action. Schumann considered this comparison important enough to devote to it a long and lively discussion of the aesthetic consequences of a technical change:

The first difference is between the earlier and the contemporary style of playing the piano, showing how we have now added a wealth of new means, trying to outdo the older style in brilliance and fullness. Of course, on the other hand, the original naiveté contained in the first outpouring of youth appears to have been completely suppressed in the present form of the work.

In order to make it easier for the reader to judge the original form and the changes made to it, I have chosen several openings:

No. 1 original [1826]:

The same now [1837]:

No. 5 original:

The same now:

No. 9 original:

The same now:

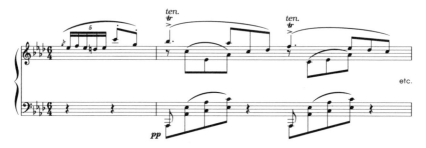

The similarities and differences are obvious. In general, the underlying moods of the openings have remained the same, although they are now embellished with richer figuration and overflowing harmonies. Everything is more emphatic. In the course of the pieces, however, the new edition exhibits so many departures from the original that the latter often disappears entirely.

It would be a waste of time to attempt a critique along the usual lines—to look for parallel fifths and false relations, for example. You have to *hear* compositions like this. The composer had to wring them from the piano with his hands; his hands have to convey them to us by means of the piano. And you also have to *see* the composer. Seeing any virtuosity is an uplifting, strengthening experience, all the more so when we see the composer struggle with his instrument and tame it, forcing every tone to obey him. These are truly formidable, frightening études for at most ten or twelve people in this world. (Schumann 1889, 2, 218f.)

Schumann notes the kinship of Liszt's musical ideas to the "ideas of French Romantic literature, among whose great minds he [Liszt] lived." This reference brings to mind Plekhanov's thesis on the non-simultaneity of success in literary and musical Romanticism. Plekhanov's thesis is based on a comparison between the fortunes of Victor Hugo and Hector Berlioz. If in this context, however, one replaces the name of Berlioz with that of Liszt, the extent to which Plakhanov's argumentation is unsubstantiated becomes apparent. Although the difference between

Liszt's and Berlioz's chances for success cannot be explained by "spiritual factors," it certainly can be explained by the nature of the musical instruments the two composers employed. The great master of instrumentation required the large orchestra to enact his innovations, while Liszt was able to exhibit his on a single keyboard instrument. Berlioz was clearly referring to this aspect of artistic activity when he said to Liszt (slightly varying a bon mot of Louis XIV): "You can . . . say: I am the orchestra! I am the chorus! Again, I am the conductor!"

Piano Production as Social Factor

Thus, apart from its aforementioned style-generating influence, Liszt's instrument reinforced the dominance of the artist, who was not only creator and performer but orchestra, chorus, and conductor all in one. Furthermore, the sheer volume of sound the new instrument could produce contributed to the image of the sovereign virtuoso. And this image, because it fit perfectly the Romantic idea of the virtuoso, itself increased his popularity with the public.

It is highly unlikely that anyone will ever succeed in researching all the effects and repercussions of the factors promoting Liszt's success and blocking Berlioz's. Nonetheless, the attempt to reveal these factors is not without results, for unlike biographical reconstruction, sociology does not aim at the individual case but rather is concerned with underlining the process of change that influences the basis of artistic creation. Such a process of change was begun by the production of pianos for the middle-class domestic music market, for which the instrument was universally usable. Max Weber pointed out this economic factor in the evolution of music:

> In the eighteenth century piano-builders, above all the Germans, were still great artisans who were personally involved in building and experimenting (like Silbermann). Machine-made mass production of the piano occurred first in England (Broadwood), then in America (Steinway) where first-rate iron could be cast for the construction of the frame. Moreover, iron helped overcome the numerous climatic difficulties that could affect a general adoption of the piano. Incidentally, climatic difficulties also stood in the way of its adoption in the tropics. By the beginning of the nineteenth century the piano had become a standard commercial object produced for stock.

> The wildly competitive struggle of the factories played a role in the development of the instrument. So, too, did the virtuosi, relying on the publicity potential of the press and exhibitions. Finally, analogous to the sales promotion techniques of breweries, the instrument manufacturers even had concert halls of their own (especially in Berlin). These forces brought about that technical perfection of the instrument which

alone could satisfy the ever-increasing demands of the composers. The older instruments were no longer adequate even for Beethoven's later creations.

Orchestra works could be made accessible for home use only in the form of piano transcriptions. Chopin was an example of a first-rank composer who restricted himself entirely to the piano. Finally Liszt, the great virtuoso, elicited from the instrument all imaginable expressive possibilities (Weber 1958, 122).

Thus the traveling piano virtuosi also had an advertising effect on behalf of piano makers (which does not mean that they always allowed themselves to be used for advertising purposes). At any rate, what these virtuosi offered was audible proof of the new instrument's musical advantages. In this way the piano was accorded first place among instruments, becoming the principal instrument of an entire musical culture. The soft, five-octave keyboard instrument of Mozart's time had become a seven-octave virtuoso pianoforte, able to replace an entire orchestra.

Factor as Conceptual Model

Liszt's 1832 piano version of Berlioz's *Symphonie fantastique* (which had premiered in 1830) quickly reached more listeners than did orchestral performances of the work. Liszt underscored the connection between the priority of economics, technically perfected construction, and the sonic universality of the modern piano:

> In my opinion the piano is first in the hierarchy of instruments. It owes this importance to the harmonic power it alone possesses. . . . In its seven octaves, it embraces the compass of an orchestra, and our ten fingers suffice to reproduce the harmonies created by an ensemble of one hundred musicians. Thus it is possible to present works with one instrument which would otherwise remain unknown due to the problems involved in assembling an orchestra. Owing to the progress already made and the incessant efforts of pianists, the instrument's adaptability increases from day to day. We can play broken chords as on the harp, long sustained notes as on wind instruments, staccati, and thousands of passages that would once have been possible only on other instruments. Due to the projected improvements in piano construction, we will surely have available that variety of sounds which we so far lack. (Liszt, quoted in Rehberg 1961, 91)

This example is meant to illustrate that psychology alone does not suffice to grasp the changes in musical activity and behavior. (I am referring again to Plekhanov's interpretation of social psychology.) A subtle theory of factors, similar to the one outlined by Labriola, is better suited to provide a model for the most important effects, repercussions, and interactions. To be sure, we must not lose sight of the fact that this is a model. As such, only those factors have been selected and reproduced from the complexity of events that can be shown to be of significance for the structure of these events or for the change of this structure. No model "can contain all the qualities of the represented reality. The model is only a model with respect to specific qualities and relationships" (Frey 1967, 90).

Chapter 9 *The Work of Art: Product and Factor of Social Activity*

The theory of factors and the concept of model do not establish how factors are selected and models constructed. In each case it is up to the researcher to decide whether to limit the inquiry, for example, to factors of economy or technology, of ideology or artistic technique. Such limited efforts are well suited to explaining the action of given factors or groups of factors. To be sure, although a research strategy of this kind is not only permissible in special cases but also quite productive, it is doomed to failure if it aims at providing the most faithful overall picture of a social process.

Taine Supplemented by Guyau

Of course, several aspects of the overall picture cannot be discovered if the concept of factors is applied mechanically—if it interprets the work of art wholly as a *product* of society and not as a *factor* of social activity as well. This dialectic relationship between work of art and society was examined by Jean-Marie Guyau (1854–1888). In *L'art au point de vue sociologique*, which was published after Guyau's death by his mentor and stepfather Alfred Fouillée, the chapter called "Genius as a Socially Formative Force" contains a very important addition to the ideas of Hippolyte Taine:

Taine's incomplete theory concerning the relationship between social milieu and artistic genius must be supplemented by a theory based on the opposite principle. Taine assumes that the individual genius is produced by the preexisting milieu; one must assume that the individual genius produces a new milieu or a new phase of the milieu. Both of these ideas are essential parts of the truth. (Guyau 1923, 42)

It has been correctly stated that, whereas neither Guyau nor Taine created a sociology of art, they both deserve credit for having opened the way for just such a discipline (Bastide 1977, 31). But Guyau's thesis that the work of art (he speaks of "genius," but he means its products) has the power to produce milieu is too vague. He does not state the conditions under which this theory can apply. If one attempts to track down the conditions, the theory turns out to be not at all general. Its validity is limited because it presupposes the creation of the autonomous work of art and it would require a more precise definition of the term "genius." Genius can, of course, be understood in a general way as personified creativity in the arts or, in a concrete historical sense, as a sociological category that is tied to given economic and social conditions (Zilsel 1926).

The Work of Art as a Force That Creates Milieu

Nonetheless, Guyau's addition to Taine's thesis of milieu represents a major advance for argumentation in the sociology of art, for it reveals the interaction between genius and milieu, between a work of art and society. The interaction—which is ascertainable in some, though not all, eras of music history since the Renaissance—can be seen especially in the process of the establishment of a musical public during the nineteenth century and the ensuing institutionalization of concert life. In his study *Structural Changes of the Public*, Jürgen Habermas forcefully demonstrated that the modern middle-class concert audience is not the product of a social shift but that, instead, the change of social structure regarding music is responsible for creating the audience (Habermas 1968, 51). The founding of concert organizations and the institutionalization of orchestras played a significant part in the creation of the middle-class musical public. These developments were, however, based on the idea that organizations and institutions were needed to provide adequate performances of masterworks. For the nineteenth century, this meant the works of Beethoven. The Paris Société des Concerts (1828), for example, came into being as a result of François Antoine

Habeneck's efforts to bring about an adequate performance of Beethoven's "Eroica." Other concert organizations in Europe were founded in order to create the conditions necessary to perform Beethoven's symphonies. Efforts in musical education were also justified along these lines: the founding of the Society of the Friends of Music conservatory in Vienna (1817) is an example. According to its statutes, students were not to learn how to play instruments solely suited to their "self-gratification" but were to gain musical proficiency in order to perform ensemble works. It should come as no surprise, then, that initially a "singing school" was founded—to which were soon added courses for violin (1818), cello (1820), woodwinds and horn (1821/22), trumpet (1827), and trombone and contrabass (1831)—but there was no piano instruction to speak of until the thirties (cf. Perger/Hirschfeld 1912, 323–324).

Beethoven as Leading Figure

Concert programs from the early days of the Vienna Conservatory show the meaning of musical activity at that time more clearly than statements by its founders or the nature of its courses. The Vienna Society of the Friends of Music held forty-six concerts between 1817 and the end of 1827, the year of Beethoven's death. Twenty-seven works by Beethoven appear in their programs, followed by seventeen works, or parts of works, by Mozart. Works by other composers make up the relatively small remainder. Furthermore, works by Beethoven were usually performed in their entirety, not in excerpt. With the exception of the third and fourth movements of the Ninth Symphony, all of Beethoven's symphonies were performed in these concerts during the composer's lifetime, some of them twice (Nos. 1, 3, 4, 5, 7, 8), with the Second Symphony being given three times.

These programs prove Beethoven's dominance in the Society's programming and show that not only the courses of study at the Conservatory but also the concert programs were intended to provide knowledge of musical works of art, primarily those of Beethoven. This phenomenon clearly demonstrates the repercussions of existing works on musical practice. The orchestra concert open to the general public created a new musical audience subject to special rituals, which often sought their justification in Beethoven. I am not suggesting that European concert life would not have come about without Beethoven's remarkable creations, yet the abundant material we have certainly shows that, at the least, Beethoven's works accelerated this process. What is more, Beethoven not only legitimated but was the central figure in this emerging ritual. We find this not only in statements by E. T. A. Hoffmann, who, in 1813, uses the words "divineness" and "consecration" to describe Beethoven's instrumental works but also in the contemporary announcement of the founding of the Royal Philharmonic Society in London, which declared its desire to serve the "genius of the great masters."

Phenomena of this kind reveal that sociologists should devote their attention not only to the social origins of a musical work of art but also to the *impact of the work on society*. This means, then, that what we now like to call the history of the reception of a musical work should be understood not only as society's reception of this work but also as the influence of the work on society. Dominik Hartmann's attempt to analyze the history of Beethoven's fame is therefore a genuine sociological task. He intends to demythologize—which was also the intent of Maurice Ravel's and Leoš Janáček's aggressive anti-Beethoven declarations during the Beethoven year of 1927—but he is far more interested in deciphering the forces inherent in Beethoven's work (cf. Hartmann 1970).

Perhaps Guyau's most important contribution is that he emphasized this aspect of the sociology of art. Nonetheless, his approach has been misinterpreted on a number of occasions. Some authors believe he represented sociology based on the actions of genius. H.-P. Thurn wrote, for example, that Guyau contains only "reminiscences of the philosophical aesthetics of Hippolyte Taine and his theory of milieu," although the previously quoted excerpt proves that Guyau meant for his theory about the influence of genius on society to supplement Taine's thesis about the influence of society on genius. Thurn, however, writes of the "myth of genius supported by Guyau" (in Silbermann 1979 B, 42), as if Guyau had wished to replace the idea of milieu's power to create art with that of art's power to create milieu.

The attempt to draw this kind of contrast between Taine and Guyau can probably also be explained in part by the need, which had been growing since the second half of the nineteenth century, to place thinkers in one of two camps: the materialistic interpretation of history or the idealistic. The view that placed society at the center of interest was for a long time negatively linked to the opinion that the individual has no appreciable influence on society. The concept of a society "without great names" was most prominent among the coarsest representatives of the materialist camp. At any rate, this view could carry weight as a historiographical corrective to the conviction that history resulted solely from the actions of major figures. But in considering the history of art and music from the sixteenth century to the present, such a one-sided view was in danger of ignoring the finished work of art and its effects on society; the work of art is regarded to be a mere "thing" and not, as Durkheim understood it, the crystallization of social activity.

Reception and Renaissance

From this juncture the road led to a sociology of art that was content to find the "sociological explanation" for the creation of given works or styles of art by carefully, and not impartially, applying selected ideas from Marx or Taine. The concentrated social force of transmission to the contemporary society, or subsequent societies, played almost no part in sociological interpretations of this kind. But social phenomena such as reception and renaissance cannot be perceived, much less explained, without taking into consideration the social energy stored in the work itself. It is surprising that the social effects of an artwork could be underestimated to such an extent, because Jacob Burckhardt had pointed out quite early what he called the characteristic ability of higher cultures "to experience renaissances" (Burckhardt 1978, 49). We would certainly be underestimating the situation if we sought to explain artistic renaissance only in the structure of our society and not also in the nature of the art society has chosen to revive. It would make just as little sense to limit oneself to deriving the constantly changing interpretation of works of art by successive societies—that is, the historical reception of works of art—only from the spirit of those societies, without asking if and to what extent these works of art are suited to such reinterpretations.

The history of the reception of music substantiates the utility of Guyau's thesis as well as Taine's. I have already mentioned that the concert audience and the institutions of musical life connected with it evolved in large part because of "the works themselves" (cf. Blaukopf 1972, 15). There can be no doubt that the reception accorded Johann Sebastian Bach's music (which has taken a variety of forms from Mozart/ Swieten to Forkel, Mendelssohn, and others up to the present) cannot be explained without recourse to the society receiving it, or without referring to the special features of a work suited to this kind of changing reception. What we today regard as misleading interpretations of works by Mozart and Haydn (for example, regarding them as rococo or playing them without appoggiaturas, as was done in Mahler's day) must either be present in the works themselves or, if one wishes to dispute this, something of the work's meaning must still be present in its misinterpretation. Even the concepts of "misinterpretation" and its opposite, "historically faithful performance practice," demand sociological criticism. Although these concepts seem to express the obvious, what appears to be obvious to us very seldom coincides with the social fact we wish to approach. Wilhelm Furtwängler expressed this very pointedly in his "Remarks on the Performance of Old Music" (1932): if

we wish to be truly historically faithful, we must "attempt to reconstruct the old ensemble, and especially the old rooms, but along with
these the 'mentality' of the audience of the period" (Furtwängler 1954,
58). This suggests that even a "historically faithful" performance creates
a different effect today than it would have at the time the music was created or first performed.

Metamorphosis of the "Christmas Oratorio"

The transformation of a musical work of art can result from the structure of the work itself, as was the case with Johann Sebastian Bach's
"Christmas Oratorio." Each of the six sections of the work was originally intended to be performed, independent of the others, on the
church holidays between Christmas and Epiphany, that is, over a two-
week period. The work therefore consists of six cantatas, each of which
had a place in the service after the reading of the gospel and before the
singing of Luther's creed. In Leipzig during Bach's time, the cantatas
functioned as part of the religious service, which included a sermon
often lasting more than one hour. Thus the cantata itself "lasted barely
half an hour, a time limit seldom exceeded" (Dürr 1971, 38). In other
words, the music was inextricably bound up with the religious service.

In modern performance practice, the music is removed from its historical context. Concert performances and recordings bring together
music that was in Bach's time tied to the liturgy; they produce a new totality that could not have been intended as such when the music was
created, but which powerfully arouses our aesthetic interest. The connecting of six separate cantatas that were meant to be integrated into the
religious service, the exclusion of the surrounding liturgical elements,
the combining of the cantatas into an oratorio performed as a single
unit, and the relocation of the music outside the church into the secular
sanctity and consecration of the concert hall—all this is surely the result
of adapting the music to norms of acting, thinking, and feeling that belong to a society different from Bach's. Yet the question also arises as to
whether this process of transplantation is inherent in the musical work
of art, or whether the work itself contains features that predestine it for
such social transplantations. The nature of the music itself apparently
calls for it to be transferred from the church into the concert hall, to undergo the transition from religious inspiration to aesthetic enjoyment.
In making this transition, the work also generates its influence on the
thinking, feeling, and musical activity of a different society.

The Assumed Harmony between Society and Art

Guyau meant precisely this kind of influence when he spoke of the ability of genius to produce a "new milieu or a new stage of the milieu." Such an active role comes to the fore in those societies—again I am using Burckhardt's expression—that are capable of artistic renaissance. In general, the presence of self-contained works of music, or works that can be interpreted as such, is a prerequisite.

Many writings on socio-musicology have paid scarce attention to the resulting subtlety of the relationship between music and society. The effect of the musical work of art on the musical milieu has seldom been investigated; the effect of a work beyond its own time has been analyzed only in exceptional cases. In general, scholars have been content to give summary information about the presumed social conditions for the creation of given musical works, thereby assuming harmony of social and artistic development. Sociological theories of this kind claimed to be based on Karl Marx. As I will demonstrate, this was and still is unjustified.

Chapter 10 *The Problem of the Sociology of Art in Marx*

Much of the literature on the sociology of art that follows the ideas of Karl Marx proceeds from a very mechanical view that the economic factor is dominant. The virulence of this view can be explained, in part, by the connection between Marxian ideas and present-day social criticism and politics. But although Marx advocated a more subtle interpretation of the relationship between art and the social base, he saw to it that his ideas on the subject remained unknown for decades. For this reason, if no other, I have chosen to discuss his ideas at this point.

In the preface to his *Critique of Political Economy*, published in 1859, Marx writes:

> It is not the consciousness of people that determines their being, but rather their social being which determines their consciousness. At a certain stage of development, society's material forces of production stand in contradiction to the existing position of production or—this is simply the legal expression—the legal position concerning property within which they had previously moved. These positions suddenly change from the developed forms of the forces of production into their chains. What follows is an era of social revolution. Once the economic foundation changes, the entire immense superstructure is revolutionized at a greater or lesser rate. In considering such revolutionary changes one must always distinguish between the material revolutionary change in the economic conditions of production, which can be observed in a scientifically objective fashion, and the legal, political,

religious, artistic, and philosophical, in short, ideological forms in which people become conscious of this conflict and in which they settle it. (Marx 1971, 15)

In this discussion, Marx aims primarily at establishing a clear distinction between the "scientifically objective" characteristics of a society's economic base and the ideas people have of changing that base. His aphoristically pointed wording is not, however, intended to speak to the kind of relationship between the economic base and the superstructure (religious, artistic, philosophical, and other). The previously quoted comments from Friedrich Engels's correspondence demonstrate that an interpretation of art in the Marxian sense is not content with this or some other general formula.

The "Suppressed" Manuscript of 1859

In all likelihood, the mechanical, stereotyped application of Marxist teachings about base and superstructure would not have been so successful if everything Marx had conceived and written about art prior to 1859 had been published at the time. This was not the case, however. Marx let it be known in the preface to his 1859 book that he had "suppressed a general introduction" that he had "dashed off." This introduction, unpublished at the time, contains several sections which deal with the relationship between art and society in a far more reasoned out and concrete fashion than would have been possible in his programmatic formulations or as margin notes in his detailed economic argumentations. The manuscript of this introduction was discovered more than forty years later in Marx's estate and was made available for the first time in 1903 in the journal *Neue Zeit*. The text shows Marx's ideas on art in a better light. That this was not accomplished more generally is surely due to the fact that following the Russian Revolution of 1917 attention was devoted to those passages in Marx's writings that were relevant to the artistic needs of the Soviet state, be they the agitatorial needs of the twenties or the officially decreed aesthetics between 1930 and 1956.

I am devoting special mention to these circumstances because they had consequences for a certain type of Marx reception, most of all among those who were taken with his ideas. Marx did not leave a systematic treatment of the problems of art. The art historians and sociologists of art who followed in his footsteps were entirely dependent on a few scattered statements about art and literature, in addition to the general considerations on the philosophy of history in which art is mentioned marginally, if at all. Although Friedrich Engels warned several times after Marx's death against a mechanical application of Marxian ideas to art and the history of art, this did not suffice to avert misinterpretations. It is unfortunate that the aforementioned text did not come to light until twenty years after Marx's death, for it would have well illustrated the circumspect and, in many respects, pioneering way in which Marx dealt with questions of the relationship between art and society. That this document was unable to prevent the continued proliferation of simplistic Marxist interpretations of art cannot be explained by the history of the sociology of art alone, because it is clear that political motives also played a role.

The text by Marx that I have chosen to single out is not a study on the sociology of art, although it does contain certain ideas about questions of methodology in the sociology of art. Marx concisely demonstrates the difficulties and limitations of a method seeking to derive artistic activity directly or indirectly from the economic base of society; he implicitly distances himself from the idea of progress that Spencer purported to see in the arts; he emphasizes the contradictions between social and artistic development; he formulates as a problem the effect of a work of art beyond its time and society, thereby going beyond Taine's ideas; indeed, he goes as far as Guyau, who was denounced as "mythicizing genius" because he states that the work of art itself creates an "audience with a sense for art and capable of beauty." The following three passages, along with my commentary, come from the Introduction to the *Critique of Political Economy*, which became known in 1903.

Contradiction Between Social and Artistic Development

Marx writes in the manuscript he had "dashed off" without a final proofreading:

> It is a well-known fact that certain periods of artistic efflorescence do not coincide in the least with the general development of society, including its material foundation which represents, as it were, the skeleton of its organization. For example, the Greeks compared to the moderns, or Shakespeare. It has even been recognized that certain art forms, the epic poem, for example, could never have been created in their epochal, classical form once the production of art as such appears. That is to say that within art itself certain eminent forms are only possible at an undeveloped stage of artistic development. If this is the case for the relationship of the various arts to each other, this is less apparent in the relationship of art as a whole to the general development of society. The only difficulty involved is to formulate these contradictions in a general fashion. Once these are particularized they are also explained. (Marx 1971, 258)

Marx is clearly referring to the difficulty of creating a general theory concerning these contradictions. He also distances himself from a method which sees the contingency of the superstructure on the base as a prefabricated formula that merely has to be applied to the artistic revolution. He emphasizes the fact that it is difficult to "formulate these contradictions in a general fashion"; no claim is made to this being possible. His remarks would seem to indicate that specifying and thereby explaining contradictions of this kind is one of the tasks for the sociology of art.

The Effect of the Work of Art Beyond its Own Time

Even if we succeed in understanding how a work of art grew out of a given social situation, the question still remains as to how works of art that owe their existence to a given situation can retain their aesthetic validity under wholly different social conditions. According to Marx:

> The difficulty does not consist in understanding the fact that Greek art and epic poetry are linked to certain social conditions. The difficulty is that they still provide us with aesthetic pleasure and are, in a certain respect, regarded as standards and, for us, unattainable models. (Marx 1971, 259)

Marx points out a problem brought into focus by the materialistic view of history—one, to be sure, important for every sociology of art. When a given society (S1) produces a given kind of art (A1), and the conditions exist for the creation of A2 but not A1 in another society (S2), how is it possible for A1 to have aesthetic validity in society S2 or, as Marx says, "provide us with aesthetic pleasure?" A distinction must obviously be made between the conditions of creation and the conditions of reception. Ancient art and the epic poem are simply examples of a phenomenon we also encounter in the history of music. The very concept of the "Classical," as employed in the history of music and as impressed on the general consciousness, documents the continuing relevance of the problem. If works of art retain their social resonance once the social conditions in which they were created have long since ceased to exist, this means that, once created, the work of art itself can and must become a "factor" of further artistic development. As we will presently see, Marx also discusses in this same text the "active role" of the work of art as a social factor.

Repercussions of the Work of Art on Society

Marx deals with this question within the context of discussing the relationship between production and consumption. He shows that, in the economic sense, not only is production determined by consumption but consumption is also determined by production. Although he refers to production and consumption in the economic sense, he also turns in passing to artistic production, which he clearly understands to be an active factor with an effect on the consumption of art. According to this, the art object (the work of art) is not only the product of a human need but, in turn, also produces this need in people.

> Production not only supplies the need with a material, but also [supplies] the material with a need. Once consumption has gone beyond primitive grossness and immediacy . . . the object itself mediates the drive. The need which this fills is created by the perception of it. The art object, like every other product, creates an art-loving public capable of enjoying beauty. Consequently, production produces not only an object for the subject, but also a subject for the object. (Marx 1971, 238)

One of my objectives in citing these quotations is to demonstrate the inadequacy of a simplistic interpretation of history that unjustly claims to be Marxian. My principal aim, however, is to draw attention to the methodological subtlety of this formulation. It is remarkable that a thinker such as Marx, who certainly could not be accused of underestimating the importance of the economic factor, insists on emphasizing the contradictions between economic and artistic development, on recognizing as a problem the effect of the work of art outside its social framework, and on underscoring the role of the work of art in the "production" of an audience receptive to this work of art. These are three important areas of sociological research, which are also of interest to music.

Chapter 11 *Economics, Leisure, and Lifestyle*

Identifying contradictions between economic development and artistic development reveals the limitations of argumentation that seeks to trace all artistic activity directly to economic (and social) factors. Even a presumed dominance of the economic factor is not always directly applicable, as the analysis of concrete phenomena shows, but often makes itself felt through a large number of intermediaries. This makes it impossible to arrive at a "general law" for these contradictions; they must be identified in each case:

> As the constant for the investigation of conditions under which arts and sciences are constituted, economics remains an objective factor which, although it does not reach the act of artistic and scientific creation, does however form the basis upon which this comes about. (Althaus 1971, 18–19)

All the same, it is also advisable to uncover the direct effects exerted by the economic structure of society upon lifestyle and, therefore, artistic activity.

Thorstein Veblen's Theory of the Leisure Class

The American sociologist Thorstein Veblen (1857–1929) made an attempt of this kind in *The Theory of the Leisure Class,* published in 1899. The existence of the leisure class posits an economic system which creates so much surplus value as "to admit of the exemption of a considerable portion of the community from steady application to a routine labor" (Veblen 1973, 25). According to Veblen, the salient characteristic of this class is "conspicuous leisure." It is part of human nature, he continues, that the conventional proof of wealth, that is leisure, turns into a form of compulsion and "fixes it in men's habits of thought as something that is in itself substantially meritorious and ennobling, while productive labor at the same time and by a like process becomes in a double sense intrinsically unworthy" (Veblen 1973, 45). Veblen cites "nonmaterial goods" as a preferred area for elevated leisure. He can be interpreted to mean that interest in these matters represents conformity to the collective norm applicable to a certain class, that is, a *fait social* as understood by Durkheim:

> Such evidences. . . are quasi-scholarly or quasi-artistic accomplishments and a knowledge of processes and incidents that do not conduct directly to the furtherance of human life. So, for instance, in our time there is the knowledge of the dead languages and the occult sciences; of correct spelling; of syntax and prosody; of the various forms of domestic music and other household art. (Veblen 1973, 48)

In this and many other passages Veblen combines his theoretical discussion of the leisure class with social criticism applicable only to the American society of the period. Nonetheless, his main thought runs throughout the book: that in certain societies demonstrative, economically untenable consumption is considered compulsory for the leisure class and that this consumption also has economic roots.

Veblen's argumentation has the weakness of applying his generally exaggerated characterization to all "leisure classes" without distinction and without differentiating between the behavior of leisure classes in different types of societies. The general nature of Veblen's statements could lead us to misinterpret them as "laws" applicable to both the patronage of Renaissance princes and the tax breaks granted to American bankers in the twentieth century for purchasing art, for the patrons of Baroque gala operas as well as for the industrial sponsors of modern concerts. This does not, however, lessen the fundamental usefulness of Veblen's line of reasoning. He draws attention to an economic factor which is suited to influencing the lifestyle of a class. As Veblen shows, this lifestyle also extends to the employment of servants whose nonproductive work (in an economic sense) contributes to the prestige of the leisure class, and who therefore carry out their masters' orders by indulging in what Veblen calls "vicarious leisure." This vicarious leisure should not, however, be considered idleness. The leisure "of the servant class exempt from productive labor is in a way a performance exacted from them, and is not normally or primarily directed to their own comfort." In general, a servant's leisure takes the form of special service that "is directed to the furtherance of his master's fullness of life" (Veblen 1973, 56). According to Veblen, the activity of a musician employed at a ruler's court should be interpreted as vicarious leisure.

The concept of a leisure class that initiates vicarious leisure in order to cultivate conspicuous consumption is ideally suited to understanding the economic and intellectual foundations of the cultivation of music at court. This concept must, however, be highly differentiated in order to arrive at an understanding of concrete historic phenomena. The general tendency toward conspicuous consumption at the Gonzaga court in Mantua during Monteverdi's lifetime produced different musical results from that at the residence of Frederick the Great. Indeed, even parallel developments such as those in Mannheim and Vienna between 1740 and 1778 cannot be understood with Veblen's general formula; they require more subtle analysis. Testing Veblen's model on this segment of music history— the Mannheim school and Viennese preclassicism—is worthwhile.

Mannheim and Vienna after 1740

At the beginning of this century, music history concentrated on the search for the "precursors" of Viennese classicism (Haydn, Mozart, and Beethoven). Hugo Riemann claimed to have found Haydn's predecessors in the Mannheim school, especially Johann Stamitz, whereas Guido Adler assigned this function to the Viennese school of preclassicism (Wagenseil, Monn, etc.) (cf. the summary of this controversy in Flotzinger MG 2, 95–96). Proponents of both points of view supported their contentions with manuscripts and evidence documenting reciprocal influence without going into the social contexts in which the musical development had taken place in Vienna and Mannheim.

Conspicuous splendor played a crucial role in the plans of the Elector Karl Theodor, who reigned in Mannheim from 1743 to 1778. He indulged not only in erecting new buildings but in expanding his instrumental ensemble as well. In 1756, the court orchestra consisted of ten first violins, ten second violins, four violas, four cellos, and two basses, a total of thirty string instruments. The Elector had musicians brought to Mannheim from near and far, for, according to Charles Burney, music was his "favorite and most constant pastime." Typically, the active artists here played more than one instrument, some even appeared as singers, and many also composed. This versatility went hand in hand with specialization. Compositions for solo instruments, for example the Concerto for Violin and Orchestra in C major by Johann

Stamitz (1717–1757), which documents his virtuosity on the instrument, are proof of this. Bringing such experienced musicians together in an ensemble led to a high degree of professionalism and technical prowess (unified bowings and refined dynamics, with the famous "Mannheim crescendo"). The result was "an army of generals, equally as able to draw up a battle plan as to fight in it," said Burney.

There can be no doubt that this trend-setting orchestra laboratory was the result of Elector Karl Theodor's conspicuous consumption. During his reign the prince invested no less than thirty-five million florins in the cultural life of his residence (Becker 1980, 5).

Maria Theresa's policy on the arts was completely different. Her accession to the throne in 1740 was a turning point: "The consequences for music, especially those resulting from the abandoning of the Spanish court ceremony, were far-reaching. For this reason alone the problem of style is inseparable from that of social function" (Gruber in MGÖ 2, 80).

The principles that Maria Theresa applied to the cultivation of music at court were not at all conditioned by "conspicuous consumption." Veblen's paradigm cannot be applied here. It must be said, however, that this was not the result of the subjective will of the ruler but the consequences of economic factors. Frugality was not only demanded by the Seven Years' War but also by the economic axioms of the state, which was based on productivity, industry, and education, and not "unproductive" luxury. According to a Theresian memorandum:

> Once the needs of state are taken care of, a sovereign owes it to his lands and subjects, including the poor, to do everything to ease their lot, but under no circumstances to squander the collected monies on entertainments, grandeur, or pomp. (Maria Theresa 1980, 131)

This is proof, then, that under certain social conditions a significant segment of the leisure class does not behave as Veblen's overly general theory would have us expect. Economic thought—also in the sense of the dominant mercantilism of the day—was concerned with modernizing the political system and with economic progress. This affected music. An end had to be put to Baroque festive operas; music, too, had to be organized with an eye to cost effectiveness. Although Burney regretted not being able to witness an opulent Baroque opera during his visit to Vienna, he praised the abolition of this genre as a humane act, with a typically English combination of economic rationality and humanity (Burney 1959, I, 125).

Business Ethics and the Cultivation of Music

Following the death of the court music director Johann Josef Fux in 1741, "the Imperial court orchestra began to lose its central importance; Maria Theresa's difficult position . . . forced her to cut expenditures, of which the musical institutions were those most adversely affected" (Orel in MGG 14, 609). To be sure, the cuts dictated by military spending are responsible only in part. Much more crucial in this regard is the mercantilistic economic attitude present in a number of documents. For example, the educational book, containing ninety-nine didactic illustrations, which the Empress commissioned in 1769 for her son Archduke Ferdinand (Rottenberg 1769), contains an illustration depicting beggars, musicians, and actors at the lowest level of the social hierarchy. Although this classification had a long tradition, it must also be viewed as a statement on this phase of the country's historic development. Grouping beggars, actors, and musicians together is one with the rejection of entertainment and extravagance.

Leopold Mozart's efforts to secure a post for his son with Archduke Ferdinand provide still more evidence. Ferdinand, educated in the spirit of the schoolbook that had been presented to him by his mother, the Empress, at Schönbrunn Palace in 1769, asked Maria Theresa for advice in this matter. Her answer of 12 December 1771 has been preserved:

> You ask whether you should take the young Salzburg musician into your service. I do not see why you should have to employ a composer or other such useless people. Should it nevertheless please you, I would not wish to prevent you from doing so. I am simply telling you not to burden yourself with such useless people. By all means avoid granting titles to such persons as if they were in your service. When such people roam around the world like beggars, it discredits service. (quoted in Paumgartner 1967, 111–112)

This letter reads like a commentary to the illustrations in Ferdinand's book, revealing an attitude toward economics related to what Max Weber termed the business ethics of puritanism. In my opinion, it shows that economic factors, in this case the need to stimulate the production of goods and provide funds for investment through accumulation, were the dominant force, going beyond religious denominations.

The consequences of these Theresian business ethics for musical life were not only organizational in nature. A 1754 decree ("Norma-Verordnung") orders that public plays and concerts may be held only 210 days of the year. A 1754 order prohibits the use of trumpets and kettle drums in church music (this was, to be sure, observed only a short time). Everything within Imperial jurisdiction, then, was aimed at frugality and sobriety, which were in accord with the hard work demanded.

To be sure, this trend of the times had little effect on the cultivation of music by the middle class, and even less by the aristocracy. Nonetheless, there was no central impulse for promoting musical pomp in the Habsburg capital during the age of Maria Theresa. The Empress's attitude toward the consumption of music was, then, diametrically opposed to the musical policy of Karl Theodor in Mannheim. This attitude placed limitations on musical activity; the professionalization and specialization of the orchestra characteristic of Mannheim did not reach Vienna until later. In Vienna, on the other hand, emphasis was placed on an active middle-class cultivation of music, not strictly separated from that of the aristocracy, which found its noblest expression in a new type of chamber music, as later created by Haydn and Mozart.

In Mannheim, the orchestra of this period was an expression of the "conspicuous consumption" described by Veblen. The musicians Karl Theodor employed in his residence were treated as anything but inferiors: they enjoyed the esteem of the prince, who commanded them to "vicarious leisure," and they contributed to the prince's prestige (Veblen 1971, 68–69). The music performed there was "cabinet music," largely intended for the ruler and those surrounding him, and less for those who were permitted to take part as tolerated guests:

> Musical performances in the Knights Hall are soirees at court. One converses at small tables at tea, playing cards while Stamitz, Cannabich, Holzbauer conduct their symphonic works or chamber music by Richter, Toeschi, Filtz, and other representatives of the Mannheim school is played. Exceptionally, friends and art-loving burghers are permitted to listen, standing. (Walter 1952, 110)

While the Empress's policies of economic and social reform at the court in Vienna were linked to cutting back on music, Prince Karl Theodor prepared the ground for a grandiose musical efflorescence. Ignaz Holzbauer, a brilliant composer who was later admired by Mozart and previously active at the Vienna Burgtheater, was also attracted by Mannheim. In 1753, Holzbauer was appointed "Court Conductor in Chief," staying in Mannheim until his death in 1785. Yet this fertilization of the musical field in Mannheim is linked to economic and social policies distinctly different from those of Maria Theresa:

> The bright side is mitigated by the dark side of social conditions, consisting largely of replacing the original municipal administration and the free middle class with civil servants brought to court from the outside. Hence it follows that Karl Theodor's efforts on behalf of the arts and sciences were in reality mere points of light meant to edify and amuse the upper circles of the society of the period. (Oeser 1904, 326)

The comparison between Vienna and Mannheim shows how multifarious the relationships between economics and the cultivation of music can be. Even more important, it shows how imperative it is to take the specific features of a particular economic situation into account, rather than only its general characteristics, when interpreting the behavior of the leisure class.

Musical Progress and Social Stagnation

The creation of a progressive workshop of orchestral culture in Mannheim can therefore not be attributed to progressive cultural convictions of the time. On the contrary, it resulted from the conspicuous consumption of a prince indifferent to economic and social reforms.

The musicians of the period were fully aware of the rank of the Mannheim orchestra. Leopold called it "undoubtedly the best in Germany" in a letter (from Schwetzingen) dated 19 July 1763. When Wolfgang Amadeus Mozart received a letter from his father in 1778 saying that he was considering placing his son again in the service of the archbishop of Salzburg once he [Wolfgang] returned from Paris, the younger Mozart vehemently rejected the idea. The well-traveled young man did not contrast what he considered the unacceptable practices in Salzburg with any of the large musical institutions of Central Europe; his ideal was the Mannheim orchestra:

> Ah, if only the orchestra were organized as they are in Mannheim! Indeed I would like you to see the discipline which prevails there and the authority which Cannabich wields. There everything is done seriously. Cannabich, who is the best conductor I have ever seen, is both beloved and feared by his subordinates. Moreover he is respected by the whole town, and so are his soldiers. But certainly they behave quite differently from ours. They have good manners, are well dressed, do not go to public-houses and swill. (*The Letters of Mozart and His Family*, 832–833)

Mozart recognized that Mannheim created the institutional basis upon which the specific values of purely instrumental music could flourish. Although certain compositional techniques—such as *durchbrochene Arbeit* (filigree work), in which themes were distributed among various instruments (first seen in the quartets of Haydn and Mozart)— were developed primarily in Vienna, it cannot be denied that the orchestral characteristics of the classical Viennese symphony owe a great deal to the experiments performed in Mannheim. That the spirit of the Mannheim orchestra infused Mozart's work, beginning in 1778, is incontestable. Clearly, the term "milieu," which Taine used to explain the creation of works of art, must be given a broader meaning. Whenever musical communication is internationalized, it is not only the immediate milieu that affects musical practice; experiences resulting from interregional or international exchange also contribute. In these cases we usually speak of stylistic influences, but I believe this reduction to purely stylistic elements is too limiting; it ignores the ideological forces at work behind the notes.

Ideological Evaluation of Instrumental Music

Of growing importance in music during the eighteenth century was thematic development and composition in which themes are distributed among different instrumental groups obeying their own, specifically musical laws. The idea of autonomous instrumental music—music not written for a specific occasion but conceived as a work in its own right—is manifest in all of its consequences beginning with Joseph Haydn's quartets, written "in a quite new special manner" (1781). But this idea had already played a part in the philosophy of the Enlightenment. Denis Diderot thought that the idea of the beautiful as a realization of relationships should be applied to music. He wrote in 1751 that secondary voices should either support the expression of the leading voice or "add new ideas which the theme demands and which the leading voice is unable to express" (Bardez 1975, 127–128). Although Jean-Jacques Rousseau, in his *Lettre sur la musique française* (1753), quotes this theoretical anticipation of the later compositional style of Haydn's quartets, he adds a commentary that reverses Diderot's thesis: the principal voice takes precedence, and the accompaniment should have no melodic role, supplying no more than coloration.

Diderot, then, takes an isolated stance with his views on music, allowing, if not furthering, purely instrumental music. In general, purely instrumental music was of little importance to the politically-oriented Encyclopedists, who valued the effects of the performances of the *bouffonists* as more important than the abstract playing with sounds. According to Jean le Rond d'Alembert, the words *bouffonist*, republican, *frondeur*, atheist, and materialist were considered to be synonyms. In 1760, d'Alembert published an essay entitled "De la liberté de la musique." In it, the author, who was quite a modern thinker for his time, labels as superfluous what we today consider to be the specific achievement of Viennese preclassicism and the Mannheim school:

> All purely instrumental music, without rhyme nor reason, speaks neither to the mind nor to the soul and merits the question asked by Monsieur Fontenelle: "Sonata, what do you want from me?" The authors who compose instrumental music create only empty noise. (d'Alembert 1772, 448)

This attitude is entirely understandable in the context of a rationalist culture, such as that of the French Encyclopedists, concerned with shaping the world through education. For them, purely instrumental music was linked to an attitude of ostentatious, non-rational behavior which could be that of a leisure class, but did not express the interests of an aspiring bourgeois intellectual class.

"Sonata" and Freedom of Thought

At that time the intellectual and philosophical relations between Mannheim and Paris were as close as the musical. The Mannheim court, at which Voltaire was a visitor, advocated an Enlightenment philosophy, not of the comprehensive democratic character of the thought of the French Encyclopedists, but restricted to the education and entertainment of the aristocracy. D'Alembert's book on the freedom of music reached Mannheim quickly, where it was read by the Elector's private secretary Cosmo Alessandro Collini (1727–1806), who wrote a commentary that has come down to us:

> In an essay bearing the title "Freedom of Music," one was somewhat astonished to find the musician forbidden to compose what he wants. Just as the freedom of thought leads to reason, so does the sonata lead to perfection in music. Sonatas are absolutely necessary. They accustom the musician to think, if I may say so, in music, and through them one can become acquainted with the particular way in which the musician thinks. (Collini, quoted in Bopp 1925)

As a result of what at first sight appears to be a paradoxical concatenation of economic and ideological factors, Mannheim, the venue of conspicuous, princely musical consumption, became a place in which progressive trends in composition were supported not only in practice but with philosophical arguments as well. This example shows the limited range of a sociological interpretation that is concerned only with the verifiable economic consequences of leisure in a society and reinforces the importance of taking all potentially relevant factors into consideration. In such cases, contemporary sociology speaks of "multivariate consideration" (e.g. Rosenmayr 1966, XLIV). The need for multivariate analysis, illustrated by the historical phenomenon I have treated here, applies equally to empirical social research of contemporary music. In this case, it will also be necessary to compare the direct musical findings with a large number of nonmusical factors that create or change a given musical practice.

One must, however, be careful when considering colloquial definitions of social phenomena and the vocabulary used in this context. Collini's statement, that freedom of thought and sonata are parallel, sounds democratic, indeed Jacobin, to our ears. Yet the expression "freedom of thought" as used by the electoral official does not carry the meaning we attach to it. For enlightened counselors in the cabinets of princes and emperors during the eighteenth century, this freedom was confined to certain subjects; it was not a general freedom but rather the prerogative of those considered capable of putting thought to good use. The attitude of the most zealous of the reformer emperors, Joseph II, also confirms this restrictive interpretation of the concept of freedom.

The term "sonata," as used by Collini in his polemic against d'Alembert, presents fewer difficulties. To him it was essentially a synonym for "purely instrumental music." We can assume that d'Alembert may have meant the chamber music widely played and published in Paris at the time (cf. Newman 1963, 605). Nonetheless, the argumentation of d'Alembert and Collini is on the same level, for sonata and symphony were still to a certain extent synonymous, both in definition and in practice. The six orchestra trios, opus 1, by Johann Stamitz, a member of the Mannheim group, are an example. They were published in Paris in 1755 with a title indicating the possibility of performance by soloists or orchestra.

That Mannheim was a musical frontier, with composition rapidly changing from a style tied to the figured bass to one of free symphonic texture, can be seen from attempts at historically authentic performances of this music. Recordings (Mannheim School 1980) convey a vivid sonic image in which both the pioneering role of Johann Stamitz and the mastery of Ignaz Holzbauer are discernible. It is interesting to note that this tradition diminished after the Elector left Mannheim in 1778. Once again, this confirms the crucial role played by the conspicuous court consumption of the prince in allowing music to flourish in Mannheim. Nonetheless, I cannot agree with the statement that the mission of the Mannheim school was "in fact over by 1757" (Adler 1930, 2, 776), because its influence continued far beyond that year, and the lasting impression and clear influence of Mannheim orchestral culture on Mozart reveals the importance of this city for the music of the period.

A comparison of Mannheim with Vienna provides impressive evidence for the nonparallel nature of economic-political progress on the one hand and musical progress on the other. It further shows that a hothouse of musical culture, set up owing to the wish of a prince eager for pomp, itself becomes a factor capable of exerting a lasting influence on musical practice in more than one place.

Chapter 12 *Georg Simmel's Contribution to the Sociology of Music*

The attempt to work with sociological categories in music clearly shows that sociological argumentation is unable to dispense with the assistance of other disciplines. The German sociologist Georg Simmel (1858–1918) emphasized this long ago. In his study *Über sociale Differenzierung* [On Social Differentiation] (Simmel 1890), Simmel stressed the fact that sociology was dependent upon using the results of other sciences as "semi-finished products" subject, as it were, to sociological finishing. Simmel therefore considered sociology a "science to the second degree," an "eclectic science to the extent that its materials are the products of other sciences" (Simmel 1890, 2).

This definition could create the impression that other sciences merely supply "material" for which sociology provides the meaning. Quite likely this distinction would widen the gulf between overemphasizing reality and playing with meaning. In fact, there are traces of this gulf in much of traditional German sociological thought. One result is the previously mentioned use of verbose analogy rather than argumentation. Even Simmel was not immune to this tendency. He

> preferred not to indulge merely in illustrating theoretical statements, but in argumentation by analogy, a procedure which Max Weber counted against him. Weber concluded that crucial aspects of Simmel's methodology were unacceptable, often regarding the results of his writings with reserve, and more often than not simply rejecting them. (G. Eisermann in Silbermann 1979 B, 73)

Simmel's sociology is not a "closed system" (F. Bülow). Those who wish to reduce sociology to observing the forms of social relationships divorced from their historical content encourage the arbitrary, subjective side of his explanations. Fortunately, Simmel is far from consistent in this respect, to which fact we owe a series of observations that can be regarded as contributions to the sociology of art. For example, in his study on picture frames, first published in 1902, he draws attention to the necessary (for purposes of art history) distinction between frameless art and framed art. His intention is to gain more concrete access to the social preconditions for panel painting on the one hand and the art of musical performance on the other. Characteristically, Simmel does not pursue the historical and social dimension of the questions he poses but limits himself instead to a description of the function of the picture frame. The frame "excludes the entire surroundings and, therefore, the observer of the artwork as well. The frame thereby helps place the artwork at the distance from which it alone can be enjoyed aesthetically" (Simmel 1922, 47).

Simmel's subtly worded aphorisms are more philosophically than sociologically oriented. Many of them may seem to be "semi-finished products," to use Simmel's terminology, meant to serve a sociology concerned with concrete social phenomena. His study of picture frames is ideally suited to this end, not only in the fine arts but in music as well. In both arts the transition from a socially frameless artistic practice rooted in life to a separation of the artistic aspect from reality is a process that appears to be linked to social givens. The picture frame, the separation of the picture from its background, demonstrates this transition and in turn contributes to creating the "distance" Simmel believed was conducive to the development of linear perspective. Music's advance from being closely tied to life to becoming a firmly established reality in a self-contained composition corresponds to the emergence of framed art. These parallels cannot be dismissed as mere analogy if the common social roots of both phenomena can be demonstrated. A number of studies (Sachs 1918, Besseler 1959, Blaukopf 1972) have taken such an approach. Simmel's failure to do so does not lessen his contribution in having outlined the problem. Those areas of sociology where Simmel was systematic contain virtually none of the categories potentially applicable to music sociology. His *Sociology*, first published in 1908, bears the telling subtitle *Studies on the Forms of Socialization*, thereby underscoring the formal character of his ideas, at a remove from any real substance. Nonetheless, this work contains two brief sections that are significant to the sociology of music.

Hearing and Seeing in the Metropolis

Simmel's formal approach to sociological thought occasionally enables him to pinpoint phenomena which would otherwise easily elude the attention of cultural studies. One such phenomenon is the relationship between hearing and seeing. Simmel was able to show that this relationship can change, that it can be influenced, for example, by the density of housing settlements. In this case, too, he falls back on a formal characteristic, yet Simmel characterizes the facts clearly enough when he writes, "We see more people in the metropolis, yet the number of those we acoustically perceive is small" (Simmel 1923, 486). To the best of my knowledge, this is one of the earliest statements on the social significance of the variable relationship between acoustic and optical perception. It is not surprising that this observation comes from a thinker with a good musical education as well as an understanding for the psychology of the fine arts. A contemporary of Simmel's, the Viennese folklorist Michael Haberlandt, had a similar double interest. A great admirer of the composer Hugo Wolf, Haberlandt was one of the founders of the Hugo Wolf Society. He deplored the loss of the sense of hearing in modern civilization. The eye had asserted its right to rule; the passive nature of hearing, "originally a biological necessity, is, however, becoming a mortal weakness in culture" (Haberlandt 1900, 180). While Haberlandt fought against the noise created by modern civilization, Simmel observed that the deindividualization of communication occurring in large cities is the result of the loss of individual hearing experiences.

Both men's observations come together in one phenomenon with which acoustic ecologists did not begin to deal until many decades later. Attention has only recently been devoted to the consequences of these changes, including those for music (Schafer 1971 and 1977). Today there is little doubt that the acoustic environment is also part of what Taine called milieu; the concrete shape of acoustic stimuli used by music is also determined by the environment that forms man's everyday acoustic life, from which music must stand out. I will have occasion to say more on this topic in chapter 22. Of course, Simmel's theses must be modified for the metropolis of today because the number and character of individual persons and things one perceives aurally have been altered by electroacoustic transmission and reproduction. This does not, however, alter the fact that Simmel was one of the first to point out the social significance of the relationship between hearing and seeing.

Ownership of Musical Works

Another result of Simmel's purely formal comparison of the audible and the visible is his analysis of the relationship of both of these to ownership. In general, Simmel writes, ownership is possible only for visual objects, whereas that which is merely audible ceases to exist the moment it is heard, therefore discounting ownership. He then continues:

> It is an odd exception when, during the seventeenth and eighteenth centuries, the great families strove to own pieces of music destined for them only and which were not permitted to be published (Simmel 1923, 487). It was part of the high position of a house to own pieces of music reserved for it alone. (Simmel 1923, 488)

What Simmel calls an "odd exception" is to be understood as a norm growing out of the conspicuous consumption Veblen recognized as being characteristic of a "leisure class." As I previously mentioned, this form of consumption clearly existed in Mannheim between 1740 and 1778, but not at the Viennese court during the same period. Nonetheless, this kind of conspicuous leisure did exist in the courts of lesser princes of the Habsburg Empire during that period.

The court of Prince Paul Anton Esterházy (1710–1762) serves as an example. When the prince moved to Eisenstadt in 1761, he immediately set about expanding the orchestra. He engaged Joseph Haydn as assistant court orchestra director that same year. The document drawn up for this engagement—it is closer to a decree of employment than to a contract—sets down, among other things, the following:

> Upon order of His Most Serene Highness, the Assistant Court Orchestra Director shall be obliged to compose such works of music as demanded by His Serene Highness, as well as not to communicate, much less allow to be copied, new compositions, except with previous knowledge and permission and instead to compose them for His Highness alone. (quoted in Geiringer 1959, 36)

This princely decree, which Haydn signed on 1 May 1761, clearly proves that this form of ownership of musical creations—which seems to contradict Simmel's logic—was perfectly suited to the social situation of a prince's court during the eighteenth century. Veblen's idea of vicarious leisure implies that everything performed and created by "assistants" served the prestige of the lord and had to be owned by him.

Although Simmel did not explain this historical "exception," which he called "odd," he must be thanked for drawing attention to these social circumstances.

For the sake of completeness, I must mention here that what Simmel calls an exception is by no means rare in the history of musical practice. In his inaugural address at the University of Amsterdam in 1953, Jaap Kunst dealt precisely with ownership of music, which he terms a "sociological link." Kunst assumes that, in the public mind, the freedom to perform any work has always universally applied. "Nonetheless, this view is utterly false" (Kunst 1953, 1). He cites modern examples: the exclusive performance rights to Richard Wagner's *Parsifal*, which the Bayreuth Festival retained for decades; Béla Bartók's Concerto for Viola and Orchestra, which the composer reserved for the violist William Primrose; and the famous example from Mozart's time, the Miserere by Gregorio Allegri, which was allowed to be performed only in the Sistine Chapel and which it was strictly forbidden to copy. Astonishingly, Mozart wrote down the work from memory after hearing it once, as Leopold Mozart proudly announced to his wife in a letter dated 14 April 1770. He went on to say that, although Wolfgang had managed to write it down, he did not want this secret "to fall into other hands" so as to spare him from being reproached by the Church.

Explanations by Ethnomusicology

Jaap Kunst does not pursue these examples from Western musical culture, using them simply to state that outside Western culture "the reserving of certain compositions and certain musical instruments for certain occasions, persons, or groups is quite customary." He deals with the sociological ties of individual instruments or compositions in non-European cultures and classifies these ties systematically, naming five kinds of ties for compositions (including non-notated music) known to ethnomusicological research (Kunst 1953, 2–3):
1. Compositions bound to certain persons
2. Compositions reserved for given festivities or occasions
3. Forms of compositions allowed to be performed only by male or female persons
4. Compositions whose performance is reserved for a given person
5. Compositions whose performance is reserved for a given group (tribe)

The term "sociological ties in music," which Jaap Kunst chose for this social linking of certain music with certain people or groups of people or occasions, agrees with the facts because we are dealing with collective norms that have penetrated into the social (collective) consciousness and represent a *fait social* in Durkheim's sense.

Other ethnomusicologists (e.g., Merriam 1964, 82ff.) also addressed the institutional involvement of musical processes in social life. From all their explanations, one is inclined to surmise not only that the crowned heads of Europe reserved the right to certain music for the economic reasons associated with belonging to a self-assertive leisure class but also that the idea of ownership was fed by older traditions. Once again recourse to ethnomusicology is fruitful in solving sociological questions concerning modern Occidental music.

As a young man, Georg Simmel also attempted to incorporate ethnology into his ideas on music. I owe my knowledge of Simmel's forgotten interest in ethnomusicology to K. Peter Etzkorn (1964), who brought to my attention Simmel's *Psychologische und ethnologische Studien über Musik* [Psychological and Ethnological Studies on Music] which first appeared in 1882. Here Simmel contests Darwin's thesis that music developed historically before speech. For Simmel, speech came first: "the song at its source was speech, intensified by affect, both as to rhythm and modulation" (Simmel 1882, 264). He believed the order of development was speech, vocal music, instrumental music. Although the ethnographical material Simmel refers to does not seem to be convincing, his effort is of fundamental importance because he points out that "empirical work in this area is possible and can have fruitful theoretical implications" (Etzkorn 1964, 107). Simmel did not follow this direction in his later work in sociology. Yet it seems all the more significant that he recognized the methodological connection between sociomusicology and ethnomusicology in 1882, indeed before the publication of the pioneering study by Alexander John Ellis. Moreover, Etzkorn credits Simmel with having touched upon two important series of questions in the sociology of art—the taxonomy of types of music and the development of "taste groups," although, to be sure, he did it in only a general, formal way.

Chapter 13 *Combarieu and French Sociology*

One of the earliest attempts to systematically incorporate sociological ideas into musicological thinking was made by Jules Combarieu (1859–1916) in, among other works, *La Musique, ses lois, son évolution*, published in 1907. The book's title somewhat recalls "Progress: Its Law and Cause," the essay in which Herbert Spencer presented some of his fundamental ideas on sociology in 1857. Combarieu's work refers not only to Spencer but to Auguste Comte, Gabriel Tarde, and Marcel Mauss as well.

Studies of the link between anthropological and sociological findings, especially those of the Durkheim student Marcel Mauss (1873–1950), influenced Combarieu's thought. Combarieu seeks to put an end to the perspective that has the history of music beginning with the ancient Greeks. He contends that the Greeks have distorted our view of the whole of humanity far too long (Combarieu 1907, 184). Although Combarieu attempts to consider the ancient Orient and all later non-European cultures in his effort to understand the "social role of music," he is unable to manage without creating a paradigm for at least the history of European music, a model he considers to be a "law of civilization." His paradigm follows Auguste Comte's law of three stages: music passed through the theological stage with the Gregorian Chant; it reached the metaphysical stage "with the great symphonists Bach, Haydn, Mozart, and Beethoven"; and it attained the positivistic age when composers turned to realism (Combarieu 1907, 208). In this final stage, composers have done away with genres and dissolved the boundaries of form. It would be impossible, for example, to assign Claude Debussy's *Prélude à l'après-midi d'un faune* to a genre.

This rather superficial application of Comte's law of three stages is, however, not the basis of all Combarieu's reflections. One would do well to view the reference to Comte as no more than a nod to the creator of the relatively insignificant positivistic interpretation of history. This is similarly the case when Combarieu attempts to explain the origins of canon, motet, and madrigal by applying Gabriel Tarde's "law of imitation" to musical composition. Combarieu's reference to the concepts of French sociologists is far more productive when he is not content to affix sociological terms to musical facts but turns instead to detailed analysis of musical phenomena. In these instances, we come across discoveries most of which are largely still relevant today.

Invention of Music in Non-Literate Cultures

Combarieu, who also studied musicology in Berlin, was familiar with the Romantic interpretation that the folk song was created collectively. Familiar with works of sociology and anthropology, he was compelled to criticize this notion of "collective composition." He came to the conclusion that folk songs are not anonymous creations, but creations "that have become anonymous" (Combarieu 1907, 114). It is conceivable that a hundred or a thousand men worked together to build a pyramid, yet a collective of this kind would not be able "together to invent a four-bar melody."

With this thesis, Combarieu showed a path that ethnomusicology later confirmed. There is proof that "composing" exists in non-literary cultures, and that in many cases members of these cultures can make statements about this activity. Such cultures also provide examples of an individual being directed to "compose," and a person who is not able to do so being replaced by another person, who receives a service or object as "purchase price" for this activity (Merriam 1964, 166–167).

The question of the so-called anonymity of the folk music in non-literate cultures is indeed a central problem of the sociology of music. It indicates a difference (in nature) between what we call "composing" and what should probably more appropriately be called "inventing" music. Ernest Ferand (1938) attempted to show this difference by contrasting improvisation and composition:

> The difference between improvisation and composition is largely the difference in psychological principles of creation. Whereas improvised utterances seem basically to be subject to the principle of organic

growth, the primary creative characteristic of composition is planned construction. (Ferand 1938, 417)

In this regard it would not be meaningful to speak of composing in cultures without musical notation, as this term designates a particular activity that is developed on the basis of notation: composing is putting together notes that stand for music. It remains to be seen, however, whether it would be meaningful to apply the term improvisation to the invention of music in non-literate cultures. Furthermore, improvisation is sometimes intermingled with notated music, and here it has an entirely different meaning from what Ferand calls "improvisation." In these cases, "invention of music" would probably be a more appropriate a term. The result of composing, then, is a notated work; the result of inventing is non-notated.

The invention of music is, as Combarieu emphasizes and ethnomusicology seems to confirm, an individual, not a collective, act. To the extent, however, that the invention does not have a fixed, notated form, it remains open to alteration by other "inventors," perhaps even a large number of "inventors." In this sense it is the creation of a collective, but "With regard to music, the people as a collective unit are primarily a distorting force" (Combarieu 1907, 114).

Consonance and the Tonal System

Combarieu offers no consistent theory concerning the change in the notion of consonance. He regards the "tyranny" of the perfect consonances (the octave and the perfect fourth and fifth) during the Middle Ages to be, not the result of musical practices, but solely the consequence of conservative ideas. To him the victory of polyphony based on the consonant third seems to be the result of the musical inclinations of Nordic peoples coming together with the reawakening of ancient theories and doing justice to the third by recognizing it as a consonant interval.

Combarieu is far more methodical in determining the social rank of our tonal system. Rather like Max Weber after him, he proceeds from the thought that there are a vast number of possible tonal systems and that the tempered twelve-note scale does not deserve to be called a natural system, being a wholly "subjective" creation (Combarieu 1907, 123). Our system is necessarily imperfect, and only the masterpieces that have been created based on it make us forget its inherent deficiencies (Combarieu 1907, 124).

This is the distinction made by Max Weber—the distinction between the "correctness" and the "social validity" of a tonal system. While Combarieu primarily attributes social validity to works composed on the basis of our system, a French composer of his time recognized that the instruments used by a given musical culture can aid in promoting the social acceptance of their system. Camille Saint-Saëns (1835–1921) coined the expression *esprit du clavier* ("piano thinking") to describe this situation. The text in question—part of an essay on Franz Liszt—deserves to be quoted:

> Furthermore, who in our time has not felt the powerful influence of the piano? This influence began to have an effect before the piano, with *The Well-Tempered Clavier* by Sebastian Bach. Piano thinking came into existence the moment *tempered tuning* led to the interchangeability of sharps and flats, thereby making it possible to use all keys. . . . This thinking [in terms of the piano] has become a tyrannical destroyer of music through the limitless spreading of the enharmonic heresy. Virtually all modern art has its origin in this heresy. It has been too rich to be deplored; nonetheless, it is a heresy which is definitely destined to perish one day, probably in the distant future, because of the evolution to which it owes its existence. What will then remain of present-day art? Perhaps only Berlioz who, unfamiliar with the piano, had an instinctive aversion for enharmonics. His antipode in this regard is Richard Wagner—enharmonics personified—who drew the most extreme consequences from this principle. (Saint-Saëns 1899, 21–22)

Whereas Saint-Saëns concretely describes the effect of the instrument on the validity of a certain tonal system, Combarieu attributes the ascendancy of our tonal system to purely spiritual motives. This, at any rate, is one way to interpret Combarieu's assertion that the system owes its triumph to "routine," that is, to "that which sociology calls the tyrannical influence of collectivity" (Combarieu 1907, 124).

Instruments and Orchestra as "Institutions"

In another context, however, Combarieu also notes the social compulsion of already existing instruments. He specifically states that explaining this influence is a task for sociology (Combarieu 1907, 211).

> In order to exist, every composition requires certain instruments suitable for its performance; and, conversely, the quality and number of available or usable instruments exercises an undeniable influence on the nature of the composition. (Combarieu 1907, 211–212)

The direct power of musical instruments to create norms is the result. Although instruments are created to perform music, they also influence the music's character by setting its possibilities and limits. Instruments therefore belong to what Fauconnet and Mauss classify as "institution," meaning what Durkheim calls *fait social*, "the way in which certain things must be done" (König 1958, 135). This understanding of the institutional character of instrument technology is frequently overlooked as a result of the causal relationship between the manufacture and use of the instrument. Erich M. von Hornbostel demonstrated that human beings begin by compensating for imperfections in their material cultural heritage with personal dexterity "before managing to facilitate the technique of use by production technology" (Hornbostel 1903, 5). As soon as production technology is improved, there is a reaction of the new musical instrument on its use.

This effect is even greater when certain combinations of instruments develop into a standardized group that, as an apparatus available for the realization of music, attains power over composers' conceptions. The idea of this power, as advocated by Combarieu, is in agreement with the sociological ideas of his time. To be sure, Combarieu goes further than Fauconnet and Mauss by not only considering customs and fashions, prejudices, and superstitions as determining behavior but also taking into consideration the available musical instruments. It is exactly this definition which lends greater depth to the specific reflections on socio-musicology.

The importance of this idea can be seen in the effect on composition of the preestablished orchestra. Hector Berlioz regretted that the standardized make-up of the orchestra prevented the creation of monumental works with innovative instrumentation. Richard Strauss's resigned comment in his 1905 edition of Berlioz's *Grand traité d'instrumentation* (published in 1844) was that "unfortunately things are not any better today!" (Berlioz 1905, 436).

The sociological problem of the institutionalized orchestra, as well as these statements by Berlioz and Strauss, once again directs our attention to the fact that the "psychology of the age" does not alone account for a given style of composition. As I said before, Plekhanov must have been very perplexed by the fact that Berlioz took much longer to make a breakthrough in music than Victor Hugo did in literature. If sociology dealing with the arts limits itself to speculation on the history of ideas, it will be unable to analyze this type of phenomenon. The sociology of music must also take into account the material means of musical communication. It is more than surprising that Plekhanov, who claimed to represent a materialistic view of history, did not take into account the material substratum of music, whereas Combarieu did. We once again see the inherent deficiency of a type of sociology that restricts itself to general propositions and dispenses with illuminating specific musical problems.

Music historians and musicians encounter these problems far more often and characterize them more thoroughly, although they lack sociological terminology. Pierre Boulez, for example, has written about the power of the orchestra to influence behavior. Boulez considers Berlioz's remark on the cumbersomeness of the symphonic apparatus to be highly perceptive:

> In point of fact, over a long period this rigidity cramped and paralyzed a composer's imagination; it came into being as a result of fixed and tolerated dimensions that necessarily always placed the same limitations and the same conditions on the artist's expressive will. Although it is an accepted fact that the standardization of musical conditions in some sense brought with it higher professional standards, broadened the repertoire, made the concert into a social tradition—indeed an obligation—yet Berlioz could not have seen that in his day, especially in France. What he could, on the other hand, notice quite clearly was the imperious demand emanating from a musical and sociological model requiring all works of symphonic musical life to conform. (Boulez 1975, 91)

Combarieu's Method

Combarieu's mode of thought, then, includes dealing with the social compulsion inherent in achievements of musical technology. Combarieu is able to meaningfully apply to music several basic ideas from the sociology of his time. Though it is not always revealed by the vocabulary he uses, the way in which he brings out the social compulsion of a tonal system, an instrument, or a combination of instruments reveals him to be a pioneer in the sociology of music. He also identified, for example, the developed system of notation as a precondition of postmedieval Occidental music (Combarieu 1907, 189). On the whole, he believes that music "develops parallel to society by reflecting all the changes of public life, the progress of the secular mind, science, and industrial labor" (Combarieu 1907, 213). To be sure, Combarieu then remarks that his sociological approach is insufficient to understand the individual aspects of musical phenomena. This approach, he continues, merely defines the framework, and it would be childish, deplorable, and unscientific to omit purely artistic aspects.

Combarieu also characteristically uses the ideas of Charles Darwin and Karl Bücher. He does not accept Darwin's assumption that "musical sounds and rhythms were used by our demi-human ancestors during courtship" and that this is the origin of human musical activity (cf. Graf 1967). Combarieu considers this, not as a self-contained "theory," but as a hypothesis that cannot be accepted in the form expressed by Darwin. If Darwin's idea were true, the monkey would be "a better musician than the nightingale" (Combarieu 1907, 165). Darwin did not provide proof for his assertion, therefore his statement is merely a "contribution."

As we can see, Combarieu is always interested in verifying the utility of existing interpretations. This is also his approach to the theory of Karl Bücher (1847–1930) concerning the link between work and music. Combarieu recognizes the social importance of workers' songs, which can increase productivity, quoting examples from empirical surveys carried out in Danzig and Senegal (Combarieu 1907, 147), yet he avoids Bücher's generalizations (Bücher 1919), which say little about the role of rhythm in art music. Combarieu is always looking for explanations given by earlier scientists, be they musicologists, sociologists, economists, or biologists. As a rule, he resists reducing a process to "purely sociological explanations." Unlike the principle that social phenomena should be explained by only social phenomena, he formulates the thesis that "a genuinely scientific method should a priori allow a number of explanations, and not search for only one" (Combarieu 1907, 150). Combarieu, however, is not eclectic in the same way as Simmel. While Simmel's eclecticism applies only to the subject matter of sociology, Combarieu wishes to extend it to the methodology. If we replace the pejorative term eclectic in this argumentation with the more neutral words multidisciplinary and interdisciplinary, we can recognize the useful aspect of Combarieu's thought. This aspect also corresponds to his desire to link musical analysis with sociological ideas.

Chapter 14 *Musical Analysis and Sociology*

Attempts to analyze the concrete form of a musical work using sociological categories began, as far as I can tell, with Combarieu. There
appear to be three possibilities for linking musical analysis with sociology:

1. The form of the work is assigned to a given historical situation
   whose sociological aspects are expressed in the work. This method
   largely conforms to the ideas of Taine or Plekhanov. Recourse can
   also be made to concepts of social type, such as those developed by
   Comte or Marx. Combarieu's attempt, applied to music attributed
   to Johann Sebastian Bach, follows this approach. I will discuss this
   analysis in the next section.

2. Component features of a composition are identified by analysis.
   This is followed by an attempt to relate these features to structural
   features of the society during the period when the work was created. To illustrate this method, which is stricter than Combarieu's
   approach, I have chosen a recent example (Rummenhöller 1978)
   comparing the music of Bach with that of Scarlatti.

3. The different effects of a work, or group of works, during various
   periods in the history of music are treated as problems. The question as to whether the various interpretations are contained in the
   work is investigated. This type of analysis represents a concretization of the idea that the work itself has an influence on the develop-

ment of audience taste and thereby contributes to the creation of an audience suited to it. This method was first applied, at least in part, to studies of Brahms (Stahmer 1972) and Liszt (Dahlhaus 1970).

Sociological Musical Analysis in Combarieu

As I have already mentioned, Combarieu is aware, as I have already mentioned, that sociology is unable to illuminate the aesthetic genesis of a musical work of art. Nevertheless, he insists on the possibility of using the tools of sociology in explaining a work's social-historical genesis. The fifth chapter of his book contains a section entitled "Analysis of the A Minor Sonata of J. S. Bach from the Sociological Point of View." If his investigation is aimed at Bach, the chosen example is not entirely suitable for his method; the work in question—number 965 in Schmieder's catalogue, possibly composed in 1720—is of dubious authenticity. Moreover, the sonata is an adaptation of a composition by Jan Adam Reincken (1623–1722), a work from his *Hortus Musicus* for two violins, viola da gamba, and basso continuo, published in Hamburg in 1687. Given these circumstances, Combarieu's remarks on Bach must be taken with a grain of salt. That matters little, however, as he is concerned with developing the historical and social conditions of this composition. The following is a summary of Combarieu's remarks, with commentary:

1. The abstract form of the "sonata" is the final stage of a development that began with concrete form (that is, from music linked to language) and ended as an abstract form (music without words). It is possible to trace the historical stages from the sung word to purely instrumental music (Combarieu 1907, 201).

Commentary
   The instrument's identity is surely the result of historical development. The term sonata (cf. W. S. Newmann in MGG 12, 871) came about in opposition to the sung canzona, yet during the sixteenth century, the distinction between the two is by no means clear. Sonata, the feminine singular past participle of the Italian verb *sonare*, indicates the notation of something that has already been played. Such notation was not originally taken to be a creation for the future, but still—if only in the linguistic sense—a record of something past whose reproduction could be assured for the future. Sixteenth-century markings such as *per cantar o sonar* or *canzon da sonar* indicate the flexibility of the performance medium.

2. The Sonata in A Minor presents features of both the church sonata (*sonata da chiesa*) and the chamber sonata (*sonata da camera*). Two movements of the church sonata type (adagio, fugue) are followed by four movements of chamber music (allemande, courante, sarabande, gigue). The composer, then, combined secular elements with religious. This combining resulted, not from willfulness, but rather from a change of customs that now also permitted the church to be used as a concert venue (Combarieu 1907, 201–202).

Commentary

The theoretical differentiation between *sonata da chiesa* and *sonata da camera* was made by Sébastien de Brossard (*Dictionnaire de musique*, 1703), although in practice the distinction was older and was on the verge of disappearing by about 1700. Its disappearance affected the previous stylistic separation of church, theater, and "chamber." Apart from the acoustic differences that are reflected in the compositions themselves, differences of function and emotional content characterize the separation of church style, theater style, and chamber style. The church sonata can already be identified during the early seventeenth century according to its function; that is, it presumably replaced portions of the Ordinary of the Mass. Chamber music was a private form of musical activity that began for the nobility and then spread to the middle class, as can be demonstrated by its dance forms.

The development of purely instrumental works, as observed by Combarieu, goes hand in hand with the overcoming of the separation of church and chamber. An example of this "overcoming" during Bach's time are the eight sonatas by Anton Franz Maichelbeck (1702–1750), published in Augsburg in 1736. According to the title page, the sonatas were intended for "playing on both church and home keyboard instruments."

Therefore the convergence of church and home (or chamber) styles represents a social phenomenon with compositional consequences not all of which can be read from the sonata analyzed by Combarieu.

3. Combarieu notes that the style of the sonata is better suited to the violin than to a keyboard instrument. He attributes this to a "fashion" to which the composer succumbed by slipping from violin style to keyboard style (Combarieu 1907, 203).

Commentary

Of course, Bach's stylistic stance does not support this statement, which is made doubly dubious by the fact that Bach may not have arranged the sonata. But Combarieu's observation can be justified by the sonata's origins in Reincken's *Hortus Musicus,* which was written for strings.

4. Combarieu considers the first Adagio to be a Prelude without its original religious function (that of preceding a chorale). He considers this transformation to be similar to the reminiscence of the "church prelude" in the adagio introductions of several symphonies by Haydn and Mozart. The "sociological causes" of a process such as this are easy to guess: the "musical spirit" gradually freed itself from the church in the same way as the public did (Combarieu 1907, 203–204).

Commentary

In this case Combarieu is satisfied with general definitions that explain little about the concrete musical effects of the "sociological causes."

5. The Fugue is a *chorale sans paroles* (chorale without words). Combarieu merely adds that Bach "did not create the fugue" (Combarieu 1907, 204).

6. The opening church sonata is fused with the chamber sonata (actually a suite), which consists of an Adagio followed by four dance movements. The tonal and thematic unity is the result of a long historical process that Combarieu outlines as follows:
   a. dance with song
   b. dance with song and instruments
   c. instruments without song and dance
   d. a succession of instrumental pieces (suite)

Commentary

This schematic representation (Combarieu 1907, 204–205) does little to help in understanding the work under discussion, although it reveals the sociological point of departure from which Combarieu explains the development of purely instrumental music. The outline—unacceptable though it is in this global form—points to the close connection between song, dance, and instrumental music in the history of their development and to their original unity, whose dissolution deserves a more thorough analysis, which will probably have to be done with concrete analyses, not general representations. The separation of the dance from its original context in European music certainly did not come about in a single step but progressed through a number of phases, starting with the hostility of medieval monks to movement. Yet from the Renaissance onwards, the separation of bodily movement from music surely has motives quite different from those of monastic discipline. Furthermore, the inclusion of the dance accent in European art music reveals countercurrents of crucial importance to synthetic listening (Besseler 1959) and the eighteenth-century style of composition suited to it. Thus Combarieu's train of thought is, at best, a new idea in need of concretization.

In his analysis of this work, Combarieu is satisfied with ascertaining the course of the social changes that prepared the ground for its composition. His description of the work's form is rudimentary; he fails to characterize its special aesthetic qualities and does not go into the effects of Bach's work beyond his own time. The extent to which the aesthetic qualities of a work may be considered responsible for its effects beyond its own time is one of the central questions of music sociology. The importance of Bach's works for many subsequent composers—and not only for audiences—shows the active power of the "art object" in molding the musical perceptions of its producers, its reproducers, or those who consume it once it has been created. The history of music is replete with examples of the apparently inevitable discussion about the artistic richness of Bach's music. These examples confirm—more than any merely theoretical consideration—what Guyau called the "power of genius to produce milieu" and Marx designated the creation of an "art-loving public capable of enjoying beauty." If we were able to derive this power to create milieu from the social conditions of the period in which the work was created, then—or so a number of people believe—the sociology of music would be legitimized as a science that produces results. Although I am unable to subscribe to this point of view, I would nonetheless like to examine a recent effort in this direction that tries to bring out an element of the timeless influence of Johann Sebastian Bach's music.

Bach and Scarlatti

Peter Rummenhöller (1978) aims to bring out the special qualities of Bach the composer by analyzing a Bach keyboard prelude (BWV 924) and comparing it with a work of Domenico Scarlatti. He is quite successful in characterizing the qualities of the two compositions individually—the "clockwork" character of the one (Scarlatti) and the organic construction of the other (Bach). He considers the "relationship of the parts to the whole, of each detail to the totality," to be a feature of Bach's music. On the other hand, he sees the characteristic of Scarlatti's music to be, not the creation of such totality as expressed in this or other works of Bach, but rather the use of "the speculative additive principle, the calculated putting together of small and even smaller parts into a functioning whole" (Rummenhöller 1978, 113). He attributes this additive quality to feudal-absolutistic society. As Bach composed in a different, forward-looking manner, his music represents a type of creation that "must be regarded as an anticipation, an anticipation of something as yet impossible to achieve in the society in which Bach lived."

Rummenhöller thereby illuminates in another way the discrepancy between social evolution and the development of composition. For him, Scarlatti's work is the more "contemporary," while the Bach Prelude is the "old-fashioned" model. His analysis of the two works seems to provide excellent support for this thesis. Nonetheless, Rummenhöller's conclusion appears to be missing a link: the disproportionality, the old-fashionedness, of Bach's Prelude is accepted here as a given because the equivalence of compositional addition and feudal absolutism has yet to be demonstrated, having only been drawn metaphorically. Thus, Rummenhöller's claim that Bach anticipated a compositional process which would have been "impossible" in his society is surprising. It would seem that, in this respect, Bach's creative power was uninfluenced by the social system!

Adorno's writings about Bach also aim in the same direction. Though not present in the first edition of his *Introduction to the Sociology of Music* (1962), the author apparently considered the following observations important enough to add them to his "revised and enlarged edition" (1968a):

> The dynamization of the motive-thematic labor which he had made universal and which, as "labor," already exceeds the static nature of the so-called musical Baroque—this dynamization is Bach's compositional consequence as much as that of the genteel, variety-seeking style that followed. It is as if the external determinants, and perhaps an actual need of the audience, had merely strengthened and accelerated whatever productive forces were ripening inside the composition. One explanation of the parallelism might be the unity of the spirit of the time. (Adorno 1976, 206)

Adorno, then, considers Bach's motivic-thematic work to be the consequence not only "of Bach" but also of a "style following him." This formula defining Bach's work to be a consequence of what followed is similar to what Rummenhöller was later to call "anticipation." Adorno's approach is shown to be speculative by his reference to the "unity of the spirit of the age"—a generalization in place of the analytical work done by Rummenhöller. Both ideas, however, lack proof for the connection between the work of music (as such) and its social background. Of course, some listeners may claim to feel this equivalence, but that does not suffice to prove or deny its validity. One suspects that we no longer interpret Bach's aesthetic richness in relationship to the general development of society of his time *because* we still enjoy this music as art. We begin with the continuing effect of Bach's works (which we seek to explain through analysis), ascribe this continuing effect to the "anticipation" of the future, and from this deduce that the works represent something which must have been "in fact impossible" in the world to which Bach belonged. The conclusion would be—Adorno hints at it in the foregoing passage—that the importance of Bach's works is the result of his genius. In this case, we do not require sociology to arrive at this conclusion.

Unlike Adorno's Hegelian aphorism—which contrasts with the many pertinent thoughts through which Adorno enriched music sociology—Rummenhöller's analysis has informative value. Even the thought of "anticipation" of the future can be fruitful if the conditions that made this anticipation possible are investigated. There is no certainty, a priori, that these conditions are social in nature. A socio-musicology that attempts to explain everything having to do with music strictly from social matters (which would be an expansion of Durkheim's call to explain social matters strictly from social matters) will soon run into difficulties. As a rule, the individual manifestations of compositional action elude purely sociological analysis. This is why, for reasons of principle, Combarieu turned against Durkheim's thesis and wished to allow "more than one explanation." Of course social aspects, if one defines the term broadly enough, play a part: the tradition of composition, the influence of the "school," the expectations of the patron, even the acoustic characteristic of the potential place of performance, and so on. However, in order to understand the specific character of individual works or groups of works, much less his complete works, it would presumably be useful to investigate the motives that led Bach to melodize the figured bass and to transform the bass voice from a mere support for the melody into a "a voice like any other among the polyphonic group of themes" (Benary 1961, 48). Phenomena of this kind—which were to a large extent responsible for the Bach reception beginning with Mozart—can scarcely be explained satisfactorily by the "unity of the spirit of the time" or derived from the social structure of Bach's era, unless one is content to regard noncommittal metaphors as substantiation.

Rummenhöller's study has the undeniable merit of presenting the problem clearly and with analytical means, but it completely avoids the question of what the sociology of music is capable of achieving. The obligation to capture the genesis of a composer's individual works (or complete works) *in the categories of sociology* is a burden which the sociology of music cannot carry. At best, the sociology of music can track down the *socially necessary* conditions of an art product; in order to understand all the *sufficient* conditions, more arguments are required than merely sociological ones. Music sociologists would perhaps do well—following a suggestion of Bertolt Brecht's—to draw up a catalogue of questions to which they have no answers.

Work and Reception

The model of sociological analysis, as demonstrated by Combarieu on an eighteenth-century work, is inconclusive on individual points. Nevertheless, it is trend-setting because it tries to integrate an inventory of musical analysis with findings from sociological analysis. Adorno also pursued this goal, as did Rummenhöller in his analysis of Bach and Scarlatti, for example. (I must note for the sake of completeness that these efforts at integration contrast with other approaches to socio-musicology that seem to proceed from an unrelated simultaneity of modes of musicological and music-sociological thought.)

The problem of the compositional "anticipation" of the future, as formulated by Rummenhöller, points to the necessity of mutually penetrating trains of thought in socio-musicology and musical analysis. The phenomenon of the lasting (and usually uneven) effects of a musical work of art can be studied seriously only if one carefully investigates both complexes belonging to this interaction—the nature of the musical message itself and the structure of those who receive the message. What people perceive of a given musical message in a temporally and spatially delimited period, and how they receive this message, depends not only on their expectations and customs but to a large degree on the character of the message itself. I must ask the reader's indulgence for belaboring this self-evident truth. This is unfortunately necessary because a good deal of sociologizing in our time seems to ignore the fact that the process of musical communication is determined by *three main elements:* the qualities of the musical message, the qualities of the receivers, and the nature of the channel of communication (that is, "performance practice"). An understanding of musical communication therefore requires a close interweaving of musical analysis, audience research, and research into performance practice.

The sociology of music is entrusted with tracking down the interactions in each case. It is, of course, entirely legitimate for the purpose of study to select two of these three areas or to study them separately. We can begin, then, by omitting aspects associated with performance practice and devoting our entire attention to the relationship between message and receiver. A number of significant recent contributions to the history of music reception employ this method. I would like to consider two of these in greater detail. They treat the changed reception of Brahms' music and the possibility of a revision of our perception of Liszt based on his works.

Aesthetic Façade and Compositional Structure

Carl Dahlhaus (1970) attempted to compare "aesthetic façade and compositional structure" in a study on Liszt. This construct seems ideal for examining how, from one time to another, the focus of musical perception can shift from that which can be immediately grasped to the specific musical structure. Of course, these extremes apply only to ideal types. It is certainly possible to discern more subtle distinctions in individual instances. Nonetheless, the terms "façade" and "structure" suggest that different perceptual modes are possible and that different aspects can come to the fore at different times in the reception of a musical work. By the term "aspects" I mean features that are not, as a rule, read into the work by the recipient but are inherent in the work itself and which the recipient may not even grasp.

The Changing Reception of Brahms

That musicology and the sociology of music are converging is confirmed by the increasing attention musicologists are devoting to the interaction between work and recipient. They wonder, for example, how the estimation of Johannes Brahms's music can have changed so radically in the space of a few decades. How, they ask, does one explain that Anton Webern thought Brahms used exemplary composition technique and Arnold Schoenberg considered him a "progressive" composer, when in the nineteenth century both enthusiasts and detractors (such as Hugo Wolf) were equally willing to swear that his music had a "retrospective nature"? (Friedrich von Hausegger).

In a study devoted to this phenomenon, Klaus Stahmer (1972) establishes an intelligent comparison between the results of musical analysis and the sociological findings on the change in reception. He demonstrates that the works Brahms wrote beginning in 1867 "increasingly contain, on the surface, all the features of a schematicized sonata" and that Brahms simultaneously underwent a renewal, a "step-by-step accommodation of the dualistic sonata-allegro form to the monothematic variations form." This process is demonstrated through an analysis of the Clarinet Quintet, Op. 115, composed in 1891. The analysis brings out the apparent tension between the formal surface (the façade, one might call it) and the inner structure of the work. As a result of his detailed analysis, Stahmer comes to the following conclusion:

> There are considerable differences between the analytically verifiable musical data of a work of art and its reception. Reception is tied to the limitations of those who receive it. The chosen example elucidates the capacity of aural interpretation to hear what one wants to hear and

end up with in a formal pattern that completely reevaluates the composer's form. (Stahmer 1972, 166)

The immediate reception of Brahms during his lifetime, then, was based on a misunderstanding. This reception detected only *one* characteristic of his music—his loyalty to the formal façade. That Brahms's critics as well as his supporters, perceived his music this way is corroborated by this statement of Hugo Wolf: "He quite literally stuffs the notes into the good old form and the result is—a symphony" (Wolf quoted in Stahmer 1972, 155).

The view of Brahms as a formally conservative classicist was doubtless reinforced by the intransigent position of a conservative faction searching for a standard-bearer against the New German School and Liszt. Only when the antagonism of music journalists gradually diminished did the novel structure behind the façade became visible. Schoenberg's and Webern's advocacy of Brahms is simply one among many signs of this change.

Stahmer's analysis, which I have only been able to outline here, also starts out with "preliminary considerations on the sociology of music." He comes out clearly against Alphons Silbermann's view that statements concerning the work of art as such and its structure are outside the purview of socio-musicology. Stahmer demonstrates with his contribution, which is also methodologically important, the wealth of knowledge that can be brought to light through a combination of sociology and musical analysis. He directs our attention to a process I would like to call the *utilization of the musical work of art through social reception*. Different aspects of the work come to the fore in the course of this process. It would be naive to believe that such utilization could bring to light anything not already, at least in the most rudimentary form, present in the work.

"Anticipation" as Sociological Problem

This idea of a different kind of utilization is also the basis of Carl Dahlhaus's analysis of the symphonic poem *Prometheus* by Franz Liszt (Dahlhaus 1970). His study demonstrates that Liszt anticipated later styles of composition, expressed in a language that, however, "soon became obsolete." Dalhaus describes Liszt's this anticipation of Liszt's by observing

that dissonances remain unresolved as characteristic notes of the principal motif; that themes and motifs represent, not the ultimate material that cannot be traced back any further, but an abstract structure of thirds; that successive and simultaneous passages, sequences of notes, and chords are treated equally; that motifs are broken down into their individual elements—series of notes and rhythm; that the harmonic connection is established by a dissonant center—the diminished seventh chord. Individually, these observations could be considered coincidental; by coming together, they attest that it was precisely in what we scorn as "New German" music that the first vague contours of modern music came into being. Liszt proves himself to be a genius of anticipation, not in the late compositions for piano, but as early as his symphonic poems. (Dahlhaus 1970,417)

Once again we run into the term "anticipation" (*Vorgriff* in Rummenhöller; *Übersteigen* or "transcendence," in Adorno). In this case, however, the term applies, not to a mystical category, but to the tension between the surface and structural content. (Dahlhaus calls this the "contradiction between the aesthetic façade and the latent compositional structures.") The structure only appears to be an anticipation because it was not perceived by contemporaries and it became a part of consciousness only at a later time. The word "anticipation" is well-suited indeed to defining the circumstances, yet the sociology of music should be careful not to take the word teleologically, as if the artist in his work had anticipated the aesthetics of a future society.

But how can we explain the contradiction suggested by Dahlhaus and Stahmer? This may be one of those questions that music sociology cannot answer. Nonetheless, we can hazard an explanation. The contradiction is based on the knowledge that the specialization and professionalization of the work of composition not only corresponds to the way in which society functions, but that a gulf has necessarily been created between specialization in the arts and in society as a whole. Émile Zola pointed to this gulf in his essay, published in 1880, on the experimental novel. He wrote that agreement should exist between the condition of society, which is the cause, and literary expression, which is its effect. And he was surprised that "men who abolish the monarchy, abolish God, and eliminate the old order" are identical with those "who preserve the literature of that past they wish to expunge from history" (Zola cited in Bastide 1977, 43). There is a genuine problem behind the astonishment of the Naturalist propagandist, one far stronger in music than in literature. Specialized musical creativity is in a position to create forms of musical behavior not in accordance with existing society and which, possibly, presume different forms of social behavior. Not until these prerequisites exist can one speak in retrospect of "anticipation." Yet it is by no means certain which, if any, of the present-day nonconformist styles of composition will ever attain social confirmation.

This leads to the question of whether looking back at history *from the point of view of a new and different society* can produce fruitful knowledge. Dahlhaus encounters this problem with Liszt's *Prometheus*:

Is it legitimate or absurd, one might ask, for works of the nineteenth century to suspend the nineteenth-century type of aesthetic judgment and instead sketch a history of the problems of composing whose principles are formulated under the influence of the musical present? A rigorous historian would have to object. The fact, however, that this process, strange though it may seem, sometimes leads to insights that could scarcely be reached by other means should placate these critics. (Dahlhaus 1970, 419)

I believe it is precisely the insights to be gained through this process that legitimize it. To be sure, the process is only useful when the works of the past themselves can, and do, enter into the musical consciousness of the age. Should this be the case, science is indeed obligated to reconstruct what society has brought about—that is, the transplantation into society Y of a musical work of art created in society X. Only an integration of musical and sociological analysis can do justice to this task. Of course, the analysis will have to be more subtle than that of Combarieu, who merely showed the way, and it will be able to use the aforementioned projects for orientation.

Chapter 15 *Music in the Sociology of Max Weber*

The sociological analysis of musical works of art, for which Combarieu prepared the ground, is only one facet of thought on socio-musicology. Attempts like his—brilliant and knowledgeable though they may be—generally create a dichotomy between the works that are subject to musicological analysis and the social phenomena that constitute the subject matter of sociology. The link between musical data and sociological knowledge is, as it were, a purely mental act. This approach results from the division of labor among the scientific professions that led to the establishment during the nineteenth century of musicology and sociology as independent disciplines. Under these conditions, the task of music sociology seemed to be to apply already existing elements of sociological thought to music. The question was seldom asked whether sociological concepts are suited to music. In order to pose this question, a type of sociologist was required who had an intimate relationship to music and who had some familiarity with the results of musicological research, music history, and ethnomusicology. Max Weber (1864–1920), whom Karl Jaspers called "the greatest German of our age" (Jaspers 1958, 7) in a monograph first published in 1932, was such a sociologist. Although I may not be able to agree with Jasper's assessment, Max Weber's towering importance for sociology is undisputed, and his contribution to the sociology of music was crucial to the subsequent development of this discipline.

Weber began his academic career as professor of commercial law and German law in Berlin in 1893 and later became professor of political science in Freiburg (1894) and Heidelberg (1897–1903). In his valedictory lecture in Heidelberg he made the oft-quoted statement: "Most of what goes under the name of sociology is humbug" (Jaspers 1958, 61). This cutting opinion was the result of Weber's aversion to arbitrary sociological systems. He did not produce such a system. It is no accident that only one of Weber's many writings (*On Some Categories of Understanding Sociology*, published in 1913 and reproduced in Weber GAWL, 427-474) deals with sociological concepts independent of concrete issues. Most of Weber's other contributions to the methodology of sociology are contained in studies that treat specific topics: studies on the history of the trading companies during the Middle Ages, the rural labor constitution, the situation of the farm laborers East of the Elbe, the stock exchange, to give but a few characteristic examples of the diverse interests of this jurist, historian, economist, and sociologist.

At least three of his texts are absolutely essential to understanding Max Weber's ideas on music:

1. *Die Objektivität sozialwissenschaftlicher und sozialpolitischer Erkenntnis* [The Objectivity of Sociological and Socio-political Knowledge] (Weber GAWL, 146-214). In this article of 1904, Weber outlined the goals of the journal *Archiv für Sozialwissenschaft und Sozialpolitik,* of which he became editor in that year together with Werner Sombart and Edgar Jaffé.

2. *Der Sinn der Wertfreiheit in den soziologischen und ökono-mischen Wissenschaften* [The Meaning of Value-Free Judgments in the Sociological and Economic Sciences] (Weber GAWL, 489-540). This text, published in 1917, arose from a lecture given at the Vienna meeting of the Society for Social Policy in 1913 that had been received with great astonishment by Weber's colleagues in the field because of his extensive references to musical problems.

3. *Die rationalen und soziologischen Grundlagen der Musik* [The Rational and Sociological Foundations of Music] (Weber 1921, 1924 and 1972). This text consists of a fragment, not edited by Weber, that had originated in his studies on socio-musicology from around 1910 and was published from his legacy by the musicologist Theodor Kroyer after Weber's death.

I shall hereafter refer to these three works as "Objectivity," "Value-Free," and "Foundations." Although "Foundations" is generally the only work discussed in connection with Weber's socio-musicology, it does not present anything approaching a full picture of Weber's ideas on music. This is due not only to the somewhat aphoristic nature of the unrevised text but also to the assumption that the methodological basis of Weber's sociology is already known without requiring further explanation. In order to understand "Foundations" it is essential to know the methodology of "Objectivity."

"Value-Free" sheds more light on Weber's concept of music as social activity. In it Weber demonstrates several of his fundamental ideas on sociology through examples from the arts and music. These examples are not merely illustrative, proving as they do the central importance of the sociology of art and music in Weber's thought. It is therefore advisable to briefly examine the other two essays relevant to the sociology of music before dealing with the fragmentary "Foundations."

Max Weber's Method

The essay "Objectivity" was meant to outline the program of a journal for the social sciences, thus providing the opportunity to touch on methodological questions of cultural sociology. Weber described the goal of the journal as "the scientific study of the general cultural significance of the socioeconomic structure of human social life and its historical forms of organization" (Weber GAWL, 165). Clearly, the economic approach chosen here recalls the materialistic view of history and its distinction between basis and superstructure. Weber is aware of the "one-sidedness" of this program:

> The right to the *one-sided* analysis of artistic reality from specific "points of view"—in our case that of economic dependence—is, first and foremost, the purely methodological result of the fact that training the eye to observe the effect of similar types of causal categories and the constantly using the same conceptual methodological apparatus offer all the advantages of a division of labor. (Weber GAWL, 170)

Although Weber acknowledges the "scientific productivity" of such a method, he rejects the materialistic view of history as the "common denominator for a causal explanation of historical reality" (Weber GAWL, 166). His suspicion of transforming a scientifically productive method into an ideology is consistent with his call for the separation of scientific research from ethical-political value judgments.

The fact is often overlooked that this distinction from the theory of an economic "common denominator" basically concurs with the warnings uttered by Friedrich Engels (see chapter 7) and agrees even more with the ideas developed by Karl Marx in his Introduction to the *Critique of Political Economy*. As previously mentioned, this introduction was not published until 1903, so we can assume that Weber did not know Marx's text when he wrote "Objectivity" in 1904. In any case, his rejection of the materialistic view of history is directed, not against a materialistic method of research, but against confusing this productive method with an ideological principle.

If, then, Weber places the cultural importance of socioeconomic structure at the center of attention for his journal's program, he also emphasizes the limitations of this method: "The reduction to economic causes alone is in no way exhaustive for *any* area of cultural phenomena" (Weber GAWL, 169). Weber also examined this problem in the work that appears to have contributed most to his reputation, *The Protestant Ethic and the Spirit of Capitalism* (1904–05) in which he defends himself against the possible charge that he wished to replace a one-sided materialistic view with an equally one-sided spiritualistic causal view of culture and history: "Both are equally possible, yet both perform an equal disservice to historical truth if they claim to be not just preliminary work but the conclusion of the study" (Weber GARS, I:205–206).

The emphasis here is on "preliminary work" which can be performed under a number of different methodological points of view. The causal tracing of all cultural processes to individual, arbitrarily chosen factors may agree with an ideology, that is, an ethical-political judgment, yet it "merely demonstrates our ignorance" (Weber GAWL, 167). In a concealed allusion to Hippolyte Taine, Weber opposes explaining cultural phenomena wholly through "race," "milieu," or "historic moment" (Weber GAWL, 167). Hackneyed rules of this type are to be overcome through training in methodology.

The Concept of Ideal Type

The cultural sciences are forced to work with terms in order to classify given phenomena, for example, concepts of style and form in musicology. Attempting to investigate the meaning of such concepts for consistently methodical research, Weber demonstrated that this type of concept formation is peculiar to the humanities and, to a certain extent, indispensable. "Political economy" and "craft," "feudalism" and "capitalism," and "literary language" represent concepts with whose help "we seek to conceive and understand reality" (Weber GAWL, 193). They are created to mentally put observed phenomena in order. Weber calls such concepts "ideal types." He does not mean "ideal" in the common sense of the word, for there are "ideal types of brothels as well as religions"; instead, he emphasizes that they are mental constructs.

What is an Ideal Type?

> An ideal type is arrived at through unilateral intensification of one or
> more points of view and becomes a uniform configuration through the
> combination of a wealth of isolated phenomena, which may be diffuse
> and discrete to a greater or lesser degree, or not at all, but which fit into
> these unilateral points of view. Being a utopia, this configuration, with
> its conceptual purity, is nowhere to be found in empirical reality. It is
> the task of historiography to determine in each case how close to that
> ideal image reality comes. . . . When cautiously applied for purposes
> of investigation and illustration, however, the concept has its particu-
> lar use. (Weber GAWL, 191)

Music, too, cannot be studied as a social phenomenon without such
ideal types. The concepts "participatory music" and "performance
music" (Besseler 1959), sociological by their very nature, are surely
ideal types, for they combine isolated phenomena nowhere to be found
in their conceptual purity. Nonetheless, they perform a highly important function in understanding phenomena. The academic concept of
"sonata form" is a mental construct serving a specific purpose, though
it does not relieve us from determining in each case the extent to which
the concrete sonata does or does not correspond to the abstract ideal
type.

We must, of course, follow Weber's advice to be careful in coining
ideal types. Interpreted as a blank check for creating arbitrary mental
constructs, the concept of ideal types invites abuse. Paul Lazarsfeld
(1965) pointed out with some justification that to find out "how Weber
really worked" (Lazarsfeld 1965, 40) one would do best to forget
Weber's definition of the ideal type, for Weber sought concrete proof in
all areas rather than evading proof by resorting to ideal-type constructs.
As Lazarsfeld asserts, it would be wrong to raise the concept of ideal
type to a central category of sociology in order to avoid empirical
research:

> In the end, all the talk about ideal types leads nowhere, but it can point
> to a genuine problem of social research. For the theorist of science, the
> only way to find a solution is to analyze empirical studies and not the
> manifestations of those who represent this tradition. (Lazarsfeld 1965,
> 41)

Max Weber's interpretation of ideal type probably does not contradict Lazarsfeld's demand. Ideal-type concepts ("capitalism," "performance music," "sonata form") represent attempts to classify the results

of empirical investigations. "The researcher would like to create an order that did not exist originally but that represents a planned classification" (Lazarsfeld 1965, 43). Max Weber also proceeds in this fashion. At the same time, however, his wordy definition of "ideal type" emphasizes that he intends it to be seen, not as identical with the concept of average, but as a classificatory construct with which to measure individual phenomena. This interpretation is in accord with that of a major ethologist:

> The abstraction of type is absolutely indispensable in order to be able to conceptualize the completely different deviations brought about by different causes and to analyze these causes. To this end, it would be useless if one were to attempt to define the average of the largest number of individual cases as typical or "normal." From the medical point of view, for example, the average man is indeed completely different from the "normal" one, that is the ideally healthy man. (Lorenz 1978, 61)

It goes almost without saying that Weber also used ideal-type constructs in his subsequent discussions of socio-musicology (Occidental music, music based on chordal harmony, and so on). His main contribution to scientific theory was to have proved the classificatory value of ideal types, which he advised should be used with caution and whose limits he recognized. He correctly points out that Marxian laws and patterns of evolution, which also have "ideal-type natures" (Weber GAWL, 205), posit deviation from the ideal type in every case. The idea-structures of an age, that is, the trains of thought peculiar to an epoch, can also be classified as ideal types. "Christianity" and "Christian Middle Ages" are categories which have no exact equivalent in reality but are, rather, "pure mental configurations we create" (Weber GAWL, 197). In order to construct ideal types, it is essential that they not be influenced by value judgments. Value judgments can be the *object* of sociological research, but they cannot become an *instrument* of research. This explains Weber's call for a research method with, ideally, intercultural validity. Using "Chinese" to represent all members of other cultures, Weber asserts "that methodically correct scientific argumentation in the social sciences must also be recognized as correct by a Chinese if it is to achieve its purpose" (Weber GAWL, 155). He (the "Chinese") must also recognize it as conclusive when he proceeds from the fact that an analyzed ideal does not correspond to his own ethical imperative. In this quite modern approach, Weber thus emphasizes that research results should have intercultural validity.

Value-Oriented Interest and Aesthetic Evaluation

The direction research takes is, of course—as Weber emphasized a number of times—determined by value-oriented interest: "The object of study and the extent to which this study extends into the infinity of the causal nexus, is determined by the notions of value held by the researcher and current in his time" (Weber GAWL, 184). This value orientation in the area of research is characteristic for the choice of what Weber calls the central problem of music sociology from the point of view of modern Europeans, that is, the question of "why harmony, which derived from almost universal polyphony, developed only in Europe and during a certain period of time, whereas everywhere else the rationalization of music took another, usually opposite direction" (Weber GAWL, 521). This statement, from the "Value-Free" essay is formulated more clearly in "Foundations":

> Why did polyphonic as well as harmonic-homophonic music and the modern tonal system develop out of the widely diffuse preconditions of polyphony only in the Occident? Such preconditions were at least as strong in other regions of the world and notably so in Hellenic antiquity and in Japan. (Weber 1958, 83)

These ideas also provide a general description of the direction Weber took in socio-musicological research.

It cannot be emphasized often enough that Weber did not think of the sociology of art as a "hyphenated sociology," that is, a mechanical, superficial application of sociological categories to art. He strove, instead, for integration:

> Anyone who wishes to achieve something in the history of art, purely empirical though these studies may be, requires the ability to "understand" artistic production. It goes without saying that this is inconceivable without the *ability* to make aesthetic judgments, that is, the ability to evaluate. (Weber GAWL, 524)

Weber does not mean that aesthetic evaluation is to be used as scientific proof; quite the contrary. All that matters here is the ability to judge, because this presumes an intimacy with art without which there can be no sociology of art.

Weber was on an intimate basis with art and music as demonstrated not only by his writings, but also by a wealth of details provided by his wife, Marianne, in the biography she wrote of her husband (Weber 1926). It is therefore surprising that in many evaluations of Weber's intellectual achievement, his relationship to art and music is either ignored or treated with little regard for the facts. An extreme example is Reinhard Bendix's attempt at an intellectual portrait of Weber. His book does not look into Weber's contribution to the sociology of art and music and goes so far as to miss the mark in characterizing Weber's work on the sociology of music (Bendix 1964, 347). I therefore consider it all the more necessary to shed light on Weber's relationship to music. Only thus can it be proved that Weber did not lack the ability of aesthetic judgment he required of others. I consider this important because I support the view that research in the sociology of music cannot be fruitful without a very close relationship to music.

Weber's Relationship to Music

Weber, who received some musical education as a child, played the piano when he was young (Baumgarten 1964, 482). His interest in music, the theater, and the fine arts was always intense, as proved by many of his letters. He planned to write a book on the sociology of art soon after the first edition of *The Protestant Ethic and the Spirit of Capitalism* was published, and he "made the first attempt in this direction about 1910, in the midst of other works, by investigating the rational and sociological foundations of music" (Weber 1926, 349). The excerpts of letters from this period quoted by Marianne Weber are filled with critical and occasionally extremely penetrating discussions of concert and opera performances. He fully supported *Salome* by Richard Strauss, although he must have been formed by the aesthetic norms of the nineteenth century. Eduard Baumgarten reports that Weber bought a piano at this time and allowed himself to be initiated into the secrets of Wagner by a lady pianist friend:

> Mina Tobler is preparing Max and Marianne for the festival in Bayreuth—*Tristan*. Max Weber saw the great score for the first time at her house. He says, extremely perplexed, "I should have a technique like this; then I would finally, as I should, be able to say many things separately, one after the other, and yet at the same time." (Baumgarten 1964, 482–483)

This reference to a *Tristan* performance in Bayreuth might lead one to believe that Weber was in the Bavarian town as early as 1906 (the only year during this time in which *Tristan* was in the Bayreuth repertoire). Yet his systematic interest in music was apparently not yet aroused at this time, and Weber does not seem to have gone deeply into music until about 1910. The performance of *Tristan* which he attended, and for which he had been prepared, took place in Munich in 1912. Before that he had witnessed a performance of *Parsifal* in Bayreuth. He rejected the "impertinence that one should regard this as a religious work," and considered *Meistersinger* to be much the greater work of art. In addition to his interest in specific works of music, of which I have given only a few, sketchy indications, Weber was well read in the scholarly literature on music. His exploration in music sociology "lead him into the most remote regions of ethnology and the most difficult studies concerning tonal mathematics and symbolism" (Weber 1926, 349).

Music in Sociological Argumentation

Music for Weber was more than just a theme of sociology; he went so far as to make it an example of sociological argumentation. Weber's need to communicate his ideas must have been so overwhelming that he occasionally forgot whether those with whom he wished to share them had the aesthetic ability and knowledge required for understanding. A theologian colleague of Weber's recalls an invitation to a Weber lecture, which was held in 1912 or 1913:

> None of us could decipher the invitation: "Sociology of the Muses?" What's gotten into him! To our great astonishment, he sat down at the piano, demonstrated pieces from the theory of harmony, and went on from there to the most unexpected things. This, we said afterward, is the most unheard of thing he has ever done. We were utterly perplexed and stunned. I understood virtually nothing. Almost none of us knew what a third was. (Baumgarten 1964, 483 n.)

Others were similarly astonished in 1913 when, at a meeting of the Union for Social Policy in Vienna, Weber read a paper on the problems surrounding value judgments in the social sciences. He took this opportunity to support his interpretation with a resumé of his studies on the sociology of art, and especially music, putting a majority of the listeners "into a rage" because, in their view, he only told anecdotes (Baumgarten 1964, 482).

His colleagues' reaction illuminates a crucial aspect of his sociology: Weber did not respect the barriers academic science placed between disciplines in the name of a pragmatic division of labor. He counteracted theory devoid of facts with factually-based argumentation. The so-called anecdotes that Weber told at the Vienna meeting in 1913 were an integral part not only of his sociology of music but of his sociology in general; not only did they illustrate his trains of thought but they formed links in the chain of his argumentation.

Fortunately, Weber does not seem to have been irritated by his colleagues' astonishment. With his characteristic perserverance, he stuck to his personal way of representing the value judgment problem. "As they did not wish to listen to him, he repeated his argument at equally painstaking length" (Baumgarten 1964, 483) in the published form of this lecture in 1917.

To this day, it must unfortunately be said, the text has not received the appreciation it deserves. In general, sociologists are still inclined to regard Weber's thoughts on music as a mannered stylistic device, while musicologists are unhappy about the music being burdened with reflections on the theory of science. It is all the more important to consider the lecture at this juncture; because Weber was no longer able to revise his "Foundations" of socio-musicology, the "Value-Free" text became the most comprehensive authentic source of his thoughts on the discipline.

Weber's Concept of Progress

Weber's "Value-Free" essay played an important role in the long discussion on methodology that has gone down in the literature as the "value-judgment debate" (cf. Ferber 1965). For my purposes, the passages in Weber's essay that deal with questions about the sociology of art and music deserve closer attention.

There is a fundamental difference between Weber's method and those upheld by several of his contemporaries in the field. Whereas, for example, Gustav Schmoller (1838–1917) proceeded from the supposedly increasing agreement on value judgments, Weber was of the opinion that science should not be content with conventional unanimity: "In my opinion, the specific function of science appears to be the precise opposite; that which is conventionally self-evident becomes a problem" (Weber GAWL, 502). Turning the conventional into a problem like this is one of the foundations of Weber's reflections on the sociology of art. Seeing from this point of view, Weber does not regard perspective in painting or harmony based on the tempered tonal system in music as self-evident; rather he sees them as phenomena sociology is almost obligated to pose as problems. He is concerned with shedding light on the creation of such "conventions"; for sociologists they are not "correct," but merely socially "valid." The prerequisites of this validity require investigation.

Weber's disagreement with the concept of progress in sociology arises from this line of thought. To him, the question of whether one can call the increasing differentiation—heterogenization in the Spencerian sense— "progress" is exclusively a matter of terminological expedience. In this regard, Weber mentions Georg Simmel's view that social differentiation can also be considered an increase in "inner wealth" and raises the objection that this cannot be decided by an empirical discipline. Weber's critique of Simmel's speculative thesis is also of significance to the sociology of art because it implicitly opposes applying an evaluative concept of progress to the history of art and music.

Weber concedes that it is impossible to *study* art without an evaluative concept of progress for single, narrowly defined areas. Here the idea of progress means verifying the extent to which an individual artistic phenomenon, or group of phenomena, fulfills a given artistic intent. (Weber's concept of artistic intent is an ideal-type construct that, as remains to be demonstrated, has its origins in the thought on art history of his time). Taken in this sense, then, progress in art reflects the degree to which an ideal-type artistic intent is realized. Trite though this definition of progress may be, it is not, according to Weber, "meaningless as such." I might add that the limited utility in musicology of such an evaluative concept of progress is supported, for example, by the notion of "minor masters," which we apply to a large number of composers who approach the ideal-type concept of artistic intent to a lesser degree than do the "great masters."

The situation is different for the *empirical history of art* and the *empirical sociology of art*. In Weber's view, the concept of progress as value judgment has no place in these disciplines. They do require, however, a technical, rational concept of progress "wholly confined to ascertaining the technical *means* used for a given artistic purpose" (Weber GAWL, 520). In Weber's opinion, the study of technical means and their evolution—that is, progress in the purely technical sense—is the domain of art history and the sociology of art, because facts about technical means and their influence on artistic intent can be ascertained wholly empirically, without aesthetic evaluation. (Weber GAWL, 520). Weber supplements this draft of the working program for the sociology of art with examples intended to demonstrate the productivity of the program. The following is a summary:

1. For *Gothic architecture* the technical solution of an architectural problem (the vaulting of a certain kind of room) was of crucial importance. This primarily technical revolution converged with emotions that were largely socially and religiously conditioned. "Consideration of the objective, technical, social, and psychological conditions of the new style exhausts the purely empirical task of the history of sociology and art" (Weber GAWL, 521).
2. With respect to the technical aspects of *painting*, Weber refers to the art historian Heinrich Wölfflin (1864–1945) and especially to his work *Die klassische Kunst* [Classical Art], which originally appeared in 1899. Wölfflin later expanded on the method in his *Kunstgeschichtliche Grundbegriffe* [Basic Concepts of Art History]. In an afterword written in 1933, Wölfflin expressed his fundamental agreement with Weber's thesis: "A change in 'mood' is not reflected by art regularly and automatically, as a change of feeling is reflected in the expressions of the human face; the expressive apparatus is not the

same for different epochs" (Wölfflin 1960, 274). Weber draws attention to this expressive apparatus and its changes, that is, to the technical means of art.

3. In *music*, Weber names as examples of the crucial role of technical means:

   a. the change in musical tuning as a precondition for the "creation of the third in its harmonic meaning"

   b. the creation of a rational notation, "without which modern composition would be inconceivable" (Weber GAWL, 522)

   c. the achievements of monasticism, which "rationalized popular polyphony for its own purposes without realizing the magnitude of its contribution" (Weber GAWL, 522)

   d. the adoption and rationalization of dance meter brought about by specific forms of life in Renaissance society, such dance types being the "father of the musical forms resulting in the sonata" (Weber GAWL, 522)

   e. the construction of the piano, "one of the most important technical means of modern musical development" (Weber GAWL, 522)

All of these, Weber adds, are examples of "progress" in technical means which had a powerful effect on the history of music: "The empirical history of music will be able to, and will have to, elaborate on these components of historical development without undertaking an *aesthetic* valuation of the musical works of art" (Weber GAWL, 523).

The foregoing shows the direction Weber wished the sociology of music to take. The historical and ethnological material that served as the basis of this view is set down fragmentarily in "Foundations," unpublished during Weber's lifetime. Weber's vital interest in this argumentation in socio-musicology is shown by the fact that he took it up again toward the end of his life. In a short preface to his *Gesammelte Aufsätze zur Religionssoziologie* [Collected Essays on the Sociology of Religion], published in 1920, he described the inextricable connection between the sociology of music and cultural research as a whole. He was interested in the concatenation of circumstances that had led to "cultural phenomena that have developed in a direction of universal significance and validity (or so we would like to think), which appeared here in the Occident, and only here." (Weber GARS, I). Among these Occidental cultural phenomena of potential universal validity, Weber includes capitalism, rational science, the separation of home and workplace, a specialized class of civil servants, the rational structure of law, and last, but by no means least, the particular form of Western music. This short preface to his essays on the sociology of religion is a concise summary of everything he had previously written on this topic. Weber uses this opportunity to place his thoughts on the sociology of music in what he considers a universal historical context:

> It would appear that the musical hearing of other peoples was better developed than ours today; at any rate, it was not less acute. Various kinds of polyphony, the playing together of many instruments, and the practice of descant have been found in widespread parts of the earth. Furthermore, all of our rational musical intervals have also been calculated and known elsewhere. But many musical practices are unique to the Occident: composed harmonic music (both counterpoint and chordal harmony); tonal material formed on the basis of three triads with the harmonic third; our chromatic scale with its enharmonics, which have been interpreted harmonically (and not by interval) since the Renaissance; our orchestra with the string quartet at its core and its particular organization of the wind ensemble; the use of figured bass; our system of notation (without which the composition and performance of modern works of music would be impossible); our standard musical forms—sonatas, symphonies, operas (although program music, tone painting, alteration of pitch, and chromaticism occur in a wide variety of musics); and all of our basic instruments—organ, piano, violin. (Weber GARS, I, 2)

This quotation reads like the outline for a more comprehensive study that Weber was not able to finish—although as he told his wife in 1912, he intended to "write about certain social conditions" that were responsible for the specific nature of the development of Western music.

The Fragment on the Sociology of Music

Although the manuscript entitled *The Rational and Sociological Foundations of Music* (Weber 1921, 1924, 1972), published after Weber's death by Theodor Kroyer, does not reach the objective that Weber described to his wife, it does consist of research notes meant to provide the basis for that project. As has been correctly noted, this work "is difficult to read, abstract and complicated, seemingly confused and disjointed, and lacking a table of contents and section headings" (Wiora 1930). Nevertheless, "Foundations" was soon received with respect and understanding. In 1925, Anatoli V. Lunacharsky (1875–1933), then People's Commissar for Education in the Soviet Union, published a long review of "Foundations." Despite political and ideological reservations, he termed Max Weber's text "virtually ideal for finishing in the factory of Marxism" (Lunacharsky 1971, 160).

He regretted, however, much as Walter Wiora was to do soon thereafter, that the text failed to include detailed discussions on sociology and methodology. The book, which Lunacharsky reviewed in full, seems to him to be only "a brief sketch that neither in its definition of its task nor in its results deals exhaustively with the problem of the sociological survey of the nature and history of music" (Lunacharsky 1971, 176).

I hope I have made sufficiently clear that "Foundations" was not intended to create a sociology of music. Even the title under which Theodor Kroyer published the work in 1921 does not seem to be Weber's. In his preface, Kroyer mentions the "great difficulty" he experienced with Weber's often undecipherable handwriting. Kroyer's statement that he "only altered what was patently wrong, but nothing else" (Weber 1924, VII) is surprising. That Weber's book has not received much subsequent attention from musicology may also be due to the fact that it was only available as an appendix to the two volumes of Weber's *Wirtschaft und Gesellschaft* [Economy and Society] totalling over 1,100 pages. Not until 1972 was a separate edition published (Weber 1972) — and then without Kroyer's preface, which might have enlightened the reader as to the problems involved in editing the text. The American translation (Weber 1958), published by two sociologists and a musicologist who shared the translating and editing, affords easier access to "Foundations." This edition gives the essence of Weber's ideas on sociology in the introduction and identifies many of Weber's sources in an appendix. These reveal that Weber did more than evaluate the musicological and sociological literature; he also utilized the sound recordings that had been collected in the phonogram archive, founded in Berlin in 1905. The text clearly indicates that Weber knew the literature concerning these recordings. We can even surmise that he heard the "demonstration collection" of phonographic recordings assembled by Erich M. von Hornbostel, which were available immediately following the First World War, if not earlier (Hornbostel 1963). In any event, Weber writes that "only recently has empirical knowledge of primitive music through sound recordings supplied materials for a more adequate picture of the origins" (Weber 1958, 33). This statement also has methodological significance, for it indicates the need for cooperation between ethnomusicology and the sociology of music.

With this attempt to reveal the framework of Weber's thought on music sociology, I have by no means exhausted the wealth of his texts in this narrowly circumscribed field. In dealing with individual, select problems in the sociology of music, however, I will again have occasion to discuss several of Weber's important contributions.

Chapter 16 *The Transition to the Perception of Chordal Harmony*

In his attempt to pin down features of the evolution of Occidental music, Max Weber came across the problem of the transition from the "horizontal" to the "vertical" way of conceiving musical composition. With our present-day perception of music, which interprets as a unity—an intentional unity—whatever is heard simultaneously, it is difficult to imagine a mode of listening based on the relative independence of individual parts. Indeed, it must seem odd to us that a composer thinks primarily in terms of individual parts and interprets the resultant ensemble of a number of parts merely as a product, albeit a controlled one. Part of the difficulty lies in the difference between the listener's and the composer's relationship to the music; it is one thing to participate in the musical act and another to allow a number of musical events forming a unified whole to affect one, as it were, from the outside. To use Besseler's terms, this distinction is the difference between *participatory* music and *performance* music. In Europe the transition to music for performance also brings the gradual change to chordal harmony, which Max Weber described in terms of ideal type:

> Thus, pure chordal harmony thinks musically in two-dimensional terms: vertically across the staff lines and, at the same time, horizontally alongside these lines. Contrapuntalism operates first monodimensionally in a horizontal direction and only then vertically, for the chords are not born from chordal harmonies and uniformly constructed configurations but arise, so to speak, by chance from the pro-

gressions of several independent voices requiring harmonic regulation. (Weber 1958, 68)

The context in which Weber places this thesis reveals that he uses the terms "counterpoint" and "chordal harmony" to denote two consecutive historical stages of musical behaviorß, in regard to both composition and listening. Despite the triumph of chordal harmony, sixteenth- and seventeenth-century music still contains clear traces of horizontal thinking. For example, Johannes Cochlaeus (1479–1552) stated in his book on music, published in Cologne in 1507, that a skilled composer writes parts separately, though he admits that it is good for beginners, who have yet to master consonances and clausulae, to notate all parts simultaneously ("simul componere"). He does not, then, regard thinking in terms of simultaneously sounding parts to be a prerequisite for composing; the overall result is the sum of the individual parts which must, of course, be written so as to relate to one another according to the rules governing consonances and clausulae. Composition still does not aim primarily at the overall sound, which is why it is not notated as a score in the modern sense. But, to those who have yet to master the linking of horizontal musical ideas according to the rules, a score arrangement is a permissible, even recommended, aid. In other words, what Weber calls "two-dimensional" musical thought should be seen, originally, as the result of the various one-dimensional concepts, and the score is not yet the finished musical work but merely an aid to the composer. Such an aid is the "Tabula compositoria" mentioned by Auctor Lampadius (1500–1559) in his *Compendium musices* (Bern 1537), a device apparently used by composers in order to view a composition at a glance. Siegfried Hermelink studied the history of the notion and function of the tabula compositoria, identifying this and a number of similar "composing devices" as forerunners of the modern score:

> The tabula compositoria was made of a material which could be written on and erased (wood or slate, with pieces of parchment, leather, and canvas treated with plaster and varnish), of various sizes (some perhaps as large as a table top), with etched staff lines. There are two kinds of staves corresponding to the two different working methods: (a) composition with the "scala compositoria" (*scala decemlinealis*), in which the entire composition was recorded on a single system consisting of ten lines. . . ; (b) composition "per systemata" (*supra quinque lineas*), the method used by those proficient in composition. In the latter system the tabula compositoria consists of individual five-line systems, which form a score resulting from the sum of the work's individual parts. There is clear proof that both of these types existed around 1500. From the very beginning, both types used vertical dividing lines

(*cancellae*) one or two bars apart, whose purpose was to organize note values. (Hermelink 1961, 227–228)

That the idea of the relative independence of horizontal musical ideas survived in musical practice into the seventeenth century is confirmed by the preface to the *Cento concerti ecclesiastici* (1602) of Ludovico Viadana (1560–1627). He compares the idea of the musical totality of a work with a musical practice not yet adopted by the whole of society:

Honored reader, a number of reasons have caused me to compose this type of *concerti*, although the principal one was the following: I had observed that at times individual singers, when they wished to sing together with the organ *a tre*, or *a due*, or with one voice, were forced to restrict themselves to one, two, or three voices in five, six, seven, or eight-part motets for want of compositions suited to their purpose. Yet, removed from the context of other voices with which they were linked by imitation, cadences, contrapuntal counterparts, and other compositional devices, these parts became full of long, repeated pauses, lacking cadences and melody, so that the result was poor and tasteless. Moreover, the interruptions of the words, often present only in the deleted parts and sometimes even containing unsuitable interpolations, make this kind of singing imperfect, dull, or amateurish; this is not pleasant for those listening, quite apart from the fact that it is also awkward for the singers. (German translation quoted in Haack 1974, *Notenteil*, VII–VIII)

This preface marks a historic transition. Viadana describes the composer's desire to control the work in performance as an innovation which has not yet been generally accepted, contrasting it with an older practice which he describes as "not pleasant for those listening." This, together with similar evidence, shows that we are dealing with different structures of musical activity, thinking, and feeling, namely, those structures which Max Weber attempted to define — perhaps unsuccessfully — as "counterpoint" and "chordal harmony." His use of the terms "horizontal" and "two-dimensional" is more apt, as "dimension" seems the most obvious way to characterize these two different structures of musical activity. Curt Sachs, for example, expressed the transition studied by Max Weber as follows:

The spatial principle in music is harmony because it contrasts the two-dimensional melody of music with a third dimension and places the single note — as the visual arts place a point in space — in a two-fold relationship to the other notes of the melody *and* to the other notes of the chord. (Sachs 1918, 458) This feeling of space, growing increasingly stronger, finally had to lead to what we today call harmony, that is, to chords that through logical linking produce a feeling akin to that of three-dimensionality, which is the basis not only of single notes but of the melody as a whole. (Sachs 1918, 461)

The sole difference between Weber's and Sachs's use of the word *dimension* is that the former attributes two dimensions to harmony, while Sachs describes it as having three. This difference results from an interpretation that characterizes a certain approach to musical activity through analogy with the representation of space in the visual arts. I will later demonstrate the objective utility of this analogy.

Structures of Musical Activity

We can compare the two-dimensional and three-dimensional approaches to musical activity by using ideal types to bring out their individual structures. We are best able to distinguish these structures by interpreting musical activity as a social phenomenon. This method proceeds, not from the subjective consciousness of the person involved in the activity (although it takes account of this consciousness), but rather from the observable regularities, the "particular kinds of acting, thinking, and feeling whose basic characteristic is that they exist outside of individual consciousness" (Durkheim 1963, 4). To Durkheim, musical activity is a "sociological fact" (*fait social*). By classifying different kinds of musical activity, it is possible to bring out the inner consistency of the ideal-type behavior, what might be termed the "structure of musical activity." In this context, Sachs's concepts of "two-dimensionality" and "three-dimensionality"—not the concepts themselves, but the totality of social activity connected with them—would be classified as different structures of musical activity. Each of these concepts is governed by certain systems of rules that incorporate social and technical elements. Thus, seen as ideal types, the two-dimensional structure goes along with *participatory music*, whereas the three-dimensional is linked to *performance music* and the division between those listening and those performing.

Working out ideal-type structures of musical activity is intended not merely to *describe* circumstances but rather to *understand* them. Historically, the transition from one manner of listening to another did not take place abruptly. Moreover, the development of new structures did not necessarily result in the complete disappearance of previous structures (cf. Parsons 1970, 625), as Adorno's types of musical conduct (1976, 1–20) illustrate. By formulating ideal-type structures for musical activity, music sociologists create a conceptual instrument of measurement that can be used to evaluate specific developments.

Latin Theory and Italian Practice

Studying the transition from two-dimensionality to three-dimensionality clearly shows how useful ideal-type structures can be. The transition, which began at the latest during the fifteenth century and required several centuries for completion, was initiated by two closely linked social and technological phenomena: the increase in the number of persons desiring formal musical training and the invention of the printing press. The *Practica musicae* of Franchinus Gafurius (1451–1522) was not originally published in learned Latin, as tradition demanded, but as *Tractato vulgare de canto figurato* (Milan, 1492) in an Italian translation by Francesco Caza, a student of Gafurius's. The original version of *Practica musicae* was published four years later. In his dedication to the "invincible Duke of Milan," Gafurius points out that, unlike other disciplines, the goal of music is not wholly speculative, being also practical, and that his work serves not only the few involved in research but the general good as well. Gafurius also presented an abridged Italian version of the work twelve years later, "upon request," so that those who did not know Latin would be able to take advantage of it (cf. Young 1969, XXXI). The fact that Gafurius gave a venerable Latin title—*Angelicum ac divinum opus musicae*—to the Italian version of his work (Milan 1508) is another indication that change was gradual. The Latin title is, as it were, the last resistance to the trend of musical theory spreading from the "artes liberales" to musical activity.

The Concept of the Composer

The concept of the composer also came into being at this time. Edgar Zilsel pointed out the social and economic bases of this concept in his study *Die Entstehung des Geniebegriffes* [The Emergence of the Concept of Genius]:

> Not until the number of those engaged in intellectual activity increased, the printing press was invented, and a wide, middle-class public more interested in cultural than religious matters came into being was the way paved for the vigorous growth of the metaphysics of fame. (Zilsel 1926, 210)

This process also brought about a reevaluation of the so-called mechanical arts, one largely determined by the relationship of workers to the means of production. In the ancient city practical skills were not looked upon favorably because such activity was considered the province of slaves. Medieval monks and the freer artisans of the late medieval town provided the basis for a revaluation of practical activity, because work no longer rested entirely on physical strength (as with slaves) but also on the acquisition of technical knowledge. "Renaissance sensibility apparently recognized a class of people who worked with their hands but required a certain amount of knowledge, a group comprising artists, technicians, and at times musicians, instrument makers, and physicians" (Zilsel 1926, 150).

As this brief survey shows, the perception of the terms "music" and "musician" was influenced by the ruling ideology's attitude toward activity and productive work. For Boethius (ca. 480–524), who was considered the highest authority in the field during the Christian Middle Ages, a *musicus* was one who "possesses insight into the mathematical laws of music, but not the practical musician; for the composer is guided only by natural instinct, not sure knowledge, and a practicing musician cannot be esteemed more than an artisan" (Ruhnke in MGG 9, 950).

The social stigma of ancient society still clung to practical activity; this attitude continued, albeit with modifications, well into the feudal society of the Middle Ages. *Musica*, defined as pure theory, was included among the seven free arts (grammar, dialectic, rhetoric, geometry, arithmetic, astronomy, and music) because mental accomplishment was considered worthy of the free and because, as a speculative discipline, it had no discernible connection to the largely mechanical work of slaves and serfs.

Consequently, the structure of ancient and feudal societies and the social evaluation of productive work peculiar to these structures exerted direct influence on the definition of *musica* and on the esteem in which practical musical activity was held. The feudal Middle Ages, which had transformed slaves into serfs enjoying an entirely different social position, assigned new importance to musical practice. Theory and practice were integrated into a hierarchical system: the authority on theory (*musicus*) contrasted with the practicing musician (*cantor*). The Venerable Bede (eighth century) insists on this distinction; the one group understands music, the other performs it. This definition, which makes a neat separation between knowledge and activity, reappears often in Medieval treatises. Guido d'Arezzo adopts it in the eleventh century, adding that he who does something without understanding it is called a beast (nam qui facit, quod non sapit, diffinitur bestia). Guido's statement contains a didactic attitude toward practical activity rather than the old disparaging one—an attitude that is confirmed by Guido's efforts in music pedagogy, which were aimed at imbuing musical activity with elements of knowledge. A teacher at the cathedral school in Arezzo who began as a Benedictine monk, Guido thereby summed up the tendency, always present in monastic work, to conduct musical activity in the liturgy according to intelligible norms. He thus cleared the way for an interpenetration of musical theory and practice.

In order for these changes in attitude to take full effect, however, additional changes were required in the social structure. A social revaluation of practical work was only possible after the development of a market economy, cities, an urban middle class, free artisans, and a rudimentary form of capital for commerce—principally in northern Italy and the Netherlands. Practicing and composing musicians were able to attain social rank, although initially this was not because of their musical activity but rather because of other social functions. It is worth noting, however, that musical activity gradually lost its social stigma. Composing could also help one attain social status, although the term "composer" as a profession is first recorded in documents toward the end of the fifteenth century, and then only sporadically.

Gafurius draws the conclusions of this new situation in his treatise *Practica musicae*, published in 1496. For him, as he states in the preface, music is "not, like the other disciplines, a merely speculative pursuit; it reaches out into practice" (Young 1969, 5). The Latin original (Musica . . . exit in actum) shows even more clearly the intention furthered by changed social conditions. In order to fully appreciate this new attitude toward musical practice, one has to place it against the social background of the period. Although the described social change allowed composing to attain higher social status, the time was not yet ripe for the recognition of a unified *work*, the intact *res facta*, much less for the final breakthrough to the chordal-harmony or "three-dimensional" concept described by Max Weber and Curt Sachs. In attempting to prove this thesis, it is not possible to document the musical behavior of, for example, the sixteenth century using only literary and pictorial sources. Heinrich Besseler demonstrated, however, that analyzing musical documents also provides sociological information. He characterizes the music of this time as "prose melody," a type of writing which remained tied to the word, carefully avoiding both repetition and symmetry (Besseler 1959, 20). Besseler attempts to derive the "listener's behavior" from this evidence:

> A musical motif can be taken up by other parts in such a way as to have the effect of a repetition. Yet the imitation of a motif, even continuous imitation in all parts, applies only to the section of the text to which it belongs. The following section presents new material. And since, for the whole work, there is no repetition or correspondence, just as there is none within the individual sections, the listener must carefully follow how the piece of music is put together from ever-new elements. In this art the intellectual content, not the music itself, is of primary importance. It is assumed that the listener will follow the text section by section and understand the motifs from the words. (Besseler 1959, 21)

Besseler considers the word "listening" to be too neutral for this type of behavior; he therefore suggests designating the behavior of the listener to such prose melody as "perceiving" (*Vernehmen*). Besseler's attempts to derive the structure of behavior from musical data—he has done the same for periods other than the sixteenth century—are important achievements. By expressing his interpretation of music as social activity without referring to sociological theories, Besseler reveals himself to be a pioneer in a line of socio-musicological thought that agrees in many details with the reflections of Max Weber.

Preliminary Stages of Complete Chordal Harmony

Of course, an objection can be raised to Besseler's analysis. It seems unlikely that the term *listener*, in our sense of the word, is appropriate for the basically "horizontal" prose melody of the sixteenth century; it is more likely that the "listeners" of the period were not a genuine audience but consisted instead of those who made the music and those who *recreated* it as they listened. Besseler's convincing thesis that performance music, in the new sense of the term, did not come about until the seventeenth century supports Helmut Haack's (1974, 60) position that this was not a "division between performers and listeners" but rather a group of persons taking part in a liturgical or secular act. In other words, the polyphonic vocal writing of the sixteenth century is to be regarded primarily as a musical group activity manifested in "horizontal" prose melody, largely devoid of the behavior of an audience listening, as it were, "from the outside." *The rules of consonance and part-writing therefore governed the behavior of both the performers and the active listeners, but they did not govern the totality of the chordal-harmonic impression.*

Chords in horizontally constructed music typically result from individual voices and have no independent aesthetic value of their own. This method of composition, which does not object to a fourth part being added to an already existing three-part composition, corresponds to a certain type of listening that Besseler terms "perceiving." As Bourdieu (1969, 166) has stated, the rise of the aesthetic mode of perception in the true sense of the term is the result of a transformation from the artistic method of production into one directed at totality.

This transformation was only initiated, not wholly accomplished, during the Renaissance. Neither the appearance of the incipient forms of printed scores (first in an organ part of Adriano Banchieri's *Concerti ecclesiastici*, 1595) nor the introduction of the figured bass as "harmonic shorthand" led to the old structures of musical behavior being immediately abandoned in favor of a new chordal-harmony, or "three-dimensional" structure. This applies as well to Viadana's *Concerti ecclesiastici* of 1602, which were long considered revolutionary because, as Manfred Bukofzer remarks (1977, 27), they are based more on the polyphonic than on the monodic principle; put another way, they are conceived more horizontally than vertically (three-dimensional chordal harmony).

Viadana's method of composition, taken in Bourdieu's sense of artistic method of production, is not as completely committed to aesthetic totality as one would assume from the passage in Viadana's preface to his *Concerti* quoted on page 127. The concept's intermediate form, neither entirely horizontal nor completely one of chordal harmony, is consistent with a world view influenced by the "transition from the feudal to a middle-class view of life" (Borkenau 1976). Unlike the industrial society to come, this epoch does not focus on scientifically understanding the work process but is satisfied with dividing work into individual units, as in the age of manual production. The method of composition is also closer to craft than to art in our usual sense of the word. Neither listening nor composition is primarily concerned with the totality of what is performed, which is one of the reasons why chordal harmony, the linking of "three-dimensional" musical components, cannot as yet play the major role. It is as if both the composer and the listener were not yet capable of surveying the musical work as a unity in *all* its dimensions, despite the use of *tabulae compositoriae* (erasable tables), which enabled one to see the totality; despite the beginnings of printed scores, which fostered this type of listening; and despite the figured bass, which now seems almost to force this comprehensive perspective of music.

Chordal Harmony and Linear Perspective

The term "three-dimensionality" suggests comparison with perspective in the visual arts, discovered in the Renaissance. I have made an attempt to demonstrate this parallel between chordal harmony and linear perspective (Blaukopf 1972, 83-97), and a number of theses on this topic have been supported by recent research (cf. Edgerton 1976 and bibliography). Of course, the comparison with painting (and drawing) is not conclusive, particularly if regarded as one of mere analogy. Nonetheless, it must be apparent that the rise of the idea of artistic genius, the creation of a work as a totality, and the integrity of the concept of a work are closely linked to the rise of linear perspective on the one hand and of chordal harmony in music on the other. Although in both cases the ground was prepared by artistic rather than scholarly efforts, the door to artistic expression was opened by theory—through the discovery of the vanishing point in the former and of temperament in the latter.

Because history has shown that seeing in perspective is not a natural but a learned behavior, the parallel between linear perspective and chordal harmony is of great importance to the sociology of art and music. Linear perspective is "not innate. It must be learned" (Edgerton 1976, 80). Unless I am mistaken, this allegation is also supported by the findings of developmental psychology. Sociology has dealt with this problem only since the beginning of the twentieth century, and anthropology has recently produced important findings in this area. W. Hudson, for example, demonstrated in 1969 that for certain African peoples the perception of space and the conception of pictures is influenced to some extent by formal education but to a greater extent by general environmental factors. In general, linear-perspective drawings are hard to understand in cultures not used to them (see Segal 1966, Walker 1979).

Identifying a form of familiar visual behavior as not natural provides us with a key to understanding the characteristics of "three-dimensional" listening. Ethnomusicological findings proved long ago that this, too, is not innate but the result of a historical learning process that presumably first took place in Occidental music. Research in the history of art and musicology suggests, then, that the relationship between chordal harmony and linear perspective is not arbitrary or merely metaphorical. Both phenomena share a common social basis, despite the fact that the development of the new way of seeing involved different factors from those that brought about the new way of listening. Once again, we are shown how productive intercultural comparisons can be when they concern the study of structures of musical behavior in European history.

Ideal-Type Concepts in Music Sociology

Creating structures of musical behavior in terms of ideal types is meant to illustrate changes of behavior. We must not succumb to the temptation of clinging to the structural pattern in individual cases; instead we must attempt to uncover concrete modes of behavior from existing evidence. Then either the pattern will be confirmed or, more likely, it will have to be modified—even though it was derived from observations. For example, an analysis of the transition from the sixteenth-century prose melody founded on participation to the later chordal harmony of the performance-oriented culture immediately shows that this transformation is made up of minute changes. Whereas these changes can be measured by established ideal-type structures, they cannot be classified according to such structures.

Something needs to be said at this point about the logic of the terms used. Concepts such as "participatory music" (*Umgangsmusik*), "performance music" (*Darbietungsmusik*), "chordal harmony," and "counterpoint" are inadequate for describing historical reality. (See chapter 23.) They merely serve to clarify the structure of certain aspects of musical behavior; that is to say, they function as what Weber calls "borderline concepts." *They are not the goal of sociological research but merely expedients in the quest for knowledge* (cf. Weber GAWL, 208–209). The task of music sociology does not end with the creation of this kind of ideal-type category; it begins there. The same is true in formulating ideal types for the evolutionary trends we are dealing with. If the transition from "two-dimensional" to "three-dimensional" musical practice and the rise of performance music associated with it can be construed as an ideal-type tendency, this is simply meant to illustrate changes in musical practice through the creation of borderline concepts. The next step must be, in all analyses of concrete details, to examine real conditions. The ideal-type construct is at best a compass for the sociology of music, never a panacea. Historically, the change to chordal-harmony performance music, which I have broadly outlined here, did not come about in an ideal-type pattern either. The transitions were in part continuous and in part erratic, sometimes entailing setbacks. No ideal-type construct is able to do justice to the actual historical developments or to the fluid transitions which must be investigated.

Viadana's aforementioned *Concerti ecclesiastici* provide an illustration of such a gradual transition. Although they contain the beginnings of chordal harmony and a new awareness of tonality, the figured bass in these *Concerti* does not lead to a continuous three-dimensional conception because

> the musical completion of the composition by the figured bass accompaniment must take into consideration that contrapuntal voice-leading operates in a particular way in this music; the accompaniment, which has absolutely nothing to do with modern figured bass playing as influenced by harmonic theory, must be adequate for the compositional substance. (Haack 1974, 253)

Instead of chords, "supplemental parts" are inserted between the written parts to complete the overall structure according to the old horizontal concept. The harmonic analysis from a later period cannot be applied to this early seventeenth-century music:

> Not until the end of the seventeenth century did one begin to grasp the vertical component of figured harmony, whereas composers around 1600 were still far from conceiving music primarily in harmonic terms or thinking in terms of keyboard patterns as conceived by the eighteenth century. When an organist is praised ca. 1600, his abilities in strict contrapuntal playing are always stressed. (Haack 1974, 185–186)

It would hardly be possible to express the particular characteristics of this structure of musical behavior more clearly. We are dealing with the transition from the old prose melody to the chordal harmony associated with performance art, a performance art directed at an audience listening "from the outside." Venice offers an example of this change, which soon found expression in the appearance of musical repetition and symmetry. Heinrich Schütz, who had already been to Venice in 1609, related that during his second visit in 1628 he felt that "everything has very much changed since I was here the first time, and there is considerably more and better music to be heard at the tables of princes, and for comedies, ballets, and similar stage performances" (Schütz quoted in Brodde 1972, 110).

Several years later, in 1637, the first opera house was opened in Venice. The creation of a public attending performances brought about what Besseler, again proceeding from an analysis of the music, called *active listening*. It is now the listener who "correlates, by listening, the parts that the composer created. To listen to sections of music in relation to each other is a characteristic of the period after 1600" (Besseler 1959, 41). Composition moves from the flow of prose melody to symmetrical grouping, from mensuration to metrical accent, from text interpretation to periodic melody. This transformation of structures of musical behavior, which took place during the seventeenth century, also affected the music theory of the period.

Signs of Structural Change in Descartes

The transition is reflected in *Musicae Compendium* by René Descartes (1596–1650), written in 1618. This treatise contains the following new aspects:

1. In his argumentation, Descartes proceeds not from the music but from the listener: "The purpose of musical sound is, in the final analysis, to please and to arouse various emotions within us. . . . All of the senses are capable of pleasure. . . . The theme must be made so as not to be too difficult and confusing to the mind." (Descartes 1978, 3)
2. Descartes makes the listener's understanding of music his most important criterion: "A theme is more easily grasped by the mind the less heterogeneous its parts." (Descartes 1978, 5)
3. Consideration of musical section or period from the *listener*'s perspective brings Descartes to the conclusion that "our imagination grasps music as a single unity made of many similar bars." (Besseler 1959, 39)
4. The demand for the listener to be able to follow all individual elements leads Descartes to recommend a well-ordered structure. This is guaranteed if music is created "from 8, 16, 32, or 64 and more met-

rical divisions. . . . If this is so, once we hear the first two divisions we immediately grasp them as one, and when we hear the third we link this to the first two as well." (Descartes 1978, 7)

5. The foregoing is a virtual program of how performance music should act with respect to the listener. Also, Descartes must have based his remarks on *dance music* from the late sixteenth century, with its characteristic single pattern and *bar accent*. (cf. Besseler 1959, 27–28, and 39)

6. "When, in 1618, for the first time in the history of musicography, Descartes proceeds not from music as such but rather from listening and imagination, he characterizes the new situation." (Besseler 1959, 41)

The "new situation" as outlined at the theoretical level by Descartes— or as I call it, the formation of a new structure of musical behavior—has been treated a number of times in the musicological literature (cf. e.g. Bukofzer 1977, 392). The task of the sociology of music is to go beyond merely identifying this social change; only by tracking down the social and technical factors that may be involved can the sociology of music explain how a change in the purpose of musical activity, a change of "artistic intent," comes about.

Chapter 17 *Artistic Intent as a Sociological Concept*

To the best of my knowledge, Max Weber's use of "artistic intent" has yet to arouse interest in the literature on the sociology of art. This is not, however, an arbitrary turn of phrase but a term that has been used and discussed in aesthetics since the 1890s.

The Ideas of Alois Riegl

Alois Riegl (1858–1905) introduced this concept. The Austrian art historian undertook to use the description of individual artistic manifestations to obtain an overall picture of the evolution of art. Riegl was less interested in the "cult of individual facts" (Riegl 1929, 54) than in investigating the principal artistic trends of an age or region. He wished to limit himself in the positivist sense (Riegl 1929, 59–60) to analyzing the manifestations of artistic production, the only definite given, and deriving artistic intent from them. Like Max Weber, he rejected the notion of evolution, much less "progress," in the arts. Riegl was chiefly reinforced in this conviction by his studies of late Roman art. In his opinion, the loss of the observation of nature at the end of Antiquity was proof that evolution could not be applied to artistic production. How was it possible, Riegl asked, that "the same people who were able to reproduce the human face to the point of perfection during the Roman Empire could be enthusiastic about rigid Byzantine puppets a few centuries later" (Riegl 1929, 9)? A change of artistic intent was the only possible explanation.

Riegl did not understand artistic intent merely as the subjective intention of the creator of art, but as a collective creative principle. Artistic intent is not ascertained by philosophical speculation but is derived from each artistic manifestation. Hans Sedlmayr, in his introduction to Riegl's *Collected Essays* (Riegl 1929, XVIII), was basically correct in pointing out the similarity between Riegl's concept of artistic intent and the sociological concept of "objective collective will," emphasizing the collective nature of artistic intent. Artistic intent is a sociological concept comprising the artistic intentions peculiar to a society, class, or group.

Of course, if unsupported by observable facts, this construct carries with it the danger of mystification. In fact, Arnold Hauser accused Riegl of conceptual mysticism: "He [Riegl] thinks of the artistic approach of an epoch as if it were an active person obtaining recognition for his purpose, often against the strongest resistance, and sometimes succeeding without the knowledge, even against the will, of his supporters" (Hauser 1951, 3, 171). This objection might justifiably be raised against some—I will not go into this here—of Riegl's evidence in art history; I believe, however, that this does not affect Riegl's methodology. He was always concerned with ascertaining artistic intent in concrete works of art. What is more, he also strove to "obtain a broader base" (Riegl 1929, 63) for understanding artistic intent by including political, religious, and scientific intent in his analysis:

> If one subsumes the common intent in all sectors of culture under the term "world view," it can be said that, although the visual arts are not determined by the then current world view, they do, for all intents and purposes, run parallel to it. (Riegl 1929, 63)

Riegl regards this linking of research in the arts to research in other areas of culture as the "true future task" of what he called comparative cultural history. This statement of purpose and its fundamentally empirical orientation not only invalidate the accusation made decades later by Hauser but also set a goal to be shared by sociology and musicology.

Application to Musicology

A distinguished example of this common goal is expressed in a passage from the academic inaugural address delivered by the musicologist Guido Adler at the University of Vienna in 1898. In this address, Adler underscored not only the insoluble connection between musicology and the study of art; he also emphasized the dependence of all intellectual production "on all kinds of social, economic, and political conditions." Although Adler did not at the time use Riegl's concept of artistic intent, he did, much like Riegl, outline a broadening of the base of argumentation, which he also understood as a task for the future:

> As the true field of musicological research will be studied with increasing success, future generations will have the new task of unraveling all these linking threads. That which has so far been achieved in this field commonly known as cultural history cannot be regarded as wholly valid. (Adler 1899, 35)

Adler's view that music depends on the social, economic, and political conditions does not indicate a preconceived allegiance to the materialistic approach to history; rather this view was forced upon him by the results of his work in musicology. Adler proceeded from an idea of value whose duality he later clearly expressed. He distinguished between the intrinsic value of a musical work of art, which he termed "more subjective," and its extrinsic value, which can be ascertained objectively by "taking into account its importance for stylistic development" (Adler 1919, 142). The method that Adler intends to apply is of particular interest because it is similar to Riegl's. Adler even came to use the term "artistic intent" in Alois Riegl's sense. I will return to this later.

Adler spoke of the "value" of a musical work in terms of the history of development. He also spoke more precisely of "developmental significance," meaning the role of a work, as revealed by its structure, in the subsequent development of the art of music. An absolute minimum of materials is required to demonstrate the chain of development. Adler, however, demands that research not be limited to analysis of what is considered to be a masterwork, a requirement that effectively demonstrates the empirical basis of his scientific method ("positivistic" in Riegl's sense of the word):

> The large quantity of works of art must be taken into consideration. Sometimes these are, at first sight, insignificant features in relatively weak, that is, inferior, pieces that assume increasing importance for the progress of the stylistic development of an art form. For example, in the course of the great evolutionary process from the dominance of the suite to the autocratic rule of the cyclical sonata, transitional passages or repetitions of thematic groups or reuse of thematic elements, which appear in otherwise unremarkable pieces, are of wide-reaching importance for the development of sonata form. And we do not find these features in masters of the first rank but in middling and lesser masters who assemble such components for a new artistic intent. (Adler 1919, 143)

The attempt to more precisely define style and stylistic change brings Adler to the realization that he cannot proceed from recognized masterpieces alone but must turn to "the large quantity of works of art." Scholarship must take into account all the artistic manifestations at work in an era, not just the small number of masterworks that have succeeded beyond their era through a process of historical selection. The elements of a new artistic intent in the making can be derived in this way, as Adler demonstrates in his illustration of the transition from the suite to the cyclical sonata.

Artistic Intent and Statistics

A sociological aspect was thus introduced to the history of art and music. Where attention had previously been devoted primarily to the iconographic in art history and to the findings of music philology in music history (with preference for manifestations included in one's own view of art), interest was now directed toward the wide spectrum of artistic manifestations operative during a given era. The idea of a collective creative principle, that is, a socially valid "artistic intent," grew not from philosophical speculation but from the realization that investigating artistic intent as a socially operative intellectual force could succeed only through analyzing the large quantity of artistic manifestations. Whereas aesthetic worth had previously been the principal criterion for the selection of the works of art and music to be analyzed, the principle of value-free selection of the works to be studied now came to the fore. Adler's reference to the "large quantity" implicitly contains the idea that the investigation of developmental trends in compositional practice must be supported by a representative sample in the statistical sense.

The ideas of Riegl and Adler also mark a general change to the social-statistical way of thinking in aesthetics and musicology. This concept, developed during the nineteenth century as a result of thought concerning human society, proceeds on the assumption that reflection without observation of facts cannot lead to the desired success. The Belgian mathematician and precursor of sociology Adolphe Quetelet (1796–1874) was one of the first to recognize that "given the variety and complexity of human actions and interactions, psychological and social problems should best be dealt with statistically, because only this approach leaves room for the variability and diversity of human nature" (Haseloff 1965, 9n). Subsequent attempts by cultural statistics to derive the characteristic data of a large number of phenomena by investigating a representative sample reveal the correlation between the analysis of the sample and the general knowledge obtained from it.

Each concretely circumscribed "artistic intent" also represents such general knowledge, ideally derived from an analysis of the most representative sample possible. It goes without saying that in historical studies the strict statistical rules for creating a sample can rarely be maintained. But Adler's call for the "large quantity of works of art" is to be understood as a recommendation to come as close as possible to this precise scientific rule. In my opinion, because Adler's method is not the result of considerations of principle but rather of his investigation into a subject (music), his recommendation is even more significant than would be one deduced wholly from the theory of science. It demonstrates that *the subject itself demands such a method*.

Riegl applied this procedure in his pioneering studies on the art industry of late Rome (Riegl 1973); Adler used this method as the basis for many of his writings on music history. The term "artistic intent," coined by Riegl and adopted by Adler, is therefore by no means a conceptual mystification; rather it is a useful category derived from concrete analysis. Adler's and Riegl's thoughts leading to this term converge with the ideas of social research derived from statistics.

Technology and Artistic Intent in Max Weber

Adler's insistence on the importance of "the large quantity of works" by "middling and lesser masters" derives from the observation that it is precisely in this large group that certain specific characteristics can be objectively identified. His reference to the elements of a new artistic intent in this group (in this case, sonata form) has a parallel in the works of Max Weber: "Technological 'progress' has quite frequently manifested itself at first in works that are extremely mediocre from an aesthetic point of view" (Weber GAWL, 523). Once again, reflections on aesthetics and sociology converge. One must not, however, overlook the fact that Max Weber undertook an analysis of the relationship between "technological development" and artistic intent that was more profound than Adler's and different from Riegl's. Closer examination of the difference between Weber and Riegl is revealing.

Riegl developed his theory of artistic intent in opposition to the view of Gottfried Semper (1803–1879) that the work of art is a product of intended use, raw materials, and technology. Riegl set his "spiritual" interpretation against Semper's "material" one: the crucial aspect is artistic intent, while intended use, raw materials, and technology are merely "friction coefficients" within the overall product (Riegl 1929, 9).

Whereas Riegl viewed technology as having a purely negative, obstructive function, Weber held that it also influenced artistic intent (Weber GAWL, 519ff.). He was not, however, satisfied with this general statement but attempted to support his contention with evidence from the history of painting, architecture, and music. His most instructive examples come from the history of music and illustrate his understanding of how the progress of technology influenced the development of music.

Weber's conception of the sociology of art, then, lends far greater weight to technical means than does Riegl's. In Weber's view, certain changes in artistic intent are made possible through the availability of particular technical means. Technology thereby has occasional repercussions on artistic intent. Contemporary sociology of art has accepted this view, for example, in deriving new points of aesthetic departure from the new technical possibilities of reproducing art in the twentieth century (Benjamin 1963). Recent development has shown the relationship between technology and artistic intent so clearly as to require no further proof. A striking example is found in the new creative modes stimulated by film. Similarly, the emergence of much experimental music would be unthinkable without the availability of electronically synthesized sound. A large number of twentieth-century concepts in aural aesthetics owe their existence to electronically produced sounds, electronic amplification, the mixing console, and the reverb unit.

Max Weber, however, recognized the specific effects of technology on aesthetics long before the period in which they became so clearly visible and audible. The core of his argumentation is the claim that science must, above all, investigate the seemingly self-evident. In every period of art, including our own, creative principles and artistic intent lose their normative character as an object of scientific study: "When the normatively valid becomes an object of *empirical* study it loses its normative character as object; it is treated as "existing" and not as "valid" (Weber GAWL, 531). It is characteristic of Weber's thought and his profound knowledge of music that he uses a musical example to illustrate this thesis: "Every description of the Pythagorean theory of music must accept the—to the best of our knowledge—'incorrect' calculation that twelve fifths equals seven octaves" (Weber GAWL, 531). This statement also implies that the technical preparation of the tonal material, that is, the selection of the pitches of the continuum, can be done in various ways and that the sociology of music must avoid judging other tonal systems from the point of view of that with which we are familiar. Each of these systems is to be regarded as "existing" and can claim "validity" only within a certain historical context. Yet the trend of artistic intent also depends on such validity. In this sense, Weber's interpretation of the relationship between technology and art differs from the conception developed by Riegl.

Chapter 18 *Christianity and Desensualization*

Sing not today psalms with the angels,
that you might tomorrow dance again with the demons.
—Ephrem the Syrian, fourth century

In his attempt to elucidate the artistic intent upon which the "Late Roman art industry" (ca. 300–800 A.D.) was based, Alois Riegl concludes by referring to the literary sources used to support the results of his analysis (Riegl 1973, 393 ff.): the writings of Saint Augustine (354–430).

Augustine's conversion to Christianity radically altered his view on the meaning of beauty. In an early work, since lost, he saw beauty not in God but rather in the tangible phenomena of the visual arts, dance, music, and poetry. His new interpretation is characterized by the subordination of the idea of beauty to the idea of God. The writings of Saint Augustine were to have such far-reaching consequences that they determined the role of music in the liturgy during a large part of the Christian Middle Ages. What is more, they played a dominant role in the desensualization without which the particular development of Occidental music may not have been possible.

A work from the end of the fourth century entitled *Quaestiones et responsiones ad Orthodoxos* states: "It is not singing as such which belongs to the level of a child, but rather singing accompanied by soulless instruments and dancing and stamping" (quoted in Blaukopf 1972, 18). Other sources from the period also demand such disciplined behavior, and Augustine's thought is wholly in line with this attitude. His personal achievement, however, consists in having clearly brought out the conflict between religious fervor and the sensual joy of music—a conflict that he himself had experienced with great intensity during his transition from paganism to Christianity. There is a passage in Augustine's *Confessions* which vividly portrays his vacillation in his assessment of the role of music in the church. It is as though Augustine's autobiography anticipated for the next millennium all the arguments in favor of the musical organization of the service and against the predominance of sensual-musical joy in the liturgy:

> But I am often deceived by this pleasure of my flesh, to which the mind should not be given over to be enervated. The bodily sense only deserves to be admitted because of the reason; but often, instead of being content to follow behind reason, it tries to go ahead of reason and take the lead. So in these matters I sin without realizing it, only realizing afterward that I have sinned.
>
> But at other times, when I am overanxious to avoid being deceived in this way, I fall into the error of being too severe—so much so that I would like banished both from my own ears and those of the Church as well the whole melody of sweet music that is used with David's Psalter—and the safer course seems to me that of Athanasius, bishop of Alexandria, who, as I have often been told, made the reader of the psalm employ so very small a modulation of the voice that the effect was more like speaking than singing. But then I remember the tears I shed at the singing in church at the time when I was beginning to recover my faith; I remember that now I am moved not by the singing but by the things that are sung, when they are sung with a clear voice and correct modulation, and once again I recognize the great utility of this institution. So I fluctuate between the danger of pleasure and my experience of the good that can be done. I am inclined on the whole (though I do not regard this opinion as irrevocable) to be in favor of the practice of singing in church, so that by means of the delight in hearing the weaker minds may be roused to a feeling of devotion. (Augustine 1963, 242–243)

What is the cause of this change of heart documented by Augustine, and how did this reorientation of "artistic intent" in religious services come about? We can gain understanding by analyzing the process through which ancient society, with its "barracked," soulless slaves, was replaced by a feudal order that gradually restored to the productive population what slaves had never possessed: family, property, and souls. Max Weber was the first to describe this transformation process and its causes in his study entitled *Die sozialen Gründe des Untergangs der antiken Kultur* [The Social Causes of the Fall of Ancient Culture], first published in 1896. His picture of the process, a subject much discussed by historians, has met with criticism and rejection (cf. Alfons Deopsch in Hübinger 1968). The central idea of Weber's argumentation, however—the transition of an economic structure primarily based on slaves and money to one largely founded on barter and feudalism—

still seems to be valid, as demonstrated by Santo Mazzarino (1973, 153–154).

Social Preconditions for Change During Late Antiquity

In connection with this social transformation, the changed position of lower-class working people is significant. Weber characterizes this change as follows:

> By reinstating (his) slaves in the single family as hereditary subjects, the lord secured the offspring and thereby a constant source of labor, which he could no longer obtain by resorting to the shrinking slave market that disappeared completely during the Carolingian period. He shifted the risk which he, the lord, bore in maintaining slaves on the plantation to the slaves themselves. This gradual, yet progressive development had far-reaching consequences. A powerful social process of change came about in the lowest strata of society: family and property were returned to them. And I would simply like to mention in passing that this took place parallel to the triumphal progress of Christianity; it is hard to imagine that this religion would have found support among the slaves, yet the unfree African farmers during the age of Augustine were already supporters of a sect. (Weber 1956b, 14)

The social structure of the North African society in which Augustine, Bishop of Hippo (located in present-day Algeria), preached his views was not unlike that which later spread throughout Europe. This surely also explains the subsequent effect of his doctrines on the whole of Medieval Europe. The positive attitude toward labor, which resulted from the economic necessities described by Max Weber, is derived from Augustine's doctrines—the contempt for knowledge for its own sake and the spiritualization of the hierarchical norms that governed not only religious life but also the attitude toward music. In the sixth book of his treatise *De Musica*, the only music that Augustine recognizes as worthwhile is "that which contributes to stimulate and deepen Christian faith, thereby conforming to the tasks and goals of the Christian Church" (Hüschen in MGG I, 852). This restriction applied to productive work as well as to the liturgy. Augustine writes in *The Manual Labor of Monks*:

> Religious songs can easily be sung during manual labor. . . . Do we not know that every worker's heart and mouth are filled with light and even dissolute theater songs without causing him to interrupt his work? What then is there to prevent the servant of God from working with his hands and yet meditating "on the law of the Lord" and singing hymns of praise to the "name of the Lord on High?" Of course, he needs spare time in which to learn what he later repeats from memory. (Augustine, quoted in Frank 1975, I, 77)

This document is especially significant because it not only confirms the continued existence (as would have to be assumed) of "light" and "dissolute" music, but also the disapproval of everyday familiarity with music. This defensive attitude characterizes the efforts of Medieval monasticism, which began around 520 with the founding of the Benedictine Order. Music serves the word of God, the community consists of men who pray with a single voice (*una voce dicentes*), their speechsong guided not by the voice but by the heart (*non voce sed corde*). The above is directed at a desensualization of music, at separating song from body movement, also from instruments to some extent, and certainly from ecstatic dance.

Disembodied Music

We are confronted, then, not only with a desensualization of music but also with a disembodiment unparalleled in history. Most discussions of Medieval Christian aesthetics stress that music was subordinate to the word.Yet this is only one side of the innovation brought about by the trend to densensualization and disembodiment. The separation of music from gesture and dance also provided the basis for reflection on specifically musical aspects. It was precisely Christianity's ideological "hostility to the body" that provided the basis for the subsequent autonomy of music. This thought dovetails with Max Weber's sociological idea that gives monasticism credit for rationalizing polyphony "without realizing the magnitude of its contribution." Although Weber's works contain no reference to the significance of what I have called disembodiment, there is evidence that he was no stranger to this idea. A student of Weber's, who also contributed to the sociology of music, notes in his *Recollections of Max Weber*:

> He [Max Weber] explained to me and a few friends his theory of the factors that had lead to the creation of purely instrumental music, in particular in the form of the suite, sonata, and symphony, a theory not contained in the posthumous manuscript entitled "Sociology of Music." In brief, the theory is that Christianity is the only scripture religion without a ritual dance. That is, it shuns the body in horror. This makes possible bodiless music that is not primarily rhythmically oriented and can therefore turn to melody to a degree unknown elsewhere. (Honigsheim 1963, 248)

As Honigsheim himself writes, one must not regard this abbreviated outline of Weber's reasoning as a complete theory. It does, however, serve to show that Weber regarded "bodiless music" as a distinctive social phenomenon to which he ascribed consequences in the development of European music. Honigsheim continues to term

Weber's view as untenable "at least in this form," pointing to the ritual dance in Seville and in the early Coptic church. Moreover, the hostility to the body in the Zarathustran religion of ancient Persia did not produce results analogous to those in European music. One could also add that the cultural history of ballet includes frequent references to dance in the Christian liturgy of Europe (Gregor 1944, 129ff.). Of course, there are countless examples to the contrary, which will not be mentioned here; an indication of the wealth of literature (e.g. Hammerstein 1962 and 1974) will have to suffice. Sources denouncing dance and certain instruments as "diabolical" and anti-Christian reveal that Christianity as a religion tended to be hostile to dance; that is, we are dealing with an ideal-type tendency that prevailed against practice, albeit not always or completely.

The Separation of Words and Music

This transformation, whose most salient feature is the separation of music from body motion, also produced a new relationship between words and sound:

> The powerful rhythm of choral psalmody reveals a different dimension, derived from that of "soulful" singing imbued with the spirit. The music that now rushes by with its own energy, arises from new spiritual sources. The unity with language is shattered. (Besseler 1979, 31)

This break between language and music cannot be emphasized enough if we wish to understand the structure of musical behavior brought about by the Christianity of late Antiquity and the early Middle Ages. We are dealing with the separation of the "musical" from a complex originally consisting of a close interweaving of language, music, and motion. We are, of course, compelled to speculate on the nature of this complex, which goes back to the early history of mankind. But all known phenomena lead us to assume "that an undifferentiated method of communication existed in remote times, one that was neither speech nor music but which possessed the three features they hold in common: pitch, stress, and duration" (Nettl 1972, 136). The fact that in African cultures "music is so much a part of tradition that certain messages can only be passed on in sung form" (Ki-Zerbo 1980, 31) may be offered in evidence.

The Christian liturgy began the process of differentiating between music and language. If we are to believe Honigsheim, Max Weber regarded the separation of musical and bodily expression as highly significant for the development of "pure music" in European history. He points to the *separation of music and movement that was tied with the differ-*

entiation between music and speech. This aspect of the structural change in musical behavior is perhaps more significant than the development of spiritualized music. Musicology regards this structural change as the crucial prerequisite for the development of Occidental music:

> Confining as the limits of tonal range and musical expressive possibilities were initially [i.e. during late Antiquity], the crucial step was taken and the new ground discovered upon which the history of European music was to take place. Its major epochs also always mark a fundamental reorganization of the relationship to the spoken word, until languageless instrumental music prevailed during the Baroque age and composition was governed by musical-spiritual powers alone, which appeared for the first time in the highly melismatic song of late Antiquity. (Besseler 1979, 31)

This statement confirms, in part, Max Weber's sociological thesis, although it suggests a not insignificant correction: not only hostility to the body but the entire process of differentiation—the separation of linguistic, musical, and bodily expression—is characteristic for the new behavioral structure. Studying the relationship between music and language leads to a similar conclusion concerning the changes brought about by the Christian liturgy:

> We are dealing, not with a structure containing music and language, but with a Western language provided with music (for this specific purpose). . . . The word must be audible, because for the community the word exists only in its sung form, not as scripture. Yet as sacred word it cannot sound as natural, subjectively colored speech. It requires an interpretation preserved in music. This is the beginning of Western music: the liturgical text is the gate through which music enters into Christian-Western intellectual history. (Georgiades 1954, 7–8)

It is difficult for us today to imagine the *breaking apart* of language and music, because we find the separation of these two areas to be the norm. We find it even more difficult to imagine the original *unity* of these areas as expounded in musicological and ethnomusicological studies. Recent advances in understanding the physiology of the brain are useful in explaining these difficulties.

Language and Music in Brain Physiology

By observing persons with brain damage, brain research has ascertained that analytical, logical, and speech functions reside in the left hemisphere, while the processing of musical information takes place primarily in the right (Kinsbourne 1975, Damásio 1977, Franklin 1978). We therefore speak of the dominance of the left hemisphere, the half of the brain associated with speech. In order to understand the structures of speech and musical behavior, it is important to know that this division of functions does not appear to be inborn. Left-brain dominance has come about gradually in the course of history (Kinsbourne 1975, 111). Moreover, left-brain dominance does not emerge in individuals until approximately ten years of age (Regelski 1977, 38). This would seem to confirm the hypothesis of a fundamental layer, as much ontogenetic as phylogenetic, in which speech and music still constitute a unity and in which the logical processing of acoustic information is part of a largely gestalt processing. Hence, the view supported by Besseler and Georgiades that the unity of word and tone in music died out in late Antiquity does not contradict the findings of cerebral physiology.

Examining physiological data is not enough, however, to obtain a comprehensive understanding of the change in the structure of musical behavior under discussion, for there can be no doubt that the development of musical behavior is also closely linked to the development of linguistic behavior. To the best of my knowledge, musicology and linguistics do not yet provide sufficient information on this subject. But it is encouraging to see that linguistics, like musicology, is devoting increasing attention to human social behavior and has come to the conclusion "that present-day demands on linguistics can only be fulfilled if it is thoroughly reoriented from a science dealing with the structure of language toward a science concerned with the behavior of speaking human beings" (Heeschen 1972, 8). Only by combining this type of linguistics with musicology can we obtain knowledge capable of supporting, modifying, or invalidating the hypothesis of the structural change of musical behavior during late European antiquity.

Research in brain physiology has clearly demonstrated the importance of linguistic behavior in the processing of information in the brain. The division of cerebral functions identified through research in Europe and America does not constitute a biological constant. Recent tests show that

> the left cerebral hemisphere of the Japanese receives a wide range of sounds—not just linguistic sounds (consonants and vowels) but also such non-linguistic sounds as the utterance of human emotions, animal cries, Japanese musical instruments, the sound of a running brook, wind, waves, and certain famous temple bells. The range of sounds Westerners receive in the left hemisphere is conspicuously narrower, apparently limited to syllables made up of both consonant and vowel sounds. (Tsunoda 1978, 3)

The division of brain function characteristic of Japanese can also be found in Americans and Koreans brought up in Japan, whereas Japanese brought up in the United States and Brazil have the same division as the people of those countries. Language, then, influences the distribution of tasks in the human brain. It is remarkable that the Japanese process the sound of Japanese musical instruments and the sound of certain temple bells in the left hemisphere of the brain, while the sound of Western musical instruments is processed primarily in the right. This is still more evidence that music is not all the same and that different structures of musical behavior and perception can be identified as far back as where information is processed in the brain.

Analytical and Structural Interpretation of Music

Misgivings have rightly been expressed at the hasty application of the results of research in brain physiology to music and to music pedagogy in particular (Franklin 1978), especially because the overwhelming majority of physiological studies are not aimed at obtaining information about music. Furthermore, the schematic assignment of musical information to the right hemisphere of the brain does not adequately explain the processing of musical information. A number of experimental set-ups have demonstrated that experienced musicians have a tendency to listen "analytically," a function performed by the left hemisphere, but the contention that musicians and non-musicians process musical stimuli differently (Franklin 1978, 42) is not unanimously supported by those in the field. Thomas G. Bever and Robert J. Chiarello (quoted in Franklin 1978) have conjectured that, owing to their training, musicians are inclined to process a melody as a series of notes in the left half of the brain, whereas non-musicians tend to admit the melody as a whole into the right half of the brain. Other researchers recognize that musical training influences the processing of musical information by the left hemisphere of the brain (Damásio 1977, 151–152).

To date, the findings of brain physiology that are relevant to the study of the structures of musical behavior can be summarized as follows:

1. The dominance of the left cerebral hemisphere is the result of human social development and not a "natural" development
2. Linguistic behavior plays a part in this development
3. It appears to be proved that the oldest elements of language were linked to the right (i.e. the "musical") cerebral hemisphere
4. Ontogenesis repeats the phylogenetic development that results in the dominance of the left half of the brain

5. In persons "experienced" in the modern sense of the term, the processing of musical information is presumably not limited to the right ("musical") half of the brain, but also takes place analytically in the left hemisphere

This breakdown easily conforms to a pattern of the development of musical behavior in Europe along ideal-type lines. The Christian liturgy of late Antiquity paved the way for the differentiation between music and language. The ground was thus prepared for the protracted process at the end of which music finally became an autonomous art. The logical-analytical view of music, represented by such concepts as variation, development, counterpoint, and so on, came into being late in the historical development of the art. "Musical logic" in Hugo Riemann's sense of the term, or "synthetic listening" in Besseler's, are achievements of eighteenth-century European musical culture. Yet this type of analytic-synthetic listening has not universally prevailed. Other types of listening, largely non-analytic and non-synthetic, continue to have their place in society, and are still, as is common knowledge, predominant in popular music.

Even in "serious" music, which seems to encourage analytic-synthetic reception, we must not suggest that we are dealing with a primarily logical way of listening linked to the processing of musical information by the left hemisphere of the brain. The attempt to define music as the art of "thinking in sounds" (Combarieu 1907) and the call for "fully adequate hearing" (Adorno 1976, 5) merely indicate a limit toward which a part of musical behavior strives or—in the opinion of some—should strive. In any case, the right hemisphere of the brain retains the visual and emotional decoding function peculiar to it. Regelski (1977) has drawn attention to the consequences of this fact for musical pedagogy and has indicated the necessity in music education of not allowing the cognitive aspects to dominate the visual-emotional.

The various possibilities of processing musical information in the human brain are also demonstrated by the biological foundations of the conventional distinction between popular and "serious" music. Such a distinction is possible only when musical behavior is directed, to a socially significant degree, at creating independent musical complexes that require analytic-synthetic listening. Therefore, according to the historical development of musical behavior, this distinction could only have been drawn relatively recently: not until musical behavior left direct contact with life, at least in part, and reached the level of performance music did it begin to delimit itself from other, colloquial forms of behavior.

Revolt against Spiritualization

Another precondition for the rise of autonomous performance music in European history is the previously mentioned disembodiment, or spiritualization, of musical behavior. The history of European music is filled with evidence of revolt against this disembodiment. The utterances of Church fathers and Papal decrees directed against such revolt must be seen in this light. Several forms of recent musical behavior imbued with bodily motion (rock, disco) are similar rebellions against disembodiment, with their precursors in the "dance frenzies" of the fourteenth century, the "waltz madness" of the nineteenth century, and the manifestations of "liberating participation" in post–World War I Europe inspired by Dixieland and jazz. All of these movements are opposed to the static seriousness demanded by high performance art, and they document an apparently elementary human need in conflict with the static calm required by complex performance music.

Effects on the Autonomic Nervous System

The findings of music therapy and neuropsychology also support the thesis that behavior corresponding to autonomous music is artificial. Music therapy contributes to understanding the difference between participatory and popular music on the one hand and serious performance music on the other. The rationale for using music as medical treatment is that musical information can be processed by patients in whom, for example, the speech center of the brain is damaged or destroyed. Even more important, music has a direct effect on the autonomic nervous system: it influences cardiac activity, respiratory rate, blood pressure, and endocrine secretions (Harrer 1975 and 1977). Autonomic effects are induced by mere changes in volume. At volumes in excess of 60 phons, changes take place *independent of the will of the listener* and without regard for his mental attitude to the musical stimulus. Psychiatrists have recorded states attained under the influence of music that border on ecstasy (Critchley 1977).

This interaction of a whole complex of autonomic changes explains the magic and ecstatic effect produced by music, and provides a biological basis both for the ritual magic of certain non-European cultures and for many of the excesses recently seen at rock or pop concerts. To be sure, the difference between natural ecstasy and modern frenzy is not only quantitative but qualitative. Whereas the earlier effect was brought about by the human voice and mechanical musical instruments, the modern fury depends on the use of amplifiers that accelerate the autonomic intoxicated state and multiply its effect.

Sociology must take into consideration the biological aspects of musical behavior. Thus all attempts at interpreting the "magical" effects of music in various cultures are doomed to failure if they consider only the undeniably important ideological aspects and ignore the influence of music on the autonomic nervous system, which lies beyond human control. The effect of acoustic stimuli on the autonomic nervous system is the virtual key to understanding the suggestive effects of music. The verifiable change of pulse rate in response to a crescendo/decrescendo drum roll, the measurable adjustment of breathing rate to a tempo change in the music, and the listener's involuntary motor activity as a result of music—all point to the biological bases of musical effects.

Acoustic Perception and Motor Activity

The connection between acoustic perception and expression on the one hand and motor activity on the other also clarifies the special cultural achievement of Christianity in disembodying music during late Antiquity and the early Middle Ages. This achievement can be defined as the beginnings of a *mutation* of musical behavior, for it strove to implement an unprecedented separation of motor activity from music in spite of the fact that the unity of the two elements must, by and large, be regarded as "natural." A number of figures of speech ("to shout someone down," "music that sets your feet tapping") still reflect this unity. The posture assumed during the performance of a musical work of art by a listener trained in the Occidental tradition makes us forget this original unity of music, respiration, heartbeat, and motion. But the attitude of the relaxed listener, whose body is seemingly unaffected by music, is anything but "natural"; rather it is learned behavior, a recent product of European musical culture that is largely attributable to the musical-liturgical practices of Christian monasticism.

The exclusion of music from the original unity of word, tone, and motion resulted from a historical process of differentiation (in the sense of Spencer, although he would have been unable to characterize the specific process). This separation is, moreover, a special case in the history of music, a particular mutation of musical behavior that is quite artificial. Despite the fact that this special development has produced an abundance of musical works of art, we must not use its underlying behavior as the point of departure for judging other musical cultures whose character and development we wish to understand. In many non-European cultures, pure music has not been separated from the more complex behavioral fabric. The same is true, to a large extent, in Occidental popular and participatory music. These musics are therefore closer to what Erich M. von Hornbostel (1925) defined as the "unity of the senses." (The expression may be obscure, but it is based on a rich experience in ethnomusicology).

Neuropsychology confirms that this unity is a biological fact, for "muscular activity can be caused through stimulating 'purely' sensory cortical fields" (Guttmann 1974, 155). Since a strict separation between the motor and the sensory cannot be determined in the cortical area of the brain, we speak of "motosensorial" or "sensomotor" zones. It is therefore apparent that the interrelation, not the division, of bodily movement and music is inherent in human nature. This background clearly shows the revolutionary importance of the change in musical behavior begun during late Antiquity—the disembodiment and, at the same time, the separation of music from the word, both conditioned by a new social function of music, a new "musical intent."

Chapter 19 *Mutations of Musical Behavior*

The change of musical intent during late Christian Antiquity that I have identified leads me to ask which factors could be involved in such a change and brings up the question of the relationship between musicological and sociological periodization. I propose to investigate these questions, not by applying existing paradigms of social development to musical evolution, but by *tracking down the possible social factors in musical practice itself.* I proceed on the thought that

> the periodization of the history of art cannot simply follow the periodizations of the history of the development of society; the task of cultural studies must be to bring out the great revolutions in the evolution of this subject. (Bürger 1974, 40–41)

This caveat not only delimits our method from arbitrary paradigms, such as those proposed by Comte, but it also opposes every attempt to force the transformational processes of musical communication into philosophical systems that serve economics or political science but lack the conceptual equipment of musical studies. I propose, not that sociology usurp music, but rather that the knowledge of structural changes in musical practice, of changes in musical intent, and of changes in the social function of musical activity (and thereby the "great revolutions") be revealed through the analysis of musical practice itself.

The Sociological Aesthetics of Charles Lalo

The Frenchman Charles Lalo (1877–1953) contributed to such a method. His contribution is contained in *Esquisse d'une esthétique musicale scientifique*, which was first published in 1908 and later appeared in an expanded version under a different title (Lalo 1939).

Characteristically, Lalo engages in a creative dialogue with the sociological writings of his predecessors Guyau, Taine, Spencer, Tarde, and Durkheim. To the best of my knowledge, this rich source of music-sociological argumentation has yet to be utilized in the literature. Even Ivo Supičić, whose informative survey of the perspectives of socio-musicology (Supičić 1971) is heavily indebted to French writings in the area, does not give Lalo the credit he deserves.

One of Lalo's basic ideas (in which he largely agrees with Weber's thoughts on the subject) is that the means of realizing music—technology as Lalo calls it—is a "social fact" in Durkheim's sense of the term (Lalo 1939, 28). Lalo accuses Taine's theory, which recognizes only three determining factors in artistic activity (heredity, environment, and historic moment), of neglecting the "internal and specific" development of artistic means, namely, technology. This consideration leads Lalo to integrate musicological and music-sociological thought. In a line of reasoning analogous to Max Weber's, he proceeds from the basic mathematical-physical fact that there is no such thing as a "natural" tonal system but that there are a number of possible forms requiring sociological explanation. Lalo's very thorough exposition of Helmholtz's classical work and Carl Stumpf's studies concerning music psychology demonstrate his desire to free the sociology of music from philosophical speculation and to direct attention to the changes in the technical substrata brought by musical activity. Lalo has therefore appropriately been called the founder of "sociological aesthetics" (Bastide 1977, 42). Interpreting the concrete technology of musical communication as an obligatory social fact (that is, a social norm) he is also able to gain insight into the individual specific structure of musical behavior. Thus, he considers harmony to be a historic-social rather than a preestablished concept: "There are ways of understanding harmony other than our own" (Lalo 1939, 224).

The richness of Lalo's ideas, which I can only hint at here, lies in the details of his comprehensive study. Nonetheless, he cannot avoid outlining a general pattern of development for Western music. To each system of technical musical means (ancient Greek melody, Christian melody, Medieval polyphony, and modern harmony) he assigns stages of youth, maturity, and decline, which he represents graphically (Lalo 1939, 257). For Lalo, of course, this is merely a means of orientation, a concession to those inclined to confuse the system with science. Lalo's achievement consists of having pointed out a number of great changes in musical behavior throughout the history of European music. I consider his remarks to be merely suggestions for further thinking, for like Lalo, I regard the choice of technical means of musical practice as the manifestation of social behavior. Needless to say, this behavior is subject to constant change, but we must distinguish between these gradual changes and the more radical alteration for which I will borrow the biological term *mutation*. This is also an ideal-type concept intended to facilitate understanding of historical processes of change. We can speak of mutation in those cases in which several aspects of musical behavior change to such a degree that we can identify a significant change in the overall behavioral structure. In the next section I will discuss a few of the significant mutations of behavior in Occidental music.

The Christian Mutation of Late Antiquity

As discussed in chapter 17, the change in musical behavior brought about by the Christianity of late Antiquity is characterized by the separation of words and music and by the spiritualization, or disembodiment, of music. That the notational system developed by the ancient Greeks was abandoned can be attributed less to the rejection of heathen practices than to the different purpose, the different "musical intent," of the Christian liturgy, which was aimed at the representation of the word, sung as if "by one voice." Yet it would probably be premature to take this to be "monophony" in our sense of the term. One must clearly distinguish between the musical *intent*, directed at unanimous manifestation, and the *result*. Without any written transmission, this result cannot be uniform; one is rather inclined to call it heterophony (Adler 1908). At this stage, heterophony is necessarily the result of intended unanimity: "One would say that heterophony is the inevitable result of the singing together of a number of people wishing to carry the same melody" (Stumpf 1911, 99). An interpretation of heterophony as "every type of ensemble based on tradition and improvisation" (Sachs in MGG 6, 330) concurs with our idea about the kind of musical activity in this era. What was actually played and sung cannot be interpreted as "monophonic" for the simple reason that the necessary directions, which could only exist in written form, did not exist. Memory was the only means for retaining the basic outline of note sequences because, as Isidor of Sevilla states in his *Sententiae de musica* (620), tones "cannot be written."

The pedagogical achievement of monasticism consisted in disciplining heterophony oriented toward unanimity, thereby prescribing the *role* each of the participants had to play. The sociological concept of role is suited to describe coherent sequences of musical behavior coordinated with the behavioral sequences of others. Historical evidence suggests that the Roman *schola cantorum* (singing school) of the eighth century was an institution charged with training for such musical-liturgical roles. We even know names of the role-players: singers of the *schola cantorum* had the official titles of *Paraphonista* and *Archiparaphonista*, which have been interpreted (though not unanimously) as meaning "singer of the fourth" and "singer of the fifth." In light of the importance of this Roman school for the vocal practices of the entire Europe missionary area (cf. Smits van Waesberghe 1955), we must assume that this notion of musical role spread to other regions. Musical behavior of this type was also practiced in the monasteries. That this was aimed at regulating the original heterophony, which it rationalized through parallel fourths and fifths, can be deduced from an early document of written music. *Musica enchiriadis*, the work of an anonymous ninth-century author, describes the behavior of two voices beginning in unison, moving to parallel fourths, and ending in unison. The modern transcription clearly shows this:

There can be no clearer proof of the intended unity together with a regulated heterophony. It has been noted, and rightly so, that this document is not an invention on the part of the writer but the fixation of a practice long in use (Sachs 1918, 457).

I therefore conclude that the so-called Medieval organum, consisting of parallel fourths and fifths, evolved not as the fruit of ecclesiastical speculation but rather as a disciplined adjustment of popular heterophony. This view contradicts a number of opinions in musicology (summarized in Reese 1941, 249ff.). It was long a dominant idea in musicology that folk song "naturally" tends to parallel thirds and sixths, a view that was refuted by ethnomusicological research (cf. Wiora 1957, 71 ff.). The original vitality of folk music sung in perfect fourths and fifths, which lived on in Europe in the "Sortisatio" into the seventeenth century (Gerson-Kiwi 1938 and Ferand 1951), has been emphasized by a number of musicologists. Solange Corbin (1960, 250), for example, takes exception to the continuing view that Medieval organal music must have been performed in a very moderate tempo; it is possible to imagine parallel fifths performed in a light, quick rhythm just as "Portuguese farmers do every day."

Here, too, recent sociological knowledge derived from human activity supports that of musicology. It sheds light on the mutation of musical behavior, brought about by Christianity between the sixth and ninth centuries, which was directed toward the separation of words and music, the disembodiment of musical expression, the absence of written music, and the rationalization of popular heterophony that finally resulted in the regulated organum of fourths and fifths.

Mutation By Descriptive Notation

The musical notation developed during the Middle Ages is less concerned with recording individual notes than with indicating the direction of melodic motion. Its purpose was to preserve the musical part of the sanctified liturgy. In order to distinguish this type of notation from that customary today, I will speak of "descriptive" and "prescriptive" notation, terms proposed by Charles Seeger (1958). Our prescriptive notation determines how something is to sound, while the older descriptive notation records how something sounded. Neumes "seem first to have come into use to describe an existing practice of recitation" (Seeger 1958, 186).

This distinction is important because it elucidates for us the practical role of the old notation and also explains the corresponding social function of the music scribe. Hucbald (840–930), the author of *De institutione harmonica*, summarizes the function of notation as *rememorationis subsidium*, that is, an aid to recalling (music). Thus, musical notation, which accompanies the words of the text, does not as yet enable the writer to add or invent something of his own. He is enjoined to place on parchment that which is dictated by the liturgical rule. He is a chronicler, not a composer. A study concerning the relationship between people and writing in the Middle Ages expresses this vividly:

> We should not translate the expression "vitium scriptoris" found repeatedly in sources as "scribal error." This is because writing is an exercise in asceticism . . . ; on the other hand, just as the parchment must be cleansed of dirt and roughness, the heart too must be purified in order to prepare good ground for the divine scriptures. The bad scribe, however, also sins when he distorts the holy texts and detracts from the praise of God; yet the good scribe saw angels all around him, the authors of the works spoke to him, indeed Christ himself consoled him for his toils. Much the same applies to singing, which was far more difficult owing to an absence of notation as we know it. The task of the *armarius* [doorman, keeper], who was also choirmaster, con-

sisted of insisting on the uniformity of singing, if necessary with the severest disciplinary measures. (Fichtenau 1946, 155–156)

One aspect of the mutation we are discussing is that it created scribes of music notation and their specific knowledge of musical practice while, at the same time, limiting their role to that of a reporter. Another aspect consists in the fact that the performance of music no longer rested entirely on memory but also on notation, which was used as an additional aid to discipline. A firmer basis was thus created for the uniformity of musical activity. It remained a peculiar feature that the behavior of individuals was not oriented toward the *totality of the musical flow* but chiefly toward *one voice*, be it the tenor or the voice next to the tenor. This particular kind of musical activity, perhaps attributable to its origins in heterophony, is confirmed in retrospect by an author writing around 1275:

> The knowledge of the ancients was chiefly oral tradition without written fixation. They paid attention to the relationship between the upper part and the lower part and taught by saying: listen carefully and remember it by singing. But they had little notational fixation and merely said: this note of the upper part coincides with this note of the lower part; and that satisfied their needs. (Latin original in Reckow 1967, translation quoted from Apel 1949, 244)

This type of interaction by singers meant that any two parts at a time conformed to the rules of concord (that is, the rules of consonance), while harmonies appeared in the overall ensemble that did not conform to these rules as seen from our perspective:

The control of the musical flow was, therefore, limited to the progression of each individual voice and its relationship to *one* of the other parts. Furthermore, a notational sign symbolized an event; it did not yet represent an abstraction of the event itself. The staff line itself, which did not come into being until about the year 1000, represented something material—the string of the monochord, which was the instrument from which singers learned their awareness of tones.

Although those entrusted with putting down notes are not as yet composers in the modern sense, they do play a certain individual role in the process of musical communication. The existence of the scribe and the presence of signs for what is performed gradually alter the old distinction between *musicus* and *cantor*: the writer becomes a bridge between pure theory and musical performance. The earliest indication of this change, which is part of the mutation we are dealing with, can be found in a work by Hermannus Contractus (1013–1054). He expects from a musicus not only a knowledge of theory ("regulariter iudicare") but also practical musical ability ("decenter modulari") and an understanding of what he calls "rationabiliter componere" (cf. Müller-Heuser 1963, 37). We must be careful not to translate "componere" as "compose." It refers, instead, to "putting together tones," which is expressed as writing because this is the practical activity it involves. The notation itself is a development of local or regional custom and is not yet codified to the extent that this writing can communicate what is to be played to those outside the immediate area. Initially, the characters could only be read where they were created (Besseler 1973, 17). Notation is not a blueprint for what is to be performed but rather an aid to singing and playing what has been handed down by tradition. The written form guarantees the continuation of this tradition and creates a model of it. A thirteenth-century chronicler wrote of Leonin (eleventh century), who collected two-part organa in a *Magnus liber organi*, that he had done so "pro servicio divino multiplicando." The purpose of recording the music was to preserve tradition. "Multiplicare" may refer to the intention of ensuring a multiple, uniform repetition of the liturgical-musical event. Nonetheless, the emergence of the music scribe created a new type of activity in musical communication. This is one of the most important elements in this mutation, which is both the prerequisite for the next mutation and, finally, for the development of the composer in the modern sense of the term.

The "Rise of the Composer"

The specialization that produced the early form of "composer" can also be traced to economic and social causes. Georg Knepler goes so far as to write that these alone, and not purely musical causes, were decisive. In a plausible attempt to explain this process, Knepler (1977, 242–243) directs his principal attention to the urbanization occurring between the eleventh and thirteenth centuries and analyzes its consequences for musical practice. In Knepler's opinion, the "intersocial assimilation" resulting from the new economic and social situation was crucial for this process of change. Several passages from the treatise *De musica*, written around 1300 by Johannes de Grocheo (active in Paris), support this hypothesis. He divides the music "which the people in Paris use" into three kinds, as listed in the following table together with the translations proposed by Johannes Wolf (1899, 84–85) and Ernst Rohloff (1943, 76–77):

Types of Parisian Music according to Johannes de Grocheo (1300)

original Latin term	J. Wolf tr.	E. Rohloff tr.
musica vulgaris	folk music	folklike music
musica mensurata	mensural music	measured music
musica ecclesiatica	sacred music	church music

More noteworthy than this classification is the fact that the author regards church music as a type that links the other two kinds, "producing something better" (Rohloff 1943, 77). What Johannes de Grocheo is referring to is the social relationship between the three spheres he has discerned, or what Knepler (1977, 226 ff.) terms "intersocial assimilation." In this virtually sociological treatise, Johannes de Grocheo also specifies the social function of several forms of *musica vulgaris*. On the whole, this simple or folklike music serves to mitigate the "innate misfortune of the human race" (Rohloff 1943, 79). The Parisian author notes of the individual types:

> The *Cantus gestualis* (Chanson de geste) must be performed for old people, the working burghers, and the lower classes while they rest from their accustomed work, so that once they have heard of the misery and misfortune of others they will be able to bear their own more easily, causing everyone to return to work with redoubled spirits. This song is thus suited to maintaining the whole state. (Rohloff 1943, 80)
> The *Cantus versualis* is meant to prevent youths from overindulging in idleness.
> The *Stantipes*, which is difficult to perform, occupies the minds of youths and girls, preventing them from thinking bad thoughts.

To the best of my knowledge this is the earliest source providing such a clear summary of the social function of entertainment music. Only a society in the process of urbanization is able to become aware of the importance of music in its functions of maintaining authority and, to put it in modern terms, using leisure time to restore the will and capacity to work.

The economic motives causing this mutation of musical practice are accompanied by a new attitude toward time, also the result of new economic conditions. As a result of urbanization, the first gear-driven clock appeared toward the end of the thirteenth century. The measurement of time begins—also for practical-economic reasons—to be established in people's minds. The music of the Church, up to then "timeless prayer" (Wendorff 1980, 130), was unable to resist this change. In the end, measuring time is also suggested, inter alia, by the connection to *musica vulgaris* described by Johannes de Grocheo. The hostility to the body of the predominantly "pneumatic," timeless singing is subjected to a first challenge. The bearers of this measured music (mensural music) are those who write notes. They show their skill in the polyphonic motets combining a number of different texts. "Sociologically speaking it was the *musicians and connoisseurs* in free association who bore the ars antiqua" (Besseler in MGG I, 687). The initial impulse toward the development of autonomous music as "art" is to be found during the period termed *ars antiqua* (ca. 1230–1320) and, even more, in the works of the *ars nova* (ca. 1320). The blow received by the anti-corporal view of music from the *ars nova* is recorded in a Papal bull promulgated at Avignon in 1322, in which the supporters of the "new school" are accused of inciting listeners to exaltation instead of meditation and to movement instead of calm (cf. Blaukopf 1972, 19).

Important though the range of this change was during the thirteenth and fourteenth centuries, its bounds were no less important. This first stage of "assembling" a musical continuum must not be considered a direct preliminary stage to composition in the modern sense. "Componere" is still more a joining together of single parts than the creation of musical totalities. Attention is still confined primarily to the horizontal motion of voices. The relation to the other parts is chiefly governed by rules that apply only at crucial junctures. The music is not written in *score* arrangement but in *part* arrangement. This requires explanation, because the idea of a score was by no means unknown. There must be a reason, then, why it was rejected. It is instructive to follow the history of the notation of European ensemble music as portrayed in Willi Apel's (1949, XXV) *Survey of Notational Systems*:

Notation for Ensemble Music

Score Arrangement	Part Arrangement

Primitive Notation
  syllables, letters,
  neumes, Dasian signs
  (ninth-twelfth century)
Square Notation
  ligatures, notes
  (ca. 1175–1250)	

	Black Mensural Notation
	  black mensural notes
	  (ca. 1260–1300)
	White Mensural Notation
	  white mensural notes
	  (ca. 1450–1600)

Partition Scores (1600–present)	

The table shows that from the ninth century to about 1250 full-score order was suitable for a musical intent directed toward uniformity. This leads to the seemingly paradoxical fact that the first appearance of the "composer" went hand in hand with the abandonment of full-score order. One would conclude—from our way of thinking—that the development should have been reversed, that someone involved in composition would be interested in setting down his creation so that he could see the whole at a glance. This paradox is, however, only in our minds. When composers first appeared in European history, they did not create works requiring scores but rather musical roles that had to be performed.

Only later did these roles fit together to become a work. The beginnings in northern France were still far from this stage. It has also been rightly said that the composer did not emerge from his anonymity until later, primarily as a result of developments in Florence: "The decisive turnabout from the principle of anonymity to identification is not to be found generally before fifteenth-century sources, especially . . . those written in Italy with mixed repertoire" (Finscher 1975, 34). Ludwig Finscher's study, the *Rise of the Composer*, is of special interest in this regard; it concludes with the preliminary conjecture that the gradual growth of interest in the individuality of the composer went along with the composer's increased interest in expressing individuality in the work.

We still have a long way to go before the professional composer emerges. The mutation I have attempted to describe here merely applies to the potential transformation of the music scribe from a reporter of past events into an author of future ones. The composition still does not fully have the character of a work, nor does that which has been created demand the overall view of a score. Yet the crucial transformation has taken place—the germ of the prescriptive function of notation.

> A notation of our kind is of more fundamental importance for the existence of such music as we possess than is orthography for our linguistic formations. . . . A somewhat complicated modern work of music . . . is neither producible nor transmittable nor reproducible without the use of notation. It cannot exist anywhere and in any form at all, not even as an intimate possession of its creator. (Weber 1958, 83–84)

From this point of view the emergence of musicians who can write notation also brings a radical change in musical culture.

> Only the elevation of many-voiced music under notational art created the composer proper and guaranteed the polyphonic creations of the Western world, in contrast to those of all other peoples, permanence, aftereffect, and continuing development. (Weber 1958, 88)

The availability of notation geared to rationalization and standard-ization contributed to the change in fortune of music in general. The "reciprocal effect of notation on music" (Dadelsen 1964, 20) strongly implies that notation is also a *fait social*, a normative system that, once it has been created, controls the structure of musical behavior. This has been expressed in a pointed yet fitting way: "Polyphony came into being with notation, it was born of writing, it is writing" (Escal 1979, 144).

Elements of Change Around 1600

The appearance, around 1600, of the full score for the notation of ensemble music suggests that from that time onward composers devoted increasing attention to the totality of the work. This striving for total control of the musical flow through writing is expressed in the *res facta*, which came into fashion about 1500. *Res facta* refers to the written record of the sum of all parts, and in practice also the result of their ensemble sound. Johannes Tinctoris (ca. 1435–1511) describes the spe-cific character of *res facta* in his *Liber de arte contrapunti* (1477). He distin-guishes between two types of counterparts to a given tenor: *scripto* (written) and *mente* (improvised). While in improvisation it is sufficient for the new part to relate correctly to the tenor, in *res facta* all voices must be related to each other. This statement illustrates the importance of writing to the new form of musical thought and activity. The com-poser is no longer merely a director who outlines the roles for the per-formers; he has instead become the creator of the overall shape of the music, the author of a work. Thus the conditions for the arrangement of parts in the score form, which came into being roughly a century later, already exist.

Tonality and Tonal System

The course of this development—which I will again follow in terms of ideal type—is, to be sure, influenced by other factors: the gradual tran-sition to autonomous performance music (which was not clearly estab-lished until the seventeenth century) and the perception of chordal harmony. I have already dealt with this extensively in chapter 16. An additional fundamental remark is required, however, concerning the problem of hearing chord-harmony and the rise of tonality in the sense we understand it.

In both the musicological and socio-musicological literature, the change to chord harmony (which can be seen most clearly in the reval-uation of the third as a consonance) is depicted as having been determined solely by a process of spiritual change. Such a point of view overlooks the fact that the size of certain intervals also changed during this epoch. For example, when a writer from the transitional period we are dealing with discusses what we call a major third, we must ask whether he is referring to the Medieval ditone (vibration ratio of 64:81) or the harmonic third (4:5).

Both of these measurements of the "third" were the object of dispute in the theory and practice of the sixteenth century. In order to explain this dispute I will illustrate both of these intervals through the measurement system introduced by Alexander J. Ellis. His system divides the octave into 1,200 (logarithmically) equal parts in such a way that the tempered half-tone to which we are accustomed receives 100 parts (cents), the whole-tone, 200 cents, and so on. The system developed on the monochord during the Middle Ages determined the "large third," the so-called ditone, through a measurement corresponding to 408 cents. The harmonic third is equal to 386 cents. In our present-day system this is replaced by the tempered major third, which is equal to 400 cents. We must therefore distinguish among three measurements of what we today call the major third:

- medieval: 408 cents
- tempered: 400 cents
- harmonic: 386 cents.

Our way of measuring a third came about as a compromise solution to the internal contradictions in the way intervals are measured, and it serves well to approximate the harmonic third because it is only 14 cents larger than the harmonic interval it is meant to reproduce. The Medieval "large third" deviates by 22 cents from the harmonic third, which is almost an eighth-tone in our tempered system.

It can easily be seen that this is a potentially crucial difference, one which is no easy matter to bring out in the real performance of Medieval music because it is difficult to produce these thirds on instruments (unless they are instruments without fixed pitch), and because it seems to be virtually impossible to bring singers, much less vocal ensembles accustomed to our music, to sing those intervals that persons trained on the Medieval monochord could presumably produce with ease. This is also why modern performances and recordings of Medieval music, in which the performers all too clearly vacillate between Medieval practice of intervals and the one to which we are accustomed, are highly problematic.

With the assistance of a computer, in which tones in Medieval tuning have been stored, we can demonstrate the aural difference between our interpretation of the third and that of the Middle Ages. A series of experiments of this type was begun at the Electro-Acoustic Institute of the Vienna Academy of Music and Performing Arts (Blaukopf 1980b). The initial results demonstrated that there is a distinct difference between our response to the sound of music from about the year 1100 performed in correct Medieval tuning and the sound of the same music performed in our tuning or one that conforms to it. This is further proof that sociological research cannot proceed from written sources but must take account of musical reality.

The change toward chordal harmony and harmonic tonality, therefore, also extends to the applied tuning. This does not mean a change in the "idea of the third" but rather a change in the interval of the third itself. (What I have said about the major third also applies, mutatis mutandis, to the minor third and the major and minor sixth as well). Carl Dahlhaus has pointed out this connection. In analyzing the development to which the tonal system was subject, between the fifteenth and seventeenth centuries, as a system of tonal relationships and tonal functions, he reached the conclusion that

> the changing position of the third from a dependent to an independent interval, the transition from the aural to the tonal quality of the leading tone, and the replacement of Pythagorean tuning (in force during the Middle Ages) with harmonic were reciprocally linked. (Dahlhaus 1968, 173–174)

The change under discussion, then, is to be seen as a syndrome of phenomena that includes not only *res facta*, full-score arrangement, chordal harmony, and music for performance but also changes in the material substrata of music, the tonal system, and its measurement of intervals.

Sociology of Tonal Systems

Reservations have been expressed against including the "sociology of tonal systems" in the sociology of music (Silbermann 1965, 257). These objections are understandable when one takes into consideration that music existed before any consciously conceived tonal systems were possible. However, at a certain stage of historical development—reached in Europe at latest with the establishment of Pythagorean tuning in the musical theory and practice of the Middle Ages—the tonal system itself became a *fait social*. A scholar well acquainted with the history of tonal systems puts it this way: "Any scale is a construct of the social mind, a phenomenon of social agreement" (Mursell 1946, 564). The twelve-note tempered tonal system with which we are familiar is also inherently social. Despite electronic composition and attempts at rebellion by the avant-garde, the system determines not only the Occidental musical practice but increasingly that of the Third World as well.

It compels us to follow a more or less set form of musical activity "that has the capability of exerting an external compulsion on the individual"—once again Durkheim's definition of the *fait social* (1967, 114). What, then, is there to prevent us from making the outward form of tonal systems an object of sociological study?

Such a sociology of tonal systems, as has already been attempted by this writer (Blaukopf 1972), can also take its point of departure from Max Weber who, to the best of my knowledge, was the first to point out that numerically "incorrect" tonal systems can also attain social validity, that "Acoustic fiction is musical reality" (Dahlhaus 1968, 171). Moreover, Weber demonstrated that the fundamental acoustic contradictions of pure tuning can be overcome by social compromises. The findings of ethnomusicology reveal the richness of each solution. A comprehensive theory of the evolution of tonal systems could, again, be developed by representing ideal-type possibilities of resolving acoustic contradictions, according to Weber's method. In my opinion, Joseph Yasser (1932) has succeeded in so doing (see also Blaukopf 1972).

Historical Stages of Recording Music

Of course, such a sociology of tonal systems cannot be seen in isolation from the broad spectrum of the sociology of music. It merely isolates that which is interwoven with the whole of social life. Thus the evolution of tonal systems is also closely linked to the development of notation. The development of notation can be outlined in stages, an approach that provides more useful knowledge than do speculative sociological systems because it throws light on activity and explains music's dependence on and independence from time and space. Curt Sachs (1948, 378) has proposed such a division:

1. *Unwritten music*—composer and performer are one person without whom the music cannot be disseminated; nor can it last except in the uncertain form of tradition.
2. *Written music*—composer and performer are separate, and modest possibilities for dissemination and duration exist.
3. *Printed music*—the possibilities for dissemination and duration are greatly increased.
4. *Recorded music*—the capability of unlimited reproduction, which is completely separate from the actual performance, provides the most possibilities for dissemination and duration in the original, authentic style of rendition.

The fourth stage was inaugurated with the invention of the phonograph by Thomas Alva Edison in 1877 and continued by the development of the phonograph record by Emil Berliner in 1896. The electrification of sound recording (beginning in 1925), and later of sound reproduction, has caused a mutation of musical practice that has been increasingly felt since the 1950s. The following chapter will discuss this change.

Chapter 20 *Mutations Through Technical Media*

In Thomas Mann's novel *Doktor Faustus* (1947) the narrator-chronicler talks of loudspeakers and amplifiers in connection with the performance of the "Apocalipsis" of the book's protagonist, composer Adrian Leverkühn. Thomas Mann attributes strange characteristics to these electroacoustic instruments, calling them an example of "easy technical facility in horror" (Engl. tr. 1948, 377).

The musical practice of the last forty years has made increasing use of this technical equipment. To an ever greater extent, electroacoustic equipment is used not only to *transmit* music, as on the radio, phonograph records, and cassettes, but to *produce* music as well. The flourishing of electronic music since the fifties would have been impossible without the refinements in technical convenience. Even more influential than the invasion of electronics into works claiming to be art, however, was the effect of new technology in the area of popular music. Pop and rock presuppose electroacoustic modification. They do not exist primarily in written form or live performance; rather they live for the most part in electroacoustic recording on tape and records.

Thomas Mann's expression "easy technical facility in horror" is an excellent characterization of the means used in participatory music. Of course, we must not elevate fear to pure terror. What is intended is more an exciting, a challenging, a stirring up of people whose autonomous nervous system is affected by this far more than their intellect. Technology provides the tools for this stirring, because there is no deviation from the sound of traditional instruments, no distortion of the human voice, and no volume, up to the threshold of physical pain and beyond, that cannot be easily produced.

Edison's invention of sound recording provided a first technical precondition for the transformation of musical communication. Further innovations were necessary to effect a mutation: electroacoustic recording via microphone, the use of electron tubes for amplification, magnetic tape recording (1946), the long-playing record (1951), and stereo (1958). During the fifties,

> technological progress in recording techniques, in the production of sound recordings, and in the development and manufacture of sound reproduction equipment were gradually achieved; taken together, these ushered in the mutation of musical communication. (Breh 1980, 7)

A crucial factor reinforcing the broad social effect of these technological advances was the introduction of FM radio, which made possible the undistorted reproduction of music in an adequate frequency range (from 40 to 15,000 hertz). The importance of the technology of mass-produced sound recordings was increased by the fact that a large proportion of radio programming consisted of playing them.

The technological transformation was not recognized immediately, and its consequences were therefore, in part, gauged incorrectly. An example of this miscalculation occurred at the conference held by the Gesellschaft für Musikwissenschaft (Society of Musicology) in May 1948 at Rothenburg ob der Tauber. One section of this conference was chaired by Erich Thienhaus, who had introduced magnetic tape into phonograph recording. The first tape recordings he had transferred to disks, organ works by Johann Sebastian Bach performed by Helmut Walcha, were presented at the conference. Of course, most participants were primarily interested in the magnetic tape recorder built by Eduard Schüller. The hope was expressed in a conference report that the new equipment would soon be made available "to research and teaching" (*Die Musikforschung* 1948, 68). The writer was obviously not aware of the importance the machine would have for musical practice, for he did not think this aspect worth mentioning.

Read today, this document from 1948 seems rather odd because we know that Helmut Walcha's organ recordings began Deutsche Grammophon Gesellschaft's highly esteemed Archiv-Produktion series and that this was the beginning of a technical-artistic solution to the problem of recording music—in West Germany a project associated with the name Erich Thienhaus who, starting in 1946, played a crucial role in training "recording engineers" at the North West German Academy of Music in Detmold. The new profession of recording engineer that has since developed is itself an aspect of the mutation that took place between 1950 and 1980. (The recording engineer and recording director play so large a role in the aesthetic result that their names are rightly listed on many LP covers).

Discomorphosis

The comprehensive character of this mutation is demonstrated by the statistics concerning production and sales of sound recordings. These data (cf. Blaukopf 1977 and 1980 D, Zeppenfeld 1978, Breh 1980, and the sources listed therein) indicate the growing economic importance of the recording industry. Together with radio, the recording industry has brought about an economic transformation in the music publishing business. The overwhelming majority of music publishers no longer derive most of their earnings from printed music but rather from the royalties earned from recording manufacturers and from radio (Dranov 1980, 97). This too can be regarded as an element of the change which French researchers have called "discomorphosis" (Hennion 1978, 25). I consider this term apt because it can encompass a number of the changes to which musical communication has been subjected owing to new technologies:

1. The adjustment of musical performance to the technical conditions of recording and playback (to a greater extent in popular music, to a lesser extent in serious music)
2. The qualitative change in musical communication by means of the specific mechanism of recording and playback
3. The change this produces in the reception of the musical message

Not only the tremendous importance but also the peculiarities of technically transmitted music permit us to speak of a "second path of musical communication" (Breh 1980, 11). The inherent possibilities for alteration—microphone placement, control-panel adjustments, editing, and so on—set this technological-artistic path apart from the previous natural ones. The final product of technological-artistic effort is not identical with that of a live performance. The "work" is ultimately present in a form "which, although it *simulates* a performance for consumers of records and tapes, actually has nothing to do with it" (Kaegi 1967, 22).

Transmission Music as a New Category

A study published more than half a century ago is the first in this form, to the best of my knowledge, that points out the difference between technologically transmitted and natural musical communication. The author states that

> the musical work of art which comes out of a loudspeaker is for many reasons no longer the same as that created by the artist, a clean distinction being required between music as art and transmitted music that seeks and finds its listeners under completely different conditions and objectives. (Winzheimer 1930, 3–4)

The term "transmission music" coined by Winzheimer is solely derived from the specific conditions of radio broadcast in his times. Winzheimer starts from the phenomenon of live broadcast. This term is of increased significance, given today's studio recordings for radio or phonograph records. The term "transmission music" has been suggested—independent of Winzheimer, it would seem—as a musical-sociological category (Niemann 1974, 49–50, and 1980). The terms *participatory* music and *performance* music are placed alongside *transmission* music, which is also to be understood as a new category of listening to music. Taken in this sense, transmission music refers to every musical communication employing an artificial-technological channel, be it a film sound track, television, radio, phonograph record, or cassette.

Technology and Musical Activity

The invasion of musical communication by technical media brought with it the fear that recorded music would pose a threat to traditional musical life and a lessening of musical activity in general. The many authors who supported this view have rightly been taken to task: "One could just as easily say that by bringing music to groups that had previously had nothing to do with it, the mass media have aroused a need for and encouraged the spontaneous cultivation of music" (Adorno 1967b).

Adorno's admonition came at the right time, because it stimulated music-sociological research to investigate the attitude of young people to the music offered by the technological media. The unexpected happened in the entertainment sector, where the paralyzing effect had been presumed: in virtually every industrialized country hundreds and thousands of young groups acquired electroacoustic instruments to make their own music. Radio and records unleashed a wave of activity; rock and pop groups proliferated (cf. Belz 1969, Bontinck 1974, and Blaukopf 1974).

These events tended to support Adorno's carefully worded hypothesis, although in a way different from what he had intended. The rock movement should have made us sit up and pay attention, because it demonstrated that the compulsions of technological musical civilization did not necessarily lead to passivity. It is understandable that science and pedagogy initially paid little attention to this phenomenon, because researchers and teachers disliked the music that sprang up. Those who thought they possessed good taste had to turn up their noses at it. Yet musical sociologists, who are condemned to lack of taste in the area of their research, could afford to note the positive aspect of this phenomenon, consisting in the fact that young people broke out of the constraints of the technological musical world to take active part.

The rejection of purely passive reception and the often desperate attempt to regain individual initiative in leisure time is a phenomenon that has been labelled as characteristic for modern industrial society (Scheuch 1972). This is proved in music not only by rock and pop groups but by the growth of overall musical activity. Precisely during this period of mutation controlled by the technological media, choirs have gained greatly in popularity as have music schools. A resumé of this development in West Germany comes to the conclusion that "Music is the only art form—and, together with sports, the most important social phenomenon—which, to a large degree, determines leisure behavior" (Suppan 1977b, 98).

Although it now seems a proven fact that the rise of media music has not led to a decrease in musical activity, we must avoid attributing the increased activity entirely to the existence of technically transmitted music. Empirical samples, so numerous that I can only refer to them in brief, merely confirm that the advance of technologically conveyed music runs parallel to intensified self-action, largely controlled by media programs (radio, records).

Material Aspects—Music as a Commodity

Today, these media offerings are regarded as a matter of course. We hardly give a thought to the material aspects of the music stored and transported on plastic discs or magnetic tape. The revolutionary character of this mutation is, however, discernible if we acknowledge the uniqueness of the transformation of musical activity into a *real object*. Before this mutation musical performance did not possess a material character. Unlike the activity of a painter or sculptor, consumption of a musician's activity was tied to the artist's presence; listeners and musicians had to come together. Paintings and sculpture could be transformed into goods in the economic sense. Musical performance remained a service and did not manifest itself as a material object. Only the composition, the plan for musical performance, could assume the character of a commodity in the form of printed music; even in industrial society the performance itself retained its economic character as a service until the beginning of the twentieth century. This fact was also discussed in nineteenth-century economic theory:

> Certain services or their utility value, the results of certain activities or work, are embodied in goods, while others do not leave a tangible result separable from the person who provides the service. For example, the service a singer performs for me satisfies my aesthetic need, but what I consume exists only in an action inseparable from the singer, and as soon as the singing, is over, so too is my consumption. (Marx 1965, I, 380)

The possibility of lending material duration to the singer's performance has also altered the economic and therefore legal nature of this service. The tangible, mass-produced object, the recording, enters the process of commercialization. This leads to the question of how to safeguard the legal claims of those involved in the creation of this product, the author and the performers. The solution for protecting the rights of the authors was based on the copyright, which has evolved since the nineteenth century. Under the pressure of the technological mutation, new solutions had to be found for performing musicians. These are codified in the legal provisions constituting so-called neighboring or residual rights (*Leistungsschutzrecht*). Moreover, the transformation of performed music into a material commodity had not only legal consequences; it led to the founding of institutions called performing rights societies that were entrusted with protecting rights and calculating claims.

Economic and Legal Consequences

The growing role of the music industry dedicated to the production of these goods also brought about economic upheavals that led to an integration of the music industry and music publishers. In addition, profit considerations demanded the consolidation of the music industries into huge conglomerates. A 1977 analysis of the prevailing trends predicted that in the near future approximately 200–300 music concerns would control roughly 80 percent of the international phonograph record and cassette market (Dranov 1980, 114). This, in turn, poses a threat to the musical sovereignty of smaller countries that do not have music industries and are therefore unable to provide opportunities for their authors and musicians (Malm 1980).

The numerous economic, legal, and cultural problems resulting from new technologies are covered in a study commissioned by UNESCO (Blaukopf 1980 D). One of these problems deserves closer attention at this juncture, the significance of duplication for musical communication. Walter Benjamin drew attention decades ago to the changed conditions of the work of art in the age when it can be reproduced, examining the aesthetic and social consequences of this reproducibility. The economic consequences, however, are just as important: unauthorized reproduction for commercial purposes ("piracy") is possible, and everyone has the opportunity to make copies of programs for private use without the copyright owner receiving reimbursement. Piracy, which has grown to considerable dimensions, especially in the Third World, has been dealt with by laws and courts in some instances. It is, however, extremely difficult to protect copyright owners in cases of private copying of recordings, owing to the anonymity of these private users. The new technologies have forced a solution by charging all potential "recorders." In the West Germany of the 1980s, a charge had to be paid for every tape recorder purchased. In Austria today, a charge is made on every tape sold according to the playing time (length) of the tape.

As I have attempted to demonstrate, the technological mutation that we take for granted has produced a large number of social consequences. Whereas some of these affect the economic, legal, and social fields related to music, others have a direct impact on musical communication as such. Contact between performers and listeners is no longer required—they no longer need to be in the same place at the same time. Furthermore, music is no longer dependent on conditions given by the shape of the space in which it is performed. Architecture has lost its direct influence on the shape of music.

Chapter 21 *Architecture and Music*

Every sociological approach must attach importance to identifying the significance of place for artistic activity. As a rule, the precise locale has less importance for literary works or works of the visual arts than for musical works. Because of the nature of musical activity, the aural product is not only the result of the acoustic sources (singing voices, instruments) but also of the way sound waves reverberate from the surfaces of the room in which the music is performed. Different conditions arise when there are no such surfaces (open-air music). Closed rooms can be classified according to the length and type of reflection of sound from the ceiling, floor, and walls.

The nature of the music room is not only a matter of room acoustics. It also contains a sociological dimension because the architectural organization of space is the result of social activity: "religious rites, gracious living, and the form of public life have an effect on the shape of a building" (Scheja 1952, 226). Consciously or unconsciously, the creator of a room influences the musical events that take place in this room. The room plays a part in the sound produced there.

Reverberation Time and Modulation Speed

One of the most important aspects of room acoustics is reverberation time, by which I mean the time required for a sound made in a room to diminish to inaudibility once the sound source has stopped. Reverberation time depends on the size of the room and the nature of the reflecting surfaces. This fact sheds light on the relationship between architecture and music, a relationship most often characterized in writings on the sociology of art merely by metaphor or analogy. It is evident that sound events occurring in quick succession must have a different musical effect in a highly reverberant Gothic cathedral than in a radio studio with low reverberation. Using this thought, I have proposed the notion of "modulation speed" (Blaukopf 1954), that is, the amount of modulation over time. What Thurston Dart (1958, 57) calls speed of harmonic change is much the same. Although eighteenth-century musical theorists did not call this "modulation speed," they were familiar with the concept. They deduced the type of music-making suited to a given performance venue from its acoustic characteristics. Thus, Johann Joachim Quantz noted in his *Versuch einer Anweisung, die Flute traversière zu spielen* [Method for Playing the Transverse Flute], first published in 1752, that harmonies must change slowly in large rooms because "in large places the constant reverberation does not die down quickly." Conversely, in a small room it is possible to play music "in which the harmony changes faster" (Quantz 1953, 170).

Today there is virtual consensus that reverberation time influences the tempo of musical interpretation because of this relationship: music with a high modulation speed demands more leisurely performance in highly reverberant rooms than in performance venues with low reverberation.

The concept of modulation speed is not clear until we move from a purely philological analysis of the work of music to the actual sound. That is, it is not enough to study the notes, because in practice not only is the distance between two related keys important, but the speed with which the transition takes place between initial key and final key. For example, it makes a difference whether a modulation from C major to G-sharp minor takes place in five seconds or fifteen seconds, whether this comes about directly or indirectly, and whether or not it contains "passing ornamental modulations."

Concert Hall and Ideal Sound

The attempt to find a correlation between types of music and reverberation time leads to the following results:

> Considering music from all periods, we arrive at reverberation times of between one and eight seconds (always assuming rooms for more than 1,200 listeners). The extreme figure of eight seconds is for music played in cathedrals, primarily during the Renaissance; the other

extreme is suited to new music. Between these values lie the ideal reverberation times for Classical and Romantic music: 1.6 to 2.1 seconds. (Winckel 1957, 1351)

The development of the ideal orchestral sound to which we are accustomed thus seems connected to the construction of concert halls with reverberation times of approximately two seconds. This precondition was created by concert halls in roughly the final third of the nineteenth century, for example:

Neues Gewandhaus, Leipzig	1866
Large Hall of the Musikverein, Vienna	1870
Concertgebouw, Amsterdam	1887
Philharmonic Hall, Berlin	1888
Carnegie Hall, New York City	1891
Grosse Tonhalle, Zurich	1895
Symphony Hall, Boston	1900
Concert Hall of the Moscow Conservatory	1901

Stylistic Categories of Room Acoustics

Up until the nineteenth century, composers and theorists were aware of the importance of the link between reverberation and music. This may be traceable to the fact that there were no standardized performance venues, meaning that the sound had to be adjusted to each place of performance. Johann Nikolaus Forkel wrote in his book on Johann Sebastian Bach published in 1802 that "in his large vocal works" (which were intended for large rooms) Bach curbed modulation while his modulatory imagination knew no bounds in his chamber music (Forkel, n.d., 57–58). This means that the distinction between *church* style, *theater* style, and *chamber* style, customary up until the eighteenth century, has a purely acoustical component in addition to the artistic one. Johann Adolph Scheibe names not only personal style and national style in his *Compendium Musices* (1730) but, in general, the style of music "according to the place and time where and when it is used" (Benary 1961, 76).

The survival of the idea that music should be modified according to its place of performance can most clearly be documented in an essay by E. T. A. Hoffmann written in 1814. He illustrates the influence of room acoustics on musical substance using a bar from the "Dies Irae" of the Mozart Requiem:

These bright, rippling figures, especially in the string instruments, disturb the calm and composure of the whole like crackling pasted-on tinsel, deadening the vocal parts and, especially in the high arched cathedral dome, creating a confusing noise. These figures are foreign to all church music; ignorance is the only excuse for using them. . . . It is right, however, that the fast notes have a great effect in the heavy violin passages; this means that it is evidently better for church performance simply to break up the longer notes of the chord into faster ones (e.g., into 16ths) than into these rippling figures. For example,

Mozart: Requiem, Dies Irae, bar 28

This same passage scored as follows:

is almost theatrical in its unrelieved dissonant form, and sounds confused in church. In general, the most seemly figures in church are those tracing the common chord, without dissonant notes, as they detract least from the power and clarity of the voices, often, in fact, reinforcing them manyfold. (Hoffmann 1814, 138–139)

Aspects of room acoustics are also important in attempts at reconstructing old music. Such projects draw our attention to the role of the music room in the social resonance of music. For example, the monumental effect of polychoral religious music after 1600

was not the result of large masses of performers, but rather of the musical-dramatic use of the large room, the projection of text and music across a powerful distance beyond that of normal human dimensions. This will to space, as it were, as a symbol of a universal order surrounding and bearing men, can be felt as the driving force behind religious music well into the eighteenth century. (Besseler 1938, 156)

Architecture and Music

The festive mass composed for Salzburg in 1628 has been used to demonstrate the role architecture plays in music:

> The effect on the listeners must have been tremendous: the music either came at them from all sides at once or their attention was directed to this or that direction by turns. The different distances of the single ensembles from the listeners and the great differences in reverberation time must have blurred the music to a certain extent, although this was certainly not felt to be unpleasant but rather as a mystical veil which simply increased the emotional value of this music. (Kolneder 1959, 554)

This excerpt also points out the spiritual effect to be assigned to room acoustical characteristics: a "mystical effect" of the music resulting from the reverberation. Music sociology is asked to decipher the particular effect of what medieval music considered to be a special phenomenon in the cathedral, the experience of transcendence that progresses from church liturgy to divine liturgy (cf. Krüger 1958, 188). The sociology of music is unable to solve this mystery without the help of room-acoustic analysis. Not until the particular room-acoustic characteristics of the Gothic cathedral are identified will it be possible to pin down the transcendental effect of the musical event.

Gothic Acoustics as a Guarantee of Gothic Liturgy

Determining reverberation time does not suffice to characterize "Gothic" acoustics. Not only is the length of reverberation (up to eight seconds and occasionally longer) important, the frequency dependence of reverberation is also significant. In other words, we have to know whether or not the reflection of sound waves is even over the entire frequency range. The stone inner surfaces of Gothic cathedrals strongly reflect low- and mid-range sounds, while the reflection of sounds over 2,000 hertz is less owing to greater absorption by the surfaces. Moreover, the shorter their wavelengths, the greater the absorption of sound waves in the air (Lottermoser 1955, 58).

This preference given by the architecture to medium and low frequencies affects listening. Our ability to locate acoustic actions depends on the proportion of high frequencies. As high frequencies are suppressed in Gothic cathedrals, worshippers imagine that the music comes from all sides. This directness of sounds that cannot be located contributes significantly to the social effect of the musical-liturgical event. The anonymity of the sound source built into the architecture is the acoustic guarantee for the internalizing of church norms and, at the same time, the basis for the view that comprehends church liturgy as part of the heavenly liturgy.

Acoustics of the Bayreuth Festival Theater

These considerations permit us to speak of an *architectural* component in music, meaning that architecture has a direct, technologically verifiable influence on musical activity. The efforts of some composers to include the performance space as an integral part of their conception, and to have a part in designing this space, did not begin in the twentieth century (Karlheinz Stockhausen, Yannis Xenakis, et al.). Richard Wagner created more than just the scores for *The Ring of the Nibelungen* and *Parsifal*; he planned the Bayreuth Festival House for them as well. The performance hall has a mid-range reverberation time of 1.55 seconds (Beranek 1962, 564). A distinct feature of the structure is the covered orchestra pit, which prevents the audience from hearing the music directly and makes sound reflection a crucial element of the listening experience. This acoustic arrangement parallels Wagner's festival ideology, which seeks to transform the audience into a homogeneous group, and reinforces the collective effect through the amphitheater shape of the auditorium. The covered orchestra pit—it has rightly been called a "mystical abyss"—in fact lends the orchestral sound a non-directional, mystical quality oddly contrasting with the clarity and directionality of the singers.

Anyone who has experienced the effect of the Bayreuth architecture on the typical Wagnerian homogeneous orchestral sound and the festive transformation of the audience into a homogeneous group will also retain the awareness of the importance of the room-acoustical factor in the social resonance of music. And this is unaffected by the fact that many famous conductors subscribe to Richard Strauss's view that "many of the boundless riches of the score are lost in Bayreuth" (Strauss 1949, 82). This attitude is fostered by a type of listening conditioned by the acoustics of most opera houses and by an analytical view of Wagner's music at a remove from the Bayreuth model. Modern recordings of Wagner's music dramas, usually with transparent orchestral sound, have contributed to strengthening this habit of analytic listening (cf. Blaukopf 1971a). Recordings of this type, however, remove the music from its traditional architectural component by subjecting it to an electronic transformation in the recording room. This transformation of musical architecture is also an aspect of the mutation we are witnessing.

Natural and Technological Communication

Musical communication changes the moment recording and playback are employed. This change also affects the room-acoustical information contained in the music. To clarify how the traditional method of communication differs from modern technological means, it will be helpful to look at the nature of the channel of musical communication. "We must distinguish transmission channels created by technology from the sensory channels that man uses with the immediate environment" (Moles 1968, 17). We are dealing with a sensory channel when the listener (L) receives the musical information emanating from a sound source (S) directly.

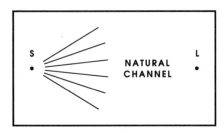

The use of a transmission channel permits a spacial and temporal separation of the reception of the musical information from the original event. The music is picked up by the microphone (M) in the recording room (R), is subjected to a transformation in the transmission channel, and reaches the listener (L) in the playback room (P) through a loudspeaker (LS).

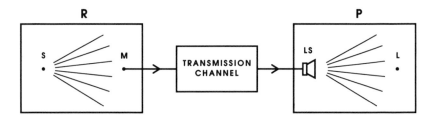

The listener's relation to music is no longer direct, but indirect. The listener's spatial impression consists of:

1. the acoustic arrangement of the recording room,
2. the changes in room-acoustic aspects in the technological part of the transmission channel, and
3. the room-acoustical characteristics of the playback room.

The social significance of this process is clear in its most general form: technology that allows us to bring the concert of a hundred-piece orchestra, by way of a sound recording, into our own home is a phenomenon unheard of in history. And this is not all there is to the transformation, because it extends to the sound itself. The fact that a symphony intended for a large concert hall is listened to in a residential room of 60-80 cubic meters must make a difference. Recording and playback must reshape what has been recorded in such a way as to make this change of rooms possible. Most of all, the dynamics are affected, although other dimensions of musical information are also involved. The spatial dimension, for example, is largely determined by the room-acoustical characteristics of the recording room but is also affected by microphone placement and electronic balance, not to mention the possibility of electronically adding resonance to recordings that have little reverberation.

Fixed and Variable Room

All of these technological devices warrant speaking of two fundamentally different types of music room—fixed and variable. Musical communication through the sensory channel corresponds to a *fixed* room whose characteristics are unchanging; the technological transmission channel corresponds to a *variable* room whose properties can be altered in the course of a single musical performance. This distinction, proposed by Fritz Winckel, makes it clear that technological development "goes beyond our natural sense of space" (Winckel 1975, 180). Electronic alteration can be taken so far that individual components of what is played can be given different reverberations. This technique, common in popular music, is also used in serious music. In certain instances the process is justified by performance directions placed in the score by the composer—the "orchestra at a distance" (*Fernorchester*) in a Mahler symphony, for example. What is fundamentally new, however, is the fact that this process is freely available. The old genres of church music, theater music, and chamber music, determined by social and acoustical factors, cease to be separate. They are replaced by transmission music, which suits the variable space of the technological channel. This is one of the most significant elements of the qualitative change in musical communication through the technological media (Blaukopf 1969).

This development of variable room affects not only composers (cf. Stockhausen 1959, Brelet 1967) but also room-acoustical arrangements in traditional music and in public life in general. For example, resonators for certain frequency ranges have been installed in concert halls (Royal Festival Hall, London) and public address systems with many speakers have been utilized in large halls and in churches. In this way, for the first time in history, architecture loses "its functional purpose and its relation to musical phenomena" (Winckel 1974, 188). The consequences of this change for musical communication as a whole are unforeseeable, yet there can be no doubt that we are dealing with a phenomenon for which there is no parallel in the history of music, one which places people in a new musical environment.

Chapter 22 *Acoustic Environment*

The knowledge that musical activity is influenced to a large degree by the acoustical characteristics of the place in which it takes place brings up another question: is this activity also influenced by the totality of acoustic stimuli to which human beings are subject? Music makes up only a part of the total human acoustic experience. Let us try to describe the total acoustic environment (TAE). This largely consists of natural sounds (N), human sounds (H), and sounds of tools, technology, and traffic noise (T). If TAE were constant for all societies there would be no reason to make acoustic environment a topic of the sociology of music because it would be impossible to attribute an influence on the change of musical practice to this factor. Since, however, the degree and composition of TAE suffers significant change through urbanization and industrialization, it is necessary to investigate the influence of TAE on musical behavior.

Although problems relating to the acoustic environment have come to the forefront of attention in recent decades, acoustic ecology has yet to provide socio-musicology with sufficient useful data. Up to now, research in this area has, understandably, been concentrated on a problem of vital interest—noise abatement. One of the few starts in utilizing acoustic research has been made by the Canadian composer and teacher R. Murray Schafer (1971, 1977). Schafer has pointed out that the proportions of N, H, and T have changed in the course of human history and that this can also have consequences for music. Schafer's estimate of the proportions for various epochs is as follows (Schafer 1971, 13):

	N	H	T
Primitive Cultures	69%	26%	5%
Medieval, Renaissance, and Preindustrial Cultures	34%	52%	14%
Postindustrial Cultures	9%	25%	66%
Today	6%	26%	68%

Although this chart is based entirely on estimates, it shows that the natural acoustic environment (N) has lost in importance, while the sounds of tools, technology, and traffic have become dominant. In other words, social-technological development has changed the composition of human aural impressions, the TAE. *Tools created by man to do work, not to produce sound, generate sound events of central importance in the human acoustic environment.* One of the chief characteristics of the change in acoustic landscape is that the level of such sound, which is regarded as "bothersome sound," or noise, is increasing in our society (figures in Schafer 1977, 185ff. and Taylor 1973, 87ff.).

Schafer has coined the apt term "soundscape" for the acoustic landscape. He points out the changes in both the composition and the quality of this "soundscape." Other, more precise, definitions followed Schafer's: "[In the preindustrial rural world] sounds are customarily isolated phenomena surrounded by profound silence. Even minimal acoustic actions can be perceived and are of importance to country dwellers" (Mark 1977, 23). But the elements of the acoustic milieu in a highly developed technological society have an entirely different character. "One thing all machine noises have in common is low informational value and high redundancy; that is, the message they carry is always the same and, in the end, boring" (Mark 1977, 24). The dominance of the redundant and the bothersome distinguishes the acoustic environment of urbanized, highly industrialized civilization from all those preceding it. Even a sociology of music interested merely in the idea of milieu as understood by Hippolyte Taine would have to have an ear for this, because acoustic milieu has a much more direct effect on musical practice than, for example, the milieus of politics or ideas.

Response by Composers

Some twentieth-century composers have tried to react creatively to this new environment. The "noise music" propagated by Luigi Russolo early in the century is an example, as are several compositions written during the twenties—*Pacific 231* (Arthur Honegger's musical portrait of a locomotive), *Ballet mécanique* (a work called "streamlined, glinting, cold" by its composer, George Antheil), *Pas d'acier* (Prokofiev), and *Iron Foundry* (Mosolov). Only since 1950 can synthetic sound be produced electronically, thereby enabling representation of machine-mechanical sounds without traditional musical stylization. This claim to contemporaneity rested on the recognition of the mechanical environment and its acoustic concomitants.

Compositions of this kind mark the relationship to a new type of environment. In general, composers previously proceeded from a pictorial stylization of the natural environment. Haydn attempted to depict nature in his great oratorios. Beethoven went further in the "Pastoral" Symphony by seeking "more expression of feeling than painting." Even Gustav Mahler began his First Symphony with a sound he described in a score note as "like a sound of nature." Not until the twentieth century did the artificial environment invade the artistic imagination, where the longing for nature has occasionally entered into an odd alliance with technology. In 1924, the year in which the painter Paul Klee created his *Zwitschermaschine*, Ottorino Respighi used such a machine in his symphonic poem *The Pines of Rome*: instead of being imitated by the instruments of the orchestra, the singing of a bird is reproduced from a phonograph recording; the name of the record company and catalogue number are included in the score.

The Volume of Music

The acoustic environment's influence on music is not exhausted by these compositional phenomena (which, incidentally, still need a systematic investigation); its effects are far more lasting and direct. An element of this influence is the increase in the noise level of our society, which creates a trend toward louder music. Measurements have shown that the noise level in so-called quiet urban dwellings has increased from about 20 phons in 1934 to about 45 phons in 1955. Philippot (1974, 56) conjectures that the volume of music has increased in order to suppress these higher levels of environmental noise. Another contributing factor is the independence of volume level from the musical instrument:

> A large portion of the music that is heard today reaches the listener's ear, not directly, but through an electroacoustic channel (loudspeaker). Consequently, the performances may have a sound volume that is no longer limited to that of the musical instruments. The fact

that the sound emanates from a point source, the loudspeaker, arouses the desire for a higher sound volume (Philippot 1974, 58).

The increase in the volume of music, prompted by the acoustic environment and made possible by the use of technological equipment, is habit-forming. This effect is most pronounced in popular music. Thus it is by now customary for theater performances of musicals to strive for the effects initially possible only in technologically enhanced music; not only is the entire sound electronically amplified, but each singing voice as well. An audience constantly exposed to this effect develops different listening expectations. In the end, unamplified performances will seem to be less impressive. People expect amplification of low frequencies in order to experience the resulting vibrations; it is satisfying to feel the presence and spatial proximity to the sound source produced by amplification in the frequencies around 3,000 hertz; the audience also understands the lyrics better when amplification of the high frequencies makes the consonants more distinct.

Hearing Sensitivity

These expectations rebound from the technological transmission of music to natural musical communication. The increases in the noise level of the industrial environment and the volume of music (as can be heard in its most extreme form in discotheques catering to young audiences) also lead to physiological changes. There is a shift in the threshold of hearing. The threshold of hearing is the sound pressure necessary to evoke an auditory sensation. When the human ear is exposed to strong acoustic stimuli for even a brief period of time, it becomes insensitive to weaker stimuli for a time, then gradually returns to normal. If, however, the ear is constantly exposed to strong acoustic stimuli, the result is a lasting increase in the threshold of hearing (cf. Bugliarello 1976, 36; Taylor 1973, 79 ff.). This loss of hearing sensitivity at low volumes is in turn one of the reasons for increasing the volume of technologically amplified music. In industrialized countries the loss of sensitivity to high frequencies increases with age; we can therefore reach the conclusion that the hearing ability and hearing expectations of people in these highly industrialized nations have changed significantly.

It thus appears that the contemporary changes in musical practice include not only the communication process of music but also the receivers of the musical message, human beings. This is to be taken as a purely ideal-type tendency that can create movements in opposition, just as the trend to building highways and atomic power plants brought about the environmental protection movement.

Music—Monetary and Time Budget

A further sign of the mutation brought about by technology is the fact that every kind of music plays a quantitatively greater role in peoples' lives. The growing role of sound recordings on the market is proof of this alone. The available information on the sales of recordings in West Germany in 1970 and 1973 shows that within a three-year period, during which movie theater receipts decreased significantly and money spent for theater, concert, and opera tickets declined by 5 percent, expenditure for phonograph records and cassettes increased by over 100 percent (Zeppenfeld 1978, 36).

Even more revealing than an analysis of private expenditure, however, is the investigation of the so-called time budget, the amount of time spent on various activities. A 1975 study (quoted in Zeppenfeld 1978, 26) cites the average weekly time spent listening to recordings by West German citizens over fourteen years of age as 81 minutes. This does not, however, cover the entire influence of recorded music on everyday life, for it is well known that a large percentage of radio broadcast time is devoted to playing industrially produced recordings. Thus, a considerable percentage of the more than eleven hours per week that a West German citizen spent listening to radio in 1975 consisted of recorded music.

The paramount role of technologically communicated music is further underscored if we take into consideration the duplicating of existing program material (records, radio) on tape. The total recording time on the blank cassettes sold in West Germany in 1977 was greater than the playing time of all the records and recorded cassettes sold during that year. By 1977 there were an estimated 330 million cassettes in West German homes (GFM 1978). Blank cassettes, which are used primarily for recording music, greatly multiply the effect of technologically transmitted music and the role it plays in everyday life. We are thus entitled to revise R. Murray Schafer's table: the sum of human acoustic experiences in highly industrialized society includes—in addition to natural sounds, human sounds, and the sounds of tools, technology, and traffic—a crucial new element, recorded and transmitted music. *Whereas the occurrence of music was previously both temporally and spatially separate from the acoustic environment, transmitted music (of every type) has now become a continuous presence.*

Characteristics of Transmission Music

Technology has not only changed the importance of music in the time budget, thereby altering its social role, it has also had an effect on the nature of transmission music itself. The following elements of this qualitative change have been established as the result of studies in this area:

1. The variable room, as previously defined, becomes the normal listening situation.
2. The technological manipulations used in recording popular music produce identification mechanisms of the "music of the lonely crowd;" this phenomenon has been described in detail (Sønstevold 1968) and its sociological importance has been indicated (Adorno 1968, 242).
3. The standard short playing time of pieces of popular music, for which there is no longer a technological reason since the introduction of the long-playing record, has created a "short-winded" type of popular music; the use of fade-ins and fade-outs shows that this music belongs to the everyday acoustic world. This music imperceptibly rises above everyday noises and again is lost in these noises (environmental and equipment).
4. Although hi-fi technology has attained a high standard of distortion-free reproduction, most replay units do not meet the DIN 45 500 standard governing minimum distortion because they have limited frequency response. Studies (Bergeijk 1960, 208) have shown that the use of such equipment causes habituation in listeners.
5. Recording, broadcast, and reproduction technology have become more important for listening. There are still no systematic studies about the influence of electroacoustic media on auditory expectations. One of the few important studies on this subject comes to the conclusion "that various pieces of music transmitted electrically are judged less on the basis of their general musical character than on the frequency range of the performance" (Kötter 1968, 15) and that, under certain conditions, an "increase of the high frequencies is considered to be advantageous" (Kötter 1968, 75).

Sociology and Technology

The phenomena briefly listed above not only shed light on the far-reaching consequences of electroacoustics in musical communications; they also elucidate the role played by this particular new type of communication in the sociology of music. It thus seems naive to believe that socio-musicology could manage with sociological categories alone, studying only the effect of music but not the nature of the music itself. Just as it is not possible to understand the development of Liszt's piano style without considering the musical instrument he used, analyzing the transformation of musical life during the period from 1950 to 1980 is impossible without taking into consideration the nature of the technological means that led to this transformation. Electroacoustic equipment has earned the status of a tool (instrument) of musical communication. Describing the consequences of this innovation is one of the most important tasks of a socio-musicology that, following Max Weber, regards the history of the technological means of music to be its proper domain. It is still possible to come across the view in the socio-musicological literature that this concept is not "sociological" in the true sense of the word because it establishes a connection between musical practice and the technological evolution of communication. Those who espouse this view want only to trace the relations of music to methods of production and politics, class struggle, and ideology. They should be reminded that technological development is also the result of social change and that it, in turn, influences this change. The mutation of musical life as I have presented it here would not have been possible without the shortening of the working day that has taken place since the beginning of our century, without increased leisure time, and without the related expansion of a music industry that makes available products for use during leisure time. Yet this overall development could not have taken place without the invention of sound recording, the electron tube, the transistor, and so on. The present and future effects of the evolution of musical technology cannot be deduced directly from the structure of the economy, the social structure, political movements, and ruling ideologies. It is thus fitting to examine the consequences of technological change separately in order to verify the crucial features of the changes in the acoustic and musical environment.

Chapter 23 *Audience Research*

I have not used the terms "light music" and "serious music" as socio-logical categories because, in distinguishing the main types of musical behavior, it seems more apt to start from the social context to which these behaviors belong. Heinrich Besseler's notions of "participatory music" and "performance music," based on the historic-comparative method, meet this requirement. The application of the sociological-typological method also establishes that the distinction is useful. The two terms are characterized as follows:

> PARTICIPATORY MUSIC—historically, the primary part of music culture, distinguished by predominantly standardized creative principles; emphasis is on the performer (interpretation); reception is predominantly spontaneous. Immediate functionality assures a relatively wide basis of consumption in society, thereby preserving the continuity of the music's communicative power.

> PERFORMANCE MUSIC—historically, the secondary part of musical culture, especially during the nineteenth and twentieth centuries; emancipated from immediate functionality, emphasis is on the authorized originality of the musical work, its aesthetic effect, and its ethical and increasingly noetic meaning (Karbusický 1975a, 59).

Participatory music, which forms the "communicative foundation of all musical culture" (Karbusický 1975a, 33), includes not only what we call "folk music" but another area of vital musical practice not usually classified as either art music or folk music. The Argentine ethnomusicologist Carlos Vega (1898–1966) proposed the term "mesomúsica" (intermediate music) for this field of popular music, a notion which has entered the literature in Latin America. Vega defines "mesomúsica" as

> the complex of musical creations . . . which can be classified functionally as entertainment, social dance, public functions, ceremonies, school classes, games, and so on, and which the audience in those classes of society that participate in modern cultural forms of expression has made its own, or has accepted. In the course of recent centuries, due to improved means of communication, the dissemination of "mesomúsica" has been furthered to the extent that in today's world only more or less primitive native peoples and those groups that have not been completely accepted into modern society can escape its influence. . . . "Mesomúsica," then, is present alongside art music in the awareness of segments of the population who have moved from rural areas to the cities, just as it plays a role alongside folklore in the life of the rural population. (Vega 1966, quoted in Aretz 1977, 39–40)

Folk music and "mesomúsica," then, would be classified under my notion of participatory music, while art music would be included under the term performance music. (I must point out, however, that the participatory or performance classification is not linked to the music itself but to how it is used. Folk music played in a concert hall can assume the nature of performance music, while the *Hungarian Dances* of Brahms or Tchaikovsky's *Nutcracker* can, under certain conditions, become participatory music.)

Categories

For reasons discussed in the previous chapters, it seems appropriate to recognize transmission music, as used by Bernhard Winzheimer (1930) and defined by Konrad Niemann (1974 and 1980), along with participatory and performance music. This category is needed to characterize a musical practice that fits into the social context in a new, technological way. The notion of transmission music does not exist on the same level as the other two, but is parallel to them. Transmission music can assume the character of either participatory or performance music. This relationship might be represented as in this diagram, in which the solid lines indicate regular classification and the broken lines refer to different, less common ties in Occidental music:

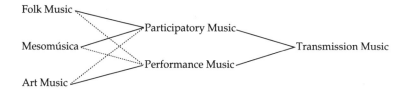

The Rise of the Audience

Participatory music requires audience involvement, while performance music is produced for passive listeners. The rise of the audience is linked to the development of performance music. A public is created wherever "modern" living conditions prevail. Tran Van Khe was able to demonstrate how an audience is gradually coming into being in the countries of Asia. The number of listeners per musical event is increasing along with a decrease in participation (Tran Van Khe 1963). Observing this transformation process under way in the countries of the Third World is apt to help us understand how the notion of audience evolved in Occidental music as well. The twentieth-century technological mutation leads to a further change in audience structure (cf. Krenek 1973). To the best of my knowledge, this change, which I have also pursued in another connection, was first pointed out by Heinrich Besseler in his habilitation address of 1925: "Radio has truly turned the public into a limitless, utterly atomized mass. In addition, the gramophone has eliminated the common temporal link" (Besseler 1975, 51)

Research Goals and Methods

This new situation created by technology has made it necessary to investigate the make-up and desires of the anonymous public. Suitable methods were developed, not by sociology, but by market and public-opinion research. Now these methods are part of communication science. The initial goal was to establish the number of persons listening to broadcasts, the composition of this group of listeners, the effect of radio information, and so on. This "recipient research" was later supplemented by "content research" and "communication research" (cf. the survey in Silbermann 1973b, 38ff.). These projects later converged with (albeit largely unsystematic) attempts to identify "different art-audience types" (Silbermann 1979 A, 148), proceeding from a historical point of view, from empirically verifiable degrees of education and socialization, or from other criteria. The most productive method for socio-musicology was soon revealed to be radio audience surveys commissioned by radio broadcasting companies. These strove to obtain an overall picture of the anonymous public by questioning a portion of this audience, a "representative sample" in the statistical sense. Such a sample exists

> when by random selection a representation of the whole with respect to the observed features has been surveyed and when each (though not too small) portion of the population sample is representative. Features of the population or of the globality which were not yet considered relevant at the beginning of the study must also be proportionally rendered. (Haseloff 1965, 111)

The data obtained on this basis permits inferences on the characteristics of the entire public as to amount of listening, education level, income, age, rating of the program, preferences, time budget, and so forth, according to how the questions are asked. As a rule, most of these projects are directed at the radio program as a whole and not just at the musical programming. Nonetheless, a number of these surveys also provide information of potential use to the sociology of music. The methodic utilization of these surveys has, as far as music is concerned, made only slight progress within communication science: "The interest of communication science in music is inversely proportional to the importance music has attained in the electronic media and via phonograph records" (Ronneberger 1979, 5). This deficiency can only be explained in part by the walls erected by scientific disciplines because, from their own analyses, communication experts must have long been aware of the quantitatively enormous importance of music in the electronic media. A more likely reason is that the methods of statistics must be adapted to the subject of study (music). The American sociologist William F. Ogburn pointed this out as early as 1932 in the largely ignored essay *Statistics and Art*: "methodological inventions arise from attacks on specific kinds of subject matter and cannot be developed apart from the special social sciences" (Ogburn 1932, 6). Communication researchers would therefore have to be familiar with music in order to carry out meaningful surveys about music.

Stumbling Blocks

Surveys involving questionnaires or interviews that deal with music are inherently more likely to run into difficulty than those that deal with voting or general consumer behavior. Two kinds of difficulties are involved. The *first* stems from the value implication attached to answering questions such as "Do you enjoy listening to symphony concerts?" and "Do you like chamber music?" Unlike questions about detergents or voting, there is an element of prestige involved. As Karl Menger (1934) has shown, this also applies to actions. The decision to take a given action is determined by

1. one's immediate desire
2. one's statements about the action
3. the maxims one wishes to follow (one's "conscience")

Where verbal statements are involved rather than decisions to act, these "general maxims" play an even greater role. There is a high probability of prestige answers, especially when the object itself suggests such an answer. The verbalization of an imagined act leads to a shift toward rational values ("conscience"), which comes to the surface particularly in those statements about objects considered to be social value symbols. It is not surprising, for example, that 84 percent of those who *do attend* music theaters in West Germany advocate public subsidy of these theaters; yet only the status of musical theater as a value symbol explains why 60 percent of those who *do not attend* are also in favor of public subsidy (figures calculated by Wiesand 1975, 11).

As a rule the coloration of an answer by "cultural conscience" is unavoidable, although control questions can sometimes eliminate this source of error. Let us assume, for example, that a newly enrolled student at an academy of music is asked to name his "favorite composer," and the response is Brahms. A subsequent control question could inquire about his "favorite work." If the answer is Brahms's Fifth Symphony, the subject apparently doesn't know that Brahms wrote only four symphonies, and one can conclude that the previous answer was probably for reasons of prestige (cf. Blaukopf 1968a, 25). This banal example should suffice to indicate one of the difficulties involved in empirical surveys about the arts.

The *second* difficulty stems from the fact that the subject is asked to respond not to music but to words referring to a given piece of music or to a specific musical genre. Let us take for example the "Music on Radio" survey commissioned by the Western German Radio (Westdeutscher Rundfunk) in 1963 (Infratest 1963). This survey employed the following methods:

1. Interview of a representative sample
2. Written survey of listeners especially interested in certain types of broadcasts
3. Psychological studio tests with small groups of listeners

One of the results recorded the distribution of interests over the various areas of music:

	listeners very or fairly interested (in percent)
1. Operettas and operetta melodies	60
2. Popular music	58
3. Folk music	51
4. Dance music	41
5. Opera programs	18
6. Classical music (general)	16
7. Classical art songs	14
8. Symphonies and symphonic works	11
9. Complete operas	10
10. Church music, organ music, and oratorios	10
11. Chamber music and solo concerts	9
12. Jazz	7
13. Contemporary serious music	6

Even those experienced in classifying given works would have difficulty placing them into the specific categories given here. Categories 2, 3, and 4 are difficult to distinguish. The word "classical" as used in category 6 has a different meaning for the musically versed listener than it does for others. As other surveys have shown, the term "jazz" is often misunderstood, being equated with "dance music" or "popular music."

Thus there seems to be little agreement between the meaning that radio specialists and interviewers attach to a given genre and the musical content that many of the respondents associate with these names. A survey conducted in London in 1969 also drew attention to this fact. Sometimes a term itself elicited a certain kind of judgment without its being associated with a musical impression: "the words 'chamber music' widely conjure up an image of something esoteric that lacks the emotional attraction of more colorful orchestral works (BBC 1964, 1:9).

The difficulty in finding genre names that are unequivocal for the respondents is reflected in tests given during the sixties and seventies by researchers into radio listening. The genre terms chosen are not internationally applicable. Revealing the uncertainty among those who plan such projects, the German study (e.g., Infratest 1963) classifies music differently from the English (BBC 1964 and 1969), which in turn differs from the French (e.g., Auzeill 1970). It must have long been clear that the chosen course was unpromising. Yet how can we overcome this problem facing audience research?

"Music Preference Test"

The Czech Radio made an attempt to solve this problem during the sixties with an applied method of listener survey (Karbusický 1964). The first account of this method published in German appeared in an East German publication (Karbusický 1966) and was later brought out in an expanded form in West Germany (Karbusický 1975b). The fundamental idea consists of not confronting the respondent with a *linguistic term* meant to trigger an idea of a certain kind of music but with *music itself*, a musical example on tape to which to react. "The principal methodology of the empirical-sociological survey is a *music preference test*" (Karbusický 1975b 286). This innovation of the survey method agrees with Ogburn's previously quoted admonition to develop a method from the nature of the subject matter. It is no accident that this innovation came about as a result of work between audience research and socio-musicology. Recent surveys increasingly proceed from the idea that the verbal questions used in information, sports, and so on, are not suited to music:

> As much as certain concepts as "symphony concerts" or "chamber music" are quite clear in the eyes of experts, they are not equally known to all lay persons. On the other hand, terms such as "jazz" are in general use but are understood in different ways. These contradictions can only be eliminated if the survey concentrates on the practice and simulates *the actual listening experience for the survey.* (SRG 1979, I)

Types of Listeners

Starting in 1979, the researchers of the Swiss Radio and Television Corporation based their work on this idea. This process is also suited to determining types of listeners, as Karbusický (1975b, 305) pointed out in his criticism of Adorno's classification of types of listeners (1976, 1ff.) The evaluation of the Swiss survey's sample in fact produced listener groups with clearly defined tastes and behaviors. The authors of this report gave these types names intended only as rough descriptions. The following is a resumé of these findings (SRG 1979, 41ff.):

1. "Folk" type (21%)
   Has few, very sharp preferences and many dislikes. Below average education, heavily superannuated, owns less playback equipment. Spends little time with music.
2. "Progressive" type (19%)
   Predilection for all types of avant-garde. Very many young people (15–24 years of age); educational level slightly above average; tends to be urban; plays an instrument more often; rarely listens to radio.

3. "Rock-Pop" type (19%)

Ninety percent younger than forty. Loves Anglo-American pop music and light baroque music; listens to Südwestfunk 3 and Radio Luxemburg; is very active musically.

4. "Poly-Listener" type (26%)

Many pop music preferences. Opposed to more serious music in the program; frequently listens to music broadcasts in the car and watches music programs on television.

5. "Classical" type (16%)

In addition to interest in "classical," above average interest in dance and light music. Below average interest in rock, pop, and folk music; prefers listening to "classical music" in concert to radio.

Over and above these classifications, which can only be fully understood by reading the report, the Swiss study is noteworthy for its insights into the musical time budget. The previously mentioned penetration of transmission music into the acoustic environment is confirmed by the following words: "Music constantly accompanies a large part of the population. Only two percent never listen to music at home" (SRG 1979, 41ff.), whereas sixty-eight percent of the group of fifteen- to seventy-year-olds agreed with the statement "I can't imagine a life without music."

Tension and Adjustment

A result such as this confirms the new role of music in people's lives and, at the same time, the transformation of the acoustic environment, which is increasingly dominated by recorded music. All of these technological changes invade the traditional structures of musical life and bring about its mutation. As I will demonstrate, these circumstances create tensions between the new technological factors and the traditional structures of musical life. Before discussing these tensions, I will address the more general question of how they can be eliminated by adjustment and, in general, *how a given structure of cultural behavior adjusts to a new factor.*

Chapter 24 *Cultural Lag*

Attempts to outline a comprehensive theory of cultural change often miscarry owing to the difficulty in organizing the wide variety of factors capable of bringing about such changes. Even in those instances where only one factor is analyzed, one soon recognizes that this factor has a potentially different meaning in different types of societies and under different cultural conditions. Sociological theory thus attaches great importance to technological changes, noting at the same time, however, that this applies especially to present-day society (Rocher 1968, 3, 57). The importance of economic factors is emphasized in the most general formulations of those sociologists who follow in the footsteps of Karl Marx. The distinction between "base" and "superstructure" (cf. chapter 10) and the assumption that the superstructure gradually adjusts to changes in the economic basis belong to a particular view of cultural change. In order to more clearly characterize cultural change, it is necessary to take into account *all possible factors*: economic, political, legal, technological, and so forth. By investigating the historical appearance of a "new factor" and its effect on cultural life, we can, as a rule, identify a process of the old adapting to the new.

Ogburn's Theory

The "cultural lag theory" developed by the American sociologist William F. Ogburn (1886–1959) deals with this change:

The strain that exists between two correlated parts of culture that change at unequal rates may be interpreted as a lag in the part that is changing at the slowest rate, for that one lags behind the other. (Ogburn/Nimkoff 1950, 592)

Ogburn names three examples of cultural lag:

1. Retaining narrow roads while increasing the speed and volume of traffic
2. Retaining the idea that "a woman's place is in the home" while shifting production out of the home
3. Retaining legislation that does not yet spell out the legal consequences of new types of accidents that are occurring in industry

The new factor or, as Ogburn calls it, the "independent variable" is almost always a scientific discovery or technological invention, but at times it is "an ideology or a non-technological variable" (Ogburn 1969, 139).

The central issue in this theory is the adjustment of an existing element to a new and different one. So long as this change has not taken place, a cultural lag exists. A sociology of culture devoted to changes in cultural modes of behavior must investigate this mechanism, diagnosing not only historical but also contemporary processes of change, as I will demonstrate further on. Such an approach is useful, because the new generating factors (the "independent variables") are not defined a priori; instead they are investigated individually to see which new element has not yet adapted to one or more existing elements.

Printed and Handwritten Music

A striking example of a lag caused by technology is the very gradual adoption of music printing during the fifteenth century. Initially, only the words of the liturgy were printed, leaving space for handwritten staves and notes. Although progress was made in solving the technical problem of printing music, the note press was forced to compete (this seems odd to us today) with handwritten music. Tradition demanded red staff lines and black notes. Rather than turning to a technologically rational solution, having both notes and staff lines the same color, music printers chose the more complicated and expensive two-color process. Printed music was suited to disseminating their product in such a way as to standardize musical practice and to impose a printed norm on performance style of both vocal and instrumental music. In spite of this fact until about 1500 there were still

many print orders for liturgical-musical works requesting staff lines only. The chorale was intentionally not fixed so that [these works]

could be used in a number of church districts. With editions containing music, the printer ran the risk of being able to sell them only to
those parishes in which these versions were in use. Editions without
music could be supplemented as required. (W. M. Luther in MGG 9,
1668)

The traditional particularism of church districts thus lagged behind the
technological innovation of printed music. This permitted prescriptive
notation as "direction" for the performance, while practice was content
to add the descriptive characters to the printed page by hand (cf. ","
page 160, for the terms "descriptive" and "prescriptive"). It took a certain amount of time before printing was fully utilized and this cultural
lag eliminated.

Artistic and Economic Factors

Compositional achievements can also function as "independent variables." The founding of orchestras and concert societies during the
nineteenth century is an example, because astonishingly many were set
up for the declared purpose of organizing adequate performances of
the Beethoven symphonies. In this instance, the new musical genre is to
be regarded as the independent variable occasioning change through
the founding of qualified, and finally professional orchestras.

During the nineteenth century, performance space underwent a
similar process of adjusting to the new genre. The building of concert
halls has correctly been attributed to the bourgeoisie's need for cultural
(status) representation, yet an artistic factor also seems to have been
involved in this change. For example, the history of the construction of
the Vienna Konzerthaus, opened in 1913 largely as a venue for orchestra music (originally conceived during the nineteenth century as a "choral hall"), would seem to support this opinion. The middle class,
politically active choral societies that originally supported the project
were replaced toward the end of the nineteenth century by a "public"
eager to hear the works of the symphonic masters. Yet these works
required a suitable performance space.

Anyone who has had the opportunity to hear Beethoven's Eroica
where it was first performed—in the Marble Hall of Lobkowitz Palace
in Vienna—will understand how this and other symphonic works had
to leave the narrow sociability of noble society for the broad performance space of the modern concert hall. The construction of concert
halls, then, also represents an adjustment to an innovation, the Classical
and Romantic symphony. (The resulting adaptation can even influence
the composer's conception; Brahms assured his publisher that he com-

posed for the Vienna Musikverein Hall and the Leipzig Gewandhaus for acoustical reasons.)

A far more direct influence occurs when economic and technological innovations cause nonadaptation and adaptation on a different level. One of the most striking phenomena of this kind is the economic dilemma of the music and music theater businesses of our times. Resulting from the economic dynamics of industrialized society—a society, moreover, that is saturated with media and awaiting a change, in Ogburn's sense of the term—this dilemma merits closer consideration.

Chapter 25 *The Economic Dilemma of the Performing Arts*

In recent years, the financial needs of musical theaters and orchestras have become a constant worry to those charged with maintaining these institutions. In West Germany the problem has led to a public discussion and to an opinion poll on cultural policy and musical theater (Wiesand 1975). The difference between expenditures and box-office receipts is not only great but apparently increasing. For three German orchestras the percentage of box-office receipts in total expenditure declined (according to Wahl-Ziegler 1978, 115) between 1969 and 1972:

Box-Office Receipts as Percent of Total Expenditure

	1969	1970	1971	1972
Berlin Philharmonic	27.4	29.8	26.6	24.3
Munich Philharmonic	19.9	16.0	14.1	14.3
Bamberg Symphony	36.4	28.8	25.4	25.4

This trend can be seen to a greater or lesser degree in all performing arts institutions—theater, musical theater, ballet, and orchestras—eliciting studies (Wahl- Zieger 1978, Netzer 1978, Leroy 1980, Dupuis 1980) that aim at tracking down the economic dynamics of the performing arts and seeking possible solutions. The first impetus in this direction came from the American researchers William J. Baumol and

William G. Bowen (Baumol 1966) who concluded on the basis of their analysis that *the disparity between receipts and costs in the performing arts will continue to grow*. Responsibility is attributed, not to inflation, mismanagement, fees for stars, or union demands, but rather to the inherent nature of enterprises concerned with the performing arts. The 1964 financial-situation audit in the United States estimated that the "gap" between receipts and expenditures for all such enterprises was between $19.5 and $22.5 million. In relation to prices of that time, this is equivalent to the cost of buying three long-range airliners or building fifteen miles of freeway. These figures indicate the expense American society had to bear to support the performing arts.

Baumol and Bowen's study also has a historical dimension. The trend of cost increase could be followed from two documents. The Drury Lane Theatre, London, showed an annual increase in costs of 1.4 percent between 1740 and 1964, as against an average general price increase of only 0.9 percent per year. A study of the budget of the New York Philharmonic Orchestra reveals a similar result over the period 1842–1964. Expenditures increased an average of 2.5 percent annually, in stark contrast to the trend of wholesale prices, which increased at a rate of only 1 percent per year during this 122-year period.

Dynamics of Productivity

One can discern the cause of this characteristically disproportionate cost increase in performing arts enterprises if one takes into consideration the role of increased productivity (the growth of work produced per working hour) in industrial society. This increase is most spectacular in the production of goods in the United States (an annual average of 2.5 percent between 1929 and 1961) and somewhat less so in service organizations (1.6 percent over the same period). Enterprises in the performing arts belong to a part of the service sector that is virtually or entirely incapable of increasing productivity. Methods employed in other branches of the economy (new technologies, capital increases, improved qualification of labor, mass production) do not apply in the performing arts. Merely to maintain the quality and quantity of production in the performing arts requires *expenditures that will constantly increase with respect to other production and services areas*. Growth of productivity, which is the blessing of industrial society, becomes the peculiar problem of the performing arts.

Baumol's Law

The inner economic dynamics of the performing arts was formulated by Baumol and Bowen and is known in the literature as Baumol's Law. This law states that the professional performing arts will increasingly burden society not only in absolute financial terms but also in terms of the share of total funds society makes available. There have been theoretical reservations about the demand for constantly increasing public subsidies based on this law. Dick Netzer (1978, 28–9), for example, argues that subsidies impede rationalization and that the additional funds could be raised by the "free interplay of forces," which essentially means raising the prices of admission.

Such a course would, however, be diametrically opposed to the stated goals of most countries as embodied in the resolutions of the European conference on cultural policy in Helsinki in 1972. These policies aim to improve access to the arts and to permit the greatest possible number of persons to enjoy the performing arts. The consistent application of this principle is, however, calculated to create a still more disproportionate increase in financial needs. If, for example, the Vienna State Opera, which requires a subsidy of roughly 1,340,000 schillings per day (calculated for 1978 in the 1979 ÖBV), gives guest performances in provincial towns, expenses increase faster than the size of the audience. Or, put another way, the costs for the final product (if we consider the seat as "final product") increase further. Thus Baumol's Law also becomes a problem of cultural policy aiming at a democratization of cultural life.

Technology and Economy

If Baumol's Law is assumed to be correct, the ability of the performing arts to survive must be questioned. The granting of additional, constantly greater funds is also rightly regarded as a political issue (Leroy 1980, 192). There are occasional hints at possible "technological" solutions in connection, for example, with inexpensive concerts of electroacoustic music (Leroy 1980, 194), but the technological media's possible role in completely or partially solving the problem has rarely been considered in any depth. Netzer mentions this role in passing:

> Income realized from orchestral recordings and televised productions of plays originally produced live may also be considered the result of productivity improvements that partly offset the rising costs of live performance. (Netzer 1978, 30)

Studies performed by the MEDIACULT Institute (Vienna) have proceeded from this idea. They have shown that the previously unhampered effectiveness of Baumol's Law is the result of "cultural lag." The mass media (film, television, radio, and sound recordings) do offer the possibility of significantly increasing the number of "seats" per performance, thereby drastically reducing the costs "per seat." Existing legal, economic, and administrative structures, however, prevent these cost cuts from having an effect on the calculations of the performing arts. Theaters, orchestra organizations, concert organizers, and the radio and recording industries are separate business and legal entities. Unified, joint program strategies (coproductions) are only possible in exceptional circumstances and require the settlement of difficult legal and financial problems. The uncoordinated coexistence of institutions that serve musical communication in our time even prevents economists from seeing that the economic dilemma of the performing arts can be overcome by the use of technological media. The economists fail to see not only that

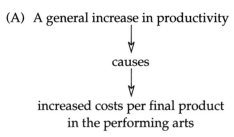

(A) A general increase in productivity

↓

causes

↓

increased costs per final product
in the performing arts

but also that

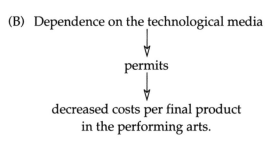

(B) Dependence on the technological media

↓

permits

↓

decreased costs per final product
in the performing arts.

If possibility (B) is not utilized (A) will take full effect, threatening the existence of the performing arts in whose survival the institutions of the technological media are vitally interested because a considerable number of their programs are taken from the performing arts. This is a glaring example of *nonadaptation* in Ogburn's sense. Owing to technological mutation, the mass media have been granted a crucial role in controlling musical life. Because these media—be they public or private—were created as independent institutions, however, they appear to be grafted onto musical life from the outside, not organically connected to it. This special status becomes virtually a textbook example of cultural lag when state-owned radio stations and state-owned opera houses, both of which are owned by the "tax payer," have a very difficult time organizing joint projects. (The many conflicts in Paris and Vienna involved in planning opera broadcasts and opera productions for television are cases in point.)

Responsibility of Cultural Policy

The picture of this mutation in our musical life would not be complete without mentioning the economic vulnerability of the performing arts and the failure of the media to adapt their structure to the reality that the performing arts are threatened. No cultural policy that professes to be democratic can completely ignore the connection between the audiovisual media and cultural development. Sociology has the task of showing the connection and characterizing the nonadaptation. The elimination of this "cultural lag," this nonadaptation, implies a whole series of organizational, legal, and administrative measures. That it is impossible to assess whether these measures can be achieved does not alter the diagnosable contradiction between the structure of the institutions and the possibilities they objectively offer.

The problem, however, goes beyond the external conditions of musical communication to the very nature of this communication. The marriage of convenience between the media and music produces, as can already be predicted, new and presumably aesthetically fruitful types of musical communication. The surrender of the performing arts to the technological media opens new creative forms, enabling hitherto little-used methods of urgency and directness to penetrate into the most intimate sphere of individual lives and giving the performing arts a place in the media reality, which today — as many studies have shown — is more real than actual reality.

Adorno rightly answered traditional reservations that media music is unable to create for the listener a meaningful relationship to music by saying that this thesis has not been proved. "Whether today one's immediate presence at performances will still assure a more vivid relation to music than will the mass media — this would have to be investigated in very carefully planned, qualitatively accentuated researches" (Adorno 1976, 130).

The side effects of the present mutation in musical practice show us that, on the whole, the technological media have not been detrimental to musical activity and interest in music. One suspects the opposite.

This makes music's nonadaptation to the media potential, a feature of the present mutation, all the more important.

Aesthetic Potential of the Mass Media

An awareness of the "cultural lag" resulting from the technological reproduction of art was evident as early as the 1930s. Walter Benjamin (1892–1940), in an essay published in the *Zeitschrift für Sozialforschung* in 1936, discussed the fate of the work of art in the age of its technological reproducibility. (Benjamin 1963). Benjamin's analysis is remarkable for his historical view of the phenomenon. Using Alois Riegl's view on the change of artistic intent, Benjamin develops the idea that human sensory perception is not only naturally but historically determined (Benjamin 1963, 17). He carefully weighs what the work of art has lost by being reproducible (its "aura," its "uniqueness," its "cult value") and what it has gained (new ways of perception not "naturally" accessible and new situations not open to the original). Reproduction enables the object to approach the viewer,

> be it in the form of a photograph or in that of a phonograph record. The cathedral leaves its place to be accepted into the studio of an art lover; the choral work, which was performed in a hall or outdoors, is heard in a room. (Benjamin 1963, 15)

Although Benjamin's argumentation is largely based on the development of film, and although his reflections end in questionable political statements, his idea is of fundamental significance. He was the first one to demonstrate systematically that the technical transmission of art contains a utilizable new potential and that an investigation of this potential could and should supplant lamentations about the decline of art.

Culture Industry

It is necessary today to recall this "optimistic" view because the "pessimistic" estimates of the mutation brought about by technology still have the upper hand. These negative appraisals are oriented toward the industrialization of art and, most of all, toward the surrender of music to technology, which manufactures products for mass consumption. The pessimists are disturbed by the abandonment of art to the "culture industry," and to a certain extent rightly so.

The term "culture industry" to designate the technological-industrial complex supplying mass-media products may have been first used in this sense in *Dialektik der Aufklärung* [Dialectic of the Enlightenment] by Max Horkheimer and Theodor W. Adorno, originally published in

1947. A chapter of this book (Horkheimer 1971, 108ff.) is devoted to describing a monster, industrially produced "mass deception." In his subsequent *Résumé über Kulturindustrie* [Resumé of the Culture Industry], Adorno gave a concise definition of this phenomenon:

> The overall effect of the culture industry is that of an anti-Enlightenment; in it, Enlightenment, that is, the progressive technological control of nature, becomes, as Horkheimer and I called it, mass deception, a means of shackling the mind. It prevents the formation of autonomous, independent, consciously aware, and deciding individuals (Adorno 1967a, 69).

This basic view of social critique also entered Adorno's thought on socio-musicology.

Chapter 26 *Theodor W. Adorno*

Theodor W. Adorno (1903–1969) was, as he himself stated, "never impartial in matters concerning the arts" (Adorno 1968b, 81). Adorno's attitude was thus different from that of Max Weber, who was concerned with "understanding" social activity. Adorno brought an emphatic tone to sociology, a new language which was soon imitated in German-speaking countries. He employed a vocabulary derived from Hegel's works and an often difficult syntax in order to adequately express complexity. His use of language could also be used to obfuscate simple circumstances, though anyone who has absorbed Hegel's *Logic* and *Aesthetics* as a young person will have very few difficulties reading Adorno's writings. It is, however, regrettable that Adorno never made it easy for the reader to get to the rational heart of his thoughts. Nonetheless, it is clear that Adorno's way of expressing himself forms an integral part of what he wished to say. Anyone who is able to listen to Adorno as Thomas Mann listened to him must realize this. (It is a well-known fact that Thomas Mann's novel *Doctor Faustus* is permeated with a number of Adorno's ideas). This, then, is why it seems unjust that, in a letter to Josef Rufer dated 5 December 1949, Arnold Schoenberg accused Adorno's *Philosophy of Modern Music* of being nothing but a scholarly show concealing a lack of ideas behind "quasi-philosophical jargon." Were one to strip Adorno's ideas on music of their philosophical garb, a wealth of individual thoughts would remain, yet they would lack not only their dress but their philosophical body.

This is not the place for an exposition of Adorno's philosophy. I am simply interested in singling out several ideas from Adorno's writings on socio-musicology that have influenced and still influence the fortunes of the discipline. The writings on music take up a large portion of Adorno's collected works (the complete edition begun in 1970 is planned to reach twenty-three volumes). Every attempt to classify Adorno's sociology of music systematically is doomed to failure, as the author did not bequeath a system. He deemed it more productive to offer models of socio-musicological knowledge than to create a survey of the subject and its methods. In Adorno's opinion, such an attempt all too easily exhausts itself in "the pomposity of an academic establishment that goes so far as to convert keeping one's eyes shut into a virtue of incorruptible objectivity" (Adorno 1959, 10). On the other hand, the writer who wishes to do justice to Adorno's sociology of music runs up against a difficulty aptly described by Kurt Oppens: "How can one make this extraordinary work speak? By standing to one side and reporting, one intolerably simplifies; by selecting this or that, one misrepresents. There is only one way to communicate—by raising objections" (Oppens 1968, 15). In my opinion it would be more fruitful to call on Adorno as a witness concerning those problems of socio-musicology and those models of socio-musicological knowledge that he dealt with thoroughly. I have applied this method a number of times in previous chapters. The result is what I would like to call a "guide to reading Adorno," a kind of compass with which to find our way more easily.

Idiosyncrasies

Of course, owing to Adorno's idiosyncrasies, the compass must be constructed in such a way as to take into account the erratic movements of the needle. One of these idiosyncrasies, for example, is his vehement rejection of the work of Stravinsky, Hindemith, and Sibelius stemming from his support for Schoenberg and his school. In 1932 Adorno described their music as "not submitting unconditionally to market laws" (Adorno 1973a, 157). From the beginning he considered this relative immunity to the pernicious influences of the capitalist environment as a criterion of music worth supporting. At the beginning of Adorno's career his argumentation was still permeated with Marxist thoughts and Marxist vocabulary; later, he increasingly utilized a philosophical terminology that less clearly betrayed its origins. The apodictic character of his early writings on the sociology of music was transformed into a juggling of often ambiguous terms.

Adorno's Concept of "Material"

A striking example of this transformation is Adorno's use of the word "material" in his writings on music. In an essay published in 1930 entitled *Reaktion und Fortschritt* [Reaction and Progress], he uses this term to develop a view quite close to the ideas of Max Weber:

> Progress in art is not manifested in individual works but in their material. For unlike the twelve semi-tones with their overtone relationships traced by physics, this material is not by nature unalterable and the same at all times. (Adorno 1930, 191)

This statement would lead one to surmise that Adorno equates the concept of material with the selection of those tones in the continuum used musically. It was but a short step to the realization that the tempered twelve-note scale familiar to us is a product of history. Yet Adorno did not immediately take this step. A 1932 statement clearly shows that he had a different understanding of "material": "The material of trivial music is the outdated or debased material of art music" (Adorno 1973a, 194). In this instance, "material" is given a particular meaning, including its use. Yet the reader of Adorno's writings should not feel comfortable with this interpretation because he constantly surprises with new nuances. At one point Adorno contrasts compositional intent with compositional material (Adorno 1968b, 41) only to insist immediately afterwards on the "imminent demands of the material" and finally once again calling the compositional material "historical material." In an essay from the sixties Adorno once again makes distinction between "material, idiom, and technique" (Adorno 1968b, 105) without supplying the reader with precise definitions of these terms. Readers who were used to regarding Schoenberg's dodecaphony as a "technique" are then told that the twelve-tone principle is a "partial reorganization of the material" (Adorno 1968b, 108). Adorno then goes on to distinguish material from materiality, completely reducing it to the spiritual principle of use, by contrasting "tonality" with "today's emancipated material," namely "the twelve equal tempered semitones" (Adorno 1968b, 118).

This inconstant terminology makes it hard for even the well-disposed reader to follow Adorno's thoughts. The reader is required to imagine the ambiguous use of terms in such a way as to read them in context. The temptation not to do so leads to the risk of overlooking Adorno's most crucially important contributions to the theory of tonal material. At times these are concealed, as in a discussion of Paul Hindemith's *Craft of Musical Composition*, for example. With a reference to Max Weber, Adorno calls "the rationalization of the physical tones through tempered tuning a conscious intervention in the natural material" (Adorno 1968b, 71), adding that such an intervention becomes an "impediment to musical production" at a certain phase in history. This is one of the rare and highly significant passages in his writings where he hints at an analysis of "material" in its historical dimension and goes beyond his artificial formulation of the term "material."

The Resilience of Tonality

My attempt to illustrate the difficulty of understanding Adorno because of his changing use of a word also serves a didactic purpose. It is intended to help immunize the reader against Adorno's numerous imitators, who have adopted the vagueness of his terminology without assuming his broad outlook on the history of philosophy. These disciples of Adorno usually devote their attention to the master's social criticism, which they try hard to patch up with musical aspects. They cling to the doctrinaire aspects of Adorno's *answers* and deal less with his frequently much more profound *questions*, for example, his thesis of the "irrevocable collapse of tonality" (Adorno 1968b, 140). This assertion is explained by Adorno's origins in the Schoenberg school (he was a student of Alban Berg) as well as his profound sympathy with the musical avant-garde of the fifties and sixties. Yet this position is hard to maintain if we are willing to heed the remarkable vitality that has been retained by tonality, which has spread far during the last forty years— even into the centers of musical culture in the Third World. Whether this is to be welcomed or regretted is another matter. Music sociologists are interested in explaining this phenomenon.

Adorno addressed the issue through what he called the resilience of tonality—the fact that, although it is a social product, chordal-harmonic tonality appears to have gained autonomous power over people:

> In the musical preconscious and in the collective unconscious, tonality seems to have become second nature despite the fact that it is also a cultural product. This should explain the great resistance in the mind of the listener to grasping structures which, in their turn, are the quite consistent and necessary consequences of the evolution of tonality as a musical language. In order to visualize the difficulties in grasping modern music, one must submit the opposite question: where does the resilience of tonality as a musical language originate. (Adorno 1968b, 117)

Adorno's observation opens a wide area of research in socio-musicology and the psychology of music. It has hardly been explored, although the fruits of such work would surely be of great interest to ethnomusicology and communication studies, cultural policy, and development policy. Of course, it is easier to accompany the creations of the musical avant-garde with torrents of sociological jargon derived from Adorno than to seek answers to Adorno's more profound questions. Finding answers requires empirical research, which cannot be replaced by philosophical speculation.

Philosophy and Empirical Survey

Adorno saw his philosophy of music—which makes up a considerable part of his sociology of music—not as standing in opposition to empirical studies but rather as a necessary corrective:

> I feel misunderstood when the publications I have written on the sociology of music since I returned from my emigration [1949] are regarded as opposed to empirical research. I would like to emphasize that I not only regard these methods as important within their area but appropriate as well. The entire production of the so-called mass media is a priori ideally suited to empirical methods. (Adorno 1967a, 95)

In my view, Adorno's importance for the sociology of music consists primarily in his ability to formulate questions of crucial significance to the discipline and his recognition of the need for interdisciplinary research. He regarded the pedantic delimitation of socio-musicology—something which the steadfast have been zealously engaged in for many years—as futile. He considered a view "which would like to oblige the sociology of art to survey effects" (Adorno 1967a, 97) to be inadmissible, because the most profound relations between art and society "take shape within the works of art themselves" (Adorno 1967a, 99). Thus he rejected a method that applies sociological categories to music without closer inspection and called for the sociology of music to deal not merely with the effects of music but with the music itself. It was not necessary for Adorno to force his sociological reasoning on music; he was able to derive it from the subject, from something close to his heart, from the music. His eminent knowledge of music—he also composed—enabled him to do so; and this fact certainly contributed to making him the dominant socio-musicologist of his time.

Pioneer of Research in Popular Music

The fact that Adorno was deeply committed to the advanced art music of his age did not prevent him from recognizing the tasks set for socio-musicology in the area of popular music. As early as 1932, he raised the question as to the musical conditions for identification with hit music in an essay *Zur gesellschaftlichen Lage der Musik* [On the Social Position of

Music], originally published in 1932 (Adorno 1973a, 198). In the study *On Popular Music* (Adorno 1973b, 66ff.), published in the United States in 1941, Adorno pins down through musical analysis the concrete elements of standardization and pseudo-individualization identifiable in a "hit." Even the idea that commercially produced musical entertainment provoked "analysis of musical goods" began with Adorno. In the *Introduction to the Sociology of Music* he once again deals with the specific effect of the self-imposed analytically verifiable elements of popular music: "The *effect* of hit songs—perhaps more precisely their social role—might be defined as that of patterns of identification" (Adorno 1976, 26). Adorno believed that these patterns would have to be demonstrated primarily through musical analysis and psychology, and that we still know too little about them owing to the "backwardness of techniques of socio-musicological investigation" (Adorno 1962, 38).

During the sixties Gunnar Sønstevold and I reacted to this challenge of Adorno's. We interpreted his thesis as a task to proceed from the analysis of written music to the analysis of the sound itself, because we surmised that the electroacoustical transformation of popular music, as the listener receives it from recordings, could be part of the "patterns of identification." When I told Adorno about this hypothesis, he encouraged me to study the particular aura of popular music created by electroacoustical manipulation and to become familiar with it technologically. He added, "I know that Benjamin would also have been very much in agreement" (letter dated 16 October 1962). Adorno considered the study that had come about owing to his encouragement (Sønstevold 1968) important enough to mention in the second edition of *Introduction to the Sociology of Music* as "more detailed concrete analyses of hit songs and mechanisms of identification" (Adorno 1968a, 242 n.).

This was, however, simply the first step in a trend toward the sociological analysis of popular music that Adorno had sketched for over thirty years. In general, however, he had opened the way to including the analysis of electroacoustical communication in socio-musicology. It was only this falling in with the new line of vision traced by the technological media that made it possible to organize the studies on the rock movement whose results were published during the seventies (Blaukopf 1974, Bontinck 1974). These studies owe not only their initial impulse but also their sociological framework to the ideas of Walter Benjamin and, still more, Adorno.

Adorno's writings are filled with impulses and questions of this kind. Even when we are unable to follow Adorno, for example in his highly subjective "types of musical behavior" (Adorno 1976, 1–20), one can feel the creative challenge to continue his thoughts by correcting them. Access to his thought has been made more difficult by the fact that Adorno was not a builder of systems but a philosophizing essayist. Yet those who can be less concerned with seeking formal perfection in his aperçus than with understanding the ideas hidden behind the verbal facade will discover a wealth of suggestions. Adorno's uniqueness may consist in his style, yet his real achievement lies behind it in the concrete treatment of individual questions of socio-musicology. Those who read Adorno's works attentively will find more insights than those I have mentioned in this chapter.

Chapter 27 *Ideological Harmonization*

Many socio-musicologists are content simply to analyze the coherence between artistic activity and the characteristic social features of an epoch. Once difficulties arise in unraveling the connective threads between social structure and musical behavior, analogy is applied. This method is ideally suited to creating plausible parallels of the type: "conditions prevailing in area Y are the same as those prevailing in area X." Whether the parallel is to economics or politics, or whether it takes its direction from the "spirit of the times," the method involves constructs which are, at best, legitimized through perceptive philosophical speculation.

Adorno's sociology of music is not immune to this method when, for example, he attempts to trace the resilience of tonality to a mechanism inherent in the market economy. According to Adorno, the tonal system has "the dignity of the closed and exclusive system of the barter society whose own dynamics seek totality and whose interchangeability profoundly agrees with all tonal elements" (Adorno 1958, 18). The "profound agreement"—an entirely legitimate hypothesis—is merely stated. It suggests a coherence whose probability remains to be demonstrated. Yet Adorno does not confine himself to creating a hypothetical coherence between tonal system and economy. In another passage he even attempts to create a connection between Schoenberg's music and modern physics:

For him [Schoenberg] tonality becomes a "special case" as Euclidean space was for Einstein. His music is, however, as certainly "classical" as, according to the most recent quantum physicists, the theory of relativity of classical physics. (Adorno 1959, 331)

Convincing as such parallels may occasionally be, it would be disastrous for music sociology to pin its hopes on them. It must be admitted, however, that the tendency to combine related or even disparate thoughts in a philosophical structure is a scientific tradition. What Thomas Kuhn (1976) calls "paradigms" are nothing more than the result of such structural combinations, creating a mental link between elements whose ties are more subjective than demonstrated. Scientific theory has also recently emphasized the criterion of "external consistency"; evaluating a scientific theory or hypothesis requires, for example, "agreement . . . with other recognized theories" (Frey 1977, 245). This need for support, as I will call it, is entirely consistent with the inclination of researchers, who otherwise try to proceed without premises. It is precisely this tendency to consistency which evokes the danger that science may attribute less importance to what is empirically verifiable than to the internal consistency of a system. In fact, the danger even occasionally exists that attention may be diverted from an empirical finding that is in apparent conflict with the chosen system of thought. Charles Darwin convincingly described this mechanism in his autobiography, writing that he had to immediately write down every observation that did not agree with his ideas to avoid the risk of forgetting it (cf. Prenant 1946, 64). This danger arises from the fact that, wishing to "harmonize" our knowledge and experiences, we seek a common denominator for all our conduct. The French literary sociologist Lucien Goldmann states that "all people strive to link their thought, feeling, and behavior into a meaningful, coherent structure" (Goldmann 1978, 116).

Although the sociology of music must refrain from a premature harmonization of this kind (which is difficult enough, given the natural inclination to consistency), preferring the approach suggested by Darwin, it also has the task of investigating ideological harmonizations. In other words, ideological harmonization must not be allowed to become a *method* of socio-musicology. It is, however, a *topic* of this discipline.

The Creative Role of "Error"

Ideological harmonization of disparate elements can occasionally play a highly creative role in the arts, although it is often demonstrably "false" in objective terms. Thus, for example, a number of manifestations of serious music in the twentieth century have been led by attempts to ideologically harmonize misunderstandings about cybernetics, computer science, and psychophysics with vague aesthetic or sociological ideas. Critics may find it useful to prove the "error" of such constructions (see Schügerl 1962), yet this does not hit what music sociology must aim at—the social genesis of such "error" and the inherent aesthetic force behind it. Socio-musicology is charged with investigating precisely this genesis. It does not begin by claiming to test the correctness of an ideological harmonization but by aiming to understand it. Regardless of what went into the makeup of Richard Wagner's ideology (nationalism and incorrect interpretations of Germanic mythology, the festival idea, and the idea of the state), these are not a subject of sociological criticism but of analysis. A similar case might be the meaning of numerology for the Schoenberg school, which has been little studied to date. Irrelevant as this may have been for the reception of the works, it provides a key to understanding these compositions.

The importance of ideological harmonization is easier to discern from a certain historical distance. The task of erecting an intellectual framework for the Medieval theory of consonance was made possible by utilizing the corresponding theological framework. The thesis that there can only be three perfect consonances (octave, fourth, fifth) was based, inter alia, on the fact that these three intervals were a "reflection of the holy trinity." Of course, argumentation of this kind is not cogent to our way of thinking, yet an understanding sociology must take into account the power of this argumentation under the prevailing circumstances of the times. The ideological vitality inherent in the concept of the trinity was also crucial for the viability of a theory of consonance based upon it.

Reality of Ideal Constructs

The phenomenon of ideological harmonization is characterized by socially evident, or socially valid, ideas combined with no logical connection. This leads to a mosaic of ideas that support one another. Single ideas receive further energy from their fusion into a philosophical structure; the self-evidence of the philosophical mosaic is also transmitted to the individual parts. The attempt to question one idea is made more difficult by resistance from the entire philosophical mosaic. Should this internal resistance combine with the interests of a dominant social stratum, it is further reinforced. Quite apart from this, however, an ideologically harmonized system is resilient because the mental definition of a situation also has practical consequences for behavior. A pioneer of American sociology, William I. Thomas (1863–1947), goes so far as to attribute real consequences to ideal constructs: "When men define a situation as real this has consequences in reality" (quoted in Bernsdorf 1959, 565; also cf. Merton 1965, 144).

The most famous example of the durability of an ideological mosaic is the geocentric cosmological model. The battle against the attempt to replace it with the "Copernican" system was conducted, not with observations and experience, but with theological argumentation combined with the view of the earth as "center of the universe." Much the same applies to the Medieval theory of consonance. Theorists hesitantly and indirectly came to terms with the gradual acceptance of the third as a consonance in musical practice. A commendable table of this evolution (Gut 1976) shows this process. In the ninth and tenth century, the ditone (an interval somewhat close to our third) was not yet considered a consonance. By about 1100 we find the ditone described as an "imperfect consonance." This classification stood for a long time (with exceptions toward the end of the twelfth century) until Bartolomé Ramos de Pareja described thirds and sixths as pure consonances in his treatise *Musica practica* of 1482.

World View and Experience

Ramos de Pareja's elevation of the third went hand in hand with a telling depreciation of the fourth to a dissonance. The theoretician proceeded from the changed practice and made a conscious break with traditional patterns. He describes the definition of intervals given by previous theoreticians as demanding and difficult to understand. "He rejected the customary trust in authority and sought to find purely empirical, practical solutions for the problems which occupied the musicians and composers of his time" (Palisca in MGG 10, 1911).

It is not surprising that this attempt to leave a firmly-rooted philosophical mosaic resulted in animated discussions. They show how intensely musical thought (which must also determine musical activity to a not inconsiderable extent) was dominated by a philosophical system whose stability was derived from a coherence evident to the epoch and that was, in turn, the result of previous ideological harmonization. The thinkers between the Middle Ages and the Renaissance were all confronted with the coherence of what we would today call a "world view." That is why the new definition of consonances not only had to change the way individual facts were represented but had to revolt against the inertia of a universal ideology.

Seen in historical perspective, Ramos de Pareja's conception seems to be a reaction to the changed musical practice, which had not yet been adequately reflected in musical thought. Such a reaction, however, was made possible by the changed conditions of scientific thought, far too

numerous to mention here. It became increasingly difficult to harmonize new facts with the traditional philosophical structure. This situation characterizes the crisis of musical thought, which was similar to the
roughly contemporary crisis of astronomical thought. The situation of
the geocentric astronomy of the time has been called "scandalous"
(Kuhn 1970, 67). Nicholas Copernicus (1473–1543) had prepared the
solution to the crisis in 1514 by accepting the heliocentric system. The
line of thought taken by Ramos de Pareja had one thing in common
with that of Copernicus: the abandonment of a philosophical structure
produced by ideological harmonization, by a "paradigm" created from
the joining together of different ideas. Thus Erich M. von Hornbostel's
description of the gradual rise of harmonic polyphony as "nothing
short of a Copernican revolution" (Hornbostel 1927, 443) is not at all
metaphoric.

Old Paradigms, New Paradigms

Certainly the increased use of observation in the natural sciences and
of sensory perception in musical theory was crucial to this revolution.
It must be said, however, that this did not put an end to the tendency
toward ideological harmonization. As is characteristic of all revolutions
of thought and action, the one we are dealing with aimed beyond just
overcoming a traditional, coherent structure of ideas to developing, at
the same time, new coherences. "The decision to reject one paradigm is
always simultaneously the decision to accept another" (Kuhn 1970, 76).
This can also be seen in Ramos de Pareja's treatise, in which he is
inclined to support his musical ideas with astronomical reflections,
equating the consonances with the distances between the planets. Here
as well, in the Copernican change of musical thought, we not only
encounter the appeal to sensory perception and the rejection of traditional paradigms but also the desire to tie new ideas together in a system to be harmonized with a more comprehensive, more coherent
mosaic of ideas.

Puritanism and Music

Musical thought and activity obey the impulse to harmonization. This
desire can be demonstrated in many constructions of music theory, up
to our century. At times this tendency is also the emanation of the social
function of music itself. I have already mentioned the example of St.
Augustine's views on the musical liturgy (cf. chapter 18). In his study
Protestant Ethics and the Spirit of Capitalism, Max Weber pointed out that
religiously conceived ethics could also be decisive in social activity for

a European society after ca. 1500. The Reformation, which brought rational Christian asceticism "out of the monasteries into secular professional life" (Weber GARS 1, 117, note 2), was also suited to changing musical practice (Weber GARS, 1, 185, note 1). Critics of Weber have objected that Protestant ethics alone could not have caused this change—something he never claimed—but that economic aspects of capitalist industrialization must have been of decisive importance, most of all the insistence on thrift in the interest of the accumulation of capital. This view seems to be confirmed by Percy Scholes's comprehensive study on the attitude of the Puritans to music. Scholes has shown that English Puritanism of the sixteenth and seventeenth century was, for the most part, not hostile to music (Scholes 1969, 345) and that this alleged typically Puritan hostility to music did not appear until the end of the eighteenth century (Scholes 1969, 349). Nonetheless, one can recognize, as did Weber, that Puritan morality was suited to developing an industrialization whose rationality was hostile to art. The ideological harmonization that took place resulted from fusing the idea of a religious-methodic life with economic goals, from synthesizing predestination and economically legitimized asceticism. The task of describing these phenomena individually and comparing them with Weber's theories still remains to be done; in addition to Scholes's works, recent English musicology has provided rich material on this subject.

Genetic Link

A distinction must be made between direct technical coherence and the coherence resulting from ideological harmonization. For example, it would be incorrect to regard the connection made in ancient Chinese thought between the perfection of the tonal system and the perfection of the order of the state merely as the fruit of ideological harmonization, because we know today that the ancient Chinese tonal system was placed in a rational relationship to the system of weights and measures. The Austrian sociologist Otto Neurath pointed out the difference between direct-technical coherence and other kinds of coherence:

> The wearing of precious stones is usually consistent with a way of life founded on magic. Once the magic period is past there remains a delight in precious stones which can later be replaced by a delight in brightly-colored glass. Such glass jewelry is related to many social institutions. It is meaningless to consider them from the present situation as helping life rather than tracing them back to a time in which they appeared as the extrapolations of a real habit. (Neurath 1931, 99)

Socio-musicologists will not be able to avoid including "fossil" remainders of ancient practices in analysis. Not everything that takes places in a given musical practice can be derived from the general social conditions of the time; much of it will require an historical-genetic explanation. Adorno opposed treating this as a problem:

> At times the genetic contexts are so complex that all attempts to disentangle them remain idle and leave room for innumerable other interpretations. More essential than what comes whence, however, is the content: how society appears in music, how it can be read in its texture. (Adorno 1976, 218)

Rejecting attempts at genetic explanation may be problematic, because it appears to lend too little social weight to tradition. It will be necessary in each case to study the importance of traditional patterns of action and thought, especially where national traditions are of importance to such patterns. This could count, for example, when ideologies are themselves at the center of a process of harmonization, as in the formation of a distinct Soviet musical policy and musical aesthetics since the 1930s, for example.

Musical Policy Under Stalin

Although this view of music, imposed by decree, had more rigorous consequences on European history than many Church pronunciamentos, it has not yet been investigated, as far as I can tell, from both the social and genetic points of view. Most accounts are content with understandably irate polemics or, at best, with merely documenting the topic. Adorno went a step further, indicating what I call ideological harmonization. He pointed out that this state view of music "places elements of truth in the service of ideology" (Adorno 1956a, 47). This musical policy amounted to a regimentation not only of artistic creativity but of all musical life. The astonishing part of it was not, for example, the idea of creating a bridge between the composer and his public—because this held an "element of truth"—but the arrogance with which politicians set about creating criteria for musical creation. The resulting demand for "understandable" music "close to the people" created a great many difficulties for composers such as Shostakovich and Prokofiev. Deviation from these rules was not only considered implicitly but expressly hostile to the people and the state.

It has correctly been pointed out that the ideological attacks by the party and the state cannot be explained by the conditions of Soviet musical life during this period alone, but that they were part of a campaign that began with philosophy, literature, and the visual arts, which was only extended to music in its final phase (Werth 1949, 17–18). This, too, indicates the tendency to harmonization, the desire to bring various areas of cultural activity into line with basic philosophical views and thereby into agreement with the ruling political ideology. Still the motives are to be found not only in a striving for harmonization but far more in politics. The political maxims of a dictatorship are not only meant to affect the administration of art but are supplemented by an aesthetic conception tailored to this practice; its most pregnant and fearful expression was formulated in the order of the ruling political party (the decree of 10 February 1948).

The attempt to analyze this process demands not only taking into account the political situation of Soviet society under Stalin but also a genetic aspect—the national Russian tradition. This tradition contains an element of revolt against the autonomy of art, an element that did not begin with Tolstoy.

The beginnings of such a sociological-genetical explanation can be found in a study by Iván Vitányi (1968). Vitányi indicates the origin of anti-aesthetic dogmas in the philosophy of Pierre-Joseph Proudhon (1809–1865), whose long-ignored 1865 book on the sociology of art is now available in reprint (Proudhon 1971). As Vitányi shows, political Proudhonism, combatted by Marx, also had parallel movements in nineteenth-century Russia. Proudhon's views on aesthetics, in turn, corresponded to Tolstoy's famous essay *What is Art?* Vitányi concludes that

> there can be no doubt that the one-sidedness of [the Stalin era's] dogmatic cultural policy agrees with the line described by Proudhon; this means that its appearance was not wholly the fruit of a despotic figure, but the result of historical and social motives attributable to a transitional period. (Vitányi 1968, 337–338)

Vitányi's analysis certainly does not exhaust this theme. Yet it has the merit of attempting to represent the rise of a new cultural and musical ideology as a process that can be explained socially and genetically, rather than merely as the result of the evil (or good) deeds of single figures. Socio-musicological research which undertakes such tasks therefore enters contemporary history with all its attendant risks. (It is no accident that the Russian tradition of socio-musicology was interrupted during the Stalin period.)

The relationship between the sociology of music and musical policy is different when democratic rules are observed. Increasingly the cultural policy of a large number of states no longer merely condones the existence of socio-musicology but expects it to provide them with knowledge that could serve cultural policy. By being called upon to provide assistance in making cultural policy decisions, the sociology of music has recently been compelled to develop new questions and new methods with which to answer them.

Chapter 28 New Tasks for the Sociology of Music

The history of socio-musicology I have sketched in this book is rich in attempts to develop suitable methods for the discipline. In recent decades, new and immediately practical tasks have come increasingly to the fore, in addition to theoretical concerns. Many countries have expressed goals in the furtherance of culture and art, raising questions whose answers are increasingly expected to be provided by sociological research. The search for measures to ease the access to art and to further general participation in cultural life presupposes a knowledge of data and facts characterizing the state of cultural life. Since the sixties this has led many countries to conduct empirical surveys of a largely descriptive nature which I call "sociographic" studies.

Sociography of Musical Life

Inventories of musical life have been taken for some time. The musical travel journals of the eighteenth and nineteenth century (Burney, Reichardt, Stendhal, Berlioz, and others) supplied sociographical material still of use to historical research. In this regard, Rudolf Flotzinger (1979, 22) recalled that Carl Maria von Weber wrote *Ideen zu einer musikalischen Topographie Deutschlands* [Ideas for a Musical Topography of Germany] in 1811 as a contribution to the contemporary history of music and as orientation "for traveling musicians."

Paul Bekker's *Das deutsche Musikleben* [German Musical Life], published in 1916, represents an attempt to paint a general picture of a country's musical life. Bekker endeavored to "grasp [musical life] as a *whole* and to determine its cultural foundation so as to use this knowledge in obtaining a scale with which to evaluate isolated phenomena and their conditions of development" (Bekker 1916, 3–4). This attempt, which the author calls sociological, still offers useful points of departure. Bekker's definition of "musical life" is, however, questionable. He takes musical life as "the sum of all phenomena of public and private cultivation of music in which our relationship to the musical art is expressed in an organized fashion" (Bekker 1916, 35–36). The term "musical art" (*Tonkunst*) indicates a restriction to works of art music. However, as understood today, sociography encompasses the full range of musical practice, from folk music to the "mesomúsica" influenced by the technical media of urbanized society. Scholars have pointed this out a number of times in connection with the inventory approach and structural analysis (cf. Reinecke 1971, 5).

There is some justification in objections to turning sociography, as an inventory of musical life, into a science independent of sociology (Silbermann 1981). Of course, the underlying interdisciplinary approach should prevent sociography from becoming independent and should show that it is merely meant as a part of sociology, a method for producing data and facts that serve the sociology of music.

The principal utility of sociography lies in the collecting and ordering of information about musical practice that helps in analyzing the structure of each practice. The available means run from musical statistics "as part of social statistics" (Wilzin 1937, 12), to surveys limited in space and time such as those employed by ethnomusicology, to surveys encompassing all population groups, all genres of music, and every kind of involvement with music, which have been aptly called "socio-musicological aerial photographs" (Sokhor 1977, 75).

Inventories of this kind can provide the basis for research to attain the overall organic picture to which Paul Bekker aspired and which I call *structural analysis*. There are good practical reasons for keeping sociographic inventory and music sociology separate. It has been shown time and again that the collection of facts and data cannot be managed by the means of socio-musicology alone; help is required from other disciplines. To name only one example, an "aerial photograph" of present-day musical life is not possible without the information that can be provided by communication specialists on the evolution of media technology, by jurists on changes in copyright laws, by economists on musical production and the music trade, and by sociologists on the scope and use of leisure time.

Another task that socio-musicology has been expected to address resulted from the changed importance of music in the educational system and cultural life owing to technological changes. Because of their practical experience, music teachers chiefly felt the need to study these problems. Thus it was that the International Society for Music Education (ISME) reached the decision in 1976 to found a Commission for Music in Cultural, Educational, and Mass Media Policies, largely consisting of socio-musicologists, which has been active since that time. (See, inter alia, ISME Year Books, vol.III, 1975/76, vol.X, 1983, vol.XII, 1985 and vol. XIV, 1987).

The interest of music educators in these types of questions is easy to explain. For a long time they applied methods from a period in which the electronic media were not dominant. During the preelectronic age, the musical experience of children and young people was limited to live music. At that time, the educators who were entrusted with entering into the immediate experiences of their learners more or less knew the musical environment of children and young people. This changed with the spread of the electronic media, with the availability of new electronic musical instruments, and with the formation of pop and rock groups which not only presented themselves as professional ensembles but also as models followed by countless semiprofessional and amateur groups. Music sociologists have concerned themselves with these new patterns of musical behavior by the younger generation in industrial societies since the early 1970s (cf. Bontinck 1974), also investigating some questions touching music pedagogy, such as:

1. How can music education take into account the emotional needs stimulated and/or satisfied by the electronic media?
2. How can music education react to the changing musical environment of students?
3. What is the relationship between the acceleration of the biological development of young people and the acceleration of changes to the musical environment (soundscape)?
4. What influence do the electronic media have on the musical experiences of children before entering school, and to what extent can education make use of this?

A group of researchers from eighteen industrialized countries asked such questions as early as 1972 (cf. Bontinck 1974, 159–200), resulting in a vast number of studies documenting the concern not only of sociologists but of music educators as well.

I mention this because it seems to prove that the rapid growth of socio-musicology is not due entirely to academic motives. Immediately practical questions have also played a role: the search for suitable pedagogic orientation in the present-day technological and social mutation of musical life; the search by state, regional, and local authorities for measures to improve access of the populace to music and to improve participation in musical life; the attempt to define the influence on musical life of the electronic media and the legal provisions applying to it.

This concern with contemporary problems that started in the seventies has brought what had been a primarily theory-oriented discipline closer to the practical problems of musical life. It is worth taking a closer look at the resultant interplay between cultural, educational, and media policy on the one hand and the sociology of music on the other. Although socio-musicology and musical life had different points of departure, the present-day mutation of musical life has become the main field of interest for music sociology. The following countries, arranged alphabetically, offer a few examples that illustrate this fact. I have limited my selection to countries in which the sociology of music is already established or about to come into being.

Austria

Undertaking to create a "catalogue for cultural policy action," the Federal Ministry of Education and Art initiated a study on the country's cultural behavior (IFES 1975). This survey, in some ways inadequate for music, was supplemented by analyses of the musical behavior of young people (Bontinck 1974, Blaukopf 1974) and by regional inventories (Deutsch 1975, 1976, and 1978). Studies of this kind revealed a new development trend—the apparently spontaneous growth of amateur musical activities. In light of the many predictions that home musical activities would decline as a result of the growth of media music, this was a challenge to more closely investigate the importance of the electronic media for musical practice.

The Viennese Institute for the Sociology of Music, founded in 1965, devoted itself to this task. It also dealt, among other things, with the social status of composers (Bontinck et al. 1984); the influence of media on established musical life (Bontinck 1986); the interaction of the mass media, musical policy, and music education (Ostleitner 1987); the change of listening behavior owing to the influence of the electronic media (Bontinck 1988); the relationship of musical institutions to the electronic media (Blaukopf 1990); and the predictable need for music teachers, given the growing demand for music instruction (Mark 1990). These studies were oriented toward the ideas developed by Guido Adler as well as the sociological concepts of Max Weber. Helmut Staubmann (1988) has pointed out this particular feature of Austrian socio-musicology. Some of the works of the Institute for the Sociology of

Music were published as part of a series (*Musik und Gesellschaft* 1967–). These helped to clarify the concept of "mutation" and need not be described in detail here, as they form the basis of this book.

Belgium

A Centre d'études de sociologie de la musique was created at the Université Libre de Bruxelles in 1964, with the musicologist Robert Wangermeé as director. Wangermeé's publications reveal the wide range of topics he has covered, including the influence of the electronic media and the economics of musical institutions (Vanhulst/Haine 1988, 13–22). Wangermeé has not only enriched the discipline with his own research but helped to create a scientific climate in which a variety of current topics could be treated: the "mediatization" of music and recording companies (de Coster 1975, 1976), the strategies of the phonograph and audio-visual industries (Lange 1986, 1988, 1990), the role of music videos (Leclercq 1990), and so on.

Wangermeé's long experience as researcher, teacher, and television director has enabled him to participate in international studies and projects of the Council of Europe devoted to musical and cultural policy. One result of these activities is the most complete account to date of the conflict between culture and profits in the musical economy, prepared in conjunction with distinguished specialists (Wangermée 1990). The conclusions of this publication are of importance to research in a number of countries, providing an exhaustive analysis of the factors involved in the planning of musical policy.

Czechoslovakia

Despite the dominance of a political doctrine opposed to empirically oriented socio-musicology, several researchers managed to continue the native traditions in this discipline and carry out a series of projects during the sixties. The political difficulties associated with these aspirations were described by one of the protagonists of the movement who was forced to leave the country in 1968, working since then in Germany (Karbusicky 1975, 7–18). The astonishing development of socio-musicology during the sixties extended not only to empirical studies concerning, for example, music on the radio, or musical abilities and preferences, but also to the theoretical prerequisites of empirical research. A monograph published at the time (Fukač/Mokrý/Karbusicky 1967) included a bibliographical survey promising greater things to come.

These efforts were cut short by the Soviet invasion in 1968. Viewed in retrospect, these achievements of the sixties (later published) already reveal the restrictions placed on the writer, forcing him not to mention the names of authors who had fallen from official favor (Fukač 1972). Yet the statement that Czech socio-musicology was established during the sixties (Fukač 1972, 81) is accurate. It can be hoped that following the radical political changes of 1989 this discipline will be able to continue a tradition going back as far as Otakar Hostinský (1847–1910) and Vladimír Helfert (1886–1945) (cf. Fukač 1969).

France

Unlike many other countries with federal structures, France has a centralized system of cultural policy planning. This centralistic tradition led in the sixties to the attempt to compile statistical data on musical life (Société d'Economie 1967). This collection of data concerning "musical supply," "musical demand," and public expenditure for music was prompted by a government commission which had drawn up a catalogue of "problems of musical life" (Commission nationale 1964). The responsible ministry's establishment of a research department charged with collecting data and providing assistance in making cultural policy decisions turned out to be particularly fruitful for socio-musicology.

In 1974, this institution published a report on the cultural behavior of the population consisting of opinion poll results. The project attempted to justify itself by its benefit to cultural policy. Rather than subjective experiences and traditional methods, "rational" and "objective" findings were to furnish the basis for planning measures of cultural and art policy:

> Cultural life is burdened to such an extent with implicit value concepts, and cultural action is still so lacking in clear and coherent goals, that the objective can only be reached by means of quantified data, facts, and figures obtained by sociology. (Services des Études 1974, I, 2)

The nationwide surveys guaranteed French research a lead over the sociography of many other industrialized countries. Nonetheless, the limitations of such inventories were soon apparent. Although it was recognized that the knowledge of the structures of cultural life had been enriched by such "snapshots," it was also understood that further steps would have to be taken in order to grasp the mechanisms of the transformation of cultural life (Service des Études 1974, I, 181).

A single survey is not sufficient to trace these mechanisms. Not until the investigation is repeated at certain intervals can information be obtained about developmental trends. The French Ministry of Culture and Communication, in accord with this principle, repeated the first analysis of 1973 in 1981 and 1988–1989. The report concerning these three surveys confirms that technological improvements in audio and video over the sixteen-year period were accompanied by progressively increasing consumption of television and home music. This observation, which is also of importance for music, leads to the conclusion that the changes of cultural behavior are largely attributable to technological, economic, and social dynamics, and it is virtually impossible to influence this process with measures of cultural policy. The force of these dynamics is felt most of all in music, because the dissemination of the electronic media and the decrease in the prices of technical equipment change the musical practices of the populace more than any measure by the state (Donnat/Cogneau 1989, 6–7).

These results once again underscore the technological components of today's changes. The methodological significance of the surveys consists in the possibility that sociographical "snapshots" repeated at appropriate intervals may permit sociography to progress to sociology in the true sense of the word. Moreover, public-opinion analyses form the framework into which can be placed other studies, such as those on musical theater, concert audiences, the music industry, and "music of everyday life." Some of these studies have furthered the move from sociographic survey to theoretical reflection—particularly the work of Pierre-Michel Menger, who has analyzed the economic aspects of the existence of contemporary composers (Menger 1983) and the influence of new technologies on the change of the profession of composer (Menger 1989).

Germany

Interest in the sociographic aspects of musical life has been growing over the past decades. Cases in point are a study on the structure of the music market (Lachmann 1960) and two statistical surveys of professions in music (Sass/Wiora 1962 and 1969). The initiative for such studies often came from cultural policy rather than from academic research. In 1969, for example, the "structural analysis of German musical life" was judged to be an important task by the responsible ministers of the Länder. Their demand was met in 1973 by the Music in City Planning memorandum (Deutscher Musikrat [German Music Council], reports, bulletin no. 23), which identified themes requiring socio-musicological research. This impetus not only challenged the sociology of music to take a position but also directed the German government's attention to the economic and social situation of professions in the arts (Künstlerbericht [Artists' Report] 1975). The spectacular increase of literature during the seventies can no doubt be traced to this sensitization of the public to matters of cultural policy, for a considerable part of this literature is intended to be a tool for helping to make cultural policy decisions. Even ethnomusicology has been advised to concern itself with the musical practice of industrialized society. In the opinion of one German ethnomusicologist, field research should extend to the offices of music publishers and to the arts departments of radio and television companies. Ethnomusicologists would find these jungles no more penetrable than those in less researched areas outside of Europe (Klusen 1980, 15).

The growing interest in sociographic studies was largely answered by the survey of the Zentrum für Kulturforschung [Center for Cultural Research] in Bonn, which analyzed the status of music in statistics and cultural policy (Fohrbeck/Wiesand 1982) as well as the mutation of professions in music and the development of the job market (Wiesand 1984). Between 1984 and 1988 the Center devoted itself to the question of the influence of new technologies on musical creation, the dissemination of music, the activity of amateurs, and the reorientation of musical education. The report on this project (Wiesand 1989) provides material for answering the question about the significance of new technologies as tools for musicians and as means of distributing music.

Attention to contemporary questions has also had an effect on the development of theory. For example, the tools with which the problems of popular music were investigated have been considerably improved (cf. Rauhe 1974 and Flender/Rauhe 1989). Remarkably enough—and not only in Germany—the disciplinary fields of reference in sociology have been expanded, as stated by Vladimír Karbusicky in a critical survey. He cites the

> deepening of methodology by combining with aesthetic and psychological experimentation, the application of the theory of ideologies, the inclusion of mass musical culture, semiotics, the acculturation process pursued from an ethnological point of view, and similar transitional fields from socio-musicology to anthropology. (Karbusicky 1986, 35)

In the past, this trend existed in both Germanys, albeit with differences. The division of Germany from 1945 to 1990 has now ended, and the subordination of science to a political creed, as practiced in the German Democratic Republic, no longer exists. This might justify viewing the coming development of German socio-musicology as a unified whole. East German theoretical efforts in the sociology of music were not insignificant, as can be seen, for example, in the publications of Georg Knepler (1977) or Konrad Niemann (1980) and a number of other authors who, despite state control, exhibit independent, critical traits, proving once again that the spectacular political changes in 1989 had been prepared intellectually, if cautiously.

Most of all, this applies to an attempt by Christian Kaden (1984) to define socio-musicology. He considers sociology and historiography to be complementary disciplines. The desire to reduce socio-musicology to an auxiliary science carrying out what historiography has neglected runs the risk of saddling a lesser discipline with the burden musicology would have to carry as a whole (Kaden 1984, 22). Kaden negates the absolute autonomy of socio-musicology when he attempts to meet this demand by applying methods usually associated with other disciplines that he nonetheless wishes to see integrated into musicology. These methods include, for example, empirical-statistical surveys of the effect of rock music and information-theory analyses, of possible use in explaining the behavior of eleventh- and twelfth-century chroniclers writing neumes. Kaden's orientation toward methodology is linked to a careful avoidance of real or imagined hollow Marxian formulas. Furthermore, he admits that he does not consider his results to be perpetually valid; rather he views them as the draft of a research program to be carried out in teamwork by specialists.

Somewhat drastically put, the importance of this attitude to methodology is that it aspires to the "death of the sociology of music" as an autonomous discipline, while opening it to the entire field of musicology, which it floods with the many methods previously used to ensure a new life for socio-musicology. Similar programs were advocated earlier, yet it must be admitted that Kaden has managed to find valid reasons, which he has been able to apply convincingly in individual instances from Medieval music to contemporary mass musical culture. But whether his view will prevail depends less on its inner logic than on the ability of the established academic organization to adapt to this logic. At present there is little indication that this adaptation will be possible.

Great Britain

The fact has been deplored more than once that historically oriented musicology lacks the proper preparation to study contemporary popular music (cf. Flender/Rauhe 1989, 1). It is precisely in this area that British socio-musicology has made its most significant contributions. This is due not only to the country's scientific tradition but also to the dominant conditions in cultural policy.

Unlike many countries of continental Europe, Great Britain does not have a comprehensive government plan for furthering culture that might stimulate sociological research. Even the economic aspects of artistic life have been dealt with in relatively few studies (e.g., Blaug 1976, Myerscough 1988, Pick 1980, Priestley 1984). Activity in socio-musicology is becoming increasingly important (e.g., Peacock 1975, Leppert 1987), yet it seems that the sociology of music is not yet established in academic theory and research (Wolff 1987, 8).

One of the explanations may be that English musicology is traditionally oriented to deal with questions of socio-musicology only marginally or by way of exception. It is not surprising then that in England, of all places, the investigation of the spectacular development of popular music since the Beatles should have been initially left to sociologists. The concepts developed by the so-called Birmingham school of sociology brought about studies on new youth music (e.g. Frith 1978, Willis 1978). The sociological methods of participating observation were set against traditional academic research as a form of protest. The assertion was made, for example,

> that the most significant sociology of rock produced in Britain is not that produced in university departments or by academic research (there is, in fact, very little academic work being done on rock) but that produced by people making and listening to music, making sense of that music for themselves, in their own lives. (Frith 1982, 142–143)

Nonetheless, this attitude led to cooperation between some musicologists and sociologists and to innovative studies on popular music. Richard Middleton and David Horn began publication of the year book *Popular Music* (PM 1981), in which the ethnomusicologist John Blacking stated the thesis, remarkable for its agreement with the view of the sociologist Simon Frith, that "art does not consist of products, but of the processes by which people make sense of certain kinds of activity and experience" (Blacking in PM 1981, 12).

The editors of *Popular Music* are dedicated to the task of taking seriously the younger generation's fun with popular music. This difficult task is often met with typical British humor, emphasizing the distance between them and academic musicology. Richard Middleton, for example, declares his competence by handing out the following calling card: "Richard Middleton has been defined as a musicologist by the Universities of Cambridge and York, which tried to educate him, and by the Open University, which now employs him. Nevertheless, he tries to be human (PM 1983, IX)."

This statement has more than anecdotal value; it underscores the humanistic and interdisciplinary position that links ethnomusicologists to socio-musicologists. The articles published in *Popular Music* are proof of this. They not only deal with theoretical questions of analyzing popular music, as does Philip Tagg, an Englishman teaching at Gothenburg (PM 1982), but they also go into technological and legal aspects, as, for example, Simon Frith in his article "Copyright and Music Business," which reaches an important conclusion for contemporary socio-musicology: "For the music industry the age of manufacture is now over. Companies (and company profits) are no longer organized around making things but depend on the creation of *rights*" (Frith in PM 1988, 57).

British studies are not just concerned with the present, which is usually the center of interest for sociologists; they also attempt to examine past popular music, which in general had previously been dismissed by traditional musicology as "light music." Moreover, the role of popular music in non-Western cultures is discussed, providing important information about the present worldwide mutation.

Hungary

At an early stage, cultural research in this country became relatively independent of the influence of Soviet dogmatism. Research was performed on "everyday music" (Losonczsi 1969), and studies were carried out on "mesomúsica" with its dependence on new technologies. Pioneering work was done in studying the new role of rock music (Bacskai 1970, Vitányi 1977). Empirical surveys were placed within a theoretical framework that included not only music but "overall cultural activity" (Vitányi 1977). The sociographic element of these studies is unmistakable, because they take into account the group-specific aspects of cultural activities, the types of activities and attitudes, historical inventory, comparative analysis, cultural institutions, and even their economic aspects. The Budapest Institute for Cultural Research plays a leading role in this area with its efforts to go beyond simply describing to analyzing trends of development and tracking down their "inner motives" (Vitányi 1980a, 370). The results of this institute's cooperation with institutions and experts in many countries are partially documented in a series of publications in English (Culture and Communication, nos. 1–6, Budapest 1976–1988).

Italy

Sociographic surveys were initially undertaken because of the need to obtain reliable sources for subsidy policy. State support for musical institutions is regulated by Law no. 800 of 14 August 1967, which led to the creation of a "Musical Map of Italy" that lists these institutions and how much subsidy they receive (Associazione 1980). The tendency exists to supplement surveys of this kind with long-term studies in order to obtain data for "cultural observatories."

Italian sociology has also produced studies of popular music (e.g., Del Grosso Destreri 1970, 1972). These are aimed at "finding, through content analysis, suitable conceptual categories for registering the value and behavior patterns of the hit song as a form of mass communication" (Del Grosso Destreri 1972, 1). Methodological points of departure derive in part from Max Weber, whose concept has been described in detail (Morelli 1976). The theoretical framework has been organized in such a way as to serve the empirical investigation of the music education system. The Trent-based "Centro per l'educazione musicale e per la sociologia della musica" devoted itself to this task for a number of years (cf. Sorce Keller 1979). The stylistic changes in the oral tradition of Trentino Province was the topic of the dissertation that Italian musicologist and sociologist Marcello Sorce Keller wrote at the University of Illinois (Sorce Keller 1985). He is also responsible for fundamental reflections on the relationship between socio-musicology and ethnomusicology (Sorce Keller 1986). The connection between Italian research and the socio-musicology of other countries is dealt with in an anthology containing more than two dozen "classical" and new texts by non-Italians (Seravazza 1980).

An attempt by the University of Trieste to create a sociology of musical communication, dealing with the connection between musical expression and function, starts from theories of linguistic communication (Tessarolo 1983). The German philosopher Hegel, not Auguste Comte, is the starting point of a critical history of socio-musicological thought that also includes "contemporary sociological results of a theoretical nature" (Del Grosso Destreri 1988). A report in Italian and German on a socio-musicological conference also attended by German and Austrian researchers provides a survey of the state of research in Italy (Del Grosso Destreri 1989).

Soviet Union

There was a rich literature on the sociology of music in Russia during the twenties. A prominent example is a collection of essays entitled *Questions on the Sociology of Music* (1927). Written by A. V. Lunacharsky, the Communist people's commissar in charge of cultural policy, these essays dealt extensively with Max Weber.

Soon thereafter all sociology, including the sociology of music, fell into official disfavor. Lunacharsky's book was not reprinted until 1958; eventually it was published in an expanded new edition (Lunacharsky 1971) as a result of reawakened interest in socio-musicology. Sociological traditions were severed during the Stalin period, for they did not agree with official decrees that tried to dictate not only to scientists but to musicians as well. The only interpretation that remained in favor was the allegedly Marxian view of music as a simple reflection of social activity.

Even with the end of the Stalin Era there was no immediate return to the tradition of the twenties. One of the scholars who nonetheless devoted himself to this difficult task was Arnold N. Sokhor (1924–1977), active in Leningrad (St. Petersburg). His writings published outside the former Soviet Union (e.g., Sokhor 1974, 1975, 1977) hardly reveal what is fundamentally new in his thought. His innovation was the desire to look beyond, far beyond, the official view that music was nothing more than the reflection of social phenomena. This can clearly be seen in an essay Sokhor wrote together with Y. Kapustin that was not published until after Sokhor's death. The essay clearly approaches the idea that not only art music but all musical practice, including folk music and popular music, is the subject of socio-musicology (Sokhor 1980a, 129).

Beginning in the sixties—and not least of all owing to the influence of Sokhor—those responsible for musical life and musical education in the Soviet Union were also interested in finding out the preferences of the populace through opinion polls (Kapustin in Sokhor 1980b, 5). These empirical surveys were flawed, however, because the musicologists who turned to this activity had no sociological training. The difficulty of bringing sociology and musicology together can be read from the echo of an investigation of "music and listener" conducted in 1967 (Tsukkerman 1971 and 1972) in the cities of Sverdlovsk (Ekaterinburg) and Chelyabinsk. The survey of 8,000 music listeners, something new in the Soviet Union, suffered, as a team of Moscow experts showed, because the listeners were only asked "questions about music" and not given a "music preference test"; in other words, they were not confronted with music as such. For reasons presented in chapter 23, critics described this as the "most vulnerable spot in Tsukkerman's methodology" (Alexeyev 1974). Alexeyev and his colleagues, however, in developing their own method for investigating "mass musical taste" (Alexeyev 1979), slightly opened the door to "value-free" empirical surveys that had previously been impossible in the Soviet Union, given the official aversion to sociology in general. These surveys brought about recognition of the increasingly strong underground movements of youth music (rock and pop). The research of a Moscow group directed by G. Golovinsky and E. Alexeyev, underway since the seventies, was intended to gather information about this aspect of the "mass taste of Moscow youth" (cf. Kapustin 1983). It was revealed that what had begun in the Soviet Union as an "unofficial" rock movement owed its success to technology, that is, to the possibility of disseminating this music by tape copy (Golovinsky 1988, 61).

The overcoming of dogmatic ideologies begun by Sokhor began to bear fruit around 1985. The boundary that official cultural policy had long placed between what was considered music and what was called nonmusic finally fell. Value-free determination of facts was finally possible for socio-musicologists, and attention was increasingly directed toward "technological innovations in both the modern system of music production (electronic studios, videoclip production, and so one) and the system of music distribution by the mass media in the form of the so-called cassette-culture" (Kapustin 1990, 2). Thus the sociology of music in Russia, too, has arrived at the questions posed by the mutation of musical life under the influence of the electronic media.

Sweden

An attempt was made by the University of Gothenburg to integrate sociological research into musicology by sketching a "social-oriented musicology" that was considered to be an "endeavor by means of descriptive surveys to delineate contemporary musical activities, their state, municipal and commercial control, the musical distribution networks . . . and the importance of music to the individual" (Ling 1971, 120).

A number of studies (cf. Karlsson's bibliography 1982) owe their existence in part to the needs of music policy planning. Socio-musicology is also understood "as a scientific tool in attaining cultural reforms" (Ling/Thorsen 1988, 3). For example, the wish to run higher musical education more efficiently led in 1970 to the creation of an official organizing committee (OMUS) charged with drafting a plan to reform music education. The guidelines for a new cultural policy passed by the Swedish parliament in 1974 also contributed to stimulating research, for in order to study the cultural needs of the population, OMUS was charged with investigating the "overall situation of musical life." The Panorama of Swedish Musical Life (Tapper 1976), issued soon afterwards, was based on sociographic surveys.

One result of the studies conducted in Sweden has more than national significance: it was determined that the musical life of small countries is dependent on the international cultural and music industries. This topic was worked into The Music Industry in Small Countries, a research program begun in 1980 under the direction of Krister Malm. The field research of this project extended to four Scandinavian countries (Denmark, Finland, Norway, and Sweden), two countries in the Caribbean (Jamaica and Trinidad), and countries in four other regions (Tunisia, Kenya, Tanzania, and Sri Lanka). The results were published as a report by the University of Gothenburg's Department of

Musicology (Wallis/Malm 1984). The findings are extremely relevant for understanding the contemporary mutation of musical life as well as the "westernization" of non-Western musical cultures.

United States

Here the sociology of music is relatively unencumbered with the philosophical ballast by which the European discipline has always been burdened. For example, the bibliography of Howard S. Becker's *Art Worlds* (1982) does not contain the names Max Weber and Theodor W. Adorno. Despite the otherwise intense American reception of Weber, and although Max Weber's socio-musicological fragment has been published in English translation with a rich commentary (Weber 1958), his ideas do not seem to have left major traces in the United States. The discussion of Adorno's ideas is also limited (cf. Blomster 1976). Among the few exceptions to this rule are the writings of K. Peter Etzkorn, who edited the American edition of the socio-musicological writings of the sociologist Paul Honigsheim, part of the group surrounding Max Weber (Honigsheim 1973). Etzkorn has added a long introduction to the new edition of these writings (Honigsheim 1989) in which he expounds the relationship of sociologists to music as well as the main themes of socio-musicology. He also includes a summary of post-Adorno socio-musicology in the United States. Characteristically, Etzkorn contrasts the simplistic but long-fashionable insistence on the parallel between music and society with the far more difficult and fruitful method of empirically and logically analyzing their connection (cf. Etzkorn 1979).

John H. Mueller (1895–1965) was a pioneer of music sociology. He investigated the social reception of musical works and conceived a social history of musical taste, which he documented with a statistical analysis of the repertoire of American orchestras (Mueller 1951). Several of his studies have been published in German (Mueller 1963), occasioning some violent criticism (e.g. Kneif 1971, 133). His defenders include Desmond Mark, who wrote a well-supported appreciation of Mueller, calling him a "pioneer of socio-musicology" (Mark 1984). Mueller's analysis of the repertoire of American orchestras has nothing to do with the notion of aesthetic quality; it is meant simply as an objective description of the history of musical preferences. Such data permits the graphic representation of "life cycles" of composers in the repertoire, which may be used in determining changes in taste.

The concept of "life cycle" is related to that of "stability" (of a work in the repertoire), a term proposed by Leo Wilzin (1937, 82) following a statistical survey (Schott 1930). Mueller's method is, in fact, suited to representing tendencies in the social reception of music and to placing the history of musical taste on a statistical basis. As Mueller writes, this idea goes back to a thought of Robert Schumann's.

John H. Mueller's work has elicited some response in Europe, although it seems not to have founded a scholarly tradition in the United States. Although numerous surveys concerning music were conducted, the majority of them were carried out by communication and media researchers, not musicologists (Hamm 1988, 7). The growth of socio-musicology in the United States was directly stimulated by the economic dilemma of the performing arts described earlier and by the creation of the National Endowment for the Arts (NEA), which received considerable funding during the seventies. Sociographic data was needed in order to make meaningful use of the subsidies. The accumulation of this data proceeded not from sociological concepts, as was often the case in Europe, but from pragmatic questions of support for the arts and culture.

Work in sociography was stimulated by a conference held in Baltimore in 1977 (Cwi 1978), at which the most important topics were identified: the institutions of artistic life and their economic problems, audience research (including the public of the mass media), and the situation of artists. The reports of the Research Division, which have been published since 1976, dealt with, among other things, cultural radio programs (NEA 1977) and the public of museums and the performing arts (NEA 1978). They also offer an American counterpart of the German "Artist Report" (1975) in an analysis of the composition and income of artists (NEA 1980). The data obtained serve not only as an aid in making decisions to further the arts; they also produce sound findings with which research can operate.

The existence of the National Endowment for the Arts has also drawn attention to the role of the state in the development of the arts. Unlike the United States, the ministries responsible for art and culture in many European countries have contributed to strengthening government's responsibility for the arts. It is characteristic of cultural work "since the second half of the nineteenth century [that it] has been trying to escape from the pressure of the market" (Lange/Renaud 1988, 136). In European discussions the United States is often still depicted as the model of an economy lacking market correctives in favor of culture. This view overlooks the fact that, although the Congressional resolutions concerning the National Endowment for the Arts regard support for the arts as primarily a private and local concern, it is also termed "an appropriate matter of concern to the Federal Government" (cf. Lars Etzkorn 1990, 323).

The issue of whether the state can and should influence the arts has recently become a theme of the sociology of art and music (cf. Etzkorn

1988a). This discussion considers not only direct promotion but the effects of copyright, media law, tax law, and so on. Economics has facilitated an understanding of these problems, showing that the market economy is by definition a regulated economy in which there is a constant need to pass new legal provisions: "The issue is one of writing a set of rules and regulations, which society can live by, in an area that has not previously been important enough to merit a set of rules and regulations" (Thurow 1980, 130). Independent of this, considerations of the sociology of art have led to the realization that government inactivity in the arts also represents a form of arts policy:

> Because states have a monopoly over making laws within their own borders . . . , the state always plays some role in the making of art works. Failing to exercise forms of control available to it through the monopoly, of course, constitutes an important form of state action. (Becker 1982, 165)

Socio-musicological considerations are concerned not only with questions of cultural policy but with the economic problems of the music business as well (cf. Radich 1987 and his bibliography). The Association for Cultural Economics has directed its initiatives to particular problems of individual areas in the arts. These include such varied topics as the market structure of the pipe organ industry, the commercialization of folk culture, and the economic bases of American symphony orchestras (in Grant 1987); the cultural economics of arts funding and the economic cooperation among performing arts centers (in Hillman-Chartrand 1987); and sociographic studies on the distribution of artists and the arts in the United States (in Shaw 1987).

Studies of this kind are to a large extent the product of the discussion of art and cultural policy; they not only expand the field of socio-musicology but contribute to the variety of methods and the refinement of the theoretical equipment. The specification of the term "art worlds," previously used in a metaphorical sense, is an example of this: "Art worlds consist of all people whose activities are necessary to the production of the characteristic works which that world, and perhaps others as well, define as art" (Becker 1982, 34). Such approaches no longer concentrate exclusively on the work of art but attempt to understand "art as activity." It is not surprising, then, that Becker insists that provision must be made for the influence of the state on the production and distribution of art and that the analysis of "art worlds" must therefore also include such themes as property, intervention, support, and censorship (Becker 1982, 165–191).

Richard Peterson has developed a concept that takes into account the many factors involved in the cultural process. He names five determining constraints: law, technology, market, organizational structure, and occupational careers (Peterson 1982), and he has applied this model very convincingly to answer the question of why rock music had to appear in 1955 (Peterson in PM 1990). Becker also underscored the special role that technological development can play in the mutation of art worlds: "Some art worlds begin with the invention and diffusion of a technology which makes certain new art products possible" (Becker 1982, 311). The influence of technological innovation on musical activity and its change—and therefore also on the creation of "music worlds"—clearly appears in recent studies concerned with the importance of "loudspeaker music" in musical communication (e.g., Etzkorn 1988b). The overall process of the contemporary technologization of music is the subject of a study by Jon Frederickson (1989), which, as I will show, makes a major contribution to understanding the present mutation. Charles Hamm has offered an instructive survey of contemporary themes still waiting to be investigated. In light of the profusion of literature on the subject, however, it is impossible to support his pessimistic statement that music sociology in the United States is virtually nonexistent so far (Hamm 1988, 1).

Yugoslavia

Zagreb, the capital of Croatia, is the source of an initiative of potential significance in establishing socio-musicology within musicology. It was long held that "many musicologists do not, either in principle or in theory, include the sociology of music in the framework of musicological research, or if they admit the importance of the sociological approach, they do not accept it as the subject of a special discipline within musicology" (Supičić in IRASM 1970, 6-7). Ivo Supičić, at the time head of the Zagreb Institute of Musicology, thus characterized a deplorable state of affairs he wished to combat by creating a journalistic forum. The *International Review of the Aesthetics and Sociology of Music* (IRASM) was founded in 1970 with Supičić as its director. Researchers from a number of countries avail themselves of this platform for contributions in English, French, and German; it satisfies the urgent need to exchange the results of socio-musicological (and musical-aesthetic) research. In his first introduction to the discipline (written in French), Supičić himself emphasized the necessity of an autonomous formulation of the sociology of music (Supičić 1971). He also makes this demand in his much more comprehensive account in English (Supičić 1987), where he significantly expands on the themes by including the mass media in addition to economic and technological aspects, and by providing a bibliography (organized by topics) that was probably the most comprehensive to date (Supičić 1987, 363–476).

The foregoing survey of socio-musicological research in a few countries is, of course, incomplete. The enumeration by examples is simply meant to show what topicality the discipline has achieved as a result of the reorientation of cultural and educational policy observed in many countries. Socio-musicology, which began as an indisputably peripheral discipline, has acquired new tasks that could initially be fulfilled only hesitantly and imperfectly. A consensus has gradually grown that socio-musicology must concern itself above all with "mutations" as described in chapters 19 and 20. In so doing, the specific features of the present mutation, due to the technological recording, transmission, and production of music, have developed with increasingly clarity.

The MEDIACULT Institute has concerned itself with this phenomenon since 1969. In order to more exactly define the influence of new technologies on the destiny of cultural communication, a large number of case studies have been carried out over the past twenty years. The themes of these investigations include the audience of musical theater, economic aspects of musical theater, rock music, youth subculture, and so on (cf. the bibliography in Mediacult no. 64, June 1989). The results indicate that the analysis of contemporary musical life cannot be complete without including "extramusical" factors that influence musical communication. Collaborating on a Council of Europe project entitled Music Industries and Creativity, carried out between 1982 and 1986, provided the opportunity to investigate the musical strategies of the European recording industries and radio corporations (Blaukopf 1983 and 1985). These studies showed that the changes to which musical communication is subject are also regulated by the systems of mass communication. This applies, inter alia, to the music needs of radio and television stations, including not just playing "musical works" in the usual sense but also filling holes in the broadcast program, providing the musical background for radio and TV programs, creating so-called signature tunes for broadcast stations or programs, and integrating various kinds of music into commercial spots.

This new, "secondary use" of music (cf. Blaukopf 1985) not only influences consumer expectations but also affects the music business: the production of music serving such purposes can generate profits. Thus the production of musical video clips—originally meant to help hits reach the top ten—became profitable as soon as the broadcast companies were willing to pay for their use.

Economic aspects such as these cannot be ignored by the sociology of music. To be sure, questions of economics also played a role in the preelectronic era, as proven, for example, by the history of publishing, concert organizers, orchestras, and musical theater. The industrial-technological production and distribution of musical goods has now, however, lent more weight to the economic element, a dynamic process which influences "live music" and its institutions as well.

In this process of change, those involved in the production and dissemination of music—the phonographic and videographic industries, the authors of musical works, and the performers of music—come forward with their economic interests. The development in a large number of countries shows that the overall legal conditions are also changing to do justice to the new situation and to the interest groups involved. This is reflected in the changes to copyright law and residual rights. The mutation of legal thought characteristic of the second half of the twentieth century can certainly not be explained from the new technological-economic conditions of musical communication alone, yet the mutation seems to be crucially important for musical culture.

The singular interconnection of musical, technological, economic, and legal changes I have sketched leads to the irrefutable thought that the present mutation of musical life is of a special kind that distinguishes it from all previous mutations. Studies of this mutation should emphasize its historic uniqueness. Only thus can the abrupt change, unprecedented in the history of music, be brought out. This corresponds to the "sociology of mutations" (Balandier 1981) that distinguishes between continuous historic movement and abrupt change.

The foregoing methodological idea follows an international study of the relationship between technology and culture (Smudits 1987). It shows that the sociology of culture cannot dispense with taking into account the interconnection of cultural, artistic, technological, economic, and legal elements. Socio-musicology is also under this constraint, not in order to blur the legitimate borders between individual disciplines, but to do justice to the reality of musical life.

To get a picture of the mutation in the second half of the twentieth century and to clearly bring out the aforementioned interconnection, a comprehensive approach appears to be needed. Socio-musicology, then, is entering a new phase in which methodology will also have to be developed for broadening the field of research and for making the transition from merely accumulative multidisciplinarity to synthetic interdisciplinarity.

Chapter 29 *The Mediamorphosis of Music as Global Phenomenon*

The reflections contained in this book have been limited—with the exception of several digressions used for purposes of comparison—to Occidental cultures. But socio-musicology cannot remain within these borders, because its concept of intercultural comparison requires that the sociology of music be extended to those cultures that have so far been relegated primarily to ethnomusicology. The convergence of socio-musicology and ethno-musicology thus seems to be necessary: "Whether they merge or not, an effort should certainly be made by music sociologists and ethnomusicologists to keep better informed about each others' work" (Sorce Keller 1986, 179).

The increasing interdependence of our planet's cultures also challenges both disciplines to cooperate. Given the hitherto limited intercultural communication, it was impossible to speak of a "world history of music." Thus, until recently, it may have been sufficient to view individual musical cultures in their (relative) isolation. The present mutation has made global coherence a central theme of research. Whereas there has until recently been no universal history of music, one has now been created with the mutation induced by the electronic media.

It seems appropriate to explain the particular characteristics of this global mutation, which has no parallel among the historic mutations known to date. A prominent feature of this metamorphosis (although not its only aspect) is the dominant role of the electronic media. In order

to visualize this specific aspect, I call the present mutation the mediamorphosis of music.

Features of Mediamorphosis

The concept of mediamorphosis that I have proposed (Blaukopf 1989)
seeks to do justice to the real interconnections of all factors currently
influencing music, and at the same time to bring out the particular elements of this present mutation. These elements include

1. The quantitative, therefore economic, dominance of music played
   by the electronic media. One result of this preponderance of electronically reproduced music is that the effectiveness of measures
   taken to promote "live" music is reduced.
2. The mediamorphosis of the idea of copyright. For example, the
   income from the media use of copyrighted music cannot always be
   unequivocally assigned to individual authors, which leads to a
   "collectivization" of claims. A striking example of this is the distribution of earnings from the tax many countries impose on blank
   audio cassettes. The income from these taxes may be divided
   among authors or even be used for general social or cultural purposes.
3. The loss of the perception that music has a unique aura. "Live
   music" has an event character that is lacking in the omnipresent
   media music because of its reproducibility. Mediamorphosis creates what French sociologists have called the "banalization" of
   music.
4. The separation of music dissemination from performance practice.
   The sounds that reach the consumer's senses through the loudspeaker have not always been performed as perceived by the
   consumer.
5. The infiltration of technology not only into the dissemination of
   music but also into the creative process. All types of popular music
   have long since ceased to exist primarily as symbols a composer
   sets to paper or in the form of traditional music-making but have
   become electronically formed sound.
6. The use of the new technological apparatus for "applied media
   music." This use of technology also satisfies the demand of radio
   broadcast companies and the advertising industry for such things
   as commercial spots, jingles, signature tunes, and background
   music.
7. The increasing influence of mediamorphosis on the creation of
   "serious music." The composer who works at his desk now is
   joined by the creator of music who works in a studio with tools that

include sound synthesis, computer programs, and sampling. Ernst Krenek predicted this change in the composer's working method as long ago as 1938.

%

Several of the consequences of mediamorphosis have been treated in the literature. Jon Frederickson has written an instructive survey summarizing the results of recent research and commenting on his own observations. He emphasizes the crucial innovation—that technology "can create a simulated musical world without performers" (Frederickson 1989, 197). Moreover, he derives other aspects of contemporary musical life from this change: the expectations of the listening public are increasingly influenced by recording techniques, so "live music" tries to emulate the sound of music conveyed by technical means (ibid., 199); in music conveyed by technical means the aura of intimacy created by "live music" is replaced by greater volume (ibid., 200); the recording engineer becomes of crucial importance in ensemble music conveyed by technical means (ibid., 201); the technology that makes possible the use and transformation of individual musical performances creates copyright questions for which there are as yet no legal provisions (ibid., 202); the direct communication of musical performers characteristic of live music can be replaced by "computerized manipulation of sounds" (ibid., 204); and technology divorces music from the spatial experience associated with it, thereby changing the perception of acoustical architecture (ibid., 205).

These statements, which I have outlined here only in part, indicate the immediately practical changes resulting from the availability of new technologies. Several general tendencies of mediamorphosis emerge that are present in both industrialized and developing countries.

The global importance of these changes reinforces the previously mentioned convergence of sociological and ethnological research provoked by the mediamorphosis of music. Thus, for example, the concepts of "westernization" and "modernization," as used by ethnomusicology (e.g., Nettl 1985), are also of growing importance to sociological research.

In order to understand westernization and modernization it is absolutely essential to abandon the idea of a predetermined international order, an imperative evolution, as it were, from "lower" to "higher." The notion of such an order is based on biological, anthropological, and socioeconomic ideas that must be examined by socio-musicology because they play a role in the sociological constructions of many thinkers and because, in my opinion, they tend to hinder the value-free evaluation of facts.

Simplifying systems, which may have been of help in popularizing the theories of Charles Darwin, can in fact mislead one to interpret "development" as a process that must lead from a "lower stage" to a "higher stage." The words "evolution" and "progress" alone heavily suggest this interpretation. Modern biology, however, shows that organisms can just as easily go down as up each rung of the evolutionary ladder, which also means, for example, from the organic to the inorganic (cf. Lorenz 1978, 27). Anthropology suggests similar considerations, contending that the progress of the human race cannot be compared to a person climbing steps (cf. Lévi-Strauss 1975, 109). Socioeconomics also indicates skepticism toward a naive belief in progress. Maurice Godelier states that social evolution is not possible without retrogression and that it is impossible to speak of a "general evolution of humankind" (Godelier 1973, 128).

Analyzing the musical practice of a culture other than our own familiar one also requires that we relinquish the notion of linear "progress" for the present—at least until such a thesis becomes plausible in one or the other case, the possibility of which cannot, of course, be excluded. In principle, each musical practice must be understood within the overall cultural framework to which it belongs. The further we go back in history, and the greater the gap between a culture under investigation and the main currents of international communication, the more distinctive the musical practice will be.

The cultures of various regions are often disparate, largely independent structures—a fact that makes the concept of a "universal history of music" so problematic. Universal concepts usually have their origins in the political, economic, and cultural interdependence of all countries. Yet because this global interdependence is a recent phenomenon, it cannot form the basis for analyzing cultural processes that took place prior to the establishment of a worldwide nexus. We must not under any circumstances derive principles of a "general" evolution from this perspective. The three-stages theory of Auguste Comte violated this guiding principle by presuming that all societies pass through certain phases, thereby furthering the view that this could also apply to music.

The Utility of a Global View

Once the naive evolutionary pattern has been rejected, we are entirely justified in proceeding to a global consideration. As far as I can see, this can be profitable in at least three instances:

1. Conceivably, historical developments of musical activity exist that lead from a common point of departure to different results or, vice versa, that begin at different points and converge. For example, Hornbostel (1911) speaks of an acoustic criterion for cultural relations. A comparative method, which includes analysis of cultural forms of behavior in addition to acoustic-musical findings, is particularly rewarding in such cases. It is able to explain from the sociological point of view the extent to which historical musical convergence is contingent on social factors and the extent to which it can be seen as "coincidental," requiring further explanation.

2. All musical practices have to confront the problem of how to divide the octave, a division for which there is no physical-mathematical norm. Max Weber recommends examining how each musical practice deals with the fundamental contradictions inherent in the acoustic material. Joseph Yasser (1932) attempted—apparently without knowledge of Weber's ideas—to utilize this idea in order to understand the evolution of tonal systems. He was able to describe certain basic types of tonal system organization by means of logical analysis. In Weberian terms these models can be described as "ideal types," that is, as entities virtually nonexistent in reality in their pure form but which, applied cautiously, can be a helpful tool in investigating and illustrating. Useful as Yasser's models are, and much as they are able to stand up to empirical verification over a long period, they take little account of the "accidental forms" of the many tonal systems that are valid only within narrowly defined limits. Yasser could justify his hypothesis that tonal systems evolved in a universal pattern because, according to him, most of the "accidental" systems found in earlier forms of society were demonstrably incapable of winning acceptance beyond a small area. But the pentatonic solution of the fundamental acoustic contradiction was developed in more than one region of our planet, thereby proving the importance of this "ideal type" for actual development (Yasser 1932, 5 n.). From this point of view, it is appropriate to seek to create a theoretical pattern for a universal history of tonal systems. Such a pattern should neither guide nor replace field research in ethnomusicology. It should serve solely as an instrument of research, as a measuring instrument for empirically existing tonal systems.

3. Global aspects are likely to come to the fore where historical international interdependence exists, that is, during the era of mediamorphosis at the latest. We are witnessing a worldwide hybridization of musical practices. It is obvious that this hybridization is being directed to a large degree by Western musical practice. The outcry is all too clear that the autochthonous musical cultures

of the so-called Third World are being threatened or destroyed by the assault of the finished goods (sound recordings) distributed by the electronic media. The danger has been pointed out for Indian music, for example, that conformity to what is felt to be the "international standard" will lead to the decay or loss of a wonderful and singular music (Daniélou 1975, 12). The Arab countries are also lamenting the decay of authentic music and the loss of tradition, to the point that most Arabs no longer know "genuine" Arab music (Touma 1975, 32).

There can be little doubt that non-Western cultures do not primarily desire the transition to Western musical practices for their own needs but that strong influences from outside create the loss of authentic traditions, the acceptance of Western models, or the development of hybrid practices. To be sure, endogenetic changes in the economic and social structure of these countries also play a role by encouraging urbanization and media saturation. Yet to a large extent these changes can also be attributed to external factors, be it colonialism, unthinking acceptance of Western technologies, or even so-called development aid. Regardless of the circumstances under which new social and technological structures are accepted, they always appear to be accompanied by at least a partial loss of musical identity. One does not have to support those who would like to protect cultural identity by erecting barriers against all industrialization in order to see this process as a task for music sociology.

The fact that the acceptance of Western practices often leads to different results in different regions gives socio-musicology virtually unprecedented opportunities to make intercultural comparisons by studying the effects of Western forms of behavior on traditional societies. A striking example is the transformation of Japanese musical culture over the past 150 years. One strongly suspects that Japanese society could have produced a musical practice similar to the Western one in parallel with their industrialization and without influences from the outside. To be sure, the Western model with its particular tonal system and instruments was presented in the Japanese educational system as early as 1879, and this may have accelerated the development. But the tempo with which "westernization" took place in Japan is evidence that forces in search of something new were already present within Japanese society.

As far as I know, Occidental observers did not predict this process. Had they been asked at the time how Japan's evolution into a mighty industrial giant might have affected international music, pundits would probably have predicted that Japanese music would conquer the world. That Japan has attained, by Occidental standards, a powerful status in musical education, concert life, instrument-making, and the electronic fixing, production, and diffusion of music without simultaneously establishing their own music the world over—this must have been as surprising to Western observers as the unexpected victory of the Japanese fleet over the Russians in 1905, which marked the actual beginning of history for modern Japan.

Tasks of Universal History

The study of the transformation of music during the transition from preindustrial to modern conditions is not only an important topic of a "world history of contemporary music"; it could also provide new knowledge in understanding the musical mutations of Occidental music itself, in grasping the musical mutations at the end of the European Middle Ages and at the beginning of the seventeenth century, for example. Of course, whatever benefit a global consideration of music can yield is merely a by-product. Those interested in a universal history of music have other interests. They are dedicated to comprehending the variety of given musical cultures and understanding the processes caused by global interdependence.

An example of such efforts is the Music in the Life of Man project undertaken by the International Music Council a good many years ago. It was pointed out at an early stage of this project that a universal history of music must not be content only to expound the forms and structures of different musics, but must also determine the roles that musical activity plays in various cultures at various times (Nketia 1980, 20). The sociological dimension of the project is thus indicated as well as its necessary methodological orientation: if musical activity can assume different functions, this means that the socio-musicalogical method cannot be standardized but must be adapted to each musical culture under investigation. This point has been emphasized in a statement about the Music in the Life of Man project (Azevedo 1980, 59) and deserves to be underscored in light of the still widespread opinion that "music is the international language." The idea is itself a product of Occidental music history, because it is founded on Western-type performance music removed from a direct, confined social context. This does not, however, apply to what Pierre Joseph Proudhon called situational art (*art en situation*) in his 1865 book on the social vocation of art and what we would describe today with Besseler's term *participatory music*. "The concert is the death of music" (Proudhon 1971, 333) is a pointed way of expressing these circumstances; it alludes to the relaxation of the direct social referent and the relative autonomy of Occidental performance music, which is the exception, not the rule, in the universal history of music.

Research methods employed with a certain degree of success in studying relatively autonomous Western art music will not be adequate for participatory musics in life. It is remarkable that European musicology has also recently advocated broadening the field of study to music in life (cf. Flothius 1974), thereby aspiring to a closer connection between traditional historical research and the study of folk music and modern popular music.

Planning for the Music in the Life of Man project enlivened the discussion of methodological questions pertaining to a universal history of music. In 1989 a new basis was created for this project, administered by a center at the City University of New York, together with a new name—The Universe of Music: a History (UMH). An international team of scholars has been charged with publishing a twelve-volume universal history of music. The results of debates during the years of planning are reflected in the project description, emphasizing that the history is to be written by "authors native to the regions about which they write" and that the goal is "to capture the authentic voice of a people, to highlight the multiplicity as well as the diversity of musical phenomena, and to transmit a contextual understanding of music in life" (UMH, no.1, July 1990, 4).

The insistence on a "contextual understanding" seems to indicate the desired ethnological and sociological perspectives. The results will reveal the extent to which the aspects of mediamorphosis I have alluded to are treated. The idea of the global transformation made possible by technology strongly suggests itself, and is, as must be remarked with all due modesty, not new. As early as 1961, Walter Wiora recommended studying music from the point of view of the technological and industrial mutation. He spoke of the four ages of music, calling the fourth the age of technology and global industrial culture. The revolution brought about by this age leads not only to another change in Occidental music, comparable to the European changes around 1600 or 1750, but to a new international situation, to a "Europeanization" of the globe (Wiora 1961, 125–127).

Ethnomusicologists have accepted this process as an object of study, investigating the reactions to the Occidental influence. Bruno Nettl (1978b, 127) identifies three ideal-type reactions:

1. Preservation—aspiring to have the traditional culture remain intact
2. Complete westernization—simply incorporating the society into a Western cultural system

3. Modernization—adopting and adapting Western technology and other products of Western culture, as needed, while simultaneously insisting that the core of cultural values does not change greatly and in the end does not match those of the West

Nettl takes these tendencies as ideal-type constructs, made concrete in innumerable mixed forms. In individual cases it will no doubt be difficult to distinguish between westernization and modernization. As industrial civilization expands, the endogenous tendencies of modernization are also steered by "Occidental" forces from the outside. In the developing countries the logic of the industrial revolution usually does not take the form of a change from within but seems to be a transformation forced from the outside, as a break with the endogenous historical process (cf. UNESCO 1980, 50, 274).

It would be tempting to attribute this break with tradition entirely to the technological-industrial factor. The fact must not be overlooked, however, that ideological goals also play a role. One of these notions is the tacit and unverified idea that the acquisition of Western modes of musical behavior is a form of "progress." That such a use of the term progress is more than questionable will have to be demonstrated by examples from tonal systems and notation.

Acculturation and its Repercussions

Regardless of how one evaluates this and similar mutations, one thing appears to be certain: a process of acculturation is taking place in many cultures under the clearly dominant influence of Occidental music. The most value-free description possible of the phenomenon is required in order to survey such acculturations scientifically. As Tran Van Khe has shown (1973, 199–200), it will not be easy to attribute to Western influence every disappearance of traditional-type music-making that results from industrialization. We must distinguish between describing the *phenomenon* of acculturation (namely, the adoption of foreign instruments, the modification of singing and playing styles, and the alteration of musical language or even tonal systems), investigating its *causes*, and determining its cultural *consequences*. There are two ideal-type classes of such cultural repercussions: (a) acculturation leading to impoverishment and possible loss of cultural identity and (b) acculturation understood and felt to be an enrichment.

This distinction taken from Tran Van Khe (1973, 207), however, cannot always be made. Furthermore, those affected would not always agree with the verdict of ethnomusicologists who attempt to identify loss or enrichment.

Does Occidental music contain aspects that virtually predestine it expand to other cultures? As far as I can tell, this question is seldom asked. Indian music has never been confined by the rhythmic corset of Western music, but Occidental music may have adopted its simpler metric patterns "in order to counterbalance the complicated harmonic and melodic structure of Western music" (Nijenhuis 1974, 60). By this schematization, Western music is suited to attracting other cultures, especially when just the simplified skeleton and not the harmonic richness that goes along with it is adopted. Wiora (1961, 131) believes, for example, that the eight-bar phrase in major, with its regular alternation of tonic and dominant, has comparable structures in all cultures, explaining why it was easily adopted.

Another aspect possibly conducive to the reception of Western music is the easily grasped rationality of the Western tonal system (and the notation associated with it). I have mentioned in connection with Adorno the phenomenon of the "resilience" of the Occidental tonal system and its inherent "tonality." This system has not only retained its dominant position again and again, in spite of innumerable innovations by Western avant-garde composers, it has also been able to extend its area of influence beyond Western culture. One might therefore ask whether it possesses expansive power as well as resilience. The fact that the number of people familiar with this type of "tonality" has grown by hundreds of millions since the beginning of the twentieth century might be used to support the hypothesis that the tonality has an inner attraction. One might, of course, object that the increasing dominance of Occidental tonality is the result, not of its "inner strength," but of the "external power" of processes of industrial technology that go hand in hand with the worldwide mediamorphosis. Neither the theoretical considerations of socio-musicologists nor the laboratory tests of musical psychologists can settle this. Not until we make a synthesis of many acculturation processes now taking place will we be able to come closer to answering this question.

The Role of Notation

An important criterion needed to define the special characteristics of a form of musical behavior is its relationship to notation. I have previously mentioned (chapter 19) that the score as the end result of musical creation is a relatively recent phenomenon in Occidental music. Adorno had a simplifying, directly social explanation for the absence of score arrangement in Medieval European music. In his opinion, the handing down of music in parts and not in score could presumably be explained by the desire "to keep the *misera plebs* away from the alchemist's kitchen of counterpoint" (Adorno 1968b, 115). Although secrecy played a role in a number of cultures (cf. Hickmann in MGG 9, 1597), Adorno's interpretation is not adequate. As late as the sixteenth century, Europeans considered the score merely as a technical aid for the composer, not for music-making. The creation of the score had to be followed by its resolution ("resolutio") into separate parts. The score itself was destroyed or erased, and the creator of the music communicated to the performers solely through the parts (cf. Georgiades 1958, 217).

Not until we understand the Western score as a late development will we be able to assess other musical cultures more accurately. Most of them regard as foreign not only the score but notation as well. As Daniélou remarks (1973, 63), the percentage of music in the world that can be written down is very small. Even placing bar lines can distort and destroy the melody when one attempts to notate such musics (cf. Graf 1965, 160). The symbols developed outside the musical culture with which we are familiar—roughly fifty such systems are known—serve primarily as aids to memory and not as a rational, unequivocal representation of music.

Of course, there is also evidence for Adorno's conjecture that symbols can occasionally be used to keep secrets. These proofs, however (taking no account of the not entirely explained meaning of *musica reservata*) refer to non-Western cultures. An approximately three-thousand-year-old Babylonian clay tablet containing texts and musical symbols closes with the note: 'Secret. For initiate to show to initiate.' It can be concluded from such sources (cf. Sachs 1968, 76–77) that the secret was not contained in the notation itself but in the ritual associated with the symbolized music.

The post-1600 Occidental notion according to which "musical creation" (= composition) takes place on music paper amounts to a reversal of the original relationship. The concept of "composition" could, with some justification, also be applied to music conceived without writing. Thus a book on Indian music speaks of "improvised composition," while vocal or instrumental improvisation lasting a number of hours is called "composition" (Nijenhuis 1974, 96).

Although the notation developed in India is an aid to memory, it has never evolved into a complete picture of music (Menon 1974, 64). The prerequisite for thinking in terms of notation, as established in the Occident, is the rationalization and standardization of the tonal system. This was the basis of Max Weber's idea that the rationalization of the tonal system and the attendant rationalization of notation was a specific feature of Occidental music. Recent sociology has picked up this idea again—without referring to Max Weber, yet based on the findings of ethnomusicology. Occidental notation is seen as a two-edged sword: as "progress" and "straitjacket":

Analytic notation has become a kind of grand-historical filter, selecting some elements of sound, those which it notates, to be of musical
significance and others, those which it can notate only inadequately or
not at all, as of only secondary importance for our perception of sound
as music. (Wishart 1977, 135)

We must, then, account for the fact that the possibilities of musical
expression in our tonal system and notation are poorer in a number of
respects than are those of musical cultures not bound by the constraints
of our system. In this regard, then, the process of acculturation under
Western influence must be termed "impoverishment" rather than
"progress." The loss of expressive potential must thus be placed in the
balance sheet alongside the enrichment by Occidental music. It is difficult to decide whether the sacrifice of microintervals and ornamental
subtleties is compensated by the potential reception of chromatic harmony.

Even modern European musical history does not regard every
achievement as purely positive. The progression from equal temperament, a prerequisite to chromatic harmony, has also resulted in a loss of
expressive possibilities: "It is ironic that in equal temperament the
increased freedom to modulate from one key to another is purchased at
the expense of a lost distinction between these keys" (Benade 1976, 312).

When a musical culture built on oral tradition is confronted with
the written music of the West, a rationalization of musical activity
occurs that leads to the loss of particular musical messages for which
the Western tonal and notational system has no place. Musical communication within Occidental cultures is not only made possible by the
standardized division of the octave but by the absolute determination
of pitches by international pitch (*Kammerton*), in force since the middle
of the nineteenth century. Pitch fixation of this kind is, for example,
unknown in Indonesian gamelan music: "No two gamelan slendro or
gamelan pelog are tuned precisely the same" (Hood 1972, 5). This
reveals its distance from Western thought just as clearly as, for example,
the diversity of intervals in traditional Arab music which is far greater
than that employed in the Western tonal system. The process of rationalization, reflected and solidified by our notation, harmonizes with
the Occidental tendency to "demystify the world," as described a number of times by Max Weber (Weber GAWL, 594). Ethnomusicology also
interprets the transition from unwritten to written music as demystification in Weber's sense (cf. Blum 1978, 25–26).

Mediamorphosis intensifies this demystification on an international scale due to the weight of its musical "finished products," which
obey the rationalized pattern of tonality and are offered as sound
recordings and spread by means of ground and satellite broadcast.
Technological development thus becomes a powerful force behind the

increased worldwide dominance of the equal tempered twelve-pitch tonal system. It should not be overlooked, however, that new technical processes also contain a creative potential of possible benefit to both traditional and Western musical cultures.

Technological Processes as Creative Means

The synthetic production of sound could bring new elements into the present-day process of acculturation, for it also opens the possibility of preserving non-Western tonal systems and lends new impetus to their use. This is, for example, the basis of the hope that the "Indian way of hearing" may be retained through the technological production of Indian rhythmic models and Indian intervals (Ghatnekar 1975, 111). Having the ability to produce and store every kind of interval makes it tempting to construct equipment that can do justice to more than one tonal system. An example of such equipment is a device built for research into Indian music that is capable of reproducing fifty-two intervals within the octave (Cellier/Kudelski 1978). It can be used to produce intervals from the most varied musical cultures. To study Javanese music, a similar method that can simulate the "sound families" of many musical cultures was developed. The process defines "a set of synthetically generable sound events which are associated with an existing sound concept" (Jannssen/Kaegi 1986, 185).

This development reveals a surprising paradox: in the very epoch in which the pure special traits of non-Western musics are endangered, the new technological tool can help to preserve traditional tonal structures. Technological processes of this kind could also aid Western composers in defining where they stand. A number of attempts by twentieth-century composers to increase or refine the tonal resources of music have been blocked by the rigidity of the tonal system so deeply impressed on our consciousness. This system of norms, regardless of its undeniable aesthetic merits, excludes every subtler form of differentiation that may have been possible prior to the existence of these norms. Electronic sound production opens the door to new scales and new "sound families." Yet the works of electronic music that have been created since about 1950 seem to suggest that avant-garde composers have a hard time finding their way in an uncharted, endlessly large universe of sound and facilitating the access of listeners to this territory. Technological progress is supposed to enable composers to penetrate this broad area, yet they seem to lack a "cultural compass" which would enable them to take their bearings in this acoustical no-man's-land. The analysis of non-Western tonal systems in conjunction with efforts to understand forms of non-Western musical behavior could help the contemporary composer throw off the bonds of the accustomed tonal system to discover new musical resources. The builders of the equipment permitting fifty-two intervals within an octave have indicated the potential gain:

> Based on observations on the psycho-physiological effect of intervals corresponding to precise numerical factors, this instrument presents new possibilities for the study of extra-European music. But it also offers a sound material extremely diversified and precise to the modern composer since it permits sound effects and expressive structures completely new. (Cellier/Kudelski 1978, 1)

The way opened by mediamorphosis, then, does not have to be a one-way street; it also offers possibilities for mutual illumination that can be of benefit to the West as well. Despite the present dominance of Western paradigms, this give-and-take could be profitable to both sides. The new technologies could, on the one hand, contribute to preserving the individuality of non-Western cultures and, on the other, make it easier for Western-trained composers to develop new musical resources.

There is no way to predict whether such a mutation of the musical material, of the tonal system and its use by the composer within Occidental culture, will occur. To be sure, a number of attempts of this kind have been made in recent decades, and some of these compositional projects are indubitably of artistic merit. Yet sociology cannot be satisfied with considering avant-garde composers alone; it must study the process in its totality. It thus becomes apparent that efforts by Occidental composers to refine their sonic raw material are not motivated entirely by the existence of new technological means. They go back further.

Anton Bruckner's enthusiasm for the just-tempered fifty- five-note harmonium of the Japanese Shohe Tanaka could be interpreted as the desire for a more subtle tonal system; Claude Debussy's wish for a division of the octave into twenty-one pitches points in the same direction; and Alban Berg's addition of plus and minus signs to a number of notes in order to indicate the desired departure from tempered intonation could also be taken as an attempt to break out of our tonal system.

Questions of this type have occasionally been studied following Joseph Yasser (1932) (cf. Blaukopf 1972a, 119–120 and the literature listed). Arnold Schoenberg took a position on this problem (see Yasser 1953), yet to the best of my knowledge the literature has not dealt systematically with it or with the ideas of Bruckner, Debussy, and Alban Berg.

Western Copyright and Non-Western Reality

The traditional Western type of composer creates a written plan for the performance of his music. The written instructions he records on music paper enjoy the status of "works of art" comparable to the works of painters, sculptors, and writers. The Occident attributes to works of art aesthetic autonomy removed from reality, a view that forms part of a concept generally held by Occidental culture—that of a division between work and leisure, which results in a distinction between aesthetic experience and everyday experience. During the last two centuries the idea evolved that, although art could not regain freedom in practice, it could retain a kind of spiritual autonomy. According to this idea, receiving the message of art promotes the fraternity of mankind, as in the poem by Schiller that Beethoven set to music in his Ninth Symphony.

This accent on the liberating effect of the arts became one of the leitmotifs of European thought—in German Idealistic philosophy, in the literary works of John Ruskin and William Morris, or in the enthusiasm of Benedetto Croce for the non-logical nature of art. Croce wrote that "all the arts are music, if thereby we wish to give emphasis to the emotional origin of artistic images, excluding from their number those constructed mechanically or burdened with realism" (Croce 1983, 26). This value system, characteristic of European culture, secured for the work of art and its creator a high ideal value. Such attitudes also had practical consequences for the stance of society toward its artists, forming one of the bases for legal rules meant to provide moral and economic protection for the highly valued creations of artists. The so-called Bern Convention of 1886 (subsequently revised by later international agreements) was guided expressly by the desire "to protect in as effective and uniform a manner as possible the rights of authors over their literary and artistic works."

The copyright laws of individual states, as well as the international conventions governing copyright, are based on the Occidental idea of "intellectual property." According to this, the authors of musical works enjoy legal protection. They alone are given the right to control the public performance, reproduction, or arranging of their work. Indeed they even enjoy moral protection, for they have the right "to object to any distortion, mutilation, or other alteration" of their creations. In legal thought the work fixed in music notation was given the status of intellectual property. This Western concept is derived from the view that the composer's creative labor is expressed in the fully notated *res facta*. It is appropriate to use the Latin expression from the fifteenth century because it indicates the complete notation of the work as distinct from a merely fragmentary one that leaves room for improvisation.

The application of copyright principles oriented to such a *res facta* is characteristic of Western musical thought. Yet precisely this mode of thought creates problems when applied to non-Western musical cultures. The Western concept leads to a higher legal status being granted to the written form of aesthetically unpretentious music than to extremely artistic music developed without notation. By Western standards, a musician who has been creating non-notated music for many years and is able to perform it with extreme dexterity is not an author and is therefore unprotected. If, however, a far less artistically gifted musician manages to put that music, which he has not created, on paper he is considered the legal author entitled to the rights of use and economic benefits of the "work" he has "created."

The idea of the copyright protection of musical works evolved from the particular conditions of artistic creation in the Occident. The unmodified application of the concept to the musical life of other cultures contradicts their special needs and original values. Thus traditional, non-notated music can be mutilated and used for financial gain without the creator of this music or the community to which this creator belongs receiving compensation. The electronic media offer ample opportunity for economically exploiting the non-notated musical legacy of other cultures.

Attempts have recently been made to put an end to this abuse. It appeared that not only is the problem acute in developing countries but the folk music of industrialized countries is subject to the same dangers from mediamorphosis. To counteract these dangers, a Fund for Folk Music was created in Sweden to which those who use collective (folk) musical property pay voluntary fees. Members of this free agreement include the Swedish Copyright Association, the phonograph industry, and the radio corporations.

The challenge to traditional music by mediamorphosis is also reflected in the legal measures of a number of developing countries. These measures are founded on the notion that the economic exploitation of collective musical property should entail fees, which in turn can be used to promote and develop the national musical culture. In Bolivia, for example, a 1968 state decree proclaimed traditional music to be part of the national legacy. This decree states that such music can be used in technological media only with the permission of the ethnomusicological department of the ministry of culture upon payment of a copyright fee. Monies thus earned are used to preserve the national musical legacy (Aretz 1974, 123).

A similar attempt to extend copyright law to traditional music was made in Senegal in 1973. Among other things, this law states that commercial public performances or recordings of folk music require permission from the national collecting society, granted for a fee. The monies thus generated must be used for the benefit of authors.

A recent example of this new trend to confront the economic constraints of mediamorphosis is the copyright law that went into effect in Ghana in 1985. The law contains a noteworthy juristic innovation, stating that the rights to folklore belong to the state "as if the Republic were the original creator of the work." To my knowledge, this statement is the clearest to date of the notion that the state, as representative of the collectivity, is entitled to act on behalf of the (usually anonymous) creators of folk music.

Laws of this kind clearly reveal the difference between Western notions of law on the one hand and the needs of developing countries on the other. It seems difficult for Western minds to grasp this difference. In order to do so a correct description and evaluation of traditional musical activity is required. Can it be called creative or is it merely repetitive? Are we permitted to judge the creative importance of this kind of musical activity by its originality and innovation, as in the West, or do other criteria apply? These questions are of importance not only for the music, but for the entire area of arts and crafts in non-Western countries, and they have been asked a number of times about African cultures. The answers are also valid for music in traditional cultures. In these cultures creativity is not synonymous with innovation and originality: "The creativity comes rather through the individual development of particular skills in organizing or performing something that is essentially traditional" (Ottenberg 1975, 215–216).

Our aesthetic and legal notions derived from notated music are unable to do justice to the diversity of cultures. The call for new legal regulations is long overdue because the dynamic of mediamorphosis has turned the attack by Western norms on the musical cultures of other societies into a central problem, one that can be solved (cf. Blaukopf 1990b).

The Occidental understanding of the musical work as a *res facta*, a work complete for all times, clashes with the understanding many other cultures have of music. It also entails a different understanding of musical time. The precise definition of "beginning" and "end" of music is not universal.

Music and Time

Very frequently participatory music in life does not derive its beginning and end from musical structure but rather from the logic of the event of which it is a part. The obligatory rules characteristic of Western culture do not apply even to liturgy linked to a text. The recitation of the

Koran can begin in the middle of a Sura and stop before its end (Touma 1975, 142). The question of how the musics of foreign cultures are heard and how unexpected musical experiences fit into one's own overall experiences has, to the best of my knowledge, yet to be investigated systematically. An instructive illustration is found in the reactions of a European who, when confronted for the first time with Indian music, recognizes no clear divisions between "warming up" (e.g., tuning the instruments) and the "performance." He patiently waits for the beginning only to find out suddenly "that the performance *has* in fact already begun" (Crossley-Holland 1966, 105).

Participatory music must also not take its orientation from the familiar notion of length of performance. Every attempt to separate such music from its situational context and to describe it "in itself," without taking into account the non-musical elements of what is going on, is a violation of its nature. Even the otherwise praiseworthy efforts of ethnologists to rescue traditional music from oblivion via tape recordings runs into this cultural barrier. It has been shown, for example, that adapting performances of traditional Korean music to the playing time of a record falsifies it (Hey Ku Lee 1975, 57–58). The process of mediamorphosis, then, affects everything down to ethnological studies, because the technological fixation of music not only preserves the traditional material but distorts it as well. This distortion effect has also been verified for Iranian classical music (Nettl 1978a, 156).

The technological recording of traditional music, then, tendentially alters its function. Music that is meant to be embedded in a given pattern of activity becomes independent of such patterns and has imposed upon it a beginning and an end, which are nonexistent in traditional music-making and listening. At the same time, mediamorphosis brings about a new proximity of music to life. Portable radios and cassette players, equipment which has penetrated into the everyday life of Arab nomads, turn the broadcast schedule of radio stations into the regulator of the daily routine (Chabrier 1974, 39). Program announcements and jingles mark periods of time, yet the music acts as a disjointed background. This music can be either Western-style notated "works" or traditional in origin. It attains, however, a new directness, entering the life of the listeners and altering their daily rhythm. The impact on non-Western cultures of messages transported by the electronic media can be called "secondary orality," to use a fitting expression of Walter J. Ong's. Electronic technology

> has brought us into the age of "secondary orality." This new orality has striking resemblances to the old in its participatory mystique, its fostering of a communal sense, its concentration on the present moment, and even its use of formulas. But it is essentially a more deliberate and self-conscious orality, based permanently on the use of

writing and print, which are essential in the manufacture and operation of the equipment and for its use as well. (Ong 1988, 136)

Ong has devoted his attention to the technologizing of the word. It also seems useful to apply these thoughts to the technologizing of music, because they indicate a characteristic feature of mediamorphosis, a secondary ordering of life governed by the electronic media. This "secondary orality" of musical communication is particularly noticeable in non-Western cultures, yet the fact should not be overlooked that it has long since taken hold of musical practice in the industrialized countries, where almost all popular music, and even part of the electronically mediated folk music and art music, is under its influence (cf. Blaukopf 1980c, 19–20).

Tonal Character of the Singing Voice

The intrusion of Western practices into other musics presumably fosters an assimilation in the use of the singing voice. The existing differences are a warning against viewing all musics from a standard point of view. If a European listener considers the voice of an Indian singer forced and nasal, he seldom takes into consideration that to Indian listeners the European style of singing can seem "unnatural." The Western style of singing appears not to have fully prevailed until rather late (perhaps not until the seventeenth century). The findings of ethnomusicology indicate that large regions (e.g., the Near East) prefer nasal, throaty singing. The question of how universally this type of singing was practiced in the European Middle Ages has been studied a number of times (cf. Marquardt 1936, Müller-Heuser 1963). The representation of the distorted faces of angels by the brothers Van Eyck on the Ghent Altar (ca. 1430) has been interpreted as implying a nasal tonal ideal (Sachs 1959, 16–17).

What could be the social motivation of such a vocal tone? What social meaning could there be behind this norm? A hypothetical explanation has been offered for Arab-Islamic music that may be applicable to other cultures: the singer's "supernatural" inspiration prohibits him from using every-day intonation, requiring instead a supernatural, that is, an unnatural voice (Hickmann 1970, 56–57). This hypothesis once again points to the social function of musical activity as a factor that can influence activity down to the smallest details. The extent to which the acculturation accelerated by mediamorphosis may decrease or even eliminate the variety of vocal styles in the world remains an open question, one which the universal history of music will certainly seek to answer. This question is linked to a problem that the contemporary literature calls a problem of "cultural identity." The possible loss of these cultural identities through the process of acculturation has only recently begun to concern sociologists, whereas ethnologists have been dealing with it for quite some time.

Cultural Identity

The slogan of preserving cultural identity has recently become fashionable. We have slowly begun to realize, however, that the notion of cultural identity must be defined more exactly and that not everything belonging to this identity is necessarily worth preserving. The satirical songs about criminals at their public execution, sung well into the nineteenth century, may have belonged to the "cultural identity" of some nations; nonetheless, civilized countries today are glad that both the national ritual of execution and a good many barbaric songs have been forgotten.

We must therefore be careful in using the concept of cultural identity. The idea that everything should be preserved was compatible with the long-since obsolete idea of the "ahistoricity" of traditional cultures, but this is no longer consistent with a dynamic view of cultural activity. The recurrent lamentation in the ethnological literature over the decline of traditional music-making must also be seen from this viewpoint. Thus, at a symposium in Dakar (Senegal), an African musician asked the entirely justifiable question how it was conceivable that Africa could develop politically and socially while at the same time clinging unchanged to its musical tradition (Bebey 1979, 139). That which an African nation considers to be its musical advantage should not be determined by ethnologists, no matter how well-intentioned, but by those affected. They are entitled to decide how much modernization or westernization is desirable. Thus the idea that the seven-tone scale is more "progressive" than the pentatonic scale (Bebey 1979, 135) may be considered an abandonment of musical identity by some ethnologists, yet those who understand the mechanisms of social change will not be as surprised.

Even political thought seems to consider awareness of national identity entirely compatible with the spectacular acceptance of foreign forms of behavior. I therefore do not share the astonishment of an ethnologist who writes about music in the Philippines: "It is curious to note that some youthful nationalists listen more to rock music than to Philippine folk or Western classical music" (Maceda 1972, 39). The adaptation to Western patterns of the national anthems of numerous countries also betrays the combining of national ambitions with musical acculturation (cf. Blaukopf 1978).

A number of forms of originally Western behavior assume entirely new functions in the context of Third World national movements. The musicians of these nations are often even proud of not only being inundated by acculturation but of taking part in it, perhaps creatively. They do not regard it as a loss of cultural identity. They do not want outside observers to define the authentic aspects of their culture; authentic is defined as "what they really are" (Bebey 1979, 139). Statements of this kind show that many musicians in developing nations regard acculturation not as an entirely negative phenomenon but also as a challenge. This confirms the correctness of the distinction made in ethnomusicology between *passive* and *active* acculturation (cf. Gerson-Kiwi 1973, 187).

Active acculturation covers the demand heard in a number of developing countries for balanced communication with all musical cultures. The encounter with Western music is not rejected; one merely attempts to reduce it to a degree compatible with the principle of balanced international exchange. This tendency was clearly present in Nigeria during the seventies. After achieving independence (1960), this African country with a population of about seventy million underwent rapid economic, political, and cultural development, owing primarily to its reserves of raw materials. The musical consequences of this development were reflected in the *Nigerian Music Review*, founded in 1977. Not surprisingly, this country whose official language is English, alongside a multitude of local languages, also advocated the idea of "polyglot" music because the presence of foreign elements in the culture was not necessarily regarded as negative. Fears of a musical "colonization" of Nigeria were therefore rejected as unfounded, with one exception: foreign pop music (Euba 1977, 19).

Leveling and its Limits

In the cultural policy of a number of countries, the dominant influence of Western popular music has led to measures directed at weakening its leveling effects. For example, there were occasional demands for import restrictions on recordings of Western popular music, or calls for restrictions on radio programs. In 1980 Kenya attempted to begin a "national renaissance" of music by a government decree proclaiming that seventy-five percent of the music played on the radio had to be performed by Kenyan musicians. The experiment was a failure, and the decree had to be annulled. It was shown that restrictive measures by themselves were not sufficient and had to be accompanied by positive promotion of native music to be successful.

The transfer of the technologies of electronic production and reproduction of music also allows developing countries the opportunity to play an active role in the acculturation process. Even where this possibility has not been taken advantage of, total westernization and leveling (to the best of present knowledge) does not have to take place. A study of the role played by the music industry in the present-day transformation leads to the prediction of two possible outcomes:

> A global music culture available to almost everybody [will be attained] long before a corresponding worldwide homogeneity in languages, living conditions, etc. is reached. . . . [Or] a multitude of types of music arising out of new living conditions and new music technologies [will emerge], at the same time as traditional music is adapted to new environments where, albeit with some changes, it can be put to similar uses and functions as in traditional society. (Wallis/Malm 1984, 324)

Investigation of the Western elements that penetrate non-Western music comes to a similar conclusion. According to Nettl (1985) these elements include functional harmony developed in Occidental music, notation and the idea of the integrity of the "work of music," and the adoption of Western instruments. Because musical practice still provides room for the expression of individual identity, it is still possible for cultural entities, social classes, certain age groups, and minorities to retain elements of their particular repertoires and musical styles. Were one to attempt to draw a conclusion from these processes about the reaction of world cultures to the invasion of Western music, one could say

> that each [culture] has tried, sometimes at great cost, to retain some significant degree of musical identity; and that each has found ways to symbolize, in its music, the positive, negative, and ambiguous aspects of its relationship to European-derived lifeways and values. (Nettl 1985, 165)

Whatever course "international music" will take in the future, technological evolution will play a crucial role; this justifies describing the process as mediamorphosis. Of course, we must make sure not to overrate the role of technology as if it were the single, inevitable determinant of cultural events. There can be no doubt that the tool we have created in turn gains power over us. "But technology alone will not decide the outcome. People and governments do that" (Wallis/Malm 1984, 324).

Despite the vast force of mediamorphosis and its palpable effects on musical activity on a world scale, it is no guarantee that our planet must be transformed into the "global village" of Marshall McLuhan. Despite standardization of economic and technological processes, countless differences will persist in the living conditions of peoples. Abstract patterns of the changes caused by mediamorphosis are unable to do justice to these differences. The climatic conditions of social life are themselves so diverse from region to region that no general standardization of cultural forms of behavior can be expected. The French writer Albert Camus once said that one of the world's many injustices, the injustice of climate, is never discussed (Camus 1961, 37). If we replace the word "injustice" with "differences" we can see that not only economic, social, and political factors are interwoven in the structure of conditions of cultural life, but climatic ones as well. The "natural" environment is one of these factors—the composition of the landscape, the climatic zone to which it belongs, the weather conditions, and so on.

This idea was not introduced by sociologists. It was present in the writings of Hegel and Marx, just as it was contained in the idea of "milieu" as used by Hippolyte Taine. Japanese culturology has rightly made a central concept of "fudo." This word can only be approximately translated as "climate," because it fuses the features of a culture with the natural phenomena of weather and geography (East Asia 1975). On the whole, Occidental culture belongs to the temperate climatic zone. This also explains why Occidental thought is largely unfamiliar with a theoretical construct that combines natural and cultural aspects, one well suited to describing factors that control the course of musical mutations. The continuing variety of climates in this sense will also, in my opinion, tend to limit leveling on an international scale. This could ensure for quite some time to come the existence of the pluralism cherished by advocates of cultural identities.

This statement once again supports my wish for the variety of methodologies appropriate to the universal history of music. The concept of global mediamorphosis does not conflict with this demand. It is not to be taken as a "law," but merely as a hypothesis that may be falsified by empirical research.

Epilogue

I hope this book has brought out my advocacy of a plurality of inductive methods where it was necessary to discuss theories. This attitude toward method shuns extreme generalizations that go beyond what can be verified empirically. A sociology of music that seeks to do justice to its tasks will identify such flimsy constructions as intellectual ballast that can easily go to one's head and must therefore be rejected. As I hope I have shown, our discipline is on the arduous way from philosophical construct to science. The further we proceed along this path the more successful we will be in renouncing premature generalizations, abstaining from taking observation into the sphere of speculation, and distinguishing legitimate theory (understood as refutable hypotheses) from hollow, pseudo-philosophical formulas. Those who are irritated by this coolness toward all-too-immediate enthusiasm for terminological pyrotechnics can be assuaged with the thesis of an Austrian physicist who achieved fame as a novelist. Robert Musil writes at the end of *Der Mann ohne Eigenschaften* [The Man without Qualities] that "when an idea becomes sounder, the keener mind abandons wrong answers as well as some more profound questions" (Musil 1970, 1120). Those familiar with the philosophy of the twentieth century will discover in Musil's affirmation a variation on a theme contained in the final sentence of Ludwig Wittgenstein's *Tractatus logico-philosophicus*: "One must remain silent on those things one cannot speak about." The score of socio-musicology also occasionally contains the word "tacet."

Bibliographies for the Sociology of Music

The following publications contain bibliographies for the sociology of music or more detailed bibliographic references.

Blaukopf, Kurt, ed.
  1967–   Musik und Gesellschaft. Vienna: VWGÖ (Verband der wissen-
          schaftlichen Gesellschaften Österreichs). Nos. 2–18 contain biblio-
          graphic information.

Elste, Martin
  1975   Verzeichnis deutschsprachiger Musiksoziologie 1848–1973. 2 vols.
          Hamburg: Karl Dieter Wagner.

Etzkorn, K. Peter
  1989   Bibliographies in Sociologists and Music, by Paul Honigsheim.
          New Brunswick, NJ: Transaction Publishers.

Fukač J., L. Mokrý,and V. Karbusický
  1967   Die Musiksoziologie in der Tschechoslowakei. Prague: Tschecho-
          slowakisches Musikinformationszentrum.

Karlsson, Henrik
  1982   Forskning om dagens musiksamhälle, Kulturpolitisk forskning och
          utvecking, 4, Statens Kulturrad. Stockholm: Statens kulturrad.

Kneif, Tibor
  1966   Gegenwartsfragen der Musiksoziologie: Ein Forschungsbericht.
          Acta Musicologica, vol. 38.

Ministry of Culture of the USSR and the Lenin State Library, Moscow
  1978   Research in the Sociology of Music in the USSR (1967–1977). Mos-
          cow: Information Center for Problems of Culture and Art.

Namenwirth, S. Micha, and Karin van der Linden
  1982   Muziek en Maatschappij: Geannoteerde Basisbibliografie. Brussels:
          Free University.

Silbermann, Alphons
  1973   Empirische Kunstsoziologie: Eine Einführung mit kommentierter Bibli-
          ographie. Stuttgart: B. G. Teubner.

1979   *Soziologie der Kunst.* In *Handbuch der empirischen Sozialforschung,* vol. 13, ed. René König. Stuttgart: Ferdinand Enke.

Supičić, Ivo
1976–78   *Sociology of Music: A Selected Bibliography.* In *IRASM,* 7 (2) 1976, 8 (1 & 2) 1977; 9 (1) 1978.
1987   *Music in Society: A Guide to the Sociology of Music.* New York: Pendragon Press.

Bibliography

The bibliography lists sources cited in the text and others which the author found to be important; they are recommended for further study.

Acham, Karl
1979　Realgeschichte—Geschichtswissenschaft—historische Sozial-wissenschaft. In *Sozialphilosophie als Aufklärung: Festschrift für Ernst Topitsch*, ed. Kurt Salamun. Tübingen: J. C. B. Mohr

Adler, Guido
1885　Umfang, Methode und Ziel der Musikwissenschaft. *Vierteljahrsschrift für Musikwissenschaft.* 1: 5–20.

1899　Musik und Musikwissenschaft. *Jahrbuch der Musikbibliothek Peters.* Leipzig: Peters.

1908　Über Heterophonie. In *Jahrbuch der Musikbibliothek Peters.* Leipzig: Peters.

1919　*Methode der Musikgeschichte.* Leipzig: Breitkopf & Härtel. Rpt. Farnborough: Gregg International Publishers, 1971.

1930　*Handbuch der Musikgeschichte.* 2d ed. 2 vols. Rpt. Tutzing: Hans Schneider, 1961.

Adorno, Theodor
1930　Reaktion und Fortschritt. *Anbruch* 12 (June): 191–195.

1955　*Prismen: Kulturkritik und Gesellschaft.* Frankfurt: Suhrkamp.

1956a　Die gegängelte Musik. In *Dissonanzen: Musik in der verwalteten Welt.* Göttingen: Vandenhoek & Ruprecht.

1956b　Über den Fetischcharakter in der Musik und die Regression des Hörens. In *Dissonanzen: Musik in der verwalteten Welt.* Göttingen: Vandenhoek & Ruprecht. [This version is slightly different from the first one, published in *Zeitschrift für Sozialforschung.* 10: 1938.]

1958　*Philosophie der neuen Musik.* Frankfurt: Suhrkamp. [1st ed. Tübingen, 1949.]

1963　*Quasi una fantasia: Musikalische Schriften II.* Frankfurt: Suhrkamp.

1964   *Moments musicaux: Neugedruckte Aufsätze 1928–1962*. Frankfurt: Suhrkamp.
1967a   *Ohne Leitbild: Parva Aesthetica*. Frankfurt: Suhrkamp.
1967b   Soziologische Anmerkungen zum deutschen Musikleben. In *Deutscher Musikrat—Referate—Informationen*, no. 5. [Also as Anmerkungen zum deutschen Musikleben in *Impromptus*, by Theodor Adorno. Frankfurt: Suhrkamp, 1968.]
1968   *Impromptus*. Frankfurt: Suhrkamp.
1973a   Zur gesellschaftlichen Lage der Musik. In *Kritische Kommunikationsforschung*, ed. Dieter Prokop. Munich: Carl Hanser. [Originally published in *Zeitschrift für Sozialforschung*, 1: 1932.]
1973b   On Popular Music. In *Kritische Kommunikationsforschung*, ed. Dieter Prokop. Munich: Carl Hanser.
1976   *Introduction to the Sociology of Music*. New York: The Seabury Press. [Originally published as: *Einleitung in die Musiksoziologie*. Frankfurt: Suhrkamp, 1962. 2d ed., corr. and enl., 1968.]

d'Alembert, Jean le Rond
1772   De la liberté de la musique. In *Mélanges de littérature, d'histoire et de philosophie*, vol. 4. Amsterdam.

Alexeyev, E. V., G. Golovinsky, and G. Zarakhovsky
1973   Approaches to the research of musical taste [in Russian]. In *Sovietskaya Muzyka* 1.

Alexeyev, E. V., L. Boguslavskaya, and G. Golovinsky
1974   The first steps of a new science [in Russian]. In *Sovietskaya Muzyka* 7.

Alexeyev, E. V., P. Andrukovich, and G. Golovinsky
1979   Questions of the sociology of art [in Russian]. In *Questions of the Sociology of Art*, ed. Kornienko et al. Moscow: Nauka.

Allen, Warren Dwight
1962   *Philosophies of Music History: A Study of General Histories of Music 1600–1960*. New York: Dover Publications.

Althaus, Horst
1971   *Ästhetik, Ökonomie und Gesellschaft*. Bern: Francke.

Apel, Willi.
1949   *The Notation of Polyphonic Music 900–1600*. Cambridge, MA: The Mediaeval Academy of America.

Apfel, Ernst
1962   Die klangliche Struktur der spätmittelalterlichen Musik. *Die Musikforschung* 15(3):212–227.

Aretz, Isabel
1974   Music in Latin America: The Perpetuation of Tradition. *Cultures* 1 (3): 117–131.
1977 (ed.) *América Latina en su música*. Mexico City: Siglo veintiuno editores.

Aristotle
1988   *Politics*. Ed. Stephen Everson. Cambridge: Cambridge University Press.

Associazione Generale Italiana dello Spettacolo
1980   *Carta musicale d'Italia*. 5th ed. Rome: Associazione Generale Italiana dello Spettacolo.

Assunto, Rosario
1963   *Die Theorie des Schönen im Mittelalter.* Cologne: DuMont.

Attali, Jacques
1977   *Bruits.* Paris: Presses Universitaires de France.

St. Augustine
1963   *The Confessions of Saint Augustine.* Trans. Rex Warner. New York: The New American Library.

Auzeill, J. P.
n.d. [1970] Les téléspectateurs et les émissions musicales. [Study of the "Service des Études de Marché"of the French Radio and Television O.R.T.F. Paris.] Paris: O.R.T.F.

Azevedo, Luis Heitor Correa de
1948   *A musica brasiliera e seus fundamentos.* Washington, D.C.: Pan American Union, Division of Musical and Visual Arts. [Portuguese with English translation.]
1980   Preliminary study on the project of preparing a Universal History of Music and on the role of the music of Latin America and the Carribean in this history. *The World of Music* 22 (3): 56–65.

Bacskai, Erika, Péter Makara, et al.
1969   *Beat* [in Hungarian]. Budapest: Zeneműkiadó. [A mimeographed summary in English entitled "Beat Movement in Hungary from the Aspects of Music and Juvenile Sociology" was presented to the Seventh World Congress for Sociology held in Varna, Bulgaria, in 1970.]

Bardez, Jean-Michel
1975   *Diderot et la musique.* Paris: Honoré Champion.

Barzun, Jacques
1950   *Berlioz and the Romantic Century.* Boston: Little, Brown and Company. [Rev. eds. 1956, 1969 as *Berlioz and His Century*].

Bastide, Roger
1977   *Art et société.* Paris: Payot.

Baumgarten, Eduard
1964   *Max Weber. Werk und Person.* Tübingen: J. C. B. Mohr.

Baumol, William J., and William G. Bowen
1966   *Performing Arts—The Economic Dilemma: A Study of Problems Common to Theater, Opera, Music and Dance.* New York: Twentieth Century Fund.

BBC
1964   The Public for "Serious Music." Part 1: Memorandum, Part 2: Statistical results. London: The British Broadcasting Corporation.
1969   *The Tastes and Opinions of Music Programme Listeners.* London: The British Broadcasting Corporation.

Beaud, Paul, and Alfred Willener
1973   *Musique et vie quotidienne: Essay de sociologie d'une nouvelle culture.* Paris: Maison Mame.

Bebey, Francis
1969   *Musique de l'Afrique.* Paris: Horizons de France.
1979   African musical tradition in the face of foreign influence. *Cultures* 6 (2): 134–140.

Becker, Heinz
1980   Die Mannheimer Schule. Program notes to the recording "Die Mannheimer Schule" (Archiv Produktion 2723 068).

Becker, Howard S.
1977   Foreword to *Whose Music: A Sociology of Musical Languages*, ed. John Shepherd et al. London: Latimer.
1982   *Art Worlds*. Berkeley, Los Angeles: University of California Press.

Bekker, Paul
1916   *Das deutsche Musikleben*. Berlin: Schuster & Loeffler.

Belvianes, Marcel
1951   *Sociologie de la musique*. Paris: Payot.

Belz, Carl
1969   *The Story of Rock*. New York: Oxford University Press.

Benade, Arthur H.
1976   *Fundamentals of Musical Acoustics*. New York: Oxford University Press.

Benary, Peter
1961   *Die deutsche Kompositionslehre des 18. Jahrhunderts*. Leipzig: Breitkopf & Härtel.

Bendix, Reinhard
1964   *Max Weber: Das Werk*. Munich: Piper.

Benjamin, Walter
1963   *Das Kunstwerk im Zeitalter seiner technischen Reproduzierbarkeit*. Frankfurt: Suhrkamp.

Beranek, Leo L.
1962   *Music, Acoustics and Architecture*. New York: John Wiley & Sons.

Bergeijk, Willem A. van, John R. Pierce, and Edward E. David.
1960   *Waves and the Ear*. Garden City, NY: Doubleday.

Berlioz, Hector
1905   *Instrumentationslehre*. Ergänzt und revidiert von Richard Strauss. Leipzig: Breitkopf & Härtel. [Translation of *Grand traité d'instrumentation et d'orchestration modernes*. Engl. trans. New York: Kalmus, 1948.]

Bernsdorf, Wilhelm, and Friedrich Bülow, eds.
1955   *Wörterbuch der Soziologie*. Stuttgart: Ferdinand Enke.

Bernsdorf, Wilhelm, ed.
1959   *Soziologenlexikon*. Stuttgart: Ferdinand Enke.

Besseler, Heinrich
1926   Grundfragen des musikalischen Hörens. In *Jahrbuch der Musikbibliothek Peters für das Jahr 1925*. Leipzig: Peters. [Also in *Musikhören*, ed. Bernhard Dopheide. Darmstadt, 1975.] Rpt. in *Aufsätze zur Musikästhetik und Musikgeschichte*. Leipzig: Philipp Reclam jun., 1978.]
1938   Musik und Raum. In *Musik und Bild: Festschrift für Max Seiffert*. Kassel: Bärenreiter.
1950   *Bourdon und Fauxbourdon: Studien zum Ursprung der niederländischen Musik*. Leipzig: Breitkopf & Härtel.
1959   *Das musikalische Hören der Neuzeit*. Berlin (East): Akademie-Verlag. [Rpt. in *Aufsätze zur Musikästhetik und Musikgeschichte*. Leipzig: Philipp Reclam jun., 1978.]

1979 *Die Musik des Mittelalters und der Renaissance.* Wiesbaden: Akademische Verlagsgesellschaft Athenaion. [Rpt. of 1931 ed.]

Besseler, Heinrich, and Peter Gülke

1973 *Schriftbild der mehrstimmigen Musik.* Leipzig: Deutscher Verlag für Musik. (= *Musikgeschichte in Bildern,* vol. 3/5, ed. Werner Bachmann.)

Blaug, Mark

1976 *The Economics of the Arts.* London: Martin Robertson & Company.

Blaukopf, Kurt

1954 Über die Veränderung der Hörgewohnheit: Aktuelle Bemerkungen zum akustisch-technischen Einfluß auf den musikalischen Geschmack. *Schweizerische Musikzeitung* 94: 60–61.

1962 Raumakustische Probleme der Musiksoziologie. *Die Musikforschung* 15 (3): 237–246.

1968a *Zur Bestimmung der klanglichen Erfahrung der Musikstudierenden.* (Musik und Gesellschaft, 2.) Karlsruhe: G. Braun.

1968b Probleme der Raumakustik und des Hörverhaltens. In *Alte Musik in unserer Zeit,* ed. Walter Wiora. Kassel: Bärenreiter. (Musikalische Zeitfragen, 13.)

1969 Die qualitative Veränderung musikalischer Mitteilung in den technischen Medien der Massenkommunikation. *Kölner Zeitschrift für Soziologie und Sozialpsychologie* 21 (3): 510–516.

1971a Probleme der elektroakustischen Aufzeichnung der Bühnenwerke Richard Wagners. In *Beiträge 70/71* (Österreichische Gesellschaft für Musik), ed. Rudolf Klein. Kassel: Bärenreiter.

1971b Space in Electronic Music. In *Music and Technology,* ed. William Skyvington. Special number of *La Revue Musicale.* Paris: 157–171.

1972a Hymnen. *HiFi-Stereophonie* 8: 708.

1972b *Musiksoziologie. Eine Einführung in die Grundbegriffe mit besonderer Berücksichtigung der Soziologie der Tonsysteme.* 2d ed. Niederteufen, Switzerland: Niggli.

1972c Symphonie, Konzertwesen, Publikum. In *Die Welt der Symphonie,* ed. Ursula Rauchhaupt. Braunschweig: Georg Westermann.

1974 *Neue musikalische Verhaltensweisen der Jugend.* Vol. 5 of *Musikpädagogik: Forschung und Lehre,* ed. Sigrid Abel-Struth. Mainz: Schott.

1977a *Massenmedium Schallplatte: Mit einem Beitrag von Paul Beaud.* Wiesbaden: Breitkopf & Härtel.

1977b Music on Records: Sociological and Statistical Aspects. In *International Musicological Society, Report of the Twelfth Congress,* ed. D. Heartz and B. Wade. Berkeley, 1977, and Kassel, 1981.

1980a Max Weber und die Musiksoziologie. In *Festschrift für Rudolf Haase,* ed. Werner Schulze. Eisenstadt: Elfriede Rötzer.

1980b Gespeicherte Tonsysteme: Zu einem Projekt der Hochschule für Musik und darstellende Kunst in Wien. Unpublished MS. Vienna: Institut für Musiksoziologie.

1980c Akustische Umwelt und Musik des Alltags. In *Musik im Alltag,* ed. R. Brinkmann. Mainz: Schott.

1983 The Strategies of the Record Industries. In *Music Industries and Creativity, Cultural Policy Series,* no. 4. Strasbourg: Council of Europe.

| 1985a | Strategies of Music Industries and Radio Organisations. Council of Europe, Document CC-GP 11 (85) 2. Strasbourg: Council of Europe. |

1985a   Strategies of Music Industries and Radio Organisations. Council of Europe, Document CC-GP 11 (85) 2. Strasbourg: Council of Europe.

1985b   Cultural Mutation Brought on by New Technologies. *Communications* 11 (3).

1985c   L'utilisation secondaire de la musique dans les médias. *Études de Radio-Télévision*, 35 (November):45–54.

1989   *Beethovens Erben in der Mediamorphose: Kultur-und Medienpolitik für die elektronische Ära*. Heiden, Switzerland: Niggli.

1990a   Les institutions des arts du spectacle et les médias électroniques. In *Les malheurs d'Orphée*, ed. Robert Wangermée. Brussels-Liège: Pierre Mardaga.

1990b   Legal Policies for the Safeguarding of Traditional Music: Are They Utopian? *The World of Music* 32 (1): 125–133.

1979 (ed.)   *Soziographie des Musiklebens*. (Musik und Gesellschaft, 17). Karlsruhe: G. Braun.

1980 (ed.)   *Music Festivals in Europe, Including the United States, Canada and Israel*. Vienna: Doblinger.

1982 (ed.)   *The Phonogram in Cultural Communication*. Vienna, New York: Springer.

Blomster, W. V.
1976   Sociology of Music: Adorno and Beyond. *Telos*, 28 (Summer 1976).

Blum, Stephen
1978   Changing roles of performers in Meshhed and Bojnurd, Iran. In *Eight Urban Musical Cultures*, ed. Bruno Nettl. Urbana, IL: University of Illinois Press.

Bontinck, Irmgard, et al.
1984   Die Lage der Komponisten. Amt der Salzburger Landesregierung, ed. *Künstler in Österreich*. Salzburg: Landeskulturreferentenkonferenz.

1986a   The "Mediatisation" of Established Musical Life. *ISME Year Book* 13: 185–191.

1986b   The Impact of Electronic Media on Adolescents, Their Everyday Experience, Their Learning Orientation and Leisure Time Activities. *Communications* 2 (1): 21–30.

1988   Comportement d'écoute et pratique musicale. In *Musique et société*, ed. M. Vanhulst and M. Haine. Brussels: Editions de l'Université.

1989   Versuche zur Typologie musikalischer Manifestationen/Per una tipologia delle manifestazioni musicali. In *Atti del Convegno Sociologia della Musica, Annali di Sociologia* 5 (1), ed. Luigi Del Grosso Destreri. Trent: Temi Editrice.

1990   The Role of Communication Technologies in the Safeguarding and Enhancing of European Unity and Cultural Diversity. *Council of Europe, Council for Cultural Cooperation*, Document COM (90) 1b. Strasbourg. 7 August.

Bontinck, Irmgard, ed.
1974   *New Patterns of Musical Behaviour: A Survey of Youth Activities in 18 Countries*. Valley Forge, PA: European American Publishers.

1977   *Kritik der etablierten Kultur*. Vienna: Universal Edition.

Bontinck, Irmgard, and J. Breuer, eds.
1979   *Institutionen des Musiklebens in Europa*. Vienna: Doblinger.

Bopp, Wilhelm
1925   Collini über Musik und Sonaten im besonderen. *Die Musik* 17:
938.

Borkenau, Franz
1976   *Der Übergang vom feudalen zum bürgerlichen Weltbild*. Rpt. Darmstadt: Wissenschaftliche Buchgesellschaft. [1st ed. Paris, 1934.]

Boulez, Pierre.
1966   *Relevés d'apprenti*. Paris: editions du Seuil.

Bourdieu, Pierre
1969   Sociologie de la perception esthétique. In (n.a., n.e.) *Les sciences
humaines et l'oeuvre d'art*. Brussels: Témoins et Témoignages.

Breh, Karl.
1980   *Die Mutation musikalischer Kommunikation durch High Fidelity und
Stereophonie*. (Musik und Gesellschaft, 18.) Karlsruhe: G. Braun.

Brelet, Gisèle
1967   Musicalisation de l'espace dans la musique contemporaine. In
Festschrift für Walter Wiora, ed. Ludwig Finscher and Christian
Mahling. Kassel: Bärenreiter.

Brodde, Otto
1972   *Heinrich Schütz: Weg und Werk*. Kassel: Bärenreiter.

Bücher, Karl.
1919   *Arbeit und Rhythmus*. 5th ed. Leipzig: Emmanuel Reinike.

Bugliarello, George, et al.
1976   *The Impact of Noise Pollution: A Socio-Technological Introduction*.
New York: Pergamon Press.

Bukofzer, Manfred
1977   *Music in the Baroque Era*. London: J. M. Dent. [1st ed. 1947.]

Burckhardt, Jacob
1978   *Weltgeschichtliche Betrachtungen*. Munich: Deutscher Taschenbuch
Verlag.

Bürger, Peter
1974   *Theorie der Avantgarde*. Frankfurt: Suhrkamp.
1978 (ed.) *Seminar: Literatur- und Kunstsoziologie*. Frankfurt: Suhrkamp.

Burney, Charles
1959   *An Eighteenth-Century Musical Tour in Central Europe and the Netherlands*. London: Oxford University Press. [Rpt. of *The Present
State of Music in Germany, the Netherlands and the United Provinces*,
1773]

Camus, Albert
1961   *Kleine Prosa*. Reinbek: Rowohlt.

Chabrier, Jean-Claude.
1974   Music in the Fertile Crescent: Lebanon, Syria, Iraq. *Cultures* 1 (3):
35–58.

Chase, Gilbert
1976   Musicology, History, and Anthropology. In *Current Thought in
Musicology*, ed. John W. Grubbs. Austin: University of Texas
Press.

Childe, Gordon
1946   *What Happened in History*. London: Penguin Books.

Combarieu, Jules
1907   *La musique, ses lois, son évolution*. Paris: Ernest Flammarion.

Commission Nationale pour l'Étude des Problèmes de la Musique
1964   Paris: Ministère des affaires culturelles.

Comte, Auguste
1969   *Sociologie: Textes choisis par Jean Laubier*. 3d ed. Paris: Presses Universitaires.

Corbin, Solange
1960   *L'église à la conquête de sa musique*. Paris: Gallimard.

Coster, Michel de
1975   L'art mass-médiatisée: L'example de la musique classique enregistrée. *IRASM* 6: 255–268.

1976   *Le disque, art ou affaires? Analyse sociologique d'une industrie culturelle*. Grenoble: Presses Universitaires de Grenoble.

Critchley, MacDonald
1977   Ecstatic and Synaesthetic Experiences During Musical Perception. In *Music and the Brain: Studies in the Neurology of Music*, ed. M. Critchley and R. A. Henson. London: William Heinemann Medical Books.

Croce, Benedetto
1983   *Guide to Aesthetics*. Lanham, NY: University Press of America. [Translation of *Breviario di estetica*. Bari: Laterza, 1913.]

Crossley-Holland, Peter
1966   Problems and Opportunities in Listening to the Music of Another Civilisation. In *Music East and West*, ed. Indian Council for Cultural Relations. New Delhi: Indian Council for Cultural Relations.

Cuvillier, Armand
1960   *Kurzer Abriß der soziologischen Denkweise*. Stuttgart: Ferdinand Enke. [Originally publ. as *Introduction à la sociologie*. Paris: Armand Colin.]

Cwi, David, ed.
1978   *Research in the Arts. Proceedings of the Conference on Policy-related Studies of the National Endowment for the Arts*. Baltimore: Walters Art Gallery.

Dadelsen, Georg von
1964   Über das Wechselspiel von Musik und Notation. In *Festschrift für Walter Gerstenberg*, ed. Georg Dadelsen and Andreas Holschneider. Wolfenbüttel: Möseler.

Dahlhaus, Carl
1968   *Untersuchungen über die Enstehung der harmonischen Tonalität*. Kassel: Bärenreiter.

1970   Zur Kritik des ästhetischen Urteiles: Über Liszts "Prometheus." *Die Musikforschung* 23: 411–419.

1974   Das musikalische Kunstwerk als Gegenstand der Soziologie. *IRASM* 5: 11–26

1978   *Die Idee der absoluten Musik*. Kassel: Bärenreiter.

Damasio, A. R., and Hanna Damasio
1977   Musical Faculty and Cerebral Dominance. In *Music and the Brain: Studies in the Neurology of Music*, ed. M. Critchley and R. A. Henson. London: William Heinemann.

Daniélou, Alain
1973   *Die Musik Asiens zwischen Mißachtung und Wertschätzung*. Wilhelmshaven: Heinrichshofen.
1975   *Einführung in die indische Musik*. Wilhelmshaven: Heinrichshofen.
1978   *Sémantique musicale*. Paris: Hermann.

Dart, Thurston
1958   *The Interpretation of Music*. 3d ed. London: Hutchinson.

Deglin, Vadim L.
1976   Our Split Brain. *The UNESCO Courier*, January: 4–19.

Del Grosso Destreri, Luigi
1968   La sociologia della musica: situazione e prospettive. In *Studi di Sociologia* 6: 156–179.
1971   *Sociologia dell'arte?* Trent: Istituto Superiore di Scienze Sociali.
1972   *Europäisches Hit-Panorama: Erfolgsschlager in vier europäischen Ländern—Aussagen, Inhalte, Analysen*. (Musik und Gesellschaft, 12.) Karlsruhe: G. Braun.
1988   *La sociologia, la musica e le musiche*. Milan: Unicopli.
1989 (ed.) Atti di Convegno Sociologia della Musica. *Annali di Sociologia* 5 (1). Trent: Temi Editrice.

Demetz, Peter
1969   *Marx, Engels und die Dichter: Ein Kapitel deutscher Literaturgeschichte*. Frankfurt: Ullstein.

Descartes, René
1650   *Musicae compendium*. Utrecht. Rpt. of the 2d ed. (Amsterdam, 1656). In *Leitfaden der Musik*, by Renatus Descartes; ed., trans., and notes Johannes Brockt. Darmstadt: Wissenschaftliche Buchgesellschaft, 1978.

Deutsch, Walter
1975 (ed.) Lungau Report 1975: Ein musikalischer Forschungsbericht. MS. Vienna: Institut für Volksmusikforschung.
1976   *Heimatkunde des Bezirkes Scheibbs: Die Volksmusik des Bezirkes Scheibbs*. Scheibbs: Rudolf und Fritz Radinger.
1978   Bericht über die kulturelle Situation in Kremsmünster mit besonderer Berücksichtigung der Musik. Institut für Volksmusikforschung der Hochschule für Musik und darstellende Kunst in Wien. (photocopy). Vienna.

Deutscher Musikrat
1973 (ed.) Musik in der Planung der Städte. *Deutscher Musikrat, Referate, Informationen* 23. Bonn-Bad Godesberg: Deutscher Musikrat.

Deva, B. C.
1975 (ed.) *Musical Scales*. Report of Symposium, February 1973. New Delhi: Sangeet Natak Akademi.

Donnat, Olivier, and Denis Cogneau
1989   *Les pratiques culturelles des Français 1973–1989*. Paris: La Documentation Française.

Bibliography

Dopheide, Bernhard
1975 (ed.) *Musikhören*. Darmstadt: Wissenschaftliche Buchgesellschaft.
1978 *Musikhören, Hörerziehung*. Darmstadt: Wissenschaftliche Buchgesellschaft.

Dranov, Paula
1980 *Inside the Music Publishing Industry*. White Plains, NY: Knowledge Industry Publications.

Dumazedier, Joffre
1975 Review of The Use of Time. Ed., Alexander Szalai. In *Revue française de sociologie*, January-March 1975: 125–129.

Dupuis, Xavier
1980 La gestion du non marchand: Analyse économique de la production lyrique. Study by the Laboratoire d'économie sociale de l'Université de Paris (photocopied). Paris: Laboratoire d'Economie Sociale. Université de Paris I.

Durkheim, Emile
1950 *Leçons de sociologie: Physique des moeurs et du droit*. Paris: Presses Universitaires.
1963 *Les règles de la méthode sociologique*. 15th ed. Paris: Presses Universitaires.

Dürr, Alfred
1971 *Die Kantaten von Johann Sebastian Bach*. Kassel: Bärenreiter.

East Asian Cultural Studies
1975 The Present State of Research on Cultural Development in Japan. *East Asian Cultural Studies* 14. Tokyo: Centre for East Asian Cultural Studies.

Edgerton, Samuel Y., Jr.
1975 *The Renaissance Discovery of Linear Perspective*. New York: Basic Books.
1976 Linear Perspective and the Western Mind: The Origins of Objective Representation in Art and Science. *Cultures* 3 (3): 77–104.

Einstein, Alfred
1947 *Music in the Romantic Era*. New York: W.W. Norton.

Ellis, Alexander John
1885 On the Musical Scales of Various Nations. *Journal of the Royal Society of Arts* 33: 1885.

Escal, Françoise
1979 *Espaces sociaux, espaces musicaux*. Paris: Payot.

Etzkorn, K. Peter
1963 The Social Context of Songwriting in the United States. *Ethnomusicology* 7: 96–106.
1964 Georg Simmel and the Sociology of Music. *Social Forces* 43: 101–107.
1974 On Music, Social Structure and Sociology. *IRASM* 5: 43–49.
1985 Sociological Demystification of the Arts and Music: Max Weber and Beyond. In *Theory of Liberty, Legitimacy and Power: New Directions in the Intellectual and Scientific Legacy of Max Weber*, ed. Vatro Murvar. London: Routledge & Kegan Paul.

1988a   Sociology, Public Policy and Contemporary Music: Observations on Changing Support Systems for Music. Paper presented at the Conference on Sociology of Music, Gothenburg, April 1988.

1988b   Contemporary Mediated Music: Challenge to Music Education. Paper presented at the ISME Seminar on Changes in Professional Profiles of Music Educators Prompted by Technological Innovations. Byron Bay, New South Wales, Australia, July 1988.

Etzkorn, Lars
1990   Balancing Art and Politics: The Use of Peer Panels in United States Funding of the Arts. *Saint Louis University Public Law Review* 9 (1): 323–342.

Euba, Akin
1977   An Introduction to Music in Nigeria. *Nigerian Music Review* 1.

Fellerer, Karl Gustav
1963   *Soziologie der Kirchenmusik*. Cologne: Westdeutscher Verlag.

Ferand, Ernest
1938   *Die Improvisation in der Musik*. Zurich: Rhein-Verlag.
1951   "Sodaine and Unexpected" Music in the Renaissance. *The Musical Quarterly* 37: 10–27.

Ferber, Christian von
1965   Der Werturteilsstreit 1909/1959: Versuch einer wissenschaftlichen Interpretation. In *Logik der Sozialwissenschaften*, ed. Ernst Topitsch. Cologne: Kiepenheuer & Witsch.

Fichtenau, Heinrich
1946   *Mensch und Schrift im Mittelalter*. Vienna: Universum.

Finscher, Ludwig
1975   Die "Entstehung des Komponisten." *IRASM* 6: 29–45 (cf. also the discussion on this report, Ibid., 135–142.)

Flender, Reinhard, and Hermann Rauhe
1989   *Popmusik: Geschichte, Funktion, Wirkung und Ästhetik*. Darmstadt: Wissenschaftliche Buchgesellschaft.

Fleouter, Claude
1980   Fela Anikulapo, figure de proue de la musique africaine contemporaine. *Le Monde*, 28/29 September.

Flothuis, Marius
1974   Taken van de hedendaagse musicoloog. Inaugural address given at the University of Utrecht.

Flotzinger, Rudolf
1979   Soziographie in der österreichischen Musikgeschichte. In *Soziographie des Musiklebens*, ed. Kurt Blaukopf. (Musik und Gesellschaft, 17.) Karlsruhe: G. Braun.

Flotzinger, Rudolf, and Gernot Gruber
1977–1979 *Musikgeschichte Österreichs*. Graz, Vienna, Cologne: Verlag Styria.

Fohrbeck, Karla, and Andreas Wiesand, eds.
1982   *Musik—Statistik—Kulturpolitik*. Cologne: DuMont.

Forkel, Johann Nikolaus
1802   *Über Johann Sebastian Bachs Leben, Kunst und Kunstwerke*. Engl. trans. A. Mendel in *The Bach Reader*. New York: Norton, 1945.

Frank, Karl Suso, ed.
1975   *Frühes Mönchtum im Abendland*. 2 vols. Zurich: Artemis.

Franklin, Elda and David A. Franklin
1978   The Brain Research Bandwagon. *Music Educators Journal* November: 38–43.

Frederickson, Jon
1989   Technology and Music Performance in the Age of Mechanical Reproduction. *IRASM* 20 (2) December: 193–220.

Freud, Sigmund
1956   *Totem und Tabu: Einige Übereinstimmungen im Seelenleben der Wilden und der Neurotiker*. Frankfurt: S. Fischer. (Several Engl. trans.)

Frey, Gerhard
1967   *Die Mathematisierung unserer Welt*. Stuttgart: W. Kohlhammer.
1977   Wissenschaftliche Begründung bei Carnap und Popper. In *Österreichische Philosophen und ihr Einfluß auf die analytische Philosophie der Gegenwart*, vol. 1, ed. J. Chr. Marek et al. Special issue of *CONCEPTUS, Zeitschrift für Philosophie*.

Frith, Simon
1978   *Sociology of Rock*. London: Constable.
1982   The Sociology of Rock—Notes from Britain (142–154). In *Popular Music Perspectives*, ed. David Horn and Philip Tagg. Gothenburg; Exeter: International Association for the Study of Popular Music.

Frotscher, Gotthold
1963   *Aufführungspraxis alter Musik*. Wilhelmshaven: Heinrichshofen.

Fukač, Jiří
1969   Soziologische Gesichtspunkte der musikwissenschaftlichen Methoden Vladimír Helferts. In *Sborník prací filosofické Brnenské University*, 4: 67–76.
1972   The Czech Sociology of Music (Theory and Empiricism). *Society and Leisure*, 4: 81–90.

Fukač, J., L. Mokrý, and V. Karbusický
1967   *Die Musiksoziologie in der Tschechoslowakei*. Prague: Tschechoslowakisches Musikinformationszentrum.

Furtwängler, Wilhelm
1954   *Ton und Wort: Aufsätze und Vorträge 1918 bis 1954*. Wiesbaden: F. A. Brockhaus.

Geiringer, Karl
1959   *Joseph Haydn*. Mainz: Schott [Orig. publ. in Engl., New York: Norton, 1946].

Georgiades, Thrasybulos
1954   *Musik und Sprache: Das Werden der abendländischen Musik*. Berlin: Springer-Verlag.
1958   Zur Lasso-Gesamtausgabe.In *Bericht über den Internationalen Musikwissenschaftlichen Kongreß* Wien 1956. Graz: Böhlau.

Gerson-Kiwi, Edith
1938   *Studien zur Geschichte des italienischen Liedmadrigals im XVI. Jahrhundert*. Würzburg: Konrad Triltsch.
1962   Musiker des Orients—ihr Wesen und ihr Werdegang. *Studia Musicologica* 3: 127–132.

1965 The Bards of the Bible. *Studia Musicologica* 7: 61–70.
1973 The Musician in Society: East and West. *Cultures* 1: 165–193.
1980 *Migrations and Mutations of the Music in the East and West.* Tel Aviv: Tel Aviv University.

Ghatnekar, V. V.
1975 Automatic Production of Music. In *Musical Scales*, ed. B. C. Deva. New Delhi: Sangeet Natak Akademi.

Godelier, Maurice
1973 *Ökonomische Anthropologie: Untersuchungen zum Begriff der sozialen Struktur primitiver Gesellschaften.* Reinbek: Rowohlt.

Goldmann, Lucie
1978 Der genetische Strukturalismus in der Literatursoziologie. In *Seminar: Literatur- und Kunstsoziologie*, ed. Peter Bürger. Frankfurt: Suhrkamp.

Golovinsky, Grigory
1988 Rock Music and the Media: New trends in the Soviet Union. In *Man and the Mediasphere, Culture and Communication* 6. Budapest: Research Institute for Culture.

Gombrich, Ernst H.
1960 *Art and Illusion.* New York: Pantheon.
1978 *Kunst und Fortschritt.* Cologne: DuMont. [Originally publ. as *The Ideas of Progress and Their Impact on Art.* New York: Cooper Union School of Art and Architecture, 1971.]

Graf, Walter
1965 Die vergleichende Musikwissenschaft an der Universität Wien. In *Mitteilungen der Anthropologischen Gesellschaft in Wien* 95: 155–161.
1967 Biologische Wurzeln des Musikerlebens. In *Schriften des Vereines zur Verbreitung naturwissenschaftlicher Kenntnisse in Wien.* 1967 report. 107: 1–39.
1969 *Die musikalische Klangforschung.* (Musik und Gesellschaft, 6.) Karlsruhe: G. Braun.
1975 Gestaltungsmerkmale der Klangwelt und des Musikerlebens. In *Grundlagen der Musiktherapie und Musikpsychologie*, ed. Gerhart Harrer. Stuttgart: Gustav Fischer.

Grant, N. K., W. S. Hendon, and V. L. Owens, eds.
1987 *Economic Efficiency in the Performing Arts.* Akron: Association for Cultural Economics (University of Akron).

Gregor, Joseph
1944 *Kulturgeschichte des Balletts.* Vienna: Gallus.

Gruber, Gernot, Franz Födermayr, et al.
1977 Gedanken zu einer Universalgeschichte der Musik. In *Musicologia Austriaca* 1. Munich, Salzburg: Emil Katzbichler.

Gurevich, A. J.
1976 Time as a Problem of Cultural History. In *Cultures and Time*, ed. UNESCO. Paris: The UNESCO Press.

Gut, Serge
1976 La notion de la consonance chez les théoriciens du moyen age. *Acta Musicologica* 48: 20–44.

Guttmann, Giselher
1974 *Einführung in die Neuropsychologie.* 2d ed. Bern: Hans Huber.

Guyau, Jean-Marie
1923   *L'art au point de vue sociologique.* 13th ed. Paris: Félix Alcan. [First publ. in 1889.]

Haack, Helmut
1974   *Anfänge des Generalbaß-Satzes.* Tutzing: Hans Schneider.

Haberlandt, Michael
1900   *Cultur im Alltag.* Vienna: Wiener Verlag.

Habermas, Jürgen
1968   *Strukturwandel der Öffentlichkeit.* 3d ed. Neuwied: Luchterhand.

Hamm, Charles
1988   Socio-Musicology and Cultural Policy in the United States of America. In *Musiksociologisk konferens 1988,* ed. Jan Ling. Papers prepared for the Conference held at the University of Gothenburg, April 1988.

Hammerstein, Reinhold
1962   *Die Musik der Engel: Untersuchungen zur Musikanschauung des Mittelalters.* Bern: Francke.
1974   *Diabolus in musica: Studien zur Ikonographie der Musik im Mittelalter.* Bern: Francke.

Harrer, Gerhart, and H. Harrer
1975   Das "Musikerlebnis" im Griff des naturwissenschaftlichen Experiments. In *Grundlagen der Musiktherapie und Musikpsychologie,* ed. Gerhart Harrer. Stuttgart: Gustav Fischer.
1977   Music, Emotion and Autonomic Function. In *Music and the Brain: Studies in the Neurology of Music,* ed. M. Critchley and R. A. Henson. London: William Heinemann.

Hartmann, Dominik
1970   Beethovens Ruhm: Versuch einer Entmythologisierung. In *HiFi-Stereophonie* 9: 237–243.

Haseloff, O. W., and H. J. Hoffmann
1965   *Kleines Lehrbuch der Statistik.* 2d ed. Berlin: Walter de Gruyter.

Hauser, Arnold
1951   *The Social History of Art.* 4 vols. New York: Vintage Books.
1973   *Kunst und Gesellschaft.* Munich: C. H. Beck.

Heeschen, Claus
1972   *Grundfragen der Linguistik.* Stuttgart: W. Kohlhammer.

Hegel, Georg Wilhelm Friedrich
1970   *Vorlesungen über Ästhetik.* 3 vols. Frankfurt: Suhrkamp.

Helmholtz, Hermann von
1913   *Die Lehre von den Tonempfindungen als physiologische Grundlage für die Theorie der Musik.* 6th ed. Braunschweig: Friedrich Vieweg. [First publ. 1863; Engl. transl. New York, 1948.]

Hennion, A., and J. P. Vignolle
1978   Artisans et industriels du disque: Essai sur le mode de production de la musique. Paris: Centre de Sociologie de l'Innovation. École Nationale Supérieure des Mines.

Herbart, Johann Friedrich
1891   *Lehrbuch zur Einleitung in die Philosophie.* Vol. 4 of *Sämtliche Werke in chronologischer Reihenfolge.* Leipzig: Veit.

Hermelink, Siegfried
1961   Die Tabula compositoria. In *Festschrift Heinrich Besseler*. Leipzig: Deutscher Verlag für Musik.

Hey Ku Lee
1975   Impact of Western Music on Asian Music. In *Proceedings of the First Asian Pacific Music Conference* 54–60. Seoul, n.p.

Hickmann, Hans
1970   Die Musik des arabisch-islamischen Bereichs. In *Orientalische Musik*, ed. Hans Hickmann and Wilhelm Staude. (= *Handbuch der Orientalistik*, sec.1, supplement IV, ed. B. Spuler et al.) Leiden, Cologne: E.J. Brill.

Hillman-Chartrand, H., W. S. Hendon, and H. Horowitz, eds.
1987   *Paying for the Arts*. Akron: The University of Akron.

Hoffmann, E. T. A.
1919   Alte Kirchenmusik (1814). In *Musikalische Novellen und Aufsätze*, by E. T. A. Hoffmann, ed. Edgar Istel. Regensburg: Deutsche Musikbücherei.

Honigsheim, Paul
1961   Musiksoziologie. In *Handwörterbuch der Sozialwissenschaften*, vol. 7. Göttingen: Vandenhoeck & Ruprecht.
1963   Erinnerungen an Max Weber. In *Max Weber zum Gedächtnis: Kölner Zeitschrift für Soziologie und Sozialpsychologie* 15: 161–271, ed. René König and Johannes Winckelmann. (Special edition.)
1973   *Music and Society: The Later Writings of Paul Honigsheim*, ed. K. Peter Etzkorn. New York: John Wiley.
1989   *Sociologists and Music*. (Revised edition of *Music and Society*.) New Brunswick, NJ: Transaction Publishers.

Hood, Mantle
1972   Music of Indonesia. In *Handbuch der Orientalistik*, sec.3, vol. 6, ed. B. Spuler et al. Leiden, Cologne: E.J. Brill.
1980   *Music of the Roaring Sea*. Vol. 1 of *The Evolution of Javanese Gamelan*. Wilhelmshaven: Heinrichshofen.

Horkheimer, Max, and Theodor W. Adorno
1971   *Dialektik der Aufklärung*. Frankfurt: S. Fischer.

Hornbostel, Erich M.
1903   Musikalisches zum XVI. Internationalen Amerikanistenkongreß in Wien. *Zeitschrift der Internationalen Musikgesellschaft* 10: 4–7.
1911   Über ein akustisches Kriterium für Kulturzusammenhänge. *Zeitschrift für Ethnologie* 43: 601–615.
1925   Die Einheit der Sinne. *Melos, Zeitschrift für Musik* 4 (January): 290–297.
1927   Musikalische Tonsysteme. In *Handbuch der Physik*, vol. 8, ed. K. Geiger and K. Scheel. Berlin: Springer.
1963   The Demonstration Collection of E. M. von Hornbostel and the Berlin Phonogramm-Archiv. [Two records, catalogue no. FE 4175, with notes by Kurt Reinhard and George List, a joint publication of the Museum of Ethnology, Berlin, and Indiana University, Bloomington, Indiana.] New York: Ethnic Folkways Library.

Hübinger, Paul Egon, ed.
1968   *Kulturbruch oder Kulturkontinuität im Übergang von der Antike zum Mittelalter*. Darmstadt: Wissenschaftliche Buchgesellschaft.

Hudson, W.
1969   The Study of the Problem of Pictorial Perception Among Unaccultured Groups. In *Cross-Cultural Studies*, ed. D. R. Price-Williams. London: Penguin Books.

IFES [= Institut für empirische Sozialforschung]
1975   Grundlagenforschung im kulturellen Bereich (photocopy). Vienna: IFES.

Indian Council for Cultural Relations, ed.
1966   *Music East and West*. New Delhi: Indian Council for Cultural Relations.

INFRATEST
1963   Musik im Hörfunk: Was wissen wir über den Musikhörer. Munich: Infratest.

IRASM [= 1970–. *International Review of the Aesthetics and Sociology of Music.*] Zagreb: Institute of Musicology.

ISME [= International Society for Musical Education], ed.
Year Books published in conjunction with the Department of Music, University of Western Australia.

Jahoda, Marie, Paul F. Lazarsfeld, and Hans Zeisel
1978   *Die Arbeitslosen von Marienthal*. 2d ed. Frankfurt: Suhrkamp.

Jannssen, J., and H. Kaegi
1986   MIDIM-duplication of a Central Javanese Sound Concept. *Interface: Journal of New Music Research* 15: 185–229.

Jaspers, Karl
1958   *Max Weber*. Munich: Piper.

Kaden, Christian
1984   *Musiksoziologie*. Berlin: Verlag Neue Musik.

Kaegi, Werner
1967   *Was ist elektronische Musik*. Zurich: Orell Füssli.

Kapustin, Yuri
1978   The definition of the notion of "musical public" [in Russian]. In *Methodological Problems of Modern Culturology*, ed. L. V. Petrov et al. 2d series. Leningrad: Institute for Theater, Music, and Cinematography.
1979   Die Musikalität der Jugend als sozio-kulturelles Problem. In *Probleme der Kunstwirkung: Wissenschaftliche Beiträge*, ed. Dietrich Sommer. Halle-Wittenberg: Martin-Luther-Universität.
1983   60 Jahre sowjetische Musiksoziologie. *Beiträge zur Musikwissenschaft* 25: 259–271.
1990   The Impact of "Perestroika" on the Music-Cultural Situation and the Educational Policy Concept in the USSR. In *Report on the Seminar "Music Education and the Changing Media Landscape,"* ed. ISME-MEDIACULT. Vienna, July–August 1990 (typescript).

Karbusický, Vladimír
1966   Zur empirisch-soziologischen Musikforschung. *Beiträge zur Musikwissenschaft* 8: 215–240.
1975a   *Empirische Musiksoziologie*. Wiesbaden: Breitkopf & Härtel.
1975b   Zur empirisch-soziologischen Musikforschung. In *Musikhören*, ed. Bernhard Dopheide. Darmstadt: Wissenschaftliche Buchgesellschaft.

1986   Gegenwartsprobleme der Musiksoziologie. *Acta Musicologica* 58:
          35–91.
Karbuscik, Vladimír, and Jaroslav Kasan
1969   *Výzkum součastné hudebnosti.* 2 vols. 2d ed. Czech Radio. Prague:
          Czech Radio Prague.
Karlsson, Henrik
1982   *Forskning om dagens musiksamhälle, Kulturpolitisk forskning och
          utvecking,* 4, Statens Kulturrad. Stockholm: Statens kulturrad.
Käsler, Dirk, ed.
1976   *Klassiker des soziologischen Denkens.* 2 vols. Munich: C. H. Beck.
Kiesewetter, Raphael Georg
1834   *Geschichte der europäisch-abendländischen Musik.* Leipzig: Breitkopf
          & Härtel.
Kinsbourne, Marcel
1975   Minor Hemisphere Language and Cerebral Maturation. In *Foun-
          dations of Language Development,* ed. Eric H. Lenneberg and Eliza-
          beth Lenneberg. 2 vols. New York: Academic Press.
Ki-Zerbo, Joseph, ed.
1980   *Méthodologie et préhistoire africaine.* Vol. 1 of *Histoire générale de
          l'Afrique.* Paris: UNESCO.
Klausmeier, Friedrich
1963   *Jugend und Musik im technischen Zeitalter.* Bonn: H. Bouvier.
1978   *Die Lust, sich musikalisch auszudrücken: Ein Einführung in sozio-
          musikalisches Verhalten.* Reinbek.
Klusen, Ernst
1980   *Elektronische Medien und musikalische Laienaktivität.* Cologne: Hans
          Gerig.
Kneif, Tibor
1966   Gegenwartsfragen der Musiksoziologie: Ein Forschungsbericht.
          Acta Musicologica 38: 72–118.
1971   *Musiksoziologie.* Cologne: Hans Gerig.
1975 (ed.) *Texte zur Musiksoziologie.* Cologne: Arno Volk.
Knepler, Georg
1977   *Geschichte als Weg zum Musikverständnis.* Leipzig: Philipp Reclam
          jun.
Kolleritsch, Otto, ed.
1979   *Adorno und die Musik.* Vienna: Universal Edition.
Kolneder, Walter
1959   Der Raum in der Musik des 17. und 18. Jahrhunderts. *Musica* 13:
          554–558.
König, René, ed.
1958   *Soziologie.* Frankfurt: S. Fischer.
Kötter, Eberhard
1968   *Der Einfluß übertragungstechnischer Faktoren auf das Musikhören.*
          Cologne: Arno Volk.
Krenek, Ernst
1938   Bemerkungen zur Rundfunkmusik. *Zeitschrift für Sozialforschung*
          7. [Rpt. in *Kritische Kommunikationsforschung,* ed. Dieter Prokop.
          Munich: Carl Hanser, 1973.]

Krüger, Walther
1958a   *Die authentische Klangform des primitiven Organum*. Kassel: Bären-
        reiter.
1958b   Aufführungspraktische Fragen mittelalterlicher Mehrstim-
        migkeit. *Die Musikforschung* 11: 177–189.

Kubik, Gerhard
1973   Verstehen in afrikanischen Musikkulturen. In *Musik und Verste-
        hen*, ed. Peter Faltin and Hans-Peter Reinecke. Cologne: Arno
        Volk.

Kuhn, Thomas
1970   *The Structure of Scientific Revolutions*. 2d enl. ed. Chicago: Univer-
        sity of Chicago Press.

Kunst, Jaap
1959   *Ethnomusicology*. The Hague: Martinus Nijhoff.
1960   Supplement to the 3d ed. of *Ethnomusicology*. The Hague: Marti-
        nus Nijhoff.
1954   Alexander John Ellis in *MGG* 3 (1954).

Künstlerbericht = 1975 Bericht der Bundesregierung über die wirtschaftliche
        und soziale Lage der künstlerischen Berufe. Deutscher Bunde-
        stag, 7th legislative period, publication 7/3071. 13 January.

Labriola, Antonio
1902   *Essais sur la conception matérialiste de l'histoire*. Paris: Giard &
        Brière. [Rpt. Paris, London, New York: Gordon & Breach, 1970.]

Lachmann, Ulrich
1960   *Die Struktur des deutschen Musikmarktes unter besonderer Berücksich-
        tigung des erwerbswirtschaftlichen Sektors*. Ph.D. diss., University of
        Tübingen.

Lalo, Charles
1939   *Éléments d'une esthétique musicale scientifique*. 2d enl. ed. Paris:
        Librairie philosophique J. Vrin. [1st publ. as *Esquisse d'une esthé-
        tique musicale scientifique*. Paris: Félix Alcan.]

Lange, André
1986   *Stratégies de la musique: L'industrie internationale de la musique
        enregistrée et l'édition phonographique dans la Communauté française
        de Belgique*. Brussels: Pierre Mardaga.
1990   Le nouveau temps de l'industrie de la musique (1986–1989). In *Les
        malheurs d'Orphée*, ed. Robert Wangermée. Liège, Brussels: Pierre
        Mardaga.

Lange, André, and Jean Luc Renaud
1988   *The Future of the European Audiovisual Industry*. Manchester: Euro-
        pean Institute of the Media.

Lazarsfeld, Paul
1965   Wissenschaftslogik und empirische Sozialforschung. In *Logik der
        Sozialwissenschaften*, ed. Ernst Topitsch. Cologne: Kiepenheuer &
        Witsch.

Leclercq, Thierry
1990   L'age cathodique du rock: perspectives de la vidéo musicale. In
        Les malheurs d'Orphée, ed. Robert Wangermée. Liège and Brussels:
        Pierre Mardaga.

Leithäuser, Gerhard
1978   Kunstwerk und Warenform. In *Seminar: Kunst- und Literatursoziologie*, ed. Peter Bürger. Frankfurt: Suhrkamp.

Leppert, Richard, and Susan McClary
1987   *Music and Society: The Politics of Composition, Performance and Reception*. Cambridge: Cambridge University Press.

Leroy, Dominique
1980   *Économie des arts du spectacle vivant*. Paris: Economica.

Lévi-Strauss, Claude
1975   Race and History. In *Race, Science and Society*, ed. Leo Kuper. London: George Allen & Unwin.

Lilley, Samuel
1966   *Men, Machines and History*. New York: International Publishers.

Ling, Jan
1971   Music-Sociological Projects in Gothenburg. *IRASM* 2: 119–130.

Ling, Jan, and Stig-Magnus Thorsten
1988   Socio-Musicology at the University of Gothenburg, Sweden. In *Papers for the Conference held at the University of Gothenburg in April 1988*.

Lorenz, Konrad
1978   *Das Wirkungsgefüge der Natur und das Schicksal des Menschen: Gesammelte Arbeiten*. Munich: Piper.

Losonczi, Agnes
1969   Le changement d'orientation sociale dans la musique de tous les jours. In *Études sociologiques*, ed. Andreas Hegedüs. Paris: Éditions anthropos, Budapest: Corvina.
1980   *Bedarf, Funktion, Wertwechsel in der Musik: Musiksoziologische Untersuchung des Musiklebens in Ungarn nach 1945*. Budapest: Akademiai Kiadó.

Lottermoser, Werner
1955   Akustische Untersuchungen an alten und neuen Orgeln. In *Klangstruktur der Musik*, ed. Fritz Winckel. Berlin: Verlag für Radio-Foto-Kinotechnik.

Lunacharsky, Anatoli V.
1971   *In the World of Music* [Russian]. 2d ed. Moscow. Vsesoiuznoe Izdatelstvo Sovietsky Kompozitor.

Maceda, José
1972   Music in the Philippines. In *Handbuch der Orientalistik*, part 3, vol. 6, ed. B. Spuler. Leiden, Cologne: E. J. Brill.

Malm, Krister
1982   Phonograms and Cultural Policy in Sweden. In *The Phonogram in Cultural Communication*, ed. Kurt Blaukopf. Vienna, New York: Springer.

Maria Theresia und ihre Zeit
1980   Exposition catalogue. Salzburg: Residenz Verlag.

Mark, Desmond
1976   John H. Mueller und sein Beitrag zur Musiksoziologie. *IRASM* 7: 185–202.
1977   Der Mensch im Spannungsfeld der neuen akustischen Umwelt. In *Der Mensch im Spannungsfeld zeitgenössischer künstlerischer Bestre-*

bungen (Beiträge zur Lehrerfortbildung, 20). Vienna: Österreichischer Bundesverlag.

1979   *Zur Bestandaufnahme des Wiener Orchesterrepertoires*. Vienna: Universal Edition.

1990   *Musikschule 2000: Der Bedarf an Musikschullehrern*. Vienna: VGWÖ
(Verband der wissenschaftlichen Gesellschaften Österreichs).

1981 (ed.) *Stock-taking of Musical Life: Music Sociography and its Relevance to
Music Education*. Vienna: Doblinger.

Marquandt, P.

1936   *Der Gesang und seine Erscheinungsformen im Mittelalter*. Ph.D. diss.,
Berlin.

Marx, Karl

1965   *Theorien über den Mehrwert*. Teil I, Marx/Engels, *Werke*, vol. 26, 1.
Berlin (East): Dietz.

1971   *Zur Kritik der politischen Ökonomie*. Berlin (East): Dietz.

Marx, Karl, and Friedrich Engels

1953   *Ausgewählte Briefe 1843–1895 (MEB)*. Berlin (East): Dietz.

Bundesministeriums für Unterricht und Kunst (Austria)

n.d.   [1975] *Kulturpolitischer Maßnahmenkatalog*. Vienna: Federal Ministry of Education and the Arts.

Mauss, Marcel

1969   *Essais de sociologie*. Paris: Editions de Minuit.

Mazzarino, Santo

1973   *La fin du monde antique*. Paris: Gallimard.

MEDIACULT, ed.

1972–   Newsletter published quarterly in English, French, and German.
[Mediacult = International Institute for Audio-Visual Communication and Cultural Development.] Vienna.

Menger, Karl

1974   *Morality, Decision and Social Organization*. Trans. Eric van der
Schalle. Dordrecht, Boston: D. Reidel Publishing Company.

Menger, Pierre-Michel

1980   The Serious Contemporary Music Market: The Condition of the
Composer and Aid for the Composers in Europe. Council of
Europe, Document CC-COLL-MU 12, Strasbourg.

1982   The Social and Professional Position of Creative Artists in the
Field of Music in Europe. Council of Europe, Document CC-GP 11
(82) 14. Strasbourg.

1983   *Le paradoxe du musicien: Le compositeur, le mélomane et l'État dans la
societé contemporaine*. Paris: Flammarion.

1989   *Les laboratoires de la création musicale*. Paris: La Documentation
Française.

Menon, Narayana

1974   Music and Culture Change in India. *Cultures* 1 (3): 59–64.

Merriam, Alan P.

1964   *The Anthropology of Music*. Evanston, IL: Northwestern University
Press.

Merton, Robert K.
1965 Die Eigendynamik gesellschaftlicher Voraussagen. In *Logik der Sozialwissenschaften*, ed. Ernst Toptisch. Cologne: Kiepenheuer & Witsch.

Meyer, Ernst Hermann, ed.
1977 *Musik in der Urgesellschaft und den frühen Klassengesellschaften.* Vol. 1 of *Geschichte der Musik.* Leipzig: Deutscher Verlag für Musik.

Moles, Abraham
1968 *Information Theory and Esthetic Perception.* Urbana, IL: University of Illinois Press.

Morelli, Renato
1976 *Musica e razionalità nella civiltà occidentale: Concezioni della musica e sistemi pedgogici.* Ph.D. diss., Trent: Libera università degli studi.

Mozart, Wolfgang Amadeus
1938 *The Letters of Mozart and his Family.* Trans. Emily Anderson. London: Macmillan.

Mueller, John H.
1938 The Folkways of Art: An Analysis of the Social Theories of Art. In *American Journal of Sociology* 44 (2): 222–238.

1946 Methods of Measurement of Aesthetic Folkways. In *American Journal of Sociology* 51 (4): 276–282.

1951 *The American Symphony Orchestra.* Includes chap. 4, Life Spans of Composers in the Repertoire, 182–252, and chap. 7, Musical Taste and How it is Formed, 380–405. Bloomington: Indiana University Press.

1958 Music and Education: A Sociological Approach. In *Basic Concepts in Musical Education,* 57th Yearbook of the National Society for the Study of Education, 88–122. Chicago: University of Chicago Press.

1963 *Fragen des musikalischen Geschmacks.* Cologne: Westdeutscher Verlag.

Müller-Heuser, Franz
1963 *Vox humana: Ein Beitrag zur Untersuchung der Stimmästhetik des Mittelalters.* Regensburg: Gustav Bosse.

Mumford, Lewis
1952 *Art und Technics.* New York: Columbia University Press.

Mursell, James L.
1946 Psychology and the Problem of the Scale. *The Musical Quarterly* 32: 564–573.

Musik und Gesellschaft
1967– Series of publications. Vienna: VGWÖ (Verband der wissenschaftlichen Gesellschaften Österreichs).

Musil, Robert
1985 *The Man without Qualities.* New York: Putnam.

Myerscough, John, et al.
1988 *The Economic Importance of the Arts in Britain.* London: Policy Studies Institute.

Myrdal, Gunnar
1969 *Objectivity in Social Research.* Middletown, CT: Wesleyan University Press.

Namenwirth, S. Micha, and Karin van der Linden
1982   *Muziek en Maatschappij: Geannoteerde Basisbibliografie.* Brussels: Free University.

National Endowment for the Arts
1977   *Arts and Cultural Programs on Radio and Television.* Washington, D.C.: National Endowment for the Arts.
1978   *Audience Studies for the Arts and Museums: A Critical Review.* Washington, D.C.: National Endowment for the Arts.
1980   *Artists Compared by Age, Sex and Earnings in 1970 and 1976.* Washington, D.C.: National Endowment for the Arts.
1981   *Audience Development: An Examination of Selected Analysis and Prediction Techniques Applied to Symphony and Theatre Attendance in Four Southern Cities.* Washington, D.C.: National Endowment for the Arts.

Nettl, Bruno
1972   *Music in Primitive Culture.* 3d ed. Cambridge, MA: Harvard University Press. [1st ed. 1956.]
1978a   *Persian Classical Music in Tehran: The Process of Change.* Urbana, IL: University of Illinois Press.
1978b   Some Aspects of the History of World Music in the Twentieth Century: Questions, Problems and Concepts. *Ethnomusicology* 22: 123–136.
1985   *The Western Impact on World Music.* New York: Schirmer Books.
1986   World Music in the Twentieth Century: A Survey of Research on Western Influence. *Acta Musicologica* 58: 360–373.

Netzer, Dick
1978   *The Subsidized Muse: Public Support for the Arts in the United States.* Cambridge, MA: Cambridge University Press.

Neurath, Otto
1937   Inventory of the Standard of Living. *Zeitschrift für Sozialforschung* 6: 140–154. [Rpt. Munich: Kösel Verlag, 1970.]
1981   *Gesammelte philosophische und methodologische Schriften.* 2 vols. Ed. Rudolf Haller and Heiner Rutte. Vienna: Hölder-Pichler-Tempsky.

Newman, William S.
1963   *The Sonata in the Classic Era.* Chapel Hill, NC: University of North Carolina Press.

Niemann, Konrad
1968   *Experimentelle und soziologische Methoden zur Ermittlung des Musikniveaus.* Ph.D. diss., Berlin (East): Humboldt Universität.
1974   Mass media: New Ways of Approach to Music and New Patterns of Musical Behaviour. In *New Patterns of Musical Behaviour,* ed. Irmgard Bontinck. Vienna: Universal Edition.
1980   Zu einigen Fragen der Anwendung empirischer Methoden in der Musiksoziologie. *Beiträge zur Musikwissenschaft* 22: 24–36.

Nijenhuis, Emmie te
1974   *Indian Music: History and Structure.* (= *Handbuch der Orientalistik,* sec. 2, vol. 6, ed. B. Spuler et al.) Leiden, Cologne: E. J. Brill.

Nketia, Joseph H. Kwabena
1970   *Ethnomusicology in Ghana.* Accra: Ghana University Press.

1975 Understanding African Music. *National Centre for the Performing Arts Quarterly Journal* 4: 8–14.
1979 *Die Musik Afrikas.* Wilhelmshaven: Heinrichshofen.
1980 Africa in the World of Music. *The World of Music* 22 (3): 19–28.

ÖBV = Österreichischer Bundestheaterverband. 1979. Bericht 1978/79.

Oeser, M.
1904 *Geschichte der Stadt Mannheim.* Mannheim: Bensheimer.

Ogburn, William F.
1932 Statistics and Art. *Journal of the American Statistical Association* 27: 1–8.
1964 *On Culture and Social Change: Selected Papers.* Chicago: University of Chicago Press.
1957 Cultural Lag as Theory. *Sociology and Social Research* 41 (January): 167–173.

Ogburn, William F., and Meyer F. Nimkoff
1950 *A Handbook of Sociology.* 2d rev. ed. London: Routledge & Kegan Paul. [1st American ed., Boston, 1940.]

Ong, Walter J.
1988 *Orality and Literacy: The Technologizing of the Word.* London: Routledge. [1st ed. London: Methuen, 1982.]

Oppens, Kurt
1968 Zu den musikalischen Schriften Adornos. *Über Theodor W. Adorno.* Frankfurt: Suhrkamp.

Ostleitner, Elena
1980 *Musiksoziographie in Österreich.* Vienna: Universal Edition.

Ottenberg, Simon
1975 *Masked Rituals of Afikpo: The Context of African Art.* Seattle: University of Washington Press.

Parsons, Talcott
1948 The Position of Sociological Theory. Paper read at the American Sociological Society, New York, December 1947. In *Synopsis,* ed. Edgar Salin. Heidelberg: Schneider.
1970 The Impact of Technology on Culture. *International Social Science Journal* 22 (4): 607–627.

Paumgartner, Bernhard
1967 *Mozart.* Zurich: Atlantis.

Peacock, Alan, and Ronald Weir.
1975 *The Composer in the Market Place.* London: Faber Music.

Perger, Richard von, and Robert Hirschfeld
1912 *Geschichte der k.k. Gesellschaft der Musikfreunde in Wien.* Vienna: Gesellschaft der Musikfreunde.

Peterson, Richard
1982 Five Constraints on the Production of Culture: Law, Technology, Market, Organizational Structure and Occupational Careers. *Journal of Popular Culture* 16: 143–153.
1990 Why 1955? Explaining the Advent of Rock Music. *PM* 9: 97–116.

Philippot, Michel P.
1974 Observations on Sound Volume and Music Listening. In *New Patterns of Musical Behaviour,* ed. Irmgard Bontinck. Vienna: Universal Edition.

Piaget, Jean
1973　*Einführung in die genetische Erkenntnistheorie*. Frankfurt: Suhrkamp. [Engl. trans. New York: Columbia University Press, 1970.]

Pick, John, ed.
1980　*The State and the Arts*. Eastbourne: John Offord.

Plekhanov, Georgi V.
1929　*Die Grundprobleme des Marxismus*. Vienna: Verlag für Literatur und Politik. [1st publ. in 1908.]
1946a　*The Materialist Conception of History*. Moscow: Foreign Languages Publishers.
1946b　*Beiträge zur Geschichte des Materialismus*. Berlin: Verlag der sowjetischen Militärverwaltung in Deutschland.

PM
1981–　*Popular Music: A Yearbook*, ed. Richard Middleton and David Horn. Cambridge.

Prenant, Marcel
1946　*Darwin*. Paris: Editions hier et aujourd'hui.

Priestley, Clive
1984　*Financial Scrutiny of the Royal Opera House Covent Garden Ltd.* London: Her Majesty's Stationery Office.

Proudhon, Pierre-Joseph
1971　*Du principe de l'art et de sa destination sociale*. Rpt. Farnborough: Gregg International Publishers. [1st publ. Paris: Garnier Frères, 1865.]

Quantz, Johann Joachim
1953　*Versuch einer Anweisung, die Flute traversière zu spielen*. Rpt. Kassel: Bärenreiter. [Engl. trans. London, 1966. 1st publ. 1752.]

Radich, Anthony J., ed.
1987　*Economic Impact of the Arts: A Sourcebook*. Denver: National Conference of State Legislatures.

Raison, Timothy, ed.
1969　*The Founding Fathers of Sociology*. London: Penguin Books.

Rauhe, Hermann.
1974　*Popularität in der Musik: Interdisziplinäre Aspekte musikalischer Kommunikation*. Karlsruhe: G. Braun.

Reckow, Fritz
1967　*Der Musiktraktat des Anonoymus IV*. 2 vols. Wiesbaden: Fritz Steiner.

Reese, Gustave
1940　*Music in the Middle Ages*. New York: W.W. Norton.

Regelski, Thomas A.
1977　Who Knows Where Music Lurks in the Mind of Man: New Brain Research Has the Answer. *Music Educators Journal* 69 (9) May: 31–38.

Rehberg, Paula
1961　*Franz Liszt*. Zurich: Artemis.

Reinecke, Hans-Peter
1971   Zur Strukturanalyse des Deutschen Musikrats. In *Musik und Bildung* 4–11.
Riegl, Alois
1929   *Gesammelte Aufsätze.* Augsburg: Filser.
1973   *Spätrömische Kunstindustrie.* 4th ed. Darmstadt: Wissenschaftliche Buchgesellschaft. [1st ed. Vienna, 1901.]
Riemann, Hugo
1904   *Handbuch der Musikgeschichte*, vol. 1. Leipzig: Breitkopf & Härtel.
Rocher, Guy.
1968   *Introduction à la sociologie générale.* 3 vols. Paris: Editions NMH.
Rohloff, Ernst
1943   *Der Musiktraktat des Johannes de Grocheio.* Leipzig: Gebrüder Reinecke. [Also in *Die Quellenhandschriften zum Musiktraktat des Johannes de Grocheio*, by Ernst Rohloff. Leipzig: Deutscher Verlag für Musik, 1972.]
Ronneberger, Franz
1979   Musik als Information. *Publizistik, Vierteljahreshefte für Kommunikationsforschung* 24: 5–28.
Rosenmayr, Leopold
1966   *Kulturelle Interessen von Jugendlichen.* Vienna: Hollinek/Juventa.
Rottenberg, Philipp von
1769   *Institutionis archiducalis Ferdinandaeae opus pictum in tres tomos divisum.* (Instruction manual for the education of Archduke Ferdinand with 99 plates, painted by Charles Joseph Roattiers. National library of Austria. Handwritten collection. Cod. min. 33a.)
Rummenhöller, Peter
1978   *Einführung in die Musiksoziologie.* Wilhelmshaven: Heinrichshofen.
Sachs, Curt
1918   Kunstgeschichtliche Wege zur Musikwissenschaft. *Archiv für Musikwissenschaft* 1: 451–464.
1928   *Geist und Werden der Musikinstrumente.* Berlin: Remer. [Rpt. Hilversum, 1965.]
1940   *The History of Musical Instruments.* New York: W. W. Norton.
1943   *The Rise of Music in the Ancient World East and West.* New York: W. W. Norton.
1948   *Our Musical Heritage.* New York: Prentice Hall.
1959   *Vergleichende Musikwissenschaft: Musik der Fremdkulturen.* Heidelberg: Quelle & Meyer.
1968   *Die Musik der Alten Welt.* Berlin (East): Akademie-Verlag.
Sagi, Maria
1978   New Approaches to the Sociology of Music. In *Studies in the Sociology of Culture*, ed. Iván Vitányi. Budapest: Institute for Culture.
Sahlins, Marshal
1976   *Stone Age Economics.* Hawthorne, NY: Aldine de Gruyter.
Saint-Saëns, Camille
n.d. [1899] *Portraits et souvenirs.* Paris: Mesnil.

Sass, Herbert, and Walter Wiora, eds.
1962   *Musikberufe und ihr Nachwuchs I: Statistische Erhebungen 1960/61 des Deutschen Musikrates*. Mainz: Schott.
1969   *Musikberufe und ihr Nachwuchs II: Statistische Erhebungen 1965/67 des Deutschen Musikrates*. Mainz: Schott.

Schafer, R. Murray
1959   *The New Soundscape*. Don Mills, ON: BMI Canada.
1977   *The Tuning of the World*. New York: Alfred A. Knopf.

Scheja, Georg
1952   Kunst und Soziologie. In *Soziologie und Leben*, ed. Carl Brinkmann. Tübingen: Rainer Wunderlich.

Scholes, Percy A.
1969   *The Puritans and Music in England and New England*. Oxford: Oxford University Press. [1st ed. 1934.]

Schott, Sigmund
1930   Theater und Orchester. *Statistisches Jahrbuch deutscher Städte*, vol. 25. [Quoted in Wilzin 1937.]

Schügerl, Kurt
1962   Der Übergriff des Automaten: Zur Analyse eines Irrtums in der neuesten Musik. *Merkur* 16: 539–554.

Schumann, Robert
1889   *Gesammelte Schriften über Musik und Musiker*. Leipzig: Breitkopf & Härtel.

Seeger, Charles
1958   Prescriptive and Descriptive Music-writing. *The Musical Quarterly* 44: 184–195.

Segal, M. H., D. T. Campbell, and M. J. Herskovits
1966   *The Influence of Culture on Visual Perception*. Indianapolis: Bobbs-Merrill.

Seravazza, Antonio, ed.
1980   *La sociologia della musica*. Torino.

Services des Études et de la Recherche
1974   *Pratiques culturelles des Français: Données quantitatives*. 2 vols. Paris: Secrétariat d'État à la Culture.

Shaw, D. V., W. S. Hendon, and C. R. Waits, eds.
1987   *Artists and Cultural Consumers*. Akron: University of Akron Press.

Shepherd, John
1987   Towards a Sociology of Musical Styles. In *Lost in Music: Culture, Style and Musical Event*, ed. Avron L. White. London: Routledge & Kegan Paul.

Shepherd, John, et al., eds.
1977   *Whose Music: A Sociology of Musical Languages*. London: Latimer.

Silbermann, Alphons
1957   *Wovon lebt die Musik: Die Prinzipien der Musiksoziologie*. Regensburg: Bosse.
1958   Die Stellung der Musiksoziologie innerhalb der Soziologie und der Musikwissenschaft. *Kölner Zeitschrift für Soziologie und Sozialpsychologie* 10: 102–115.
1965   *Ketzereien eines Soziologen*. Düsseldorf:Econ-Verlag.

1967   Anmerkungen zur Musiksoziologie: Eine Antwort auf Theodor W. Adornos "Thesen zur Kunstsoziologie." *Kölner Zeitschrift für Soziologie und Sozialpsychologie* 19: 538–545.

1968   A Definition of the Sociology of Art. *International Social Science Journal* 20: 567–588.

1973a   *Empirische Kunstsoziologie: Eine Einführung mit kommentierter Bibliographie.* Stuttgart: B.G. Teubner.

1979a   Soziologie der Künste. In *Handbuch der empirischen Sozialforschung,* vol. 13, ed. René König. 2d ed. Stuttgart: Ferdinand Enke.

1979b (ed.)*Klassiker der Kunstsoziologie.* Munich: C.H. Beck.

1981   Review of *Soziographie des Musiklebens* (ed. Kurt Blaukopf, Karlsruhe, 1979). *Neue Zeitschrift für Musik* 142 (1): 84–85.

Silbermann, Alphons, and Udo Michael Krüger
1973b   *Soziologie der Massenkommunikation.* Stuttgart: W. Kohlhammer.

Simmel, Georg
1882   Psychologische und ethnologische Studien über Musik. *Zeitschrift für Völkerpsychologie und Sprachwissenschaft* 13: 261–305. [Rpt. in *Texte zur Musiksoziologie,* ed. Tibor Kneif. Cologne: Arno Volk, 1975.]

1890   Über sociale Differenzierung: Sociologische und psychologische Untersuchungen. In *Staats- und socialwissenschaftliche Forschungen,* vol. 10, ed. Gustav Schmoller. Leipzig: Duncker & Humblot.

1922   *Zur Philosophie der Kunst.* Potsdam: Kiepenheuer.

1923   *Sociologie: Untersuchungen über die Formen der Vergesellschaftung.* 3d ed. Munich: Duncker & Humblot. [1st publ. 1908.]

Smits van Waesberghe, Josef
1955   Neues über die Schola Cantorum in Rom. *Bericht über den 2. Internationalen Kongreß für katholischen Kirchenmusik 1954.* Vienna: Exekutivkomitee des 2. Internationalen Kongresses für katholische Kirchenmusik.

Smudits, Alfred, ed.
1987   *New Media: A Challenge to Cultural Policies—A Mediacult Report.* Vienna: VGWÖ.

Sokhor, Arnold N.
1973   How music functions under changed social and technological conditions [in Russian]. *The Musical Culture of Peoples: Report on the 7th Congress of the International Music Council in Moscow* [in Russian]. Moscow: Sovietsky Kompozitor.

1974   Young People's Leisure Time and Its Use for Musical-aesthetic Education. In *New Patterns of Musical Behaviour,* ed. Irmgard Bontinck. Vienna: Universal Edition.

1975   Die Freizeit der Jugend und ihre Ausnützung für die musikalisch-ästhetische Erziehung. In *Schule und Umwelt: Beiträge zur Schulmusik,* vol. 28, ed. Kurt Blaukopf. Wolfenbüttel: Möseler.

1977   Die Entwicklung der Musiksoziologie in der Sowjetunion. In *Sozialistische Musikkultur,* ed. J. Elsner and G. Ordshonikidse. Berlin (East): Verlag Neue Musik.

1978   The Role of culturology and sociology in researching Soviet artistic culture [in Russian]. In *Methodological problems of modern culturology* [in Russian], Series 2, ed. L. V. Petrov et al. Leningrad: Institute for Theater, Music and Cinematography.

1980a (ed.)*Questions of sociology and musical aesthetics* [in Russian]. Intro. by Yuri N. Kapustin. Leningrad: Sovietsky Kompozitor.

Sokhor, Arnold N., and Yuri N. Kapustin
1980b   Sociology and musicology.In *Questions of the Sociology of Art* (anthology). Leningrad: Institute for Theater, Music and Cinematography.

Société d'Économie
1967   *Données statistiques sur le système musical français*. Paris: Société d'Économie et de Mathématique Appliquées.

Sønstevold, Gunnar, and Kurt Blaukopf
1968   *Musik der "einsamen Masse."* Karlsruhe: G. Braun.

Sorce Keller, Marcello
1979   *Le scienze sociali e la musica*. Trent: Libera Università degli Studi.
1986   Sociology of Music and Ethnomusicology: Two Disciplines in Competition. *The Journal of General Education* 38 (3): 167–181.
1988   Some Remarks on Musical Aesthetics from the Viewpoint of Ethnomusicology. *The Music Review* 48/49 (2), May: 138–144.

Spencer, Herbert
1893   *First Principles*. 5th ed. London: Williams & Norgate.
1896   *The Principles of Sociology*, vol. 3. London: Williams & Norgate.
1966   *Essays on Education and Kindred Subjects*. London: J. M. Dent.

SRG [= Schweizerische Radio- und Fernsehgesellschaft]
1979   Musik und Publikum (Deutsche Schweiz). Studie der Abteilung Forschungsdienst (photocopy). Bern: SRG.

Stahmer, Klaus
1972   Korrekturen am Brahms-Bild: Eine Studie zur musikalischen Fehlinterpretation. *Die Musikforschung* 25: 152–167.

Staubmann, Helmut
1988   An der schönen blauen Donau ... Entstehungsbedingungen soziologischer Musikforschung in Österreich. In *Geschichte der österreichischen Soziologie*, ed. Josef Langer. Vienna: Verlag für Gesellschaftskritik.

Steinberger, Gerhard
1976   Das Phänomen der Musikalität und Fragen der Musiksoziologie im Lichte der jüngsten sowjetischen Musikforschung. *Schweizerische Musikzeitung* 116: 170–178.

Stockhausen, Karlheinz
1959   Musik und Raum. In *Die Reihe* 5, ed. Herbert Eimert and Karlheinz Stockhausen. Vienna: Universal Edition.

Strauss, Richard
1949   Bemerkungen zu Richard Wagners Gesamtkunstwerk und zum Bayreuther Festspielhaus. In *Betrachtungen und Erinnerungen*, by Richard Strauss. Zurich: Atlantis.

Stumpf, Carl
1911   *Die Anfänge der Musik*. Leipzig: Barth.

Supičić, Ivo
1971   *Musique et société: Perspectives pour une sociologie de musique*. Zagreb: Institute for Musicology.
1987   *Music in Society: A Guide to the Sociology of Music*. New York: Pendragon Press.

Bibliography

Suppan, Walter
1977a   Werkzeug—Kunstwerk—Ware. *Musikethnologische Sammelbände*
         1: Graz: Akademische Druck- und Verlagsgesellschaft.
1977b   Amateurmusik. In *In Sachen Musik*, ed. Sigrid Abel-Struth et al.
         Kassel: Bärenreiter.

Swedish Council [= Swedish National Council for Cultural Affairs]
1979   *Phonograms and Cultural Policy.* (Summary of the report in Swed-
         ish.) Stockholm: Statents kulturrad.

Szalai, Alexander, ed.
1972   *The Use of Time.* The Hague, Paris: Mouton.

Taine, Hippolyte
1903   *Philosophie de l'art.* 2 vols. 10th ed. Paris: Hachette. [The first edi-
         tion appeared in 1882. The first two chapters were first published
         in 1865.]

Tapper, Karl-Hermann, et al.
1976   *Musiken—Människan—Samhället.* Stockholm: Statens kulturrad.
         [A summary in English, German, and French entitled *Music—
         Man—Society* was published Stockholm, 1976.]

Tappolet, Willy
1947   *La notation musicale et son influence sur la pratique de la musique du
         moyen age à nos jours.* Boudry, Switzerland: Bacconière.

Tarde, Gabriel
1895   *Les lois de l'imitation: Étude sociologique.* 5th ed. Paris: Félix Alcan.

Taylor, Rupert.
1970   *Noise.* London: Penguin Books.

Tessarolo, Mariselda
1983   *L'espressione musicale e le sue funzioni.* Milan: Giuffré.

Thurow, Lester C.
1980   *The Zero-Sum Society.* New York: Basic Books.

Tokumaru, Yoshihiko
1985   Mündliche und schriftliche Tradierung in der japanischen Musik.
         Beiträge zur Musikwissenschaft 27: 110–115.

Touma, Habib Hassan
1975   *Die Musik der Araber.* Wilhelmshaven: Heinrichshofen.

Tran van Khe
1963   Le public de concert en orient devant les changements d'ordre
         sociologique. *The World of Music* 5: 16–17.
1973   Traditional Music and Culture Change: A Study in Acculturation.
         Cultures 1 (1): 195–210.
1980   For a Universal History of Music: What Is Lacking in Present-day
         Histories of Music. *The World of Music* 22 (3): 19–28.

Tsukkerman, V. S.
1971   The attitudes of various population segments toward music:
         Attempt at a sociological study [in Russian]. In *Reception of Art,*
         ed. B. S. Mailakh. Leningrad: Nauka.
1972   *Music and listener: Attempt at a sociological study* [in Russian]. Mos-
         cow: Muzyka.

Tsunoda, Tadanobu
1978   The Left Cerebral Hemisphere of the Brain and the Japanese Lan-
         guage. *The Japan Foundation Newsletter* 6 (1).

UMH
1990   *The Universe of Music: A History.* 1 July. (Newsletter publ. annually by the Center for Music Research and Documentation, City University of New York.)

UNESCO
1980   Preliminary Report of the Director General on the Medium-Term Plan for 1984–1989.

Vanhulst, Henri and Malou Haine, eds.
1988   Musique et société: Hommages à Robert Wangermée. Brussels: Éditions de l'Université de Bruxelles.

Veblen, Thorstein
1973   *The Theory of the Leisure Class.* Boston: Houghton Mifflin. [1st ed. 1899.]

Vega, Carlos
1966   La Mésomusica. In *Polifonia* 21. (Quoted from Aretz 1977, 39–40.)

Vitányi, Iván
1974   The Musical and Social Influence of Beat Music in Hungary. In *New Patterns of Musical Behaviour*, ed. Irmgard Bontinck. Vienna: Universal Edition.

1980a   Sociology of Art and Artistic Life. In *Studies in the Sociology of the Arts*, vol. 2, by Iván Vitányi. Budapest: Institute for Culture.

1978 (ed.) *Studies in the Sociology of Culture*, vol. 1. (Photocopies: Institute of Culture, Budapest.) Budapest: Institute for Culture.

1980b (ed.)Studies in the Sociology of the Arts. Selected lectures held at the 9th World Congress of Sociology, Uppsala 1978. (Photocopies: Institute of Culture, Budapest.) Budapest: Institute for Culture.

Wahl-Zieger, Erika
1978   *Theater und Orchester zwischen Marktkräften und Marktkorrektur: Existenzprobleme und Überlebenschancen eines Sektors aus wirtschaftstheoretischer Sicht.* Göttingen: Vandenhoek & Ruprecht.

Walker, David Addison
1979   *Understanding Pictures: A Study in the Design of Appropriate Visual Materials for Education in Developing Countries.* Ph.D. diss., Massachusetts University.

Wallis, Roger and Krister Malm
1980   The Interdependency of Broadcasting and the Phonogram Industry: A Case Study Covering Events in Kenya During March 1980 (mimeographed). Vienna: Mediacult Institute.

1984   Big Sounds from Small Peoples: The Music Industry in Small Countries. Series of reports from the Gothenburg University Department of Musicology, no.7. London: Constable.

Walter, Ferdinand
1952   *Aufgabe und Vermächtnis einer deutschen Stadt: Drei Jahrhunderte Alt-Mannheim.* Frankfurt: Knapp.

Wangermée, Robert
1965   *Die flämische Musik in der Gesellschaft des 15. und 16. Jahrhunderts.* Brussels: Editions Arcade.

1975   *Rundfunkmusik gegen die Kulturmoralisten verteidigt.* Karlsruhe: G. Braun.

1990 (ed.) *Les Malheurs d'Orphée: Culture et profit dans l'économie de la musique.* Liège, Brussels: Pierre Mardaga.

Webb, Beatrice
1938 *My Apprenticeship,* vol. 1. London: Penguin Books.

Weber, Marianne
1926 *Max Weber: Ein Lebensbild.* Tübingen: J. C. B. Mohr.

Weber, Max
1924 *Die rationalen und soziologischen Grundlagen der Musik.* 3d ed. Mit einer Einleitung von Theodor Kroyer. Munich: Drei Masken Verlag. [1st ed. 1921.]
1956a *Wirtschaft und Gesellschaft.* 2 vols. Studienausgabe. Cologne: Kiepenheuer & Witsch.
1956b Die sozialen Gründe des Untergangs der antiken Kultur. 2d ed. In *Soziologie/Weltgeschichtliche Analysen/Politik,* by Max Weber, ed. Johannes Winckelmann. Stuttgart: Alfred Kröner.
1958 *The Rational and Social Foundations of Music.* Trans. and ed. Don Martindale, Johannes Riedel, and Gertrude Neuwirth. Carbondale, IL: Southern Illinois University Press.
1972 *Die rationalen und soziologischen Grundlagen der Musik.* Tübingen: J. C. B. Mohr. [Does not contain Theodor Kroyer's preface for the 1921 and 1924 editions.]
1972 *GARS = Gesammelte Aufsätze zur Religionssoziologie,* 6th ed. vol. 1. Tübingen: J. C. B. Mohr [vol. 2: 1976, vol. 3: 1978].
1973 *GAWL = Gesammelte Aufsätze zur Wissenschaftslehre.* 4th ed. Tübingen: J. C. B. Mohr.

Wendorff, Rudolf
1980 *Zeit und Kultur: Geschichte des Zeitbewußtseins in Europa.* Opladen: Westdeutscher Verlag.

Werth, Alexander
1949 *Musical Uproar in Moscow.* London: Turnstile Press.

White, Avron L., ed.
1987 *Lost in Music: Culture, Style and Musical Event.* London: Routledge & Kegan Paul.

Wiesand, Andreas Johannes, and Karla Fohrbeck
1975 Bevölkerungsumfrage zur Kulturpolitik und zum Musiktheater. Part 1 of *Musiktheater—Schreckgespenst oder öffentliches Bedürfnis: Ergebnisse der "Opernstudie" des Instituts für Projektstudien Hamburg.* Mainz: Schott.

Wiesand, Andreas Johannes, ed.
1984 *Musikberufe im Wandel.* Mainz: Schott.
1985 (ed.) *Musikleben und Kulturpolitik.* Bonn: Deutscher Musikrat.
1990 (ed.) *Neue Technik—Neue Medien—Neue Musik?* Bonn: Bundesministerium für Bildung und Wissenschaft.

Wiese, Leopold von
1964 *Soziologie.* 7th ed. Berlin: Walter de Gruyter.

Willis, Paul
1978 *Profane Culture.* London: Routledge & Kegan Paul.

Wilzin, Leo
1937 *Musikstatistik: Logik und Methodik gesellschaftsstatistischer Musikforschung.* Vienna: Deuticke.

Winckel, Fritz
1952   *Klangwelt unter der Lupe*. Berlin: Max Hesses Verlag.
1955   *Klangstruktur der Musik*. Berlin: Verlag für Radio-Foto-Kinotech-nik.
1957   Akustik im festlichen Haus. *Bauwelt* 48 (51): 1349–1353.
1960   *Phänomene des musikalischen Hörens*. Berlin: Max Hesses Verlag.
1974   Space, music and architecture. *Cultures* 1 (3): 135–203.
1975   Die psychophysischen Bedingungen des Musikhörens. In *Musikhören*, ed. Bernhard Dopheide. Darmstadt: Wissenschaft-liche Buchgesellschaft.

Winzheimer, Bernhard
1930   *Das musikalische Kunstwerk in elektrischer Fernübertragung*. Augs-burg: Filser.

Wiora, Walter
1930–31 Review of *Die rationalen und soziologischen Grundlagen der Musik*, by Max Weber. In *Musik und Gesellschaft: Arbeitsblätter für soziale Musikpflege und Musikpolitik* 102–103.
1961   *Die vier Weltalter der Musik*. Stuttgart: W. Kohlhammer. [Engl. trans. 1965. New York: Norton.]

Wishart, Trevor
1977   Musical Writing, Musical Speaking. In *Whose Music: A Sociology of Musical Languages*, ed. John Shepherd et al. London: Latimer.

Wölfflin, Heinrich
1960   *Kunstgeschichtliche Grundbegriffe*. 12th ed. Basel: Benno Schwabe. [1st ed. 1915.]

Wolf, Johannes
1899–1900 Die Musiklehre des Johannes de Grocheo. *Sammelbände der Inter-nationalen Musikgesellschaft* 1: 65–130.

Wolff, Janet
1981   *The Social Production of Art*. London: The Macmillan Press.
1987   The Ideology of Autonomous Art. In *Music and Society: The Politics of Composition, Performance and Reception*, ed. Richard Leppert and Susan McClary. Cambridge: Cambridge University Press.

Yasser, Joseph
1932   *A Theory of Evolving Tonality*. New York: American Library of Musicology.
1953   A Letter from Arnold Schoenberg. *Journal of the American Musico-logical Society* 6 (1): 53–62.

Young, Irwin
1969   *The Practica Musicae of Franchinus Gafurius*. Madison, WI: Univer-sity of Wisconsin Press.

Zeppenfeld, Werner
1978   *Tonträger in der Bundesrepublik Deutschland: Anatomie eines medi-alen Massenmarktes*. Bochum: N. Bruckmeyer.

Zilsel, Edgar
1926   *Die Entstehung des Geniebegriffes: Ein Beitrag zur Ideengeschichte der Antike und des Frühkapitalismus*. Tübingen: J. C. B. Mohr.

Index